Sing Joyfully

Jack Schrader
Editor

Karen Burton Mains
Worship Resources Editor

Tabernacle Publishing Company
Carol Stream, Illinois 60188

INTRODUCTION

A mother holds her adopted infant in her arms. Having suffered the indignities of infertility—barrenness heaped high by several unsuccessful operations; expensive examinations and treatments, raised hopes/hopes dashed; now her joy is full as she watches in loving awe. She is totally preoccupied with the movement of her new son's hand, the play of a smile on his face, his eyes searching for her familiar countenance. Her finger traces the baby wrinkle on a soft wrist. She raises her head in wonder and says, "It's amazing how much time a grown person can spend watching an infant!"

Worship has been defined as *being preoccupied with God.*

Yet how little Christians know about this kind of devout attention. Some can remember that mad obsession called "falling in love" when the whereabouts, the thoughts, the actions of the beloved filled their minds. Some are often consumed with concerns for their children. Work, the planning and ordering of it, can control the worker so much that he or she becomes compulsive in its accomplishment. We humans are preoccupied with many things: successes and failures, the gaining or losing of possessions, the hurts and joys of living; but we are rarely preoccupied with God.

And yet, in a secularized age, which seems to be racing dangerously along in a rapid moral decline, we need to worship more than ever. As the late William Temple said:

> The world can be saved by one thing and that is worship. For to worship is to quicken the conscience by the holiness of God, to feed the mind with the truth of God, to purge the imagination by the beauty of God, to open the heart to the love of God, to devote the will to the purpose of God.

To be preoccupied with something indicates a total absorption; it implies (or "necessitates") a passionate giving of our attention. It means to be possessed by a thought or a concept or a person. It means to be engrossed in; to be seized with thoughts about.

How then do we learn to become preoccupied with God? By cultivating *intentionality.* By deliberately turning our minds toward divine preoccupation. By developing worship habits and working on them. Intentional worship means a worshiper is not going to church expecting that worship will just happen; but intentionality means that a worshiper is going to church determined to make worship happen—at least as far as he or she is able.

The word for "worship" in the ancient Anglo-Saxon tongue was the word "woerth-scrip" (later, "worthship")—meaning to "ascribe supreme worth to God." This exaltation, this adoration does not often happen spontaneously. It takes work on the part of humans, bogged about by the demands of materiality—by the urgent, by the necessary, but not by the spiritual. A church bulletin aptly described this dilemma: "Too many Christians worship their work, work at their play, and play at their worship." We must learn to work at our worship so that preoccupation with God becomes delightfully habitual.

One of the deadliest blows to participatory worship is the worshiper as spectator. The biblical ethic regards worship as work. *Av'dh* in Hebrew, *dienst* in German, *leitourgia* in Greek, *service* in English all have the double meaning of worship and work. In fact, liturgy means "common work"—a sacred work in which a people corporately, determined to be enamored with God, find meaningful ways to tell him of this and to remind themselves as well.

We Christians are always in danger of allowing spiritual forms to lose their meaning, to become formulaic. Think, for instance, of the hymns we sing without knowing their meaning. Think of the prayers we hear to which we do not really listen. Think of the sermons that are preached which we wish would soon end. Think of the hours of Bible study we attend which have no influence on our daily lives.

The French philosopher, Voltaire, once said, "If you want to kill Christianity, you must abolish Sunday." Contemporary Christianity is in danger of losing the meaning of the spiritual worship forms—the calls to worship, the pastoral prayers, the hymn-singing, the preaching of the Word—with a consequent diminishment of the impact of Christianity on ourselves, our families, and, inevitably, on our world and culture.

How frequently do strangers and sojourners enter our sanctuaries because they are drawn by an unexplainable sense of something remarkable? How often do people experience healing (physical and psychological and spiritual) simply because they attend a Sunday morning service? How many times does the Holy Spirit break through our complacency, convicting us of our sin, and producing tears and weeping and confession? How many times do we linger in quiet after a service is over because the presence of Christ is so real we yearn to stay longer in His company? How many times are we stirred in our souls by the Scripture readings? How many times do we sing the hymns with an inward, adamant *yes* that affirms the doctrines we are mouthing?

Sundays can be abolished by meaningless routine as surely as by boarding up the church doors. Empty worship has always been anathema to God. Amos declares for the Lord, "I hate, I despise your feasts and I take no delight in your solemn assemblies . . . Take away from me the noise of your songs; to the melody of your harps I will not listen." Israel was expelled from the land because of two lacks: her empty worship and her lack of justice. These two national sins seem always to feed one into the other. Contemporary Christians must not become guilty of these sins as well.

How do we become intentional in worship? How do we become participants rather than spectators?

Congregational participation is not developed by blaming the church staff for being inadequate worship leaders. We must make sure that as individual lay people, *we* are prepared to take our place in the congregation, eager to begin the work of worship.

In the Old Testament Jewish pattern, the Hebrew people observed Sabbath from Friday evening to Saturday evening; and for the observant Jew, that form has continued through the centuries. Jewish religious rituals have been one of the reasons for the maintenance of Jewish life despite persecution, pogroms, and dispersion. It has been said that the Jewish family did not keep Sabbath, but that Sabbath kept the Jewish family.

At a minimum, we Christians can be ready for Sunday morning by Saturday evening. We can have clothes cleaned and pressed, food ready, hearts stilled, the work of the week put aside. We can examine our souls to see if there are attitudes or deeds that are unpleasing to God which need to be confessed. One friend's grandmother raised six children alone after she was widowed, and she always made sure all the housework was done by noon on Saturday. Then she retired to her bedroom and began to study Scripture.

Another friend's mother taught her to go to church with "a full basket, not an empty one." We must begin to retrain ourselves to consider during each Saturday evening/Sunday morning: What have I to give to God and to his people? Am I ready to worship? Am I eager to be preoccupied with Him? We must learn to transform the age-old, self-centered question, What am I going to get out of the service? to, What am I going to put into the service?

We need to remind ourselves, over and over, that the focus of Sunday worship must be upon the living Christ among us. In truth, if Christ were bodily present and we could see him with more than our soul's eyes, all our worship would become intentional. If Christ stood on our platforms, we would bend our knees without asking. If He stretched out His hands and we saw the wounds, our hearts would break; we would confess our sins and weep over our shortcomings. If we could hear His voice leading the hymns, we too would sing heartily; the words would take on meaning. The Bible reading would be lively; meaning would pierce to the marrow of our souls. If Christ walked our aisles, we would hasten to make amends with that brother or sister to whom we have not spoken. We would volunteer for service, the choir loft would be crowded. If we knew Christ would attend our church Sunday after Sunday, the front pews would fill fastest, believers would arrive early, offering plates would be laden with sacrificial but gladsome gifts, prayers would concentrate our attention.

This is participatory worship.

Yet, the startling truth is that Christ is present, through His Holy Spirit, in our churches; it is we who must develop eyes to see and ears to hear Him.

A hymnal is one of the most remarkable aids to participatory worship a lay person can utilize. Within its binding and pages are contained the doctrines of the faith culled through the ages and saturated with the devotion of those saints who have been members of the church triumphant. Music by its very nature evokes the soul's response. If we allow it, music can lift our hearts to attend to God; singing heartily, suddenly we discover that for a moment, brief but powerfully, we are absolutely preoccupied with the divine.

Intentionality is important in hymnal usage. Those brief and powerful moments filled with the surprising numinous can be increased by our willing work. These songs, some ancient and some new, can also lose their meaning. The intentional hymn singer will come early enough to church (having prepared oneself to adore Christ the night before) to read through the lyrics of the chosen hymns, so that when the congregation sings, the lyrics will have meaning. The intentional hymn singer will ask: Am I making noisesome sounds or do I really believe this? Have I experienced these truths? Am I participating in this praise chorus because it is a means of expressing my preoccupation with God?

Intentional hymn singers will use their imaginations, sanctified by worship, to increase personal participation in some of the following ways: They might think about Christ bodily visiting the sanctuary; they will attempt to sing the hymns to His Presence. If they are singing about the crucifixion, they might work to see the Cross. They might think how these hymns are an expression of communion. They might remember the church through the ages: those who have suffered for their faith; the martyrs singing at the stake; Paul and Silas hymning psalms in prison. They might think about themselves, singing at this moment, bound by time, with those now absolutely spiritually alive who are no longer restricted by physicality or human history.

When this happens, when Christians learn to sing as unto God, understanding that hymns are more than a musical interlude in a printed worship program, but an aid to meaningful adoration, they may suddenly encounter the spiritual in surprising fashion. "How greatly did I weep in Thy hymns and canticles, deeply moved by the voices of Thy sweet-speaking Church!" cries Augustine. "The voices flowed into my ears, and the truth was poured forth into my heart, whence the agitation of my piety overflowed, and my tears ran over, and blessed was I therein."

One old man I know always weeps when his church sings the doxology, "Holy, Holy, Lord God Almighty." The tears run down his wrinkled cheeks. Would that we all could experience that awe, that reality which breaches the borders of the intellect and somehow reaches the affective, the guarded emotional parts of ourselves.

For truly, one day, one eternal day, we will recognize that divine presence, we will kneel in awe, our hearts will sigh, will shout, "Holy! Holy! Holy! Lord God Almighty!" We will weep for joy in the Presence of God. We will become utterly preoccupied. We will adore. We will exalt. We will worship. And this time, this one day in time, this Sunday—every Sunday, in fact, Sunday after Sunday; we are preparing our souls, practicing for that Eternity when every day will be a Sabbath without end, for that day when we will know most assuredly, Christ is here!

Karen Burton Mains

PREFACE

Psalm 33:1 exhorts, *"Sing Joyfully* to the Lord, you righteous; it is fitting for the upright to praise Him." Since scripture encourages believers thus, a hymnal becomes an important tool for corporate and individual worship.

SING JOYFULLY is the eighth major hymnal to be published by Tabernacle Publishing Company in the past 74 years. It also represents a large step forward in introducing new gospel songs, hymns, and praise choruses. While maintaining the core-list of best-loved hymns, well over 200 new songs have been included in *Sing Joyfully*, when compared with its predecessor, *Hymns of Faith*.

Certain features have been added that hopefully will stimulate creativity in corporate worship. One of these is the distribution of appropriate readings throughout the book in order to complement and amplify the themes of the hymns. We gratefully acknowledge the help of noted Christian author, Karen Burton Mains, for her work in gathering, adapting, and writing most of this material. These readings, liturgies, and prayers are thoroughly indexed for easy accessibility. Often, a reading can be used not only for personal meditation, but as a spoken introduction to a hymn that follows, thereby making it an effective worship resource. Other helpful indexes include an exhaustive Topical Index, an index of Authors and Composers, and of Copyright Owners and Sources. The latter should be utilized for all permissions to reproduce any copyrighted material.

SING JOYFULLY has been organized in a traditional manner, grouping hymns in general categories, such as Worship, Testimony, Guidance, and so forth. Each section is introduced with its own subject-title page.

The body of Christ is characterized by magnificent diversity, its goal also being to demonstrate compelling love and unity. In this same way, the creative work of all the authors and composers found in this hymnbook, testifies to the supernatural work of the Holy Spirit, enabling humans to praise and worship the Godhead through word and music. Christian believers have the best reason to sing . . . and to *SING JOYFULLY!*

The Publishers

TABLE OF CONTENTS

TABLE OF CONTENTS
(Cont.)

Praise
and
Worship

Sing joyfully to the Lord, you righteous;
it is fitting for the upright to praise him.
Psalm 33:1

A Mighty Fortress Is Our God 1

God is our refuge and strength. Psa. 46:1

MARTIN LUTHER   MARTIN LUTHER

1. A might-y for-tress is our God, A bul-wark nev-er fail-ing;
2. Did we in our own strength con-fide, Our striv-ing would be los-ing,
3. And though this world, with dev-ils filled, Should threat-en to un-do us,
4. That word a-bove all earth-ly powers, No thanks to them, a-bid-eth;

Our help-er He, a-mid the flood Of mor-tal ills pre-vail-ing:
Were not the right Man on our side, The man of God's own choos-ing:
We will not fear, for God hath willed His truth to tri-umph through us:
The Spir-it and the gifts are ours Through him who with us sid-eth:

For still our an-cient foe Doth seek to work us woe; His craft and power are
Dost ask who that may be? Christ Je-sus, it is He; Lord Sab-a-oth His
The Prince of Dark-ness grim, We trem-ble not for him; His rage we can en-
Let goods and kin-dred go, This mor-tal life al-so; The bod-y they may

great, And, armed with cru-el hate, On earth is not his e-qual.
name, From age to age the same, And He must win the bat-tle.
dure, For lo, his doom is sure; One lit-tle word shall fell him.
kill: God's truth a-bid-eth still; His king-dom is for-ev-er. A-men.

2 Holy, Holy, Holy!

They rest not day and night, saying, Holy, holy, holy, Lord God Almighty. Rev. 4:8

REGINALD HEBER   JOHN B. DYKES

1. Ho - ly, ho - ly, ho - ly! Lord God Al - might - y!
2. Ho - ly, ho - ly, ho - ly! all the saints a - dore Thee,
3. Ho - ly, ho - ly, ho - ly! though the dark - ness hide Thee,
4. Ho - ly, ho - ly, ho - ly! Lord God Al - might - y!

Ear - ly in the morn - ing our song shall rise to Thee;
Cast - ing down their gold - en crowns a - round the glass - y sea;
Though the eye of sin - ful man Thy glo - ry may not see,
All Thy works shall praise Thy name, in earth, and sky, and sea;

Ho - ly, ho - ly, ho - ly! mer - ci - ful and might - y!
Cher - u - bim and ser - a - phim fall - ing down be - fore Thee,
On - ly Thou art ho - ly; there is none be - side Thee,
Ho - ly, ho - ly, ho - ly! mer - ci - ful and might - y!

God in three per - sons, bless - ed Trin - i - ty!
Which wert and art, and ev - er - more shalt be.
Per - fect in pow'r, in love, and pu - ri - ty.
God in three per - sons, bless - ed Trin - i - ty! A - men.

Crown Him with Many Crowns 3

And on His head were many crowns . . . Rev. 19:12

MATTHEW BRIDGES AND
GODFREY THRING

GEORGE J. ELVEY

1. Crown Him with man - y crowns, The Lamb up - on His throne;
2. Crown Him the Son of God Be - fore the worlds be - gan,
3. Crown Him the Lord of life, Who tri - umphed o'er the grave,
4. Crown Him the Lord of love! Be - hold His hands and side,

Hark! how the heav'n - ly an - them drowns All mu - sic but its own!
And ye, who tread where He hath trod, Crown Him the Son of Man;
And rose vic - to - rious in the strife For those He came to save;
Those wounds, yet vis - i - ble a - bove, In beau - ty glo - ri - fied:

A - wake, my soul, and sing Of Him who died for thee, And
Who ev - ery grief hath known That wrings the hu - man breast, And
His glo - ries now we sing, Who died and rose on high, Who
All hail, Re - deem - er, hail! For Thou hast died for me: Thy

hail Him as thy match-less King Thro' all e - ter - ni - ty.
takes and bears them for His own, That all in Him may rest.
died e - ter - nal life to bring, And lives that death may die.
praise and glo - ry shall not fail Thro'- out e - ter - ni - ty. A - men.

4 Majesty

Yours, O Lord; is the greatness, the power, and the glory, the victory, and the majesty; I Chr. 29:11

Jack W. Hayford

Jack W. Hayford

Maj - es - ty, wor-ship His maj - es - ty. Un - to

Je - sus be all glo - ry, hon - or, and praise.

Maj - es - ty, king-dom auth-or - i - ty flow from His

throne un - to His own; His an - them raise. So, ex-

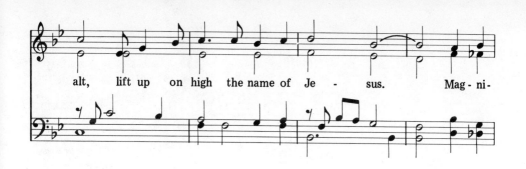

alt, lift up on high the name of Je - sus. Mag - ni-

fy, come, glo - ri - fy Christ Je - sus the King.

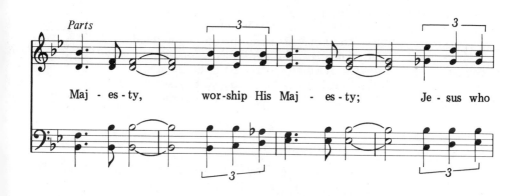

Parts

Maj - es - ty, wor-ship His Maj - es - ty; Je - sus who

died, now glo - ri - fied, King of all kings.

5   Psalm 29

Leader: A Call to Worship!
Ascribe to the Lord, O heavenly beings,
ascribe to the Lord glory and strength.
People: **Ascribe to the Lord the glory of his name;**
worship the Lord in holy array.
Leader: The voice of the Lord is upon the waters;
the God of glory thunders,
the Lord thunders over many waters.
People: **The voice of the Lord is powerful;**
the voice of the Lord is majestic.
Leader: The voice of the Lord breaks the cedars . . .
He makes Lebanon skip like a calf . . .
The voice of the Lord strikes with flashes of lightning!
The voice of the Lord shakes the desert, twists the oaks
and strips the forests bare.
People: **The Lord sits enthroned over the flood;**
the Lord is enthroned as King forever.
All: **The Lord gives strength to his people;**
the Lord blesses his people with peace.
Leader: Hear you, this day, the voice of the Lord!

I Sing the Almighty Power of God 6

O come, let us worship . . . let us kneel before the Lord our maker. Psa. 95:6

ISAAC WATTS

TRADITIONAL ENGLISH MELODY
ARR. RALPH VAUGHAN WILLIAMS

1. I sing th'al-might-y pow'r of God That made the moun-tains rise,
2. I sing the good-ness of the Lord That filled the earth with food;
3. There's not a plant or flow'r be-low But makes Thy glo-ries known;

That spread the flow-ing seas a-broad And built the loft-y skies.
He formed the crea-tures with His word And then pro-nounced them good.
And clouds a-rise and tem-pests blow By or-der from Thy throne;

I sing the wis-dom that or-dained The sun to rule the day;
Lord, how Thy won-ders are dis-played Where-e'er I turn my eye,
While all that bor-rows life from Thee Is ev-er in Thy care,

The moon shines full at His com-mand And all the stars o-bey.
If I sur-vey the ground I tread Or gaze up-on the sky!
And ev-ery-where that man can be, Thou, God, art pres-ent there.

Music from the ENGLISH HYMNAL. Reprinted by permission of Oxford University Press.

7 Great Is the Lord

Great is our Lord, and mighty in power; His understanding is infinite. Psa. 147:5

MICHAEL W. SMITH AND
DEBORAH D. SMITH

MICHAEL W. SMITH AND
DEBORAH D. SMITH

Unison

Great is the Lord, He is ho-ly and just; By His pow-er we trust in His love.

Great is the Lord, He is faith-ful and true; By His mer-cy He proves He is love.

Parts

1. Great is the Lord and wor-thy of glo-ry! Great is the Lord and
2. Great are You, Lord, and wor-thy of glo-ry! Great are You, Lord, and

wor-thy of praise. Great is the Lord; now lift up your voice, now
wor-thy of praise. Great are You, Lord; I lift up my voice, I

Copyright © 1982 Meadowgreen Music Co. All rights adm. by Tree Pub. Co., Inc. 8 Music Sq. W., Nashville, TN 37203
International Copyright Secured. All Rights Reserved. Used by Permission.

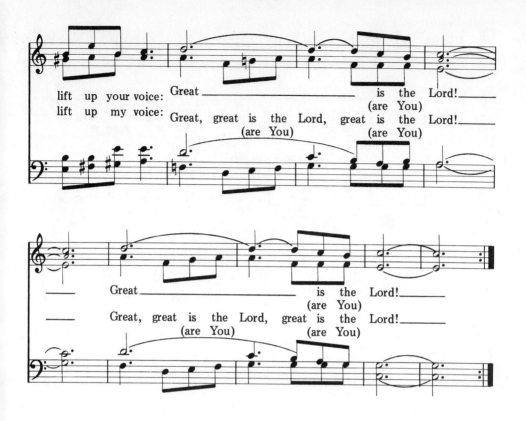

lift up your voice: Great _____ is the Lord! ____
lift up my voice: Great, great is the Lord, great is the Lord! ____
(are You)
(are You)   (are You)

____ Great _____ is the Lord! ____
(are You)
____ Great, great is the Lord, great is the Lord! ____
(are You)   (are You)

Psalm 93

Leader: A Call to Worship!
The Lord reigns, he is robed in majesty.
People: **The Lord is robed in majesty and is armed with strength.**
Leader: The world is firmly established.
People: **It cannot be moved.**
All: **Your throne was established long ago;**
You are from all eternity.
Leader: The seas have lifted up, O Lord,
People: **The seas have lifted up their voice;**
All: **The seas have lifted up their pounding waves.**
Leader: Mightier than the thunder of the great waters,
People: **Mightier than the breakers of the sea —**
All: **The Lord on high is mighty!**
Leader: Your statutes stand firm;
People: **Holiness adorns your house for endless days, O Lord!**
All: **The Lord on high is mighty!**

(NIV)

9 How Majestic Is Your Name

They shall lift up their voice, they shall sing; for the majesty of the Lord. Isaiah 24:14

MICHAEL W. SMITH

MICHAEL W. SMITH

Unison

O Lord, our Lord, how ma-jes-tic is Your name in all the

1 earth. O 2 earth. O Lord, we praise Your

Parts

name. O Lord, we mag-ni-fy Your name, Prince of

Peace, Might-y God; O Lord God Al-might - y.

Praise to the Lord, the Almighty 10

For then shalt thou have thy delight in the Almighty. Job 22:26

JOACHIM NEANDER
TR. CATHERINE WINKWORTH

STRALSUND GESANGBUCH

1. Praise to the Lord, the Al-might-y, the King of cre-a-
tion! O my soul, praise Him, for He is thy health and sal-
va-tion! All ye who hear, Now to His tem-ple draw
near; Join me in glad ad-o-ra-tion!

2. Praise to the Lord, who o'er all things so won-drous-ly reigneth, Shel-ters thee un-der His wings, yea, so gen-tly sus-
tain-eth! Hast thou not seen How thy de-sires e'er have
been Grant-ed in what He or-dain-eth?

3. Praise to the Lord, who doth pros-per thy work and de-fend
thee; Sure-ly His good-ness and mer-cy here dai-ly at-
tend thee. Pon-der a-new What the Al-might-y can
do, If with His love He be-friend thee.

4. Praise to the Lord! O let all that is in me a-dore
Him! All that hath life and breath, come now with prais-es be-
fore Him! Let the A-men Sound from His peo-ple a-
gain: Glad-ly for aye we a-dore Him. A-men.

11 Thou Art Worthy

For Thou has created all things. Rev. 4:11

PAULINE M. MILLS

PAULINE M. MILLS
ARR. JACK SCHRADER

Thou art wor-thy, Thou art wor-thy, Thou art wor-thy, O

Lord, To re-ceive glo-ry, glo-ry and hon-or, Glo-ry and

hon-or and pow'r; For Thou hast cre-a-ted, hast all things cre-

a-ted, Thou hast cre-a-ted all things, And for Thy pleas-ure

they are cre-a-ted: For Thou art wor-thy, O Lord!

Unto the King eternal, immortal, invisible, the only wise God, be honor and glory . . . I Tim. 1:17

WALTER CHALMERS SMITH   TRADITIONAL WELSH HYMN MELODY

1. Im - mor - tal, in - vis - i - ble, God on - ly wise,
2. Un - rest - ing, un - hast - ing, and si - lent as light,
3. To all, life Thou giv - est— to both great and small,
4. Great Fa - ther of glo - ry, pure Fa - ther of light,

In light in - ac - ces - si - ble hid from our eyes,
Nor want - ing, nor wast - ing, Thou rul - est in might;
In all life Thou liv - est— the true life of all;
Thine an - gels a - dore Thee, all veil - ing their sight;

Most bless - ed, most glo - rious, the An - cient of Days,
Thy jus - tice, like moun - tains, high soar - ing a - bove
We blos - som and flour - ish as leaves on the tree,
All praise we would ren - der— O help us to see

Al - might - y, vic - to - rious— Thy great name we praise.
Thy clouds, which are foun - tains of good - ness and love.
And with - er and per - ish— but naught chang - eth Thee.
'Tis on - ly the splen - dor of light hid - eth Thee! A - men.

13 Joyful, Joyful, We Adore Thee

All Thy works shall praise Thee, O Lord . . . Psa. 145:10

HENRY VAN DYKE

LUDWIG VAN BEETHOVEN

1. Joy-ful, joy-ful, we a-dore Thee, God of glo-ry, Lord of love;
2. All Thy works with joy sur-round Thee, Earth and heav'n re-flect Thy rays,
3. Thou art giv-ing and for-giv-ing, Ev-er bless-ing, ev-er blest,
4. Mor-tals join the might-y cho-rus Which the morn-ing stars be-gan;

Hearts un-fold like flow'rs be-fore Thee, Open-ing to the sun a-bove.
Stars and an-gels sing a-round Thee, Cen-ter of un-bro-ken praise.
Well-spring of the joy of liv-ing, O-cean-depth of hap-py rest!
Fa-ther love is reign-ing o'er us, Broth-er love binds man to man.

Melt the clouds of sin and sad-ness; Drive the dark of doubt a-way;
Field and for-est, vale and moun-tain, Flow-ery mead-ow, flash-ing sea,
Thou our Fa-ther, Christ our Broth-er— All who live in love are Thine;
Ev-er sing-ing, march we on-ward, Vic-tors in the midst of strife;

Giv-er of im-mor-tal glad-ness, Fill us with the light of day!
Chant-ing bird and flow-ing foun-tain Call us to re-joice in Thee.
Teach us how to love each oth-er, Lift us to the joy di-vine.
Joy-ful mu-sic leads us sun-ward In the tri-umph song of life. A-men.

Psalm 92

Leader: A Call to Worship!
It is good to praise the Lord
and make music to your name, O Most High.
People: **To proclaim your love in the morning,
and your faithfulness at night,**
Leader: To the music of the ten-stringed lyre
and the melody of the harp.
People: **You make us glad by your deeds, O Lord;
we sing for joy at the works of your hands.**
Leader: How great are your works, O Lord,
how profound your thoughts!
People: **The righteous will flourish like a palm tree,
they will grow like a cedar of Lebanon;
planted in the house of the Lord,
they will flourish in the courts of our God.**
Leader: They will still bear fruit in old age,
they will stay fresh and green,
proclaiming, "The Lord is upright."
People: **The Lord is upright!**
Leader: He is our Rock!
People: **He is our Rock!**
Leader: There is no wickedness in him.
All: **It is good to praise the Lord!
How great are your works, O Lord,
how profound are your thoughts!**

15 My Tribute

To God only wise, be glory through Jesus Christ. Rom. 16:27

ANDRAÉ CROUCH · ANDRAÉ CROUCH

How can I say thanks for the things You have done for me?

Things so un-de-served, Yet You gave to prove Your love for me; The

voic-es of a mil-lion an-gels could not ex - press my gra-ti - tude.

All that I am, and ev - er hope to be; I owe it all to Thee.

Refrain

To God be the glo - ry, To God be the glo - ry,

To God be the glo - ry For the things He has done.

With His blood He has saved me; With His power He has raised me;

To God be the glo - ry For the things He has done.

Just let me live my life; Let it be pleas-ing, Lord, to Thee.

And if I gain an - y praise, Let it go to Cal - va - ry. With His

16 How Great Thou Art

Great is the Lord, and greatly to be praised. Psa. 48:1

CARL BOBERG
TR. STUART K. HINE

SWEDISH FOLK MELODY
ARR. STUART K. HINE

1. O Lord my God, when I in awe-some won-der Con-sid-er
2. When thro' the woods and for-est glades I wan-der And hear the
3. And when I think that God, His Son not spar-ing, Sent Him to
4. When Christ shall come with shout of ac-cla-ma-tion And take me

all the worlds Thy hands have made, I see the stars, I hear the roll-ing
birds sing sweet-ly in the trees, When I look down from loft-y moun-tain
die, I scarce can take it in, That on the cross, my bur-den glad-ly
home, what joy shall fill my heart! Then I shall bow in hum-ble ad-o-

Refrain

thun-der, Thy pow'r thro'-out the u-ni-verse dis-played.
gran-deur, And hear the brook and feel the gen-tle breeze.
bear-ing, He bled and died to take a-way my sin.
ra-tion, And there pro-claim, my God, how great Thou art.

Then sings my

soul, my Sav-ior God, to Thee; How great Thou art, how great Thou art! Then sings my

soul, my Sav-ior God, to Thee: How great Thou art, how great Thou art!

Great Is Thy Faithfulness 17

His compassions fail not. They are new every morning. Lam. 3:22,23

THOMAS O. CHISHOLM   WILLIAM M. RUNYAN

1. Great is Thy faith-ful-ness, O God my Fa-ther, There is no shad-ow of
2. Sum-mer and win-ter, and springtime and har-vest, Sun, moon and stars in their
3. Par-don for sin and a peace that en-dur-eth, Thy own dear pres-ence to

turn-ing with Thee; Thou chang-est not, Thy com-pas-sions they fail not;
cours-es a-bove Join with all na-ture in man-i-fold wit-ness
cheer and to guide; Strength for to-day and bright hope for to-mor-row,

Refrain

As Thou hast been Thou for-ev-er wilt be.
To Thy great faith-ful-ness, mer-cy and love. Great is Thy faith-ful-ness!
Bless-ings all mine, with ten thou-sand be-side!

Great is Thy faith-ful-ness! Morn-ing by morn-ing new mer-cies I see; All I have

need-ed Thy hand hath pro-vid-ed—Great is Thy faith-ful-ness, Lord, un-to me!

18 El Shaddai

I am God Almighty. Gen. 17:1

MICHAEL CARD AND
JOHN THOMPSON

MICHAEL CARD AND
JOHN THOMPSON

El Shad-dai,* El Shad-dai, El El - yon na A - do-nai;

Age to age You're still the same by the

pow - er of the name. El Shad-dai, El Shad-dai,

Er - kahm - ka na A - do-nai; We will

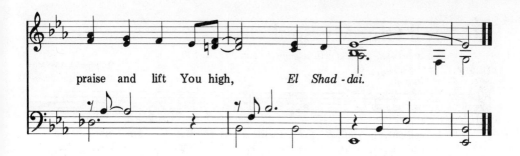

praise and lift You high, El Shad-dai.

In the Name of the Lord 19

Sing aloud unto God our strength. Psa. 81:1

PHILL McHUGH, GLORIA GAITHER AND
SANDI PATTI HELVERING

SANDI PATTI HELVERING

There is strength in the name of the Lord; There is pow'r in the name of the Lord; There is hope in the name of the Lord!

Bless-ed is He who comes in the name of the Lord!

optional repeat

20 Tell Out, My Soul

And Mary said, "My soul doth magnify the Lord." Luke 1:46

TIMOTHY DUDLEY-SMITH

WALTER GREATOREX

1. Tell out, my soul, the great-ness of the Lord! Un - num-bered bless-ings give my spir - it voice; Ten-der to me the prom-ise of His word; In God my Sav-ior shall my heart re-joice.

2. Tell out, my soul, the great-ness of His Name! Make known His might, the deeds His arm has done; His mer-cy sure, from age to age the same; His ho - ly Name, the Lord, the might - y one.

3. Tell out, my soul, the great-ness of His might! Pow'rs and do-min-ions lay their glo - ry by. Proud hearts and stub-born wills are put to flight, The hun-gry fed, the hum-ble lift - ed high.

4. Tell out, my soul, the glo - ries of His word! Firm is His prom-ise, and His mer-cy sure. Tell out, my soul, the great-ness of the Lord To chil-dren's chil-dren and for - ev - er-more!

The God of Abraham Praise 21

And God said unto Moses, I AM THAT I AM. Ex. 3:14

HEBREW MELODY
ARR. MEYER LYON

THOMAS OLIVERS

1. The God of A - braham praise, Who reigns en - throned a - bove;
2. The God of A - braham praise, At whose su - preme com - mand
3. He by Him - self hath sworn, I on His oath de - pend,
4. The whole tri - um - phant host Give thanks to God on high;

An - cient of ev - er - last - ing days, And God of love.
From earth I rise, and seek the joys At His right hand.
I shall, on ea - gles wings up - borne, To heaven as - cend;
"Hail, Fa - ther, Son and Ho - ly Ghost!" They ev - er cry.

Je - ho - vah, great I AM, By earth and heaven con - fessed;
I all on earth for - sake, Its wis - dom, fame, and power;
I shall be - hold His face, I shall His power a - dore,
Hail, A - braham's God and mine! I join the heaven - ly lays;

I bow and bless the sa - cred name, For - ev - er blest.
And Him my on - ly por - tion make, My shield and tower.
And sing the won - ders of His grace For - ev - er - more.
All might and ma - jes - ty are Thine, And end - less praise. A - men.

22 Praise, My Soul, the King of Heaven

Bless the Lord, O my soul, and forget not all His benefits. Psa. 103:2

HENRY F. LYTE

MARK ANDREWS

Unison

1. Praise, my soul, the King of heav-en, To His feet thy
2. Praise Him for his grace and fa-vor To our fa-thers
3. Frail as sum-mer's flow'r we flour-ish; Blows the wind and
4. An-gels in the height, a - dore Him; Ye be-hold Him

trib-ute bring; Ran-somed, healed, re-stored, for - giv-en,
in dis-tress; Praise Him, still the same as ev - er,
it is gone; But, while mor-tals rise and per - ish,
face to face; Saints tri - um-phant, bow be - fore Him;

Ev - er-more His prais-es sing; Al - le - lu - ia!
Slow to chide, and swift to bless; Al - le - lu - ia!
God en-dures un-chang-ing on: Al - le - lu - ia!
Gath-ered in from ev-ery race; Al - le - lu - ia!

Al - le - lu - ia! Praise the ev - er - last - ing King.
Al - le - lu - ia! Glo-rious in His faith - ful - ness.
Al - le - lu - ia! Praise the high e - ter - nal one.
Al - le - lu - ia! Praise with us the God of grace.

Te Deum (To God) 23

You are God: we praise You;
You are the Lord: we acclaim You;
You are the eternal father:
All creation worships You.
To You all angels, all the powers of heaven,
Cherubim and Seraphim, sing in endless praise:
Holy, holy, holy Lord, God of power and might,
heaven and earth are full of your glory.
The glorious company of apostles praises You.
The noble fellowship of prophets praises You.
The white-robed army of martyrs praises You.
Throughout the world the holy Church acclaims You:
Father, of majesty unbounded, Your true and only Son, worthy of all worship,
and the Holy Spirit, advocate and guide.
You, Christ, are the king of glory, eternal Son of the Father.
When You became man to set us free You did not disdain the Virgin's womb.
You overcame the sting of death,
and opened the kingdom of heaven to all believers.
You are seated at God's right hand in glory.
We believe that You will come, and be our judge.
Come then, Lord, sustain Your people,
bought with the price of Your own blood,
and bring us with Your saints to everlasting glory.

A Contemporary Version

Be Still and Know 24

Be still and know that I am God. Psa. 46:10

ANONYMOUS
ARR. JACK SCHRADER

ANONYMOUS

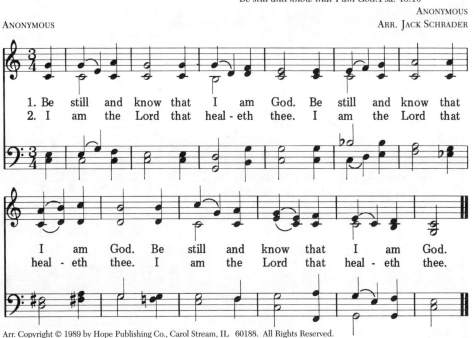

1. Be still and know that I am God. Be still and know that I am God. Be still and know that I am God.
2. I am the Lord that heal-eth thee. I am the Lord that heal-eth thee. I am the Lord that heal-eth thee.

25 When in Our Music God Is Glorified

Let everything that hath breath praise the Lord. Psa. 150:6

FRED PRATT GREEN   CHARLES V. STANFORD

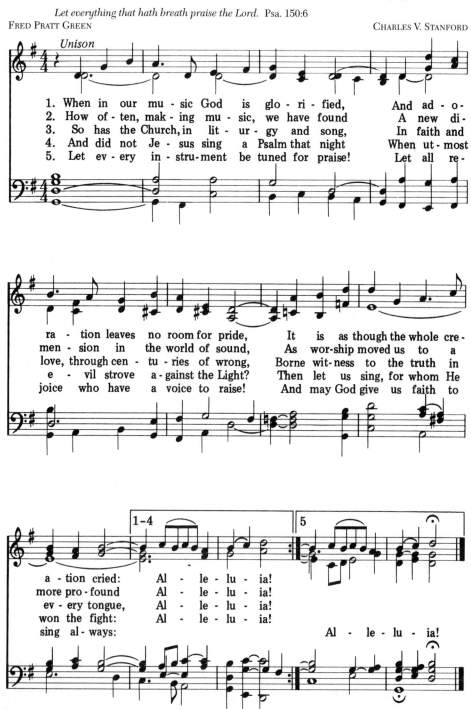

1. When in our mu - sic God is glo - ri - fied, And ad - o-
2. How of - ten, mak - ing mu - sic, we have found A new di-
3. So has the Church, in lit - ur - gy and song, In faith and
4. And did not Je - sus sing a Psalm that night When ut - most
5. Let ev - ery in - stru - ment be tuned for praise! Let all re-

ra - tion leaves no room for pride, It is as though the whole cre-
men - sion in the world of sound, As wor-ship moved us to a
love, through cen - tu - ries of wrong, Borne wit-ness to the truth in
e - vil strove a - gainst the Light? Then let us sing, for whom He
joice who have a voice to raise! And may God give us faith to

1-4

a - tion cried: Al - le - lu - ia!
more pro - found Al - le - lu - ia!
ev - ery tongue, Al - le - lu - ia!
won the fight: Al - le - lu - ia!
sing al - ways:

5

Al - le - lu - ia!

Praise the Lord Who Reigns Above 26

Praise God in His sanctuary; praise Him in the firmament of His power. Psa. 150:1

CHARLES WESLEY

FOUNDERY COLLECTION

1. Praise the Lord who reigns a - bove And keeps His court be - low;
2. Cel - e - brate th'e - ter - nal God With harp and psal - ter - y,
3. Him, in whom they move and live, Let ev - ery crea - ture sing,

Praise the ho - ly God of love, And all His great - ness show;
Tim - brels soft and cym - bals loud In His high praise a - gree;
Glo - ry to their Mak - er give, And hom - age to their King.

Praise Him for His no - ble deeds, Praise Him for His match - less pow'r;
Praise Him ev - ery tune - ful string; All the reach of heav'n - ly art,
Hallow-ed be His name be - neath, As in heav'n on earth a - dored;

Him from whom all good pro-ceeds Let earth and heav'n a - dore.
All the pow'rs of mu - sic bring, The mu - sic of the heart.
Praise the Lord in ev - ery breath, Let all things praise the Lord. A - men.

27 We Praise Thee, O God, Our Redeemer

Great is the Lord and most worthy of praise. 1 Chr. 16:25

JULIA C. CORY

DUTCH MELODY
ARR. EDWARD KREMSER

1. We praise Thee, O God, our Re-deem-er, Cre-a-tor, In grate-ful de-vo-tion our trib-ute we bring; We lay it be-fore Thee, we kneel and a-dore Thee, We bless Thy ho-ly Name, glad prais-es we sing.

2. We wor-ship Thee, God of our fa-thers, we bless Thee, Thru life's storm and tem-pest our Guide hast Thou been; When per-ils o'er-take us, es-cape Thou wilt make us, And with Thy help, O Lord, our bat-tles we win.

3. With voic-es u-nit-ed our prais-es we of-fer To Thee, great Je-ho-vah, glad an-thems we raise; Thy strong arm will guide us, our God is be-side us, To Thee, our great Re-deem-er, for-ev-er be praise!

Holy God, We Praise Thy Name 28

...Holy, Holy, Holy is the Lord of hosts... Isa. 6:3

TR. CLARENCE A. WALWORTH

KATHOLISCHES GESANGBUCH

1. Ho - ly God, we praise Thy name; Lord of all, we
2. Hark! the loud ce - les - tial hymn An - gel choirs a -
3. Lo! the ap - os - tol - ic train Join Thy sa - cred
4. Ho - ly Fa - ther, Ho - ly Son, Ho - ly Spir - it,

bow be - fore Thee; All on earth Thy scep - ter claim;
bove are rais - ing; Cher - u - bim and ser - a - phim
name to hal - low; Proph - ets swell the glad re - frain,
Three we name Thee; While in es - sence on - ly One,

All in heav'n a - bove a - dore Thee. In - fi - nite Thy
In un - ceas - ing cho - rus prais - ing, Fill the heav'ns with
And the white - robed mar - tyrs fol - low; And from morn to
Un - di - vid - ed God we claim Thee, And a - dor - ing

vast do - main, Ev - er - last - ing is Thy reign.
sweet ac - cord: Ho - ly, ho - ly, ho - ly Lord.
set of sun, Through the Church the song goes on.
bend the knee, While we sing our praise to Thee.

29 *"I believe we ought to have again the old Biblical concept of God which makes God awful and makes men lie face down and cry, 'Holy, holy, holy, Lord God Almighty.' That would do more for the church than everything or anything else."* A.W. Tozer

30
Leader: Come consider the glory of the Lord! Come exalt his holy name!
People: **Holy, holy, holy is the Lord Almighty; the whole earth is filled with his glory.**
Leader: Woe unto us! for we are people of unclean lips,
People: **And we live among a people of unclean lips.**
Leader: Come consider the glory of the Lord! Come exalt his holy name!
People: **Holy, holy, holy is the Lord Almighty; the whole earth is filled with his glory.**
All: **May we be holy unto Thee,**
for Thou alone art holy.

31 Holy Is the Lord

I, the Lord your God, am holy. Lev. 19:2

TRADITIONAL

FRANZ SCHUBERT

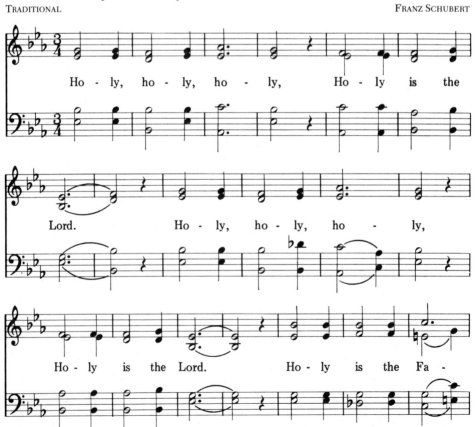

Ho - ly, ho - ly, ho - ly, Ho - ly is the Lord. Ho - ly, ho - ly, ho - ly, Ho - ly is the Lord. Ho - ly is the Fa -

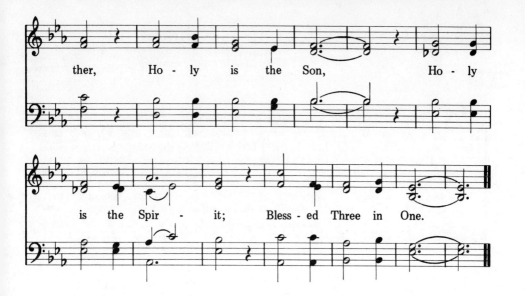

ther, Ho - ly is the Son, Ho - ly

is the Spir - it; Bless - ed Three in One.

Psalm 100

Leader: A Call to Worship!
Shout for joy to the Lord, all the earth.
Worship the Lord with gladness;
come before him with joyful songs.
Know that the Lord is God.
People: **It is he who made us, and we are his;**
we are his people, the sheep of his pasture.
Leader: Enter his gates with thanksgiving
and his courts with praise.
People: **Give thanks to him and praise his name.**
Leader: For the Lord is good!
People: **His love endures forever!**
Leader: His faithfulness continues through all generations.
People: **Shout for joy to the Lord, all the earth!**
Leader: Worship the Lord with gladness!
Come before him with joyful songs.
All: **For the Lord is good;**
His love endures forever!

33 All Creatures of Our God and King

All Thy works shall praise Thee, O Lord. Psa. 145:10

ST. FRANCIS OF ASSISI

GEISTLICHE KIRCHENGESÄNG
ARR. RALPH VAUGHAN WILLIAMS

1. All crea-tures of our God and King, Lift up your voice and with us sing
2. Thou rush-ing wind that art so strong, Ye clouds that sail in heav'n a - long,
3. Thou flow-ing wa - ter, pure and clear, Make mu-sic for thy Lord to hear,
4. And all ye men of ten-der heart, For-giv - ing oth - ers, take your part,
5. Let all things their Cre-a - tor bless, And wor-ship Him in hum-ble - ness,

Al-le - lu - ia, Al-le-lu - ia! Thou burn-ing sun with gold - en beam,
O praise Him, Al-le - lu - ia! Thou ris - ing morn in praise re - joice,
Al-le - lu - ia, Al-le - lu - ia! Thou fire so mas-ter - ful and bright,
O sing ye, Al-le-lu - ia! Ye who long pain and sor - row bear,
O praise Him, Al-le - lu - ia! Praise, praise the Fa - ther, praise the Son,

Thou sil - ver moon with soft - er gleam, O praise Him, O praise Him,
Ye lights of eve - ning, find a voice, O praise Him, O praise Him,
That giv - est man both warmth and light, O praise Him, O praise Him,
Praise God and on Him cast your care, O praise Him, O praise Him,
And praise the Spir - it, three in one, O praise Him, O praise Him,

Al-le - lu - ia, al - le - lu - ia, al - le - lu - ia!
Al-le - lu - ia, al - le - lu - ia, al - le - lu - ia!
Al-le - lu - ia, al - le - lu - ia, al - le - lu - ia!
Al-le - lu - ia, al - le - lu - ia, al - le - lu - ia!
Al-le - lu - ia, al - le - lu - ia, al - le - lu - ia! A-men.

Come into His Presence 34

Come before Him with joyful songs. Psa. 100:2

UNKNOWN   UNKNOWN

Four-Part Canon

1. Come in-to His pres-ence singing Al-le-lu - ia,   al-le-lu - ia,   al-le-lu - ia.
2. Come in-to His pres-ence singing Je-sus is Lord,   Je-sus is Lord,   Je-sus is Lord.
3. Praise the Lord together singing Worthy the Lamb, worthy the Lamb, worthy the Lamb.
4. Praise the Lord together singing Glo-ry to God, glo-ry to God, glo-ry to God.

We Will Glorify 35

To Him who sits on the throne and to the Lamb be praise and honor and glory. Rev. 5:13

TWILA PARIS   TWILA PARIS

1. We   will   glo - ri - fy   the   King   of   kings,   we   will
2. Lord   Je - ho - vah   reigns   in   maj - es - ty,   we   will
3. He   is   Lord   of   heav - en,   Lord   of   earth,   He   is
4. Hal - le - lu - jah   to   the   King   of   kings,   hal - le -

glo - ri - fy   the   Lamb;   We   will   glo - ri - fy   the
bow   be - fore   His   throne;   We   will   wor - ship   Him   in
Lord   of   all   who   live;   He   is   Lord   a - bove   the
lu - jah   to   the   Lamb;   Hal - le - lu - jah   to   the

Lord   of   lords,   who   is   the   great   I   Am.
right - eous - ness,   we   will   wor - ship   Him   a - lone.
u - ni - verse,   all   praise   to   Him   we   give.
Lord   of   lords,   who   is   the   great   I   Am.

36 We Have Come into His House

Where two or three come together in my name, there am I with them. Matt.18:20

BRUCE BALLINGER

BRUCE BALLINGER

1. We have come in - to His house and gath-ered in His name to
2. Let's for - get a - bout our-selves, and mag - ni - fy His name and

wor - ship Him, We have come in - to His house and
wor - ship Him, Let's for - get a bout our-selves, and

gath - ered in His name to wor - ship Him; We have
mag - ni - fy His name and wor - ship Him; Let's for-

come in - to His house and gath-ered in His name to wor-ship Him;
get a - bout our-selves, and mag - ni - fy His name and wor-ship Him;

O, wor - ship Him, Je - sus Christ, the Lord.

Praise the Name of Jesus 37

The Lord is my Rock and Fortress. Psa. 18:2

ROY HICKS

ROY HICKS

Praise the name of Je - sus, Praise the name of Je - sus.

He's my Rock, He's my For - tress, He's my De - liv - er - er, in

Him will I trust. Praise the name of Je - sus.

38 O sing unto the Lord a new song: sing unto the Lord, all the earth. Sing unto the Lord, bless his name; show forth his salvation from day to day.

Declare his glory among the heathen, his wonders among all people.

For the Lord is great, and greatly to be praised: he is to be feared above all gods.

For all the gods of the nations are idols: but the Lord made the heavens.

Honor and majesty are before him: strength and beauty are in his sanctuary.

Give unto the Lord, O ye kindreds of the people, give unto the Lord glory and strength.

Give unto the Lord the glory due unto his name: bring an offering, and come into his courts.

O worship the Lord in the beauty of holiness: fear before him, all the earth.

From Psalm 96

39 O Worship the Lord

O worship the Lord in the beauty of holiness. Psa. 96:9

ROBERT CLATTERBUCK

ROBERT CLATTERBUCK

1. O wor-ship the Lord in the beau-ty of ho-li-ness, O
2. O lift up the Lord till we see Him up-on His throne, O
3. Lord, qui-et my heart as I en-ter Your pres-ence, Lord,

wor ship the Lord in the beau-ty of ho-li-ness; Wor-ship the
lift up the Lord till we see Him up-on His throne; Lift up the
qui-et my heart as I en-ter Your pres-ence; Lord, Qui-et my

Lord with our hearts in ac-cord, O wor - ship the Lord.
Lord, let His name be a-dored, O lift up the Lord.
heart, tho'ts of self set a-part, Lord, qui - et my heart.

This Is My Father's World 40

The morning stars sang together, and all the sons of God shouted for Joy. Job 38:7

MALTBIE D. BABCOCK   FRANKLIN L. SHEPPARD

1. This is my Fa-ther's world, And to my lis-tening ears All
2. This is my Fa-ther's world, The birds their car-ols raise, The
3. This is my Fa-ther's world, O let me ne'er for-get That

na-ture sings, and round me rings The mu-sic of the spheres.
morn-ing light, the lil-y white, De-clare their Mak-er's praise.
though the wrong seems oft so strong, God is the Rul-er yet.

This is my Fa-ther's world: I rest me in the thought Of
This is my Fa-ther's world: He shines in all that's fair; In the
This is my Fa-ther's world: Why should my heart be sad? The

rocks and trees, of skies and seas—His hand the won-ders wrought.
rus-tling grass I hear Him pass, He speaks to me ev-ery-where.
Lord is King: let the heav-ens ring! God reigns: let earth be glad! A-men.

41 Glory Be to God the Father

To Him be glory and dominion for ever and ever. Rev. 1:6

HORATIUS BONAR

HENRY T. SMART

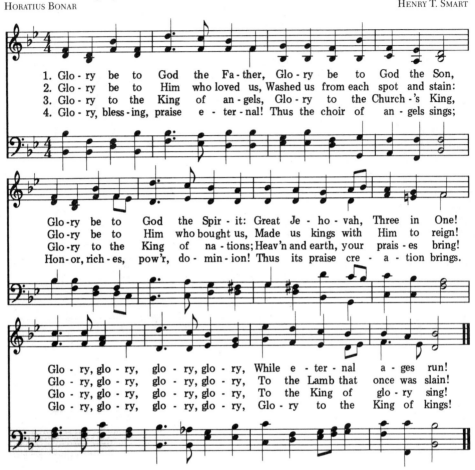

1. Glo-ry be to God the Fa-ther, Glo-ry be to God the Son,
2. Glo-ry be to Him who loved us, Washed us from each spot and stain:
3. Glo-ry to the King of an-gels, Glo-ry to the Church-'s King,
4. Glo-ry, bless-ing, praise e-ter-nal! Thus the choir of an-gels sings;

Glo-ry be to God the Spir-it: Great Je-ho-vah, Three in One!
Glo-ry be to Him who bought us, Made us kings with Him to reign!
Glo-ry to the King of na-tions;Heav'n and earth, your prais-es bring!
Hon-or, rich-es, pow'r, do-min-ion! Thus its praise cre-a-tion brings.

Glo-ry, glo-ry, glo-ry, glo-ry, While e-ter-nal a-ges run!
Glo-ry, glo-ry, glo-ry, glo-ry, To the Lamb that once was slain!
Glo-ry, glo-ry, glo-ry, glo-ry, To the King of glo-ry sing!
Glo-ry, glo-ry, glo-ry, glo-ry, Glo-ry to the King of kings!

42 All People That on Earth Do Dwell

Make a joyful noise unto the Lord, all ye lands. Psa. 100:1

GENEVAN PSALTER

WILLIAM KETHE

ED. LOUIS BOURGEOIS

1. All peo-ple that on earth do dwell, Sing to the Lord with cheer-ful voice;
2. The Lord, ye know, is God in-deed; With-out our aid He did us make;
3. O en-ter then His gates with praise, Ap-proach with joy His courts un-to;
4. For why? The Lord our God is good, His mer-cy is for-ev-er sure;

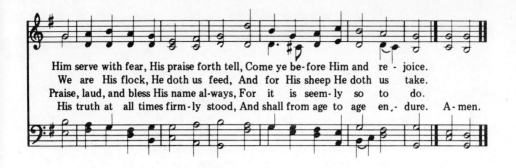

Him serve with fear, His praise forth tell, Come ye be-fore Him and re - joice.
We are His flock, He doth us feed, And for His sheep He doth us take.
Praise, laud, and bless His name al-ways, For it is seem-ly so to do.
His truth at all times firm-ly stood, And shall from age to age en-dure. A-men.

He's Got the Whole World in His Hands   43

In whose hand is the soul of every living thing . . .Job 12:10

TRADITIONAL SPIRITUAL   TRADITIONAL SPIRITUAL

Unison

1. He's got the whole world in His hands, He's got the
2. He's got the wind and the rain in His hands, He's got the
3. He's got the ti - ny lit - tle ba - by in His hands, He's got the
4. He's got you and me, broth-er, in His hands, He's got

whole world in His hands, He's got the whole world
wind and the rain in His hands, He's got the wind and the rain
ti - ny lit - tle ba - by in His hands, He's got the ti - ny lit - tle ba - by
you and me, sis - ter, in His hands, He's got you and me, broth-er,

Coda (after last stanza)

in His hands, He's got the whole world in His hands.
in His hands, He's got the whole world in His hands.
in His hands, He's got the whole world in His hands.
in His hands, He's got the whole world in His hands. He's got the whole world in His hands.

44 Psalm 33

Leader: A Call to Worship!
Sing joyfully to the Lord, you righteous;
it is fitting for the upright to praise him.
*Choir: Praise the Lord with the harp;
make music to him on the ten-stringed lyre.*
People: **Sing to him a new song;
play skillfully, and shout for joy.**
Leader: For the word of the Lord is right and true;
he is faithful in all he does.
People: **The Lord loves righteousness and justice;
the earth is full of his unfailing love.**
*Choir: By the word of the Lord were the heavens made,
their starry host by the breath of his mouth,
He gathers the waters of the sea into jars;
he puts the deep into storehouses.*
Leader: Let all the earth fear the Lord!
People: **Let all the people of the world revere him!**
*Choir: For he spoke, and it came to be;
he commanded, and it stood firm.*
Leader: Blessed is the nation whose God is the Lord.
*Choir: The eyes of the Lord are on those who fear him,
on those whose hope is in his unfailing love.*
Leader: We wait in hope for the Lord;
People: **He is our help and our shield.**
Leader: In him our hearts rejoice;
People: **For we trust in his holy name.**
All: **May your unfailing love rest upon us, O Lord,
As we put our hope in you.**
Choir: Sing joyfully to the Lord, you righteous;
People: **It is fitting for the upright to praise him.**
Leader: Praise the Lord with the harp;
make music to him on the ten-stringed lyre.
Choir: Sing to him a new song; play skillfully and shout for joy.
All: **For the word of the Lord is right and true;
he is faithful in all he does.**

(NIV)

Sing Praise to God Who Reigns Above 45

The Lord reigneth; let the earth rejoice...Psa. 97:1

JOHANN J. SCHÜTZ
TR. FRANCES E. COX

BOHEMIAN BRETHREN'S
KIRCHENGESANG

1. Sing praise to God who reigns a-bove, The God of all cre-a-tion, The God of pow'r, the God of love, The God of our sal-va-tion; With heal-ing balm my soul He fills, And ev-ery faith-less mur-mur stills: To God all praise and glo-ry.

2. What God's al-might-y pow'r hath made His gra-cious mer-cy keep-eth; By morn-ing glow or eve-ning shade His watch-ful eye ne'er sleep-eth; With-in the king-dom of His might, Lo! all is just and all is right: To God all praise and glo-ry.

3. The Lord is nev-er far a-way, But, through all grief dis-tress-ing, An ev-er-pres-ent help and stay, Our peace, and joy, and bless-ing; As with a moth-er's ten-der hand, He leads His own, His cho-sen band: To God all praise and glo-ry.

4. Thus, all my glad-some way a-long, I sing a-loud Thy prais-es, That men may hear the grate-ful song My voice un-wea-ried rais-es, Be joy-ful in the Lord, my heart, Both soul and bod-y bear your part: To God all praise and glo-ry. A-men.

46 O Could I Speak the Matchless Worth

I call to the Lord, who is worthy of praise. II Sam. 22:4

SAMUEL MEDLEY

UNKNOWN
ARR. LOWELL MASON

1. O could I speak the match-less worth, O could I sound the glo-ries forth Which in my Sav-ior shine, I'd sing His glo-rious right-eous-ness, And mag-ni-fy the won-drous grace Which made sal-va-tion mine, Which made sal-va-tion mine.

2. I'd sing the char-ac-ters He bears, And all the forms of love He wears, Ex-alt-ed on His throne: In loft-iest songs of sweet-est praise, I would to ev-er-last-ing days Make all His glo-ries known, Make all His glo-ries known.

3. Soon the de-light-ful day will come When my dear Lord will bring me home, And I shall see His face; Then with my Sav-ior, Broth-er, Friend, A blest e-ter-ni-ty I'll spend, Tri-um-phant in His grace, Tri-um-phant in His grace.

Praise Ye the Triune God 47

I will . . . praise Thy name for Thy loving kindness. Psa. 138:2

ELIZABETH R. CHARLES   FRIEDRICH F. FLEMMING

1. Praise ye the Fa - ther! for His lov - ing kind - ness, Ten - der - ly
2. Praise ye the Sav - ior! great is His com - pas - sion, Gra - cious - ly
3. Praise ye the Spir - it! Com-fort - er of Is - rael, Sent of the

cares He for His err - ing chil - dren; Praise Him, ye an - gels,
cares He for His cho - sen peo - ple; Young men and maid - ens,
Fa - ther and the Son to bless us; Praise ye the Fa - ther,

praise Him in the heav - ens, Praise ye Je - ho - vah!
ye old men and chil - dren, Praise ye the Sav - ior!
Son and Ho - ly Spir - it, Praise ye the tri - une God!

Father, I Adore You 48

True worshipers will worship the Father in spirit and truth. John 4:23

TERRYE COELHO   TERRYE COELHO

Unison I   II   III

1. Fa - ther, I a-dore You, Lay my life be - fore You; How I love You.
2. Je - sus, I a-dore You, Lay my life be - fore You; How I love You.
3. Spir - it, I a-dore You, Lay my life be - fore You; How I love You.

49 Brethren, We Have Met to Worship

Let us go into the house of the Lord. Psa. 122:1

GEORGE ATKINS

WILLIAM MOORE

1. Breth - ren, we have met to wor-ship And a - dore the Lord our God;
2. Let us love our God su - preme-ly, Let us love each oth - er too;

Will you pray with all your pow - er, While we try to preach the Word?
Let us love and pray for sin - ners Till our God makes all things new.

All is vain un - less the Spir - it Of the Ho - ly One comes down;
Then He'll call us home to heav - en, At His ta - ble we'll sit down;

Breth - ren, pray, and ho - ly man - na Will be show-ered all a - round.
Christ will gird Him - self and serve us With sweet man - na all a - round.

Holy, Holy 50

Holy, holy, holy, Lord God Almighty, which was, and is, and is to come. Rev. 4:8

JIMMY OWENS

JIMMY OWENS

1. Ho - ly, ho - ly, ho - ly, ho - ly, Ho - ly, ho - ly,
2. Gra - cious Fa - ther, gra - cious Fa - ther, We're so blest to be your
3. Pre - cious Je - sus, pre - cious Je - sus, We're so glad that you've re-
4. Ho - ly Spir - it, Ho - ly Spir - it, Come and fill our hearts a-
5. Ho - ly, ho - ly, ho - ly, ho - ly, Ho - ly, ho - ly,

Lord God al - might - y; And we lift our hearts be - fore You as a
chil - dren, gra - cious Fa - ther; And we lift our heads be - fore You as a
deemed us, pre - cious Je - sus; And we lift our hands be - fore You as a
new, Ho - ly Spir - it; And we lift our voice be - fore You as a
Lord God al - might - y; And we lift our hearts be - fore You as a

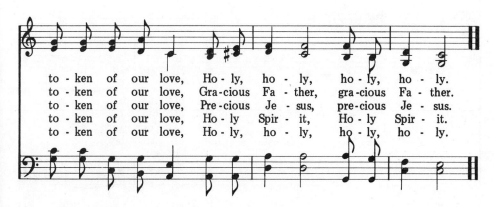

to - ken of our love, Ho - ly, ho - ly, ho - ly, ho - ly.
to - ken of our love, Gra - cious Fa - ther, gra - cious Fa - ther.
to - ken of our love, Pre - cious Je - sus, pre - cious Je - sus.
to - ken of our love, Ho - ly Spir - it, Ho - ly Spir - it.
to - ken of our love, Ho - ly, ho - ly, ho - ly, ho - ly.

51 God of the Ages

And God said, "I AM THAT I AM." Ex. 3:14

MARGARET CLARKSON

TRADITIONAL GAELIC MELODY
ARR. JACK SCHRADER

1. God of the a - ges, His - to - ry's Mak - er,
2. God of this morn - ing, Glad - ly Your chil - dren
3. God of to - mor - row, Strong O - ver - com - er,
4. Lord of past a - ges, Lord of this morn - ing,

Plan - ning our path - way, Hold - ing us fast,
Wor - ship be - fore You, Trust - ing - ly bow:
Princ - es of dark - ness Own Your com - mand:
Lord of the fu - ture, Help us, we pray:

Shap - ing in mer - cy All that con - cerns us:
Teach us to know You Al - ways a - mong us,
What then can harm us? We are Your peo - ple,
Teach us to trust You, Love and o - bey You,

Fa - ther, we praise You, Lord of the past.
Qui - et - ly sov - 'reign— Lord of our now.
Now and for - ev - er Kept by Your hand.
Crown You each mo - ment Lord of to - day.

Psalm 113

Leader: A Call to Worship!
Praise the Lord.
Praise, O servants of the Lord,
praise the name of the Lord.
People: **Let the name of the Lord be praised,**
both now and forevermore.
From the rising of the sun to the place where it sets,
the name of the Lord is to be praised.
Leader: The Lord is exalted over all the nations, his glory above the heavens.
People: **Who is like the Lord our God? —**
Leader: The One who sits enthroned on high,
who stoops down to look on the heavens and the earth?
People: **He raises the poor from the dust**
and lifts the needy from the ash heap.
Leader: He seats them with princes,
with the princes of their people.
People: **He settles the barren woman in her home**
as a happy mother of children.
Leader: Praise the Lord!
People: **Praise the Lord!**
All: **Praise, O servants of the Lord!**
Praise the name of the Lord!

(NIV)

53 You Are My Hiding Place

You will preserve me from trouble with songs of deliverance. Psa. 32:7

MICHAEL LEDNER

MICHAEL LEDNER

You are my hid-ing place, You al-ways fill my heart with songs of de-liv-er-ance when-ev-er I am a-fraid, I will trust in You. I will trust in You; Let the weak say, "I am strong in the strength of the Lord."

We Love You and Praise You 54

Enter into His courts with praise. Psa. 100:4

HARLAN ROGERS   HARLAN ROGERS

1. O how we love you and praise you, O Lord.
2. O how we thank you and wor - ship you, Lord.
3. O how we love you and hon - or you, Lord.

How we love you and praise you, O Lord.
How we thank you and wor - ship you, Lord.
How we love you and hon - or you, Lord.

With our hearts filled with praise, our voic - es we raise;
As our hearts o - ver - flow we want you to know
As our hearts o - ver - flow we want you to know

We love you and praise you, O Lord.
We thank you and wor - ship you, Lord.
We love you and hon - or you, Lord.

55 Join All the Glorious Names

Far above . . . every name that is named. Eph. 1:21

ISAAC WATTS

JOHN DARWALL

1. Join all the glorious names, Of wisdom, love, and pow'r,
2. Great Prophet of my God, My tongue would bless Thy name:
3. Jesus, my great High Priest, Offered His blood, and died;
4. Thou art my Counselor, My Pattern, and my Guide,
5. My Savior and my Lord, My Conqu'ror and my King,

That ever mortals knew, That angels
By Thee the joyful news Of our sal-
My guilty conscience seeks No sacri-
And Thou my Shepherd art; O, keep me
Thy scepter and Thy sword, Thy reigning

ever bore: All are too poor to speak His worth,
vation came, The joyful news of sins forgiv'n,
fice beside: His pow'rful blood did once atone
near Thy side; Nor let my feet e'er turn astray
grace, I sing: Thine is the pow'r; behold I sit

Too poor to set my Savior forth.
Of hell subdued and peace with heav'n.
And now it pleads before the throne.
To wander in the crooked way.
In willing bonds beneath Thy feet. A-men.

All Hail the Power of Jesus' Name 56

He hath . . . a name written, King of Kings, and Lord of Lords. Rev. 19:16

EDWARD PERRONET   JAMES ELLOR

1. All hail the pow'r of Je - sus' name! Let an - gels pros-trate
2. Ye cho - sen seed of Is - rael's race, Ye ran-somed of the
3. Let ev - ery kin - dred, ev - ery tribe, On this ter - res - trial
4. O that with yon - der sa - cred throng We at His feet may

fall, Let an - gels pros-trate fall; Bring forth the roy - al di - a-
fall, Ye ran - somed of the fall; Hail Him who saves you by His
ball, On this ter - res - trial ball; To Him all maj - es - ty as-
fall, We at His feet may fall! We'll join the ev - er - last - ing

dem,
grace,   And crown   Him, crown Him,
cribe,
song,   And crown Him, crown Him, crown Him, crown Him, crown Him,

crown

crown Him,   crown Him, And crown   Him   Lord of all. A-men.

Him,   And crown Him

57 Jesus, Name Above All Names

At the name of Jesus every knee shall bow. Phil. 2:10

NAIDA HEARN

NAIDA HEARN

Je - sus, name a - bove all names: beau - ti - ful
Sav - ior, glo - ri - ous Lord, Em - man - u - el, God is
with us, bless - ed Re - deem - er, Liv - ing Word.

58 JESUS — Praise His Holy Names!

LOVE	RESURRECTION AND THE LIFE	ROCK
SAVIOR	JESUS CHRIST OUR KING	MASTER
MESSIAH	CHIEF CORNERSTONE	TEACHER
IMMANUEL	BREAD OF LIFE	THE VINE
SON OF GOD	DAYSPRING	SON OF MAN
LORD OF ALL	RABBI	LAMB OF GOD
ONLY WISE GOD		KING OF GLORY
ROSE OF SHARON	I	MAN OF SORROWS
PRINCE OF PEACE	AM	THE SECOND ADAM
STAR OUT OF JACOB	THE	SEED OF THE WOMAN
BRIGHT AND MORNING STAR	ALPHA	WAY, TRUTH, AND LIFE
WONDERFUL COUNSELOR	AND	EVERLASTING FATHER
SON OF THE HIGHEST	OMEGA	LILY OF THE VALLEY
LIGHT OF THE WORLD		HEIR OF ALL THINGS
GREAT HIGH PRIEST		FAITHFUL AND TRUE
GREAT PHYSICIAN	THE DOOR	ANCIENT OF DAYS
GOD'S ANOINTED	HEAD OF THE BODY	GOOD SHEPHERD
WORD OF GOD	IMAGE OF THE	MIGHTY GOD
	INVISIBLE GOD	

AUTHOR AND FINISHER OF OUR FAITH

Blessed Be the Name 59

Blessed be the name of the Lord. Job 1:21

Source Unknown

William H. Clark

Arr. Ralph E. Hudson and William J. Kirkpatrick

1. All praise to Him who reigns a - bove In maj - es - ty su - preme,
2. His name a - bove all names shall stand, Ex - alt - ed more and more,
3. Re - deem - er, Sav - ior, Friend of man Once ru - ined by the fall,
4. His name shall be the Coun - sel - or, The might - y Prince of Peace,

Who gave His Son for man to die, That He might man re - deem!
At God the Fa - ther's own right hand, Where an - gel hosts a - dore.
Thou hast de - vised sal - va - tion's plan, For Thou hast died for all.
Of all earth's king - doms Con - quer - or, Whose reign shall nev - er cease.

Refrain

Bless-ed be the name, bless-ed be the name, Bless-ed be the name of the Lord;

Bless-ed be the name, bless-ed be the name, Bless-ed be the name of the Lord.

60 His Name Is Wonderful

His name shall be called Wonderful . . . Isa. 9:6

AUDREY MIEIR

AUDREY MIEIR

His name is Won-der-ful, His name is Won-der-ful, His name is Won-der-ful,

Je - sus, my Lord; He is the might-y King, Mas-ter of ev - ery-thing,

His name is Won - der -ful, Je - sus, my Lord. He's the great Shep-herd, the

Rock of all a - ges, Al-might-y God is He; Bow down be-

fore Him, Love and a - dore Him, His name is Won-der-ful, Je-sus my Lord.

Glorify Thy Name 61

Father, glorify Thy name. John 12:28

DONNA ADKINS

DONNA ADKINS

{Fa - ther,}
{Je - sus,} I love you, I praise you, I a - dore you;

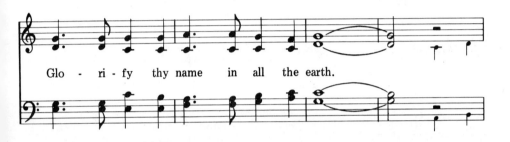

Glo - ri - fy thy name in all the earth.

Glo - ri - fy thy name, glo - ri - fy thy name,

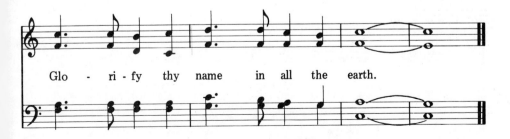

Glo - ri - fy thy name in all the earth.

62 I Will Praise Him

Worthy is the Lamb that was slain . . . Rev. 5:12

MARGARET J. HARRIS

MARGARET J. HARRIS

1. When I saw the cleans-ing foun-tain, O - pen wide for all my sin,
2. Tho' the way seems straight and nar-row, All I claimed was swept a-way;
3. Then God's fire up-on the al - tar Of my heart was set a-flame;
4. Bless - ed be the name of Je - sus! I'm so glad He took me in;
5. Glo - ry, glo - ry to the Fa - ther! Glo - ry, glo - ry to the Son!

I o-beyed the Spir-it's woo - ing When He said, "Wilt thou be clean?"
My am - bi - tions, plans and wish-es At my feet in ash - es lay.
I shall nev - er cease to praise Him— Glo - ry, glo - ry to His name!
He's for - giv - en my trans-gres-sions, He has cleansed my heart from sin.
Glo - ry, glo - ry to the Spir - it! Glo - ry to the Three in One!

Chorus

I will praise Him! I will praise Him! Praise the Lamb for sin-ners slain;

Give Him glo - ry, all ye peo-ple, For His blood can wash a-way each stain.

Our Great Savior 63

Behold . . . a friend of publicans and sinners! Luke 7:34

ROWLAND H. PRICHARD
ARR. ROBERT HARKNESS

J. WILBUR CHAPMAN

1. Je - sus! what a Friend for sin - ners! Je - sus! Lov - er of my soul;
2. Je - sus! what a Strength in weak - ness! Let me hide my - self in Him;
3. Je - sus! what a Help in sor - row! While the bil - lows o'er me roll,
4. Je - sus! what a Guide and Keep - er! While the tem - pest still is high,
5. Je - sus! I do now re - ceive Him, More than all in Him I find,

Friends may fail me, foes as - sail me, He, my Sav - ior, makes me whole.
Tempt - ed, tried, and some - times fail - ing, He, my Strength, my vic - t'ry wins.
E - ven when my heart is break - ing, He, my Com - fort, helps my soul.
Storms a - bout me, night o'er - takes me, He, my Pi - lot, hears my cry.
He hath grant - ed me for - give - ness, I am His, and He is mine.

Refrain

Hal - le - lu - jah! what a Sav - ior! Hal - le - lu - jah! what a Friend!

Sav - ing, help - ing, keep - ing, lov - ing, He is with me to the end.

64 For the Beauty of the Earth

Every good gift and every perfect gift is from above. James 1:17

FOLLIOTT S. PIERPOINT

CONRAD KOCHER
ARR. WILLIAM H. MONK

1. For the beau - ty of the earth, For the glo - ry
2. For the beau - ty of each hour Of the day and
3. For the joy of ear and eye, For the heart and
4. For the joy of hu - man love, Broth - er, sis - ter,
5. For each per - fect gift of Thine To our race so

of the skies, For the love which from our birth
of the night, Hill and vale, and tree, and flow'r,
mind's de - light, For the mys - tic har - mo - ny
par - ent, child, Friends on earth and friends a - bove,
free - ly giv'n, Grac - es hu - man and di - vine,

O - ver and a - round us lies, Lord of all, to
Sun and moon and stars of light, Lord of all, to
Link - ing sense to sound and sight, Lord of all, to
For all gen - tle thoughts and mild, Lord of all, to
Flow'rs of earth and buds of heav'n, Lord of all, to

Thee we raise This our hymn of grate - ful praise.
Thee we raise This our hymn of grate - ful praise.
Thee we raise This our hymn of grate - ful praise.
Thee we raise This our hymn of grate - ful praise.
Thee we raise This our hymn of grate - ful praise. A - men.

All Things Bright and Beautiful 65

All things were made by Him...John 1:3

CECIL F. ALEXANDER

TRADITIONAL ENGLISH MELODY

Unison

All things bright and beau - ti - ful, All crea - tures great and small,

Fine

All things wise and won - der - ful; The Lord God made them all.

1. Each lit - tle flow'r that o - pens, Each lit - tle bird that sings,
2. The pur - ple - head - ed moun - tain, The riv - er run - ning by,
3. The cold wind in the win - ter, The pleas - ant sum - mer sun,
4. He gave us eyes to see them, And lips that we might tell

D. C. al Fine

He made their glow - ing col - ors, He made their ti - ny wings.
The sun - set, and the morn - ing That bright - ens up the sky.
The ripe fruits in the gar - den: He made them, ev - ery one.
How great is God Al - might - y, Who has made all things well.

66 When Morning Gilds the Skies

His voice shalt Thou hear in the morning, O Lord, Psa. 5:3

Tr. Edward Caswall

Joseph Barnby

1. When morn - ing gilds the skies, My heart a - wak - ing cries:
2. The night be - comes as day When from the heart we say:
3. Sing, suns and stars of space, Sing, ye that see His face,
4. Be this while life is mine My can - ti - cle di - vine:

May Je - sus Christ be praised! A - like at work or prayer
May Je - sus Christ be praised! The pow'rs of dark - ness fear
Sing, Je - sus Christ be praised! Let all the earth a - round
May Je - sus Christ be praised! Be this th' e - ter - nal song,

To Je - sus I re - pair: May Je - sus Christ be praised!
When this sweet chant they hear: May Je - sus Christ be praised!
Ring joy - ous with the sound: May Je - sus Christ be praised!
Through all the a - ges long: May Je - sus Christ be praised! A-men.

67 O God, Our Help in Ages Past

Lord, Thou has been our dwelling place in all generations. Psa. 90:1

Isaac Watts

William Croft

1. O God, our help in a - ges past, Our hope for years to come,
2. Un - der the shad - ow of Thy throne Still may we dwell se - cure;
3. Be - fore the hills in or - der stood, Or earth re - ceived her frame,
4. A thou - sand a - ges in Thy sight Are like an eve - ning gone;
5. O God, our help in a - ges past, Our hope for years to come,

Our shel-ter from the storm-y blast, And our e-ter-nal home!
Suf-fi-cient is Thine arm a-lone, And our de-fense is sure.
From ev-er-last-ing Thou art God, To end-less years the same.
Short as the watch that ends the night, Be-fore the ris-ing sun.
Be Thou our guide while life shall last, And our e-ter-nal home! A-men.

All Hail the Power of Jesus' Name 68

He hath...a name written, King of Kings, and Lord of Lords. Rev. 19:16

EDWARD PERRONET
ADAPTED BY JOHN RIPPON

OLIVER HOLDEN

1. All hail the power of Je-sus' name! Let an-gels pros-trate fall;
2. Ye cho-sen seed of Is-rael's race, Ye ran-somed from the fall,
3. Let ev-ery kin-dred, ev-ery tribe, On this ter-res-trial ball,
4. O that with yon-der sa-cred throng We at His feet may fall!

Bring forth the roy-al di-a-dem, And crown Him Lord of all;
Hail Him who saves you by His grace, And crown Him Lord of all;
To Him all maj-es-ty as-cribe, And crown Him Lord of all;
We'll join the ev-er-last-ing song, And crown Him Lord of all;

Bring forth the roy-al di-a-dem, And crown Him Lord of all!
Hail Him who saves you by His grace, And crown Him Lord of all!
To Him all maj-es-ty as-cribe, And crown Him Lord of all!
We'll join the ev-er-last-ing song, And crown Him Lord of all!

69 Sing Hallelujah

Sing Praise to the Lord. Psa. 68:32

LINDA STASSEN

LINDA STASSEN

Optional Descant

Unison

Sing hal-le-lu-jah to the Lord.

Sing hal-le-lu-jah to the Lord. Sing hal-le-

Sing hal-le-lu-jah, Hal - le - lu -

lu-jah to the Lord. Sing hal-le-lu-jah, Sing hal-le-

1 **2**

jah; Sing hal-le-lu-jah to the Lord.

1 **2**

lu-jah. Sing hal-le-lu-jah to the Lord.

Come, Christians, Join to Sing 70

O come, let us sing unto the Lord. Psa. 95:1

CHRISTIAN H. BATEMAN

TRADITIONAL SPANISH MELODY
ARR. DAVID EVANS

1. Come, Chris-tians, join to sing Al-le-lu-ia! A - men!
2. Come, lift your hearts on high, Al-le-lu-ia! A - men!
3. Praise yet our Christ a - gain, Al-le-lu-ia! A - men!

Loud praise to Christ our King; Al-le-lu-ia! A - men!
Let prais - es fill the sky; Al-le-lu-ia! A - men!
Life shall not end the strain; Al-le-lu-ia! A - men!

Let all, with heart and voice, Be - fore His throne re - joice;
He is our Guide and Friend; To us He'll con - de - scend;
On heav - en's bliss - ful shore His good - ness we'll a - dore,

Praise is His gra - cious choice: Al-le-lu-ia! A - men!
His love shall nev - er end: Al-le-lu-ia! A - men!
Sing - ing for - ev - er - more, "Al-le-lu-ia! A - men!"

Music from the *Revised Church Hymnary* by permission of Oxford University Press.

71 Love Divine, All Loves Excelling

Above all these things put on charity, which is the bond of perfectness. Col. 3:14

CHARLES WESLEY   JOHN ZUNDEL

1. Love di - vine, all loves ex - cel - ling, Joy of heav'n, to earth come down;
2. Breathe, O breathe Thy lov - ing Spir - it In - to ev - ery trou-bled breast!
3. Come, Al-might - y to de - liv - er, Let us all Thy life re - ceive;
4. Fin - ish then Thy new cre - a - tion, Pure and spot-less let us be;

Fix in us Thy hum - ble dwell-ing, All Thy faith - ful mer-cies crown.
Let us all in Thee in - her - it, Let us find the prom-ised rest.
Sud-den - ly re - turn, and nev - er, Nev - er-more Thy tem-ples leave:
Let us see Thy great sal - va - tion Per - fect - ly re-stored in Thee:

Je - sus, Thou art all com - pas-sion, Pure, un-bound-ed love Thou art;
Take a - way the love of sin - ning, Al - pha and O - me - ga be;
Thee we would be al - ways bless-ing, Serve Thee as Thy hosts a - bove,
Changed from glo - ry in - to glo - ry, Till in heav'n we take our place,

Vis - it us with Thy sal - va - tion; En - ter ev - ery trem-bling heart.
End of faith, as its be - gin-ning, Set our hearts at lib - er - ty.
Pray, and praise Thee with-out ceas-ing, Glo - ry in Thy per-fect love.
Till we cast our crowns be-fore Thee, Lost in won-der, love, and praise. A-men.

O the Deep, Deep Love of Jesus 72

Having loved His own, He loved them to the end. John 13:1

TRADITIONAL GAELIC MELODY
ARR. JACK SCHRADER

SAMUEL TREVOR FRANCIS

1. O, the deep, deep love of Je - sus,
2. O, the deep, deep love of Je - sus,
3. Un - der - neath me, all a - round me

Vast, un - mea - sured, bound - less, free!
Love of ev - ery love the best;
Is the cur - rent of His love;

Roll - ing as a might - y o - cean
'Tis an o - cean vast of bless - ing,
Lead - ing on - ward, lead - ing home - ward,

In its full - ness o - ver me.
'Tis a ha - ven sweet of rest.
To my glo - rious rest a - bove.

73 Praise Him! Praise Him!

Praise Him according to His excellent greatness. Psa. 150:2

FANNY J. CROSBY

CHESTER G. ALLEN

1. Praise Him! praise Him! Je - sus, our bless - ed Re - deem - er! Sing, O Earth, His
2. Praise Him! praise Him! Je - sus, our bless - ed Re - deem - er! For our sins He
3. Praise Him! praise Him! Je - sus, our bless - ed Re - deem - er! Heav'n - ly por - tals

won - der - ful love pro - claim! Hail Him! hail Him! high - est arch - an - gels in glo - ry;
suf - fered, and bled and died; He our Rock, our hope of e - ter - nal sal - va - tion,
loud with ho - san - nas ring! Je - sus, Sav - ior, reign - eth for - ev - er and ev - er;

Strength and hon - or give to His ho - ly name! Like a shep - herd Je - sus will
Hail Him! hail Him! Je - sus the Cru - ci - fied. Sound His prais - es! Je - sus who
Crown Him! crown Him! Proph - et and Priest and King! Christ is com - ing! o - ver the

Refrain

guard His chil - dren, In His arms He car - ries them all day long:
bore our sor - rows; Love un - bound - ed, won - der - ful, deep and strong: Praise Him! praise Him!
world vic - to - rious, Pow'r and glo - ry un - to the Lord be - long:

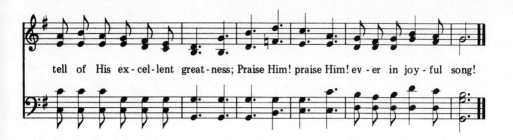

tell of His ex-cel-lent great-ness; Praise Him! praise Him! ev-er in joy-ful song!

Ye Servants of God, Your Master Proclaim 74

Salvation and glory, and honor, and power, unto the Lord our God. Rev. 19:1

CHARLES WESLEY · WILLIAM CROFT

1. Ye serv-ants of God, your Mas-ter pro-claim, And pub-lish a-
2. God rul-eth on high, al-might-y to save; And still He is
3. Sal-va-tion to God who sits on the throne, Let all cry a-
4. Then let us a-dore and give Him His right, All glo-ry and

broad His won-der-ful name; The name all vic-to-rious of
nigh— His pres-ence we have; The great con-gre-ga-tion His
loud, and hon-or the Son; The prais-es of Je-sus the
pow'r, all wis-dom and might; All hon-or and bless-ing, with

Je-sus ex-tol; His king-dom is glo-rious, He rules o-ver all.
tri-umph shall sing, As-crib-ing sal-va-tion to Je-sus our King.
an-gels pro-claim, Fall down on their fac-es and wor-ship the Lamb.
an-gels a-bove, And thanks nev-er ceas-ing, and in-fi-nite love. A-men.

75 Let's Just Praise the Lord

Lift up your hands...and praise the Lord. Psa. 134:2

WILLIAM J. AND GLORIA GAITHER

WILLIAM J. GAITHER

Let's just praise the Lord! Praise the Lord! Let's just

lift our hearts to heav - en and praise the

Lord; Let's just praise the Lord, Praise the Lord, Let's just

Fine

lift our hearts to heav - en and praise the Lord!

1. O, we thank You for Your kind - ness, We thank You for Your
2. Just the pre - cious name of Je - sus is worth - y of our

love, We have been in heaven - ly plac - es, felt bless-ings from a -
praise. Let us bow our knees be - fore Him, our hands to heav - en

bove; We've been shar - ing all the good things, the fam - ily can af -
raise: When He comes in clouds of glo - ry, with Him to ev - er

D.C.

ford. Let's just turn our praise toward heav - en and praise the Lord.
reign, Let's just lift our hap - py voic - es, and praise His name.

76   Psalm 148

Leader: A Call to Worship!
Praise the Lord.
People: **Praise the Lord from the heavens,**
praise him in the heights above.
Leader: Praise him, all his angels,
praise him, all his heavenly hosts.
People: **Praise him, sun and moon,**
praise him, all you shining stars.
Leader: Praise him, you highest heavens
and you waters above the skies.
All: **Let them praise the name of the Lord,**
for he commanded and they were created.
Leader: He set them in place for ever and ever;
he gave a decree that will never pass away.
All: **Praise the Lord from the earth!**
Leader: You great sea creatures and all ocean depths.
People: **Lightning and hail, snow and clouds,**
stormy winds that do his bidding.
Leader: You mountains and all hills!
People: **Fruit trees and all cedars!**
Leader: Wild animals and all cattle, small creatures and flying birds!
People: **Kings of the earth and all nations,**
you princes and all rulers on earth!
Leader: Young men and maidens,
old men and children!
All: **Let them praise the name of the Lord!**
Leader: For his name alone is exalted!
People: **His splendor is above the earth and the heavens.**
All: **Praise the name of the Lord!**
(NIV)

Praise the Lord, Ye Heavens, Adore Him 77

Praise the Lord from the heavens. Psa. 148:1

BASED ON PSALM 148

JOHN H. WILLCOX

1. Praise the Lord! ye heav'ns, a - dore Him; Praise Him, an - gels in the height;
2. Praise the Lord! for He is glo - rious; Nev - er shall His prom - ise fail:
3. Wor - ship, hon - or, glo - ry, bless - ing, Lord, we of - fer un - to Thee;

Sun and moon, re - joice be - fore Him, Praise Him, all ye stars of light. Praise the
God hath made His saints vic - to - rious; Sin and death shall not pre - vail. Praise the
Young and old, Thy praise ex - press - ing, In glad hom - age bend the knee. All the

Lord! for He hath spo - ken; Worlds His might - y voice o - beyed; Laws, which
God of our sal - va - tion! Hosts on high, His pow'r pro - claim; Heav'n, and
saints in heav'n a - dore Thee; We would bow be - fore Thy throne: As Thine

nev - er shall be bro - ken For their guid - ance He hath made.
earth, and all cre - a - tion, Laud and mag - ni - fy His name.
an - gels serve be - fore Thee, So on earth Thy will be done. A - men.

78 I Just Came to Praise the Lord

While I live will I praise the Lord...Psa. 146:2

WAYNE ROMERO   WAYNE ROMERO

1. I just came to praise the Lord, I just came to praise the Lord;
2. I just came to thank the Lord, I just came to thank the Lord;
3. I just came to love the Lord, I just came to love the Lord;

1,3 Fine | **2**

I just came to praise His name, I just came to praise the Lord.
I just came to praise His name, I just came to thank the Lord.   He
I just came to praise His name, I just came to love the Lord.

came in - to my life one ver - y spe-cial day, He came in - to my heart

to show me a bet - ter way; He said He would nev - er de - part,

D.C. al Fine

And this is why I sing: I just came to praise the Lord.

To God Be the Glory 79

Give unto the Lord the glory due unto His name. Psa. 29:2

FANNY J. CROSBY   WILLIAM H. DOANE

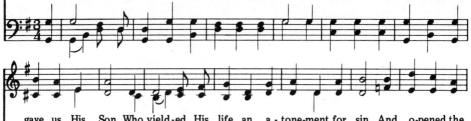

1. To God be the glo - ry, great things He hath done, So loved He the world that He
2. O per - fect re - demp-tion, the pur-chase of blood, To ev - ery be - liev - er the
3. Great things He hath taught us, great things He hath done, And great our re-joic · ing thro'

gave us His Son, Who yield-ed His life an a - tone-ment for sin, And o-pened the
prom-ise of God; The vil - est of - fend - er who tru - ly be-lieves, That mo-ment from
Je - sus the Son; But pur - er, and high - er, and great - er will be Our won-der, our

Refrain

Life-gate that all may go in.
Je - sus a par-don re-ceives. Praise the Lord, praise the Lord, Let the earth hear His
trans-port, when Je - sus we see.

voice! Praise the Lord, praise the Lord, Let the peo - ple re-joice! O come to the

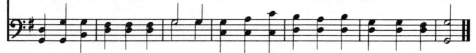

Fa-ther thro' Je - sus the Son, And give Him the glo - ry, great things He hath done.

80 Sometimes "Alleluia"

All with one accord. Acts 2:1

CHUCK GIRARD   CHUCK GIRARD

Some-times Al - le - lu - ia,   Some-times praise the Lord.

Fine
(3rd time)

Some-times gent-ly sing - ing,   Our hearts in one ac - cord.

1. Oh, let us lift our voic - es,   look toward the
2. Oh, let our joy be un - con-fined,   let us sing with

sky and start to sing.   Oh, let us now re - turn His
free - dom un - re-strained.   Let's take this feel - ing that we're

love, just let our voic - es ring.
feel -ing now, out-side these walls and let it rain.

Oh, let us feel His pres - ence, let the sound of
Oh, let the Spir - it o - ver-flow, as we are

prais - es fill the air. Oh, let us sing the song of
filled from head to toe. We love You, Fa - ther, Son and

D. C.

Je - sus' love to peo - ple ev - ery - where.
Ho - ly Ghost— we want this world to know.

81   Psalm 147

Leader: A Call to Worship!
Praise the Lord.
**People: How good it is to sing praises to our God,
how pleasant and fitting to praise him!**
*Voice One: The Lord builds up Jerusalem;
he gathers the exiles of Israel.*
He heals the brokenhearted and binds up their wounds
**People: How good it is to sing praises to our God,
how pleasant and fitting to praise him!**
Leader: Praise the Lord!
*Voice Two: He determines the number of the stars
and calls them each by name.*
Leader: Great is our Lord and mighty in power;
his understanding has no limit.
*Voice One: The Lord sustains the humble
but casts the wicked to the ground.*
**People: Sing to the Lord with thanksgiving;
make music to our God on the harp.**
*Voice Two: He covers the sky with clouds;
he supplies the earth with rain
and makes grass grow on the hills.*
*Voice One: He provides food for the cattle
and for the young ravens when they call.*
Leader: The Lord delights in those who fear him,
who put their hope in his unfailing love.
Extol the Lord, O Jerusalem.
People: Praise your God, O Zion.
*Voice One: For he strengthens the bars of your gates
and blesses your people within you.*
*Voice Two: He grants peace to your borders
and satisfies you with the finest of wheat.*
*Voice One: He sends his command to the earth;
his words run swiftly.*
Voice Two: He spreads the snow like wool and scatters the frost like ashes.
*Voice One: He hurls down his hail like pebbles.
Who can withstand his icy blast?*
*Voice Two: He sends his word and melts them;
he stirs up his breezes, and the waters flow*
Leader: Praise the Lord!
**People: How good it is to sing praises to our God,
how pleasant and fitting to praise him!**
All: **Praise the Lord!**

(NIV)

Come, Thou Fount of Every Blessing 82

The Lord daily loads us with benefits. Psa. 68:19

ROBERT ROBINSON   TRADITIONAL AMERICAN MELODY

1. Come, Thou Fount of ev-ery bless-ing, Tune my heart to sing Thy grace;
2. Here I raise mine Eb-en-e-zer, Hith-er by Thy help I'm come;
3. O to grace how great a debt-or Dai-ly I'm con-strained to be!

Streams of mer-cy, nev-er ceas-ing, Call for songs of loud-est praise.
And I hope, by Thy good pleas-ure, Safe-ly to ar-rive at home.
Let Thy good-ness, like a fet-ter, Bind my wan-dering heart to Thee:

Teach me some me-lo-dious son-net, Sung by flam-ing tongues a-bove;
Je-sus sought me when a stran-ger, Wan-dering from the fold of God;
Prone to wan-der, Lord, I feel it, Prone to leave the God I love;

Praise His name—I'm fixed up-on it— Name of God's re-deem-ing love.
He, to res-cue me from dan-ger, Bought me with His pre-cious blood.
Here's my heart, O take and seal it; Seal it for Thy courts a-bove.

83 Holy Ground

The place where you stand is holy ground. Acts 7:33

GERON DAVIS

GERON DAVIS

We are stand-ing on ho-ly ground, And I

know that there are an-gels all a-round; Let us

praise Je-sus now— We are

stand-ing in His pres-ence on ho-ly ground (ho-ly ground).

This Is the Day 84

...We will rejoice and be glad in it. Psa. 118:246

LES GARRETT

LES GARRETT

Unison

This is the day, this is the day that the Lord has made, that the
Lord has made; We will re-joice, we will re-joice and be
glad in it, and be glad in it. This is the day that the
Lord has made; We will re-joice and be glad in it.
This is the day, this is the day that the Lord has made.

85 Bless the Lord, O My Soul

All that is within me, bless His holy name. Psa. 103:1

ADAPTED FROM PSALM 103:1

TRADITIONAL

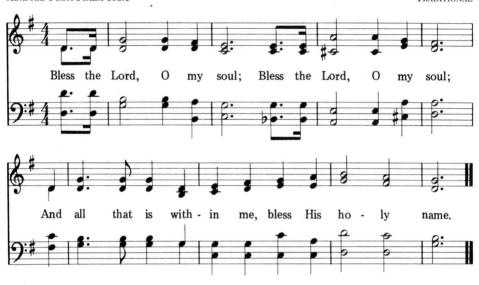

Bless the Lord, O my soul; Bless the Lord, O my soul;

And all that is with-in me, bless His ho-ly name.

86 Clap Your Hands

Clap your hands...shout to God...Psa. 47:1

JIMMY OWENS

JIMMY OWENS

Two-Part Canon

Clap your hands, all you peo-ple; Shout un-to God with a voice of tri-umph

Clap your hands, all you peo-ple; Shout un-to God with a voice of praise! Ho-

san - na! Ho-san - na! Shout un-to God with a voice of tri-umph!

Praise Him! Praise Him! Shout un-to God with a voice of praise!

Glorious Is Thy Name 87

Blessed be Thy glorious name. Neh. 9:5

B.B. McKinney

B.B. McKinney

1. Bless - ed Sav - ior, we a - dore Thee, We Thy love and grace pro-claim;
2. Great Re - deem - er, Lord and Mas - ter, Light of all e - ter - nal days;
3. From the throne of heav-en's glo - ry To the cross of sin and shame,
4. Come, O come, im - mor - tal Sav - ior, Come and take Thy roy - al throne;

Thou art might - y, Thou art ho - ly, Glo - rious is Thy match-less name!
Let the saints of ev - 'ry na - tion Sing Thy just and end - less praise!
Thou didst come to die a ran - som, Guilt - y sin - ners to re - claim!
Come, and reign, and reign for ev - er, Be the king-dom all Thine own!

Refrain

Glo - ri - ous, Glo - ri - ous,
Glo-rious is Thy name, O Lord! Glo-rious is Thy name, O Lord!

1. Glo - rious is Thy name, O Lord!
2. name, O Lord! A - men.

88 Come, Thou Almighty King

Give unto the Lord the glory due unto His name...Psa. 29:2

UNKNOWN

FELICE DE GIARDINI

1. Come, Thou Al - might - y King, Help us Thy name to sing, Help us to praise: Fa - ther, all glo - ri - ous, O'er all vic - to - ri - ous, Come, and reign o - ver us, An - cient of Days.
2. Come, Thou In - car - nate Word, Gird on Thy might - y sword, Our prayer at - tend: Come, and Thy peo - ple bless, And give Thy word suc - cess: Spir - it of ho - li - ness, On us de - scend.
3. Come, Ho - ly Com - fort - er, Thy sa - cred wit - ness bear In this glad hour: Thou who al - might - y art, Now rule in ev - ery heart, And ne'er from us de - part, Spir - it of pow'r.
4. To Thee, great One in Three, E - ter - nal prais - es be Hence, ev - er - more! Thy sov - ereign maj - es - ty May we in glo - ry see, And to e - ter - ni - ty Love and a - dore! A - men.

89 The King of Love My Shepherd Is

I am the good shepherd...I lay down My life for the sheep. John 10: 14, 15

HENRY W. BAKER

JOHN B. DYKES

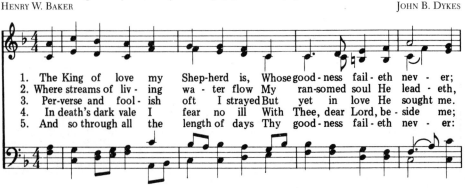

1. The King of love my Shep-herd is, Whose good - ness fail - eth nev - er;
2. Where streams of liv - ing wa - ter flow My ran-somed soul He lead - eth,
3. Per-verse and fool - ish oft I strayed But yet in love He sought me,
4. In death's dark vale I fear no ill With Thee, dear Lord, be - side me;
5. And so through all the length of days Thy good-ness fail - eth nev - er:

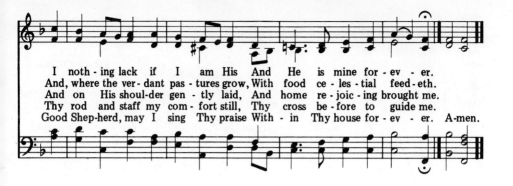

I noth-ing lack if I am His And He is mine for-ev - er.
And, where the ver-dant pas-tures grow, With food ce-les-tial feed-eth.
And on His shoul-der gen - tly laid, And home re-joic-ing brought me.
Thy rod and staff my com-fort still, Thy cross be-fore to guide me.
Good Shep-herd, may I sing Thy praise With - in Thy house for-ev - er. A-men.

O Worship the King, All Glorious Above 90

O Lord my God... Thou are clothed with honor and majesty. Psa. 104:1

ROBERT GRANT

WILLIAM GARDINER'S *SACRED MELODIES*

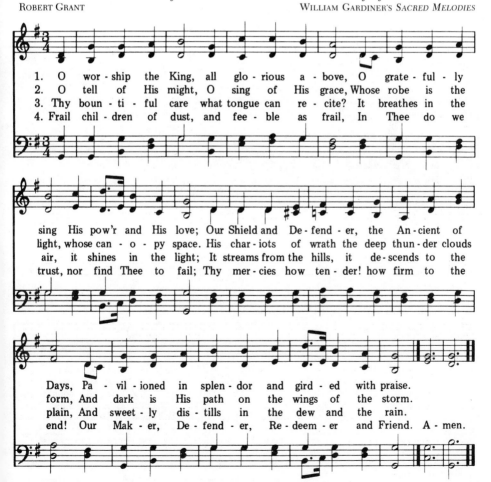

1. O wor - ship the King, all glo - rious a - bove, O grate-ful - ly
2. O tell of His might, O sing of His grace, Whose robe is the
3. Thy boun - ti - ful care what tongue can re - cite? It breathes in the
4. Frail chil - dren of dust, and fee - ble as frail, In Thee do we

sing His pow'r and His love; Our Shield and De - fend - er, the An-cient of
light, whose can - o - py space. His char - iots of wrath the deep thun-der clouds
air, it shines in the light; It streams from the hills, it de-scends to the
trust, nor find Thee to fail; Thy mer - cies how ten - der! how firm to the

Days, Pa - vil - ioned in splen - dor and gird - ed with praise.
form, And dark is His path on the wings of the storm.
plain, And sweet - ly dis - tills in the dew and the rain.
end! Our Mak - er, De - fend - er, Re - deem - er and Friend. A - men.

91 Unto Thee, O Lord

Unto Thee, O Lord, I lift up my soul. Psa. 25:1

PSALM 25:1,2

CHARLES F. MONROE

Descant (second time only)

Un-to thee, O Lord,

Unison

Un-to thee, O Lord, do I lift up my

do I lift up my soul; Un-to thee, O Lord,

soul; Un-to thee, O Lord,

do I lift up my soul. O my

do I lift up my soul. O my God,

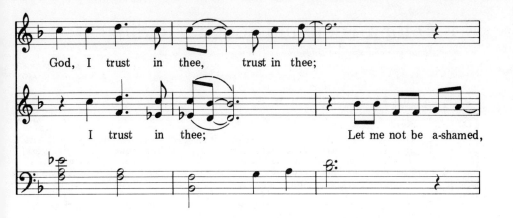

God, I trust in thee, trust in thee;

I trust in thee; Let me not be a-shamed,

repeat ad lib.

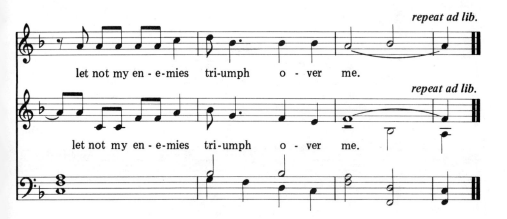

let not my en - e-mies tri-umph o - ver me.

repeat ad lib.

let not my en-e-mies tri-umph o - ver me.

Lift Up Our Souls 92

Let us not seek out of You what we can find only in You,
O Lord, peace and rest and joy and bliss, which abide
only in your abiding joy. Lift up our souls above the
weary round of harassing thoughts to your eternal Presence. Lift up our souls to the pure, bright, serene,
radiant atmosphere of your Presence, that there we may
breathe freely, there repose in your Love, there be at
rest from ourselves, and from all things that weary us;
and there return, arrayed with your peace, to do and
bear what shall please You — Amen.

E.B. Pusey

93 O for a Thousand Tongues to Sing

My tongue shall speak of Thy...praise all the day long. Psa. 35:28

CHARLES WESLEY

CARL G. GLÄSER
ARR. LOWELL MASON

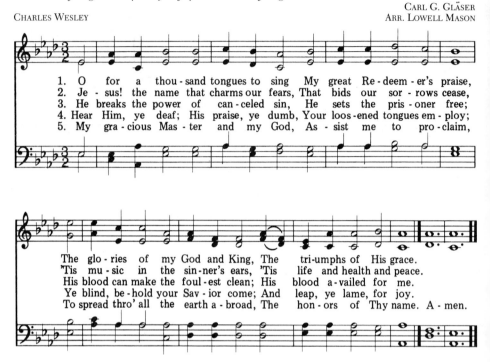

1. O for a thou-sand tongues to sing My great Re-deem-er's praise,
2. Je - sus! the name that charms our fears, That bids our sor - rows cease,
3. He breaks the power of can-celed sin, He sets the pris-oner free;
4. Hear Him, ye deaf; His praise, ye dumb, Your loos-ened tongues em - ploy;
5. My gra-cious Mas - ter and my God, As - sist me to pro-claim,

The glo - ries of my God and King, The tri-umphs of His grace.
'Tis mu - sic in the sin-ner's ears, 'Tis life and health and peace.
His blood can make the foul-est clean; His blood a-vailed for me.
Ye blind, be-hold your Sav - ior come; And leap, ye lame, for joy.
To spread thro' all the earth a-broad, The hon - ors of Thy name. A - men.

94 Lord, We Praise You

Sing unto Him; talk ye of all His wondrous works...Psa 105:2

OTIS SKILLINGS

OTIS SKILLINGS

1. Lord, we praise You, Lord, we praise You,
2. Lord, we thank You, Lord, we thank You,
3. Lord, we love You, Lord, we love You,
4. Al - le - lu - ia! Al - le - lu - ia!

Lord, we praise You, We praise You, Lord!
Lord, we thank You, We thank You, Lord!
Lord, we love You, We love You, Lord!
Al - le - lu - ia! We praise You, Lord!

Revive Us Again 95

Wilt Thou not revive us again! that Thy people may rejoice in Thee? Psa. 85:6

WILLIAM P. MACKAY

JOHN J. HUSBAND

1. We praise Thee, O God, for the Son of Thy love, For Je - sus who
2. We praise Thee, O God, for Thy Spir - it of light, Who has shown us our
3. All glo - ry and praise to the Lamb that was slain, Who has borne all our
4. Re - vive us a - gain, fill each heart with Thy love; May each soul be re-

Refrain

died and is now gone a - bove.
Sav - ior and scat - tered our night.
sins, and has cleansed ev - ery stain.
kin - dled with fire from a - bove.

Hal - le - lu - jah! Thine the glo - ry, Hal - le -

lu - jah! A - men; Hal - le - lu - jah! Thine the glo - ry; Re - vive us a - gain.

96 What a Wonderful Savior!

...And know that this is indeed the Christ, the Savior of the world. John 4:42

ELISHA A. HOFFMAN — ELISHA A. HOFFMAN

1. Christ has for sin a - tone-ment made, What a won-der-ful Sav - ior!
2. I praise Him for the cleans-ing blood, What a won-der-ful Sav - ior!
3. He cleansed my heart from all its sin, What a won-der-ful Sav - ior!
4. He walks be - side me in the way, What a won-der-ful Sav - ior!

We are re-deemed! the price is paid! What a won-der-ful Sav - ior!
That rec - on-ciled my soul to God; What a won-der-ful Sav - ior!
And now He reigns and rules there-in; What a won-der-ful Sav - ior!
And keeps me faith-ful day by day, What a won-der-ful Sav - ior!

Refrain

What a won-der-ful Sav - ior is Je - sus, my Je - sus!

What a won-der-ful Sav - ior is Je - sus, my Lord!

In Moments Like These 97

Love the Lord with all your hearts. Mark 12:30

David Graham

David Graham

In mo-ments like these I sing out a song, I sing out a

love song to Je - sus. In mo-ments like these I lift up my voice, I

lift up my voice to the Lord, sing-ing I love you,

Lord, sing-ing I love you, Lord, sing-ing I love

you, Lord, I love you; sing-ing you.

98   **Psalm 146**

Leader: A Call to Worship!
Praise the Lord.
Praise the Lord, O my soul.
People: We will praise the Lord all our lives.
We will sing praise to our God as long as we live.
Leader: Do not put your trust in princes,
in mortal men, who cannot save.
When their spirit departs, they return to the ground;
on that very day their plans come to nothing.
People: **Blessed is he whose help is the God of Jacob,**
whose hope is in the Lord his God,
the Maker of heaven and earth,
the sea and everything in them —
the Lord, who remains faithful forever.
Leader: He upholds the cause of the oppressed
and gives food to the hungry.
People: **The Lord sets prisoners free.**
Leader: The Lord gives sight to the blind.
People: **The Lord lifts up those who are bowed down.**
All: **The Lord loves the righteous.**
Leader: The Lord watches over the alien
and sustains the fatherless and the widow.
People: **But the Lord frustrates the ways of the wicked.**
All: **The Lord reigns forever!**
Leader: Your God, O Zion, reigns for all generations.
Praise the Lord!
People: **Praise the Lord!**
All: **Praise the Lord!**

99 Praise the Savior, Ye Who Know Him

Jesus Christ the same yesterday, and today, and forever. Heb. 13:8

THOMAS KELLY   TRADITIONAL GERMAN MELODY

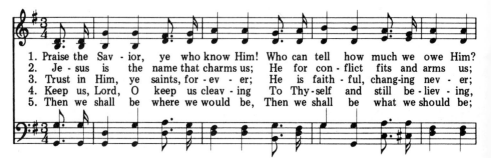

1. Praise the Sav - ior, ye who know Him! Who can tell how much we owe Him?
2. Je - sus is the name that charms us; He for con - flict fits and arms us;
3. Trust in Him, ye saints, for - ev - er; He is faith - ful, chang-ing nev - er;
4. Keep us, Lord, O keep us cleav - ing To Thy-self and still be - liev - ing,
5. Then we shall be where we would be, Then we shall be what we should be;

Glad - ly let us ren - der to Him All we are and have.
Noth - ing moves and noth - ing harms us While we trust in Him.
Nei - ther force nor guile can sev - er Those He loves from Him.
Till the hour of our re - ceiv - ing Prom - ised joys with Thee.
Things that are not now, nor could be, Soon shall be our own. A - men.

Stand Up and Bless the Lord 100

Stand up and bless the Lord your God, for ever and ever. Neh. 9:5

JAMES MONTGOMERY   AARON WILLIAMS

1. Stand up and bless the Lord, Ye
2. Though high a - bove all praise, A -
3. God is our strength and song, And
4. Stand up and bless the Lord, The

peo - ple of His choice; Stand up and bless the
bove all bless - ing high, Who would not fear His
His sal - va - tion ours; Then be His love in
Lord your God a - dore; Stand up and bless His

Lord your God With heart and soul and voice.
ho - ly name, And laud and mag - ni - fy?
Christ pro - claimed With all our ran - somed pow'rs.
glo - rious name, Hence - forth for - ev - er - more. A - men.

101 I Will Call Upon the Lord

...Who is worthy to be praised. Psa. 18:3

ADAPTED FROM PSALM 18
BY MICHAEL O'SHIELDS

MICHAEL O'SHIELDS

Lord. The Lord liv-eth and bless-ed be the Rock, And let the God

of my sal-va-tion be ex-alt - ed. The

Lord liv-eth and bless-ed be the Rock. And let the God

of my sal-va-tion be ex-alt - ed. The

alt - ed.

102 Bless His Holy Name

Bless the Lord, O my soul, and all that is within me. Psa. 103:1

ANDRAÉ CROUCH

ANDRAÉ CROUCH

Bless the Lord, O my soul, and all that is with-in me, Bless His

Fine

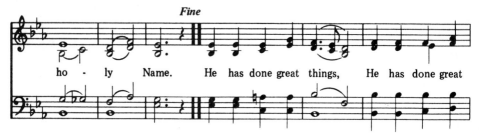

ho - ly Name. He has done great things, He has done great

D.C. al Fine

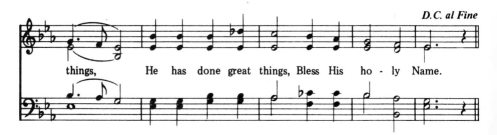

things, He has done great things, Bless His ho - ly Name.

103 He Is Lord

And that every tongue should confess that Jesus Christ is Lord. Phil. 2:11

BASED ON PHILIPPIANS 2:11

TRADITIONAL

He is Lord, He is Lord! He is ris-en from the dead and He is Lord!

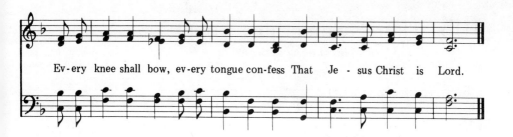

Ev-ery knee shall bow, ev-ery tongue con-fess That Je - sus Christ is Lord.

Fairest Lord Jesus 104

Thou art fairer than the children of men...Psa. 45:2

MÜNSTER *GESANGBUCH*
TR. JOSEPH A. SEISS AND ANONYMOUS

SCHLESISCHE VOLKSLIEDER
ARR. RICHARD S. WILLIS

1. Fair - est Lord Je - sus! Ru - ler of all na - ture,
2. Fair are the mead - ows, Fair - er still the wood - lands,
3. Fair is the sun - shine, Fair - er still the moon - light,
4. Beau - ti - ful Sav - ior! Lord of the na - tions!

O Thou of God and man the Son! Thee will I cher - ish,
Robed in the bloom - ing garb of spring: Je - sus is fair - er,
And all the twink - ling star - ry host: Je - sus shines bright - er,
Son of God and Son of Man! Glo - ry and hon - or,

Thee will I hon - or, Thou, my soul's glo - ry, joy, and crown!
Je - sus is pur - er, Who makes the woe-ful heart to sing.
Je - sus shines pur - er, Than all the an - gels heav'n can boast.
Praise, ad - o - ra - tion, Now and for - ev - er - more be Thine! A - men.

105 There's Something About That Name

*... Thou shalt call His name Jesus...*Matt. 1:23

WILLIAM J. AND GLORIA GAITHER

WILLIAM J. GAITHER

Je - sus, Je - sus, Je - sus; There's just some - thing a - bout that name! Mas - ter, Sav - ior, Je - sus, Like the fra - grance af - ter the rain; Je - sus, Je - sus, Je - sus, Let all Heav - en and earth pro - claim: Kings and king - doms will all pass a - way, But there's some - thing a - bout that name!

The Greatest Thing 106

Love the Lord thy God with all thy heart, soul, and strength. Mark 12:30

MARK PENDERGRASS

MARK PENDERGRASS

1. The great-est thing in all my life is know-ing You; The
2. The great-est thing in all my life is lov-ing You; The
3. The great-est thing in all my life is serv-ing You; The

great-est thing in all my life is know-ing You.
great-est thing in all my life is lov-ing You.
great-est thing in all my life is serv-ing You.

I want to know You more, I want to know You more.
I want to love You more, I want to love You more.
I want to serve You more, I want to serve You more.

The great-est thing in all my life is know-ing You.
The great-est thing in all my life is lov-ing You.
The great-est thing in all my life is serv-ing You.

107 Sun of My Soul

The darkness and the light are both alike to Thee. Psa. 139:12

JOHN KEBLE

KATHOLISCHES GESANGBUCH

1. Sun of my soul, Thou Sav - ior dear, It is not night if Thou be near;
2. When the soft dews of kind - ly sleep My wea - ry eye - lids gent - ly steep,
3. A - bide with me from morn till eve, For with - out Thee I can - not live;
4. Come near and bless us when we wake, Ere through the world our way we take;

O may no earth-born cloud a - rise To hide Thee from Thy serv-ant's eyes.
Be my last thought, how sweet to rest For-ev - er on my Sav-ior's breast.
A - bide with me when night is nigh, For with-out Thee I dare not die.
Till, in the o-cean of Thy love, We lose our-selves in heav'n a-bove. A-men.

108 Safety

I will both lay me down in peace,

and sleep:

For thou, Lord, only makest me to

dwell in safety.

Psalm 4:8

109 Begin, My Tongue, Some Heavenly Theme

My tongue will tell of your righteous acts. Psa. 71:24

ISAAC WATTS

HENRY W. GREATOREX

1. Be - gin, my tongue, some heav'n-ly theme And speak some bound-less thing:
2. Tell of His won - drous faith - ful - ness And sound His pow'r a - broad;
3. His ver - y word of grace is strong As that which built the skies;
4. O might I hear Thy heav'n-ly tongue But whis - per, "Thou art mine!"

The might - y works or might-ier name Of our e - ter - nal King.
Sing the sweet prom-ise of His grace, The love and truth of God.
The voice that rolls the stars a - long Speaks all the prom - is - es.
Those gen - tle words shall raise my song To notes al - most di - vine.

Jesus, Thou Joy of Loving Hearts 110

He...filleth the hungry soul with goodness. Psa. 107:9

ATTR. TO BERNARD OF CLAIRVAUX
TR. RAY PALMER

HENRY BAKER

1. Je - sus, Thou Joy of lov - ing hearts, Thou Fount of
2. Thy truth un - changed hath ev - er stood; Thou sav - est
3. We taste Thee, O Thou liv - ing Bread, And long to
4. Our rest - less spir - its yearn for Thee, Where - e'er our
5. O Je - sus, ev - er with us stay, Make all our

life, Thou Light of men, From the best bliss that earth im -
those that on Thee call; To them that seek Thee, Thou art
feast up - on Thee still; We drink of Thee, the Foun - tain -
change - ful lot is cast; Glad, when Thy gra - cious smile we
mo - ments calm and bright; Chase the dark night of sin a -

parts, We turn un - filled to Thee a - gain.
good, To them that find Thee, all in all.
head, And thirst our souls from Thee to fill.
see, Blest, when our faith can hold Thee fast.
way, Shed o'er the world Thy ho - ly light. A - men.

111 Rejoice, Ye Pure in Heart

Rejoice in the Lord, O ye righteous...Psa. 33:1

EDWARD H. PLUMPTRE

ARTHUR G. MESSITER

1. Re - joice, ye pure in heart, Re - joice, give thanks, and sing;
2. Bright youth and snow-crowned age, Strong men and maid - ens fair,
3. With all the an - gel choirs, With all the saints on earth,
4. Yes, on through life's long path, Still chant - ing as ye go;
5. Still lift your stand - ard high, Still march in firm ar - ray;

Your fes - tal ban - ner wave on high, The cross of Christ your King.
Raise high your free, ex - ult - ing song, God's won-drous praise de - clare.
Pour out the strains of joy and bliss, True rap - ture, no - blest mirth!
From youth to age, by night and day, In glad - ness and in woe.
As war - riors through the dark - ness toil Till dawns the gold - en day.

Refrain

Re - joice, re - joice, Re - joice, give thanks, and sing! A - men.
Re - joice, re - joice,

112 We Worship and Adore You

They sang praises with gladness and bowed their heads and worshiped. II Chr. 29:30

TRADITIONAL

TRADITIONAL

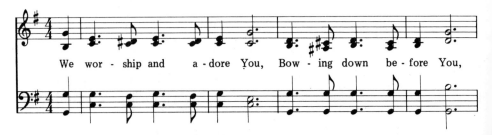

We wor - ship and a - dore You, Bow - ing down be - fore You,

Songs of prais - es sing - ing, Hal - le - lu - jahs ring - ing. Hal - le -
lu - jah, hal - le - lu - jah, hal - le - lu - jah, A - men.

Rejoice in the Lord Always 113

Rejoice in the Lord always; and again I say, Rejoice. Phil. 4:4

PHIL. 4:4

TRADITIONAL

Re - joice in the Lord al - ways, a - gain I say, re - joice! Re -

joice in the Lord al - ways, a - gain I say, re - joice! Re - joice, re - joice, a -

gain I say, re - joice! Re - joice, re - joice, a - gain I say, re - joice!

The
Church

You are ... God's people and members of God's household,
built on the foundation of the apostles and prophets,
with Christ Jesus himself as the chief cornerstone.
Eph. 2:19,20

Built on the Rock 114

And upon this rock I will build My church. Matt. 16:18

NICOLAI F. S. GRUNDTVIG

LUDVIG M. LINDEMAN

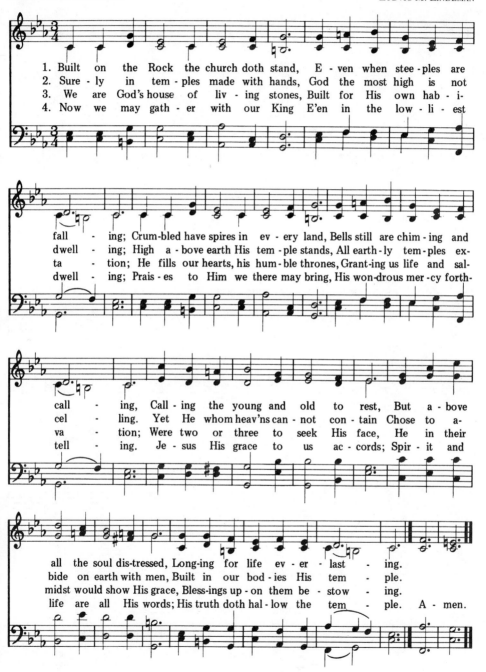

1. Built on the Rock the church doth stand, E - ven when stee -ples are
2. Sure - ly in tem - ples made with hands, God the most high is not
3. We are God's house of liv - ing stones, Built for His own hab - i -
4. Now we may gath - er with our King E'en in the low - li - est

fall - ing; Crum-bled have spires in ev - ery land, Bells still are chim - ing and
dwell - ing; High a - bove earth His tem - ple stands, All earth - ly tem - ples ex -
ta - tion; He fills our hearts, his hum - ble thrones, Grant-ing us life and sal -
dwell - ing; Prais - es to Him we there may bring, His won-drous mer -cy forth -

call - ing, Call - ing the young and old to rest, But a - bove
cel - ling. Yet He whom heav'ns can - not con - tain Chose to a -
va - tion; Were two or three to seek His face, He in their
tell - ing. Je - sus His grace to us ac - cords; Spir - it and

all the soul dis-tressed, Long-ing for life ev - er - last - ing.
bide on earth with men, Built in our bod - ies His tem - ple.
midst would show His grace, Bless-ings up - on them be - stow - ing.
life are all His words; His truth doth hal - low the tem - ple. A - men.

Text copyright © 1958 SERVICE BOOK AND HYMNAL, Reprinted by permission of Augsburg Fortress.

115 The Church's One Foundation

Other foundation can no man lay than that is laid . . . Jesus Christ. I Cor. 3:11

SAMUEL J. STONE

SAMUEL S. WESLEY

1. The Church's one foun-da-tion Is Je-sus Christ her Lord;
2. E-lect from ev-ery na-tion, Yet one o'er all the earth,
3. Though with a scorn-ful won-der Men see her sore op-pressed,
4. 'Mid toil and trib-u-la-tion, And tu-mult of her war,
5. Yet she on earth hath un-ion With God, the Three in One,

She is His new cre-a-tion, By wa-ter and the word:
Her char-ter of sal-va-tion, One Lord, one faith, one birth;
By schisms rent a-sun-der, By her-e-sies dis-tressed:
She waits the con-sum-ma-tion Of peace for-ev-er-more;
And mys-tic sweet com-mun-ion With those whose rest is won:

From heav'n He came and sought her To be His ho-ly bride;
One ho-ly name she bless-es, Par-takes one ho-ly food,
Yet saints their watch are keep-ing, Their cry goes up, "How long?"
Till with the vi-sion glo-rious Her long-ing eyes are blest,
O hap-py ones and ho-ly! Lord, give us grace that we,

With His own blood He bought her, And for her life He died.
And to one hope she press-es, With ev-ery grace en-dued.
And soon the night of weep-ing Shall be the morn of song.
And the great Church vic-to-rious Shall be the Church at rest.
Like them, the meek and low-ly, On high may dwell with Thee. A-men.

Glorious Things of Thee Are Spoken 116

Glorious things are spoken of thee, O city of God. Psa. 87:3

JOHN NEWTON

FRANZ JOSEPH HAYDN

1. Glo - rious things of thee are spo - ken, Zi - on, cit - y of our God;
2. See the streams of liv - ing wa - ters, Spring-ing from e - ter-nal love,
3. Round each hab - i - ta - tion hov-ering, See the cloud and fire ap - pear
4. Sav - ior, if of Zi - on's cit - y, I through grace a mem-ber am,

He whose word can - not be bro - ken Formed thee for His own a - bode;
Well sup - ply thy sons and daugh-ters, And all fear of want re - move:
For a glo - ry and a cov - ering, Show-ing that the Lord is near!
Let the world de - ride or pit - y, I will glo - ry in Thy name;

On the Rock of A - ges found-ed, What can shake thy sure re - pose?
Who can faint, while such a riv - er Ev - er will their thirst as - suage?
Thus de - riv - ing from their ban - ner Light by night and shade by day;
Fad - ing is the world's best pleas-ure, All its boast-ed pomp and show;

With sal - va - tion's walls sur-round-ed, Thou mayst smile at all thy foes.
Grace which, like the Lord, the Giv - er, Nev - er fails from age to age.
Safe they feed up - on the man - na Which He gives them when they pray.
Sol - id joys and last - ing treas-ure None but Zi - on's chil-dren know. A-men.

117 We Are God's People

You are a chosen people...belonging to God. I Pet. 2:9

BRYAN JEFFERY LEECH

JOHANNES BRAHMS
ARR. JACK SCHRADER

1. We are God's peo - ple, the cho - sen of the Lord,
2. We are God's loved ones, the Bride of Christ our Lord,
3. We are the Bod - y of which the Lord is Head,
4. We are a Tem - ple, the Spir - it's dwell - ing place.

Born of His Spir - it, es - tab - lished by His Word; Our
For we have known it, the love of God out - poured; Now
Called to o - bey Him, now ris - en from the dead; He
Formed in great weak - ness, a cup to hold God's grace; We

cor - ner - stone is Christ a - lone, And strong in Him we stand: O
let us learn how to re - turn The gift of love once giv'n: O
wills us be a fam - i - ly Di - verse yet tru - ly one: O
die a - lone, for on its own Each em - ber los - es fire: Yet

let us live trans - par - ent - ly, And walk heart to heart and hand to hand.
let us share each joy and care, And live with a zeal that pleas - es Heav'n.
let us give our gift to God, And so shall His work on earth be done.
joined in one the flame burns on To give warmth and light, and to in - spire.

Faith of Our Fathers 118

Earnestly contend for the faith which was once delivered unto the saints. Jude 3

FREDERICK W. FABER

HENRI F. HEMY
ARR. JAMES G. WALTON

1. Faith of our fa - thers! liv - ing still In spite of dun - geon,
2. Our fa - thers, chained in pris - ons dark, Were still in heart and
3. Faith of our fa - thers! we will strive To win all na - tions
4. Faith of our fa - thers! we will love Both friend and foe in

fire and sword: O how our hearts beat high with joy
con - science free: How sweet would be their chil - dren's fate,
un - to thee, And thro' the truth that comes from God,
all our strife: And preach thee too as love knows how,

When-e'er we hear that glo - rious word! Faith of our fa - thers,
If they like them could die for thee! Faith of our fa - thers,
Man-kind shall then be tru - ly free. Faith of our fa - thers,
By kind - ly words and vir - tuous life: Faith of our fa - thers,

ho - ly faith! We will be true to thee till death!
ho - ly faith! We will be true to thee till death!
ho - ly faith! We will be true to thee till death!
ho - ly faith! We will be true to thee till death!

119 They'll Know We Are Christians by Our Love

By this shall all men know...if ye have love one to another. John 13:35

PETER SCHOLTES   PETER SCHOLTES

Unison

1. We are one in the Spir-it, we are one in the Lord, We are one in the Spir-it, we are one in the Lord, And we pray that all u-ni-ty may one day be re-stored:
2. We will walk with each oth-er, we will walk hand in hand, We will walk with each oth-er, we will walk hand in hand, And to-geth-er we'll spread the news that God is in our land:
3. We will work with each oth-er, we will work side by side, We will work with each oth-er, we will work side by side, And we'll guard each man's dig-ni-ty and save each man's pride:
4. All praise to the Fa-ther, from whom all things come, And all praise to Christ Je-sus, His on-ly Son, And all praise to the Spir-it, who makes us one:

Refrain

And they'll know we are Chris-tians by our love, by our love, Yes, they'll know we are Chris-tians by our love.

Behold, What Manner of Love 120

How great is the love the Father has lavished on us. I John 3:1

PATRICIA VAN TINE

PATRICIA VAN TINE
ARR. LEE HERRINGTON

Be - hold, what man - ner of love the Fa - ther has giv - en un - to us. Be - hold, what man- ner of love the Fa - ther has giv - en un - to us;

That we should be called the sons of God;

That we should be called the sons of God.

121 To Be God's People

You shine like stars...as you hold out the Word of Life. Phil. 2:15,16

CHARLES F. BROWN

CHARLES F. BROWN

1. Al-might-y Fa-ther give us a vis-ion of a dy-ing world that needs Your love and care. We see the need, the yearn-ing for a Sav-ior, In Je-sus' name, grant this our prayer.

2. And when we fal-ter be Thou our com-fort; guide us as Your chil-dren that our lives may be A bea-con in this dark-ness that sur-rounds us, A light that oth-ers then may see.

Refrain

To be God's peo-ple in this place, live His good-ness, share His grace,

Pro - claim God's mer - cy   thru His Son,

be His love   to ev - er - y - one.

Him We Proclaim! 122

adapted from Colossians

Leader: God has rescued us from the dominion of darkness
and brought us into the kingdom of the Son he loves,
in whom we have redemption, the forgiveness of sins.

People: **Him we proclaim! Christ in us, the hope of glory.**

Leader: He is the image of the invisible God, the firstborn over all creation.
By him all things were created, and in him all things hold together.

People: **Him we proclaim! Christ in us, the hope of glory.**

Leader: He is the head of the body, the church;
he is the beginning and the firstborn from the dead.

People: **Him we proclaim! Christ in us, the hope of glory.**

Leader: In Christ, God's fullness we are pleased to dwell,
and through him to reconcile all things,
making peace through his blood, shed on the cross.

People: **Him we proclaim! Christ in us, the hope of glory.**

Leader: Once you were alienated from God;

People: **But now we are reconciled by Christ to God.**

Leader: Once you were enemies in your minds because of your evil behavior;

People: **But now we are holy in his sight, without blemish and free from accusation.**

Leader: God has rescued us from the dominion of darkness
and brought us into the kingdom of the Son he loves,
in whom we have redemption, the forgiveness of sins.

All: **Him we proclaim! Christ in us, the hope of glory.**

123 The Bond of Love

By this shall all men know...if ye have love one to another. John 13:35

OTIS SKILLINGS

OTIS SKILLINGS

1. We are one in the bond of love; We are one in the
2. Let us sing now, ev - ery - one; Let us feel His

bond of love. We have joined our spir - it with the
love be - gun. Let us join our hands that the

Spir - it of God; We are one in the bond of love.
world will know We are one in the bond of love.

124   I Sought My Soul

I sought my soul,
But my soul I could not see.
I sought my God,
But my God eluded me.
I sought my brother,
And I found all three.

Author Unknown

In This Very Room 125

I am in my Father, you are in me, and I am in you. John 14:20

RON AND CAROL HARRIS

RON AND CAROL HARRIS

1. In this ver - y room   there's quite e - nough love   for   one like me,
2. In this ver - y room   there's quite e - nough love   for   all of us,
3. In this ver - y room   there's quite e - nough love   for   all the world,

And   in this ver - y room   there's quite e - nough joy   for   one like me;
And   in this ver - y room   there's quite e - nough joy   for   all of us;
And   in this ver - y room   there's quite e - nough joy   for   all the world;

And there's quite   e - nough hope,   and   quite   e - nough pow'r   to

chase a - way an - y gloom, For Je-sus, Lord Je-sus, is   in this ver-y room.

126 The Gift of Love

...But the greatest of these is love. I Cor. 13:13

HAL HOPSON
BASED ON I COR. 13

HAL HOPSON
BASED ON AN ENGLISH FOLK TUNE

Unison

1. Though I may speak with brav - est fire,
2. Though I may give all I pos - sess,
3. Come, Spir - it, come, our hearts con - trol,

And have the gift to all in - spire,
And striv - ing so my love pro - fess,
Our spir - its long to be made whole.

And have not love; my words are vain;
But not be giv'n by love with - in.
Let in - ward love guide ev - ery deed;

As sound - ing brass, and hope - less gain.
The prof - it soon turns strange - ly thin.
By this we wor - ship, and are freed.

Help Us Accept Each Other 127

Be kindly affectioned one to another...in honor preferring one another. Rom. 12:10

FRED KAAN

JOHN NESS BECK

Unison

1. Help us ac - cept each oth - er as Christ ac - cept - ed us;
2. Teach us, O Lord, Your les - sons, as in our dai - ly life
3. Let Your ac - cept - ance change us, so that we may be moved
4. Lord, for to - day's en - coun - ters with all who are in need,

Teach us as sis - ter, broth - er each per - son to em - brace.
We strug - gle to be hu - man and search for hope and faith.
In liv - ing sit - u - a - tions to do the truth in love;
Who hun - ger for ac - cept - ance, for right - eous - ness and bread,

Be pres - ent, Lord, a - mong us and bring us to be - lieve
Teach us to care for peo - ple, for all, not just for some;
To prac - tice Your ac - cept - ance un - til we know by heart
We need new eyes for see - ing, new hands for hold - ing on;

We are our - selves ac - cept - ed and meant to love and live.
To love them as we find them, or as they may be - come.
The ta - ble of for - give - ness and laugh - ter's heal - ing art.
Re - new us with Your Spir - it; Lord, free us, make us one!

128 The Family of God

...His whole family in heaven and on earth. Eph. 3:15

WILLIAM J. AND GLORIA GAITHER

WILLIAM J. GAITHER

I'm so glad I'm a part of the fam-ily of God—I've been washed in the foun-tain, cleansed by His blood! Joint heirs with Je-sus as we trav-el this sod, For I'm part of the fam-ily, the fam-ily of God.

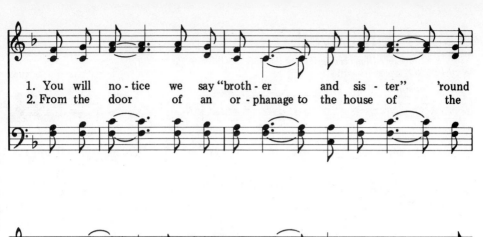

1. You will no-tice we say "broth-er and sis-ter" 'round
2. From the door of an or-phanage to the house of the

here— It's be-cause we're a fam-ily and these folks are so near; When
King— No long-er an out-cast, a new song I sing; From

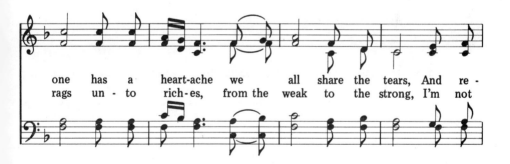

one has a heart-ache we all share the tears, And re-
rags un-to rich-es, from the weak to the strong, I'm not

D.C.

joice in each vic-tory In this fam-ily so dear.
wor-thy to be here, But, praise God, I be-long!

129 I Am Loved

We love Him, because He first loved us. I John 4:19

WILLIAM J. AND GLORIA GAITHER

WILLIAM J. GAITHER

I am loved, I am loved, I can risk lov-ing you; For the One who knows me best, loves me most. I am loved, you are loved; Won't you please take my hand? We are free to love each oth - er; we are loved.

Bind Us Together 130

Love one another, as He commanded us. I John 3:2

BOB GILLMAN

BOB GILLMAN

Bind us to - geth - er, Lord, Bind us to - geth - er with

cords that can - not be bro - ken. Bind us to - geth - er, Lord,

Fine

Bind us to - geth - er, Lord; Bind us to - geth - er with love.

There is on - ly one God; There is on - ly one King.

D. C. al Fine

There is on - ly one bod - y, That is why we sing:

131 This Is My Commandment

Love one another, as I have loved you. John 15:12

TRADITIONAL

TRADITIONAL

This is My com-mand-ment that you love one an-oth-er, that your

joy may be full. full. That your

joy may be full, that your joy may be

full. This is My com-mand-ment that you

love one an-oth-er, that your joy may be full.

Open Our Eyes, Lord 132

...That the eyes of your heart may be enlightened. Eph. 1:18

ROBERT CULL

ROBERT CULL

O - pen our eyes, Lord, we want to see Je - sus,

to reach out and touch Him, and say that we love Him.

O - pen our ears, Lord, and help us to lis - ten;

O - pen our eyes, Lord, we want to see Je - sus.

133 I Then Shall Live

Whoever seeks to save his life will lose it, and whoever loses his life will preserve it. Luke 17:33

GLORIA GAITHER

JEAN SIBELIUS

1. I then shall live as one who's been for-giv-en;
I'll walk with joy to know my debts are paid. I know my
name is clear be-fore my Fa-ther; I am His child, and
I am not a-fraid. So great-ly par-doned, I'll for-give my

2. I then shall live as one who's learned com-pas-sion;
I've been so loved that I'll risk lov-ing, too. I know how
fear builds walls in-stead of bridg-es; I dare to see an-
oth-er's point of view. And when re-la-tion-ships de-mand com-

3. Your king-dom come a-round and thru and in me,
Your pow'r and glo-ry, let them shine thru me; I know how
Name, O may I bear with hon-or, And may Your liv-ing
King-dom come in me. The Bread of Life, O may I share with

broth - er; The law of love I glad - ly will o - bey.
mit - ment, Then I'll be there to care and fol - low through.
hon - or, And may You feed a hun - gry world thru me.

Forgiveness   134

Be kind and compassionate to one another,
forgiving each other,
just as in Christ God forgave you.
Be imitators of God therefore, as dearly
loved children;
And live a life of love, just as Christ
loved us,
and gave himself up for us
As a fragrant offering and sacrifice to God.
Ephesians 4:32-5:2   (NIV)

I Love Thy Kingdom, Lord 135

Lord, I have loved the habitation of Thy house. Psa. 26:8

TIMOTHY DWIGHT   AARON WILLIAMS

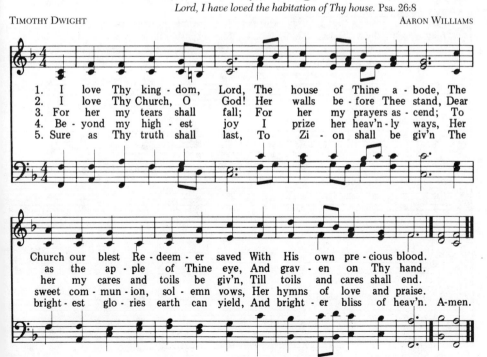

1. I love Thy king - dom, Lord, The house of Thine a - bode, The
2. I love Thy Church, O God! Her walls be - fore Thee stand, Dear
3. For her my tears shall fall; For her my prayers as - cend; To
4. Be - yond my high - est joy I prize her heav'n - ly ways, Her
5. Sure as Thy truth shall last, To Zi - on shall be giv'n The

Church our blest Re - deem - er saved With His own pre - cious blood.
as the ap - ple of Thine eye, And grav - en on Thy hand.
her my cares and toils be giv'n, Till toils and cares shall end.
sweet com - mun - ion, sol - emn vows, Her hymns of love and praise.
bright - est glo - ries earth can yield, And bright - er bliss of heav'n. A-men.

136 We're Marching to Zion

Let the children of Zion be joyful in their King. Psa. 149:2

ISAAC WATTS

ROBERT LOWRY

1. Come, we that love the Lord, And let our joys be known,
2. Let those re - fuse to sing Who nev - er knew our God,
3. The hill of Zi - on yields A thou - sand sa - cred sweets
4. Then let our songs a - bound, And ev - ery tear be dry;

Join in a song with sweet ac - cord, Join in a song with sweet ac - cord
But chil - dren of the heav'n - ly King, But chil - dren of the heav'n - ly King
Be - fore we reach the heav'n - ly fields, Be - fore we reach the heav'n - ly fields
We're march-ing thro' Im-manuel's ground, We're march - ing thro' Im-manuel's ground

And thus sur - round the throne, And thus sur - round the throne.
May speak their joys a - broad, May speak their joys a - broad.
Or walk the gold - en streets, Or walk the gold - en streets.
To fair - er worlds on high, To fair - er worlds on high.

Refrain

We're march - ing to Zi - on, Beau - ti - ful, beau - ti - ful Zi - on;
We're march - ing on to Zi - on,

We're march - ing up - ward to Zi - on, The beau - ti - ful cit - y of God.

In Christ There Is No East or West 137

You are all one in Christ Jesus. Gal. 3:28

JOHN OXENHAM

ALEXANDER R. REINAGLE

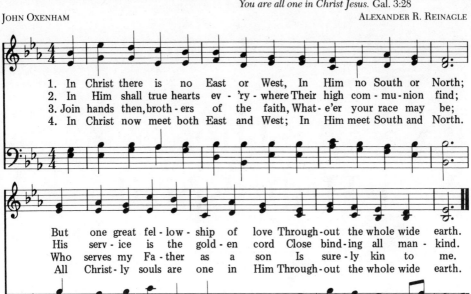

1. In Christ there is no East or West, In Him no South or North;
2. In Him shall true hearts ev-'ry-where Their high com-mu-nion find;
3. Join hands then, broth-ers of the faith, What-e'er your race may be;
4. In Christ now meet both East and West; In Him meet South and North.

But one great fel-low-ship of love Through-out the whole wide earth.
His serv-ice is the gold-en cord Close bind-ing all man-kind.
Who serves my Fa-ther as a son Is sure-ly kin to me.
All Christ-ly souls are one in Him Through-out the whole wide earth.

Words used by permission of Desmond Dunkerley.

Blest Be the Tie That Binds 138

You are all one in Christ Jesus. Gal. 3:28

JOHN FAWCETT

JOHANN G. NÄGELI; ARR. LOWELL MASON

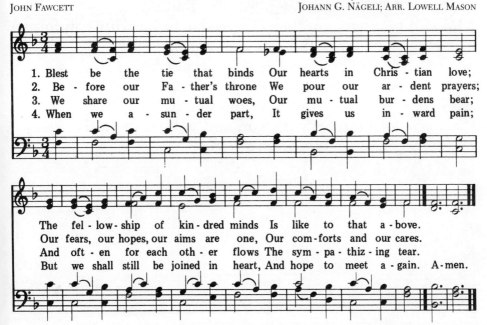

1. Blest be the tie that binds Our hearts in Chris-tian love;
2. Be-fore our Fa-ther's throne We pour our ar-dent prayers;
3. We share our mu-tual woes, Our mu-tual bur-dens bear;
4. When we a-sun-der part, It gives us in-ward pain;

The fel-low-ship of kin-dred minds Is like to that a-bove.
Our fears, our hopes, our aims are one, Our com-forts and our cares.
And oft-en for each oth-er flows The sym-pa-thiz-ing tear.
But we shall still be joined in heart, And hope to meet a-gain. A-men.

The Holy Spirit

And I will ask the Father,
and he will give you another Counselor to be with you forever
the Spirit of truth.
The world cannot accept him,
because it neither sees him nor knows him.
But you know him,
for he lives with you and will be in you.
John 14:16,17

Breathe on Me, Breath of God 139

He breathed on them, and said, Receive the Holy Ghost. John 20:22

EDWIN HATCH · ROBERT JACKSON

1. Breathe on me, Breath of God, Fill me with life a - new, That I may
2. Breathe on me, Breath of God, Un - til my heart is pure, Un - til my
3. Breathe on me, Breath of God, Till I am whol - ly Thine, Un - til this
4. Breathe on me, Breath of God, So shall I nev - er die, But live with

love what Thou dost love, And do what Thou wouldst do.
will is one with Thine, To do and to en - dure.
earth - ly part of me Glows with Thy fire di - vine.
Thee the per - fect life Of Thine e - ter - ni - ty. A-men.

Spiritual Breath 140

Almighty God,
Who alone gavest us the breath of life,
and alone canst keep alive in us the breathing of holy desires,
we beseech Thee for Thy compassion's sake
to sanctify all our thoughts and endeavours,
that we may neither begin any action without a pure intention,
nor continue it without Thy blessing;
and grant that having the eyes of our understanding
purged to behold things invisible and unseen,
we may in heart be inspired with Thy wisdom,
and in work be upheld by Thy strength,
and in the end be accepted of Thee,
as Thy faithful servants,
having done all things to Thy glory,
and thereby to our endless peace.
Grant this prayer, O Lord—Amen.

Rowland Williams

141 There Is a Balm in Gilead

Is there no balm in Gilead; is there no physician there? Jer. 8:22

TRADITIONAL SPIRITUAL

TRADITIONAL SPIRITUAL

Unison

(Ref.) There is a balm in Gil - e - ad To make the wound - ed whole,

Fine

There is a balm in Gil - e - ad To heal the sin - sick soul.

1. Some - times I feel dis - cour - aged, And think my work's in vain,
2. If you can not preach like Pe - ter, If you can - not pray like Paul,

D.C. Refrain

But then the Ho - ly Spir - it Re - vives my soul a - gain.
You can tell the love of Je - sus, And say, "He died for all."

Where the Spirit of the Lord Is 142

Where the Spirit of the Lord is...II Cor. 3:17

STEPHEN R. ADAMS   STEPHEN R. ADAMS

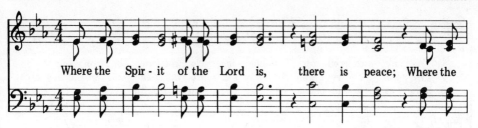

Where the Spir-it of the Lord is, there is peace; Where the

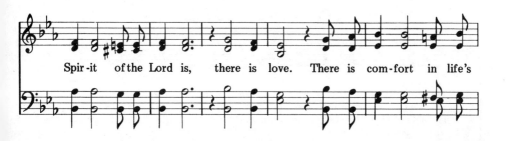

Spir-it of the Lord is, there is love. There is com-fort in life's

dark-est hour, there is light and life; There is help and

pow-er in the Spir-it, in the Spir-it of the Lord.

143 Old-Time Power

He shall baptize you with the Holy Ghost and with fire. Matt. 3:11

PAUL RADER

PAUL RADER

1. We are gath-ered for Thy bless-ing, We will wait up-on our God;
2. We will glo-ry in Thy pow-er, We will sing of won-drous grace;
3. Bring us low in prayer be-fore Thee, And with faith our souls in-spire,

We will trust in Him who loved us, And who bought us with His blood.
In our midst as Thou hast prom-ised, Come, O come and take Thy place.
Till we claim by faith the prom-ise Of the Ho-ly Ghost and fire.

Refrain

Spir-it, now melt and move All of our hearts with love,

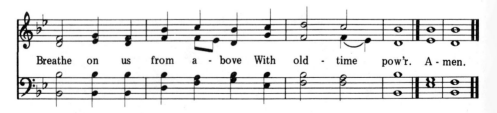

Breathe on us from a-bove With old-time pow'r. A-men.

There's a Quiet Understanding 144

Where two or three are gathered in My name, there am I... Matt. 18:20

TEDD SMITH   TEDD SMITH

1. There's a qui - et un - der-stand - ing when we're gath - ered
2. And we know when we're to - geth - er, shar - ing love and

in the Spir - it, It's a prom - ise that He gives us,
un - der-stand - ing, That our broth - ers and our sis - ters

when we gath - er in His name. There's a love we feel in Je - sus,
feel the one-ness that He brings. Thank You, thank You, thank You, Je - sus,

there's a man - na that He feeds us, It's a prom - ise
for the way You love and feed us, For the man - y

1
that He gives us When we gath - er in His name.

2 (Repeat, ad lib.)
ways You lead us, Thank You, thank You, Lord.

145 Come, Holy Spirit

In the last days...I will pour out my Spirit upon all flesh. Acts 2:17

JOHN W. PETERSON

JOHN W. PETERSON

1. The Ho - ly Spir - it came at Pen - te - cost, He came in
2. Then in an age when dark-ness gripped the earth, "The just shall

might - y full - ness then; His wit - ness thro' be - liev - ers
live by faith" was learned; The Ho - ly Spir - it gave the

won the lost, And mul - ti - tudes were born a - gain.
Church new birth As ref - or - ma - tion fires burned.

The ear - ly Chris - tians scat - tered o'er the world, They preached the
In lat - er years the great re - viv - als came, When saints would

Gos - pel fear - less - ly; Tho' some were mar - tyred and to
seek the Lord and pray; O, once a - gain we need that

© Copyright 1971 by JOHN W. PETERSON MUSIC COMPANY. All Rights Reserved. International Copyright Secured. Used by permission.

li - ons hurled, They marched a - long in vic - to - ry!
ho - ly flame To meet the chal - lenge of to - day!

Refrain

Come, Ho - ly Spir - it, Dark is the hour, We need Your fill - ing, Your

love and Your might - y pow'r; Move now a - mong us, Stir us, we

D. C.

pray, Come, Ho - ly Spir - it, Re - vive the church to - day!

Coda

Re - vive the church to - day! Re - vive the church to - day!

146 Surely the Presence of the Lord Is in This Place

In Thy presence is fullness of joy. Psa. 16:11

LANNY WOLFE   LANNY WOLFE

Sure - ly   the pres-ence   of the Lord   is   in this place;   I can

feel   His might-y   pow- er   and His   grace.   I can

hear   the brush of an-gels' wings,   I see glo - ry on each face;

Sure - ly   the pres - ence   of the Lord   is   in this place.

Blessed Quietness   147

He shall give you another Comforter, that He may abide with you forever. John 14:16

MANIE P. FERGUSON

W.S. MARSHALL

ARR. JAMES M. KIRK

1. Joys are flow-ing like a riv-er, Since the Com-fort-er has come;
2. Bring-ing life and health and glad-ness, All a-round this heav'n-ly Guest,
3. Like the rain that falls from heav-en, Like the sun-light from the sky,
4. See, a fruit-ful field is grow-ing, Bless-ed fruit of right-eous-ness;
5. What a won-der-ful sal-va-tion, Where we al-ways see His face!

He a-bides with us for-ev-er, Makes the trust-ing heart His home.
Ban-ished un-be-lief and sad-ness, Changed our wea-ri-ness to rest.
So the Ho-ly Ghost is giv-en, Com-ing on us from on high.
And the streams of life are flow-ing In the lone-ly wil-der-ness.
What a per-fect hab-i-ta-tion, What a qui-et rest-ing place!

Refrain

Bless-ed qui-et-ness, ho-ly qui-et-ness, What as-sur-ance in my soul!

On the storm-y sea He speaks peace to me, How the bil-lows cease to roll!

148 The Comforter Has Come

I will pray the Father, and He will give you another Comforter. John 14:16

FRANK BOTTOME

WILLIAM J. KIRKPATRICK

1. O spread the ti-dings 'round wher-ev-er man is found, Wher-
2. The long, long night is past, the morn-ing breaks at last, And
3. Lo, the great King of kings with heal-ing in His wings, To
4. O bound-less love di-vine! how shall this tongue of mine To

ev-er hu-man hearts and hu-man woes a-bound; Let ev-ery Chris-tian
hushed the dread-ful wail and fu-ry of the blast, As o'er the gold-en
ev-ery cap-tive soul a full de-liv-'rance brings; And through the va-cant
wond-'ring mor-tals tell the match-less grace di-vine—That I, a child of

tongue pro-claim the joy-ful sound: The Com-fort-er has come!
hills the day ad-vanc-es fast! The Com-fort-er has come!
cells the song of tri-umph rings; The Com-fort-er has come!
hell, should in His im-age shine! The Com-fort-er has come!

Refrain

The Com-fort-er has come, the Com-fort-er has come! The

Ho-ly Ghost from Heav'n, the Fa-ther's prom-ise giv'n; O spread the ti-dings

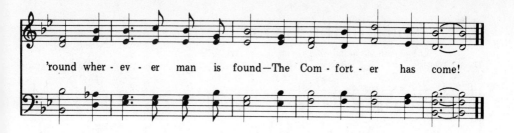

'round wher - ev - er man is found—The Com - fort - er has come!

Gracious Spirit, Dwell with Me 149

A new spirit will I put within you. Ezek 36:26

THOMAS T. LYNCH

RICHARD REDHEAD

1. Gra - cious Spir - it, dwell with me: I my - self would gra - cious be;
2. Truth - ful Spir - it, dwell with me: I my - self would truth - ful be;
3. Might - y Spir - it, dwell with me: I my - self would might - y be;
4. Ho - ly Spir - it, dwell with me: I my - self would ho - ly be;

And with words that help and heal Would Thy life in mine re - veal;
And with wis - dom kind and clear Let Thy life in mine ap - pear;
Might - y so as to pre - vail Where un - aid - ed man must fail;
Sep - a - rate from sin, I would Choose and cher - ish all things good,

And with ac - tions bold and meek Would for Christ my Sav - ior speak.
And with ac - tions broth - er - ly Speak my Lord's sin - cer - i - ty.
Ev - er by a might - y hope Press - ing on and bear - ing up.
And what - ev - er I can be, Give to Him who gave me Thee! A - men.

150 Spirit of the Living God

I will pour out in those days of my Spirit...Acts 2:18

DANIEL IVERSON   DANIEL IVERSON

Spir - it of the liv - ing God, Fall fresh on me. Spir - it of the liv - ing God, Fall fresh on me. Melt me, mold me, fill me, use me. Spir - it of the liv - ing God, Fall fresh on me.

151 Come, Holy Spirit, Dove Divine

We are buried with Him by baptism...Rom. 6:4

ADONIRAM JUDSON   H. PERCY SMITH

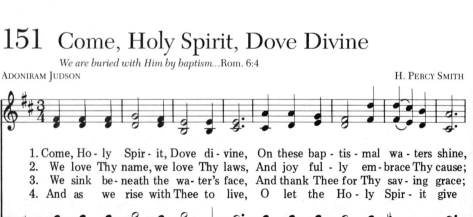

1. Come, Ho - ly Spir - it, Dove di - vine, On these bap - tis - mal wa - ters shine,
2. We love Thy name, we love Thy laws, And joy - ful - ly em - brace Thy cause;
3. We sink be - neath the wa - ter's face, And thank Thee for Thy sav - ing grace;
4. And as we rise with Thee to live, O let the Ho - ly Spir - it give

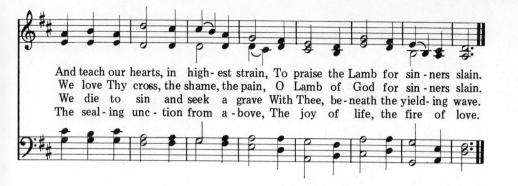

And teach our hearts, in high-est strain, To praise the Lamb for sin-ners slain.
We love Thy cross, the shame, the pain, O Lamb of God for sin-ners slain.
We die to sin and seek a grave With Thee, be-neath the yield-ing wave.
The seal-ing unc-tion from a-bove, The joy of life, the fire of love.

O Breath of Life 152

Wilt Thou not revive us again?...Psa. 85:6

BESSIE P. HEAD   MARY J. HAMMOND

1. O Breath of Life, come sweep-ing through us, Re - vive Thy
2. O Wind of God, come bend us, break us, Till hum - bly
3. O Breath of Love, come breathe with - in us, Re - new - ing
4. Re - vive us, Lord! Is zeal a - bat - ing While har - vest

church with life and pow'r; O Breath of Life, come, cleanse, re -
we con - fess our need; Then in Thy ten - der - ness re -
thought and will and heart; Come, Love of Christ, a - fresh to
fields are vast and white? Re - vive us, Lord, the world is

new us, And fit Thy church to meet this hour.
make us, Re - vive, re - store, for this we plead.
win us, Re - vive Thy church in ev - ery part.
wait - ing, E - quip Thy church to spread the light. A-men.

153 Sweet, Sweet Spirit

Behold, how good and how pleasant it is for brethren to dwell together in unity! Psa. 133:1

DORIS AKERS   DORIS AKERS

Unison

1. There's a sweet, sweet Spir - it in this place, And I
2. There are bless - ings you can - not re - ceive Till you

know that it's the Spir - it of the Lord; There are
know Him in His full - ness, and be - lieve. You're the

sweet ex - pres - sions on each face, And I
one to pro - fit when you say, "I am

know they feel the pres - ence of the Lord.
going to walk with Je - sus all the way."

Sweet Ho - ly Spir - it, Sweet heav-en-ly Dove, Stay right here

with us, Fill - ing us with your love, And for these

bless - ings we lift our hearts in praise; With-out a

doubt we'll know that we have been re - vived When we shall leave this place.

154 Spirit of God, Descend upon My Heart

If we live in the Spirit, let us also walk in the Spirit. Gal. 5:25

GEORGE CROLY

FREDERICK C. ATKINSON

1. Spir - it of God, de - scend up - on my heart; Wean it from
2. I ask no dream, no proph - et ec - sta - sies, No sud - den
3. Hast Thou not bid us love Thee, God and King? All, all Thine
4. Teach me to feel that Thou art al - ways nigh; Teach me the
5. Teach me to love Thee as Thine an - gels love, One ho - ly

earth, through all its puls - es move; Stoop to my weak - ness, might - y
rend - ing of the veil of clay, No an - gel vis - it - ant, no
own, soul, heart and strength and mind. I see Thy cross—there teach my
strug - gles of the soul to bear, To check the ris - ing doubt, the
pas - sion fill - ing all my frame; The bap - tism of the heav'n - de-

as Thou art, And make me love Thee as I ought to love.
o - p'ning skies; But take the dim - ness of my soul a - way.
heart to cling: O let me seek Thee, and O let me find.
reb - el sigh; Teach me the pa - tience of un - an - swered prayer.
scend - ed Dove, My heart an al - tar, and Thy love the flame. A - men.

155 Come, Holy Spirit, Heavenly Dove

The love of God is shed abroad in our hearts by the Holy Ghost...Romans 5:5

ISAAC WATTS

JOHN B. DYKES

1. Come, Ho - ly Spir - it, heav'n - ly Dove, With all Thy quick - n'ing pow'rs;
2. In vain we tune our for - mal songs, In vain we strive to rise;
3. And shall we then for - ev - er live At this poor dy - ing rate?
4. Come, Ho - ly Spir - it, heav'n - ly Dove, With all Thy quick - n'ing pow'rs;

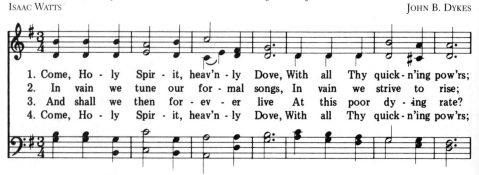

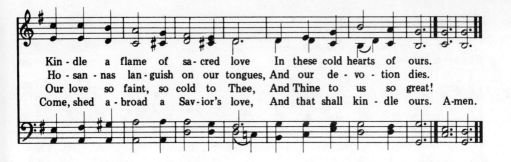

Kin - dle a flame of sa - cred love In these cold hearts of ours.
Ho - san - nas lan - guish on our tongues, And our de - vo - tion dies.
Our love so faint, so cold to Thee, And Thine to us so great!
Come, shed a - broad a Sav-ior's love, And that shall kin - dle ours. A-men.

Ancient Prayer 156

O God,
Who hast taught us to keep all Thy heavenly
commandments by loving Thee and our neighbour;
grant us the spirit of peace and grace,
that we may be both devoted to Thee
with our whole heart,
and united to each other with a pure will;
through Jesus Christ our Lord—Amen.

A.D. 460

Speak, Lord, in the Stillness 157

Speak, Lord; for Thy servant heareth. I Sam. 3:9

E. MAY GRIMES   HAROLD GREEN

1. Speak, Lord, in the still - ness While I wait on Thee;
2. Speak, O bless - ed Mas - ter, In this qui - et hour;
3. For the words Thou speak - est, They are life in - deed;
4. All to Thee is yield - ed, I am not my own;
5. Fill me with the know - ledge Of Thy glo - rious will;

Hushed my heart to lis - ten In ex - pect - an - cy.
Let me see Thy face, Lord, Feel Thy touch of power.
Liv - ing bread from heav - en, Now my spir - it feed!
Bliss - ful, glad sur - ren - der, I am Thine a - lone.
All Thine own good pleas - ure In Thy child ful - fill. A-men.

158 Pentecostal Power

I will pour out my Spirit. Joel 2:28

CHARLOTTE G. HOMER

CHARLES H. GABRIEL

1. Lord, as of old at Pen-te-cost Thou didst Thy pow'r dis-play,
2. For might-y works for Thee, pre-pare And strength-en ev-ery heart.
3. All self con-sume, all sin de-stroy! With ear-nest zeal en-due
4. Speak, Lord, be-fore Thy throne we wait; Thy prom-ise we be-lieve,

With cleans-ing, pu-ri-fy-ing flame De-scend on us to-day.
Come, take pos-ses-sion of Thine own, And nev-er-more de-part.
Each wait-ing heart to work for Thee. O Lord, our faith re-new!
And will not let Thee go un-til The bless-ing we re-ceive.

Lord, send the old-time pow'r, the Pen-te-cos-tal pow'r!

Thy flood-gates of bless-ing on us throw o-pen wide!

Lord, send the old-time pow'r, the Pen-te-cos-tal

pow'r, That sin-ners be con-vert-ed and Thy name glo-ri-fied!

Holy Spirit, Light Divine 159

Not by might nor power, but by my Spirit, says the Lord. Zech. 4:6

ANDREW REED

LOUIS M. GOTTSCHALK
ARR. BY EDWIN P. PARKER

1. Ho - ly Spir - it, Light di - vine, Shine up - on this
2. Ho - ly Spir - it, Power di - vine, Cleanse this guilt - y
3. Ho - ly Spir - it, Joy di - vine, Cheer this sad - dened
4. Ho - ly Spir - it, all di - vine, Dwell with - in this

heart of mine; Chase the shades of night a - way,
heart of mine; Long hath sin with - out con - trol
heart of mine; Bid my man - y woes de - part,
heart of mine; Cast down ev - ery i - dol throne,

Turn my dark - ness in - to day.
Held do min - ion o'er my soul.
Heal my wound - ed, bleed - ing heart.
Reign su - preme, and reign a - lone. A - men.

160 Showers of Blessing

There shall be showers of blessing...Ezek. 34:26

DANIEL W. WHITTLE

JAMES McGRANAHAN

1. There shall be show-ers of bless - ing: This is the prom-ise of love;
2. There shall be show-ers of bless - ing — Pre-cious re - viv - ing a - gain;
3. There shall be show-ers of bless - ing: Send them up - on us, O Lord;
4. There shall be show-ers of bless - ing: O, that to - day they might fall,

There shall be sea - sons re - fresh - ing, Sent from the Sav - ior a - bove.
O - ver the hills and the val - leys, Sound of a - bun-dance of rain.
Grant to us now a re - fresh - ing, Come, and now hon - or Thy Word.
Now as to God we're con - fess - ing, Now, as on Je - sus we call!

Refrain

Show - ers of bless - ing, Show - ers of bless - ing we need:
Show - ers, show - ers of bless - ing,

Mer - cy - drops 'round us are fall - ing, But for the show - ers we plead.

Fill Me Now 161

...Be filled with the Spirit. Eph. 5:18

ELWOOD H. STOKES

JOHN R. SWENEY

1. Hov - er o'er me, Ho - ly Spir - it, Bathe my trem - bling heart and brow;
2. Thou canst fill me, gra - cious Spir - it, Though I can - not tell Thee how;
3. I am weak - ness, full of weak - ness, At Thy sa - cred feet I bow;
4. Cleanse and com - fort, bless and save me, Bathe, O bathe my heart and brow;

Fill me with Thy hal - lowed pres - ence, Come, O come and fill me now.
But I need Thee, great - ly need Thee, Come, O come and fill me now.
Blest di - vine, e - ter - nal Spir - it, Fill with pow'r and fill me now.
Thou art com - fort - ing and sav - ing, Thou art sweet - ly fill - ing now.

Chorus

Fill me now, fill me now, Je - sus, come and fill me now;

Fill me with Thy hal - lowed pres - ence, Come, O come and fill me now.

Prayer

—————————————

Very early in the morning, while it was still dark,
Jesus got up,
and went off to a solitary place,
where he prayed.
Mark 1:35

What a Friend We Have in Jesus 162

By prayer...with thanksgiving let your requests be made known unto God. Phil 4:6

JOSEPH M. SCRIVEN   CHARLES C. CONVERSE

1. What a Friend we have in Je - sus, All our sins and griefs to bear!
2. Have we tri - als and temp - ta - tions? Is there trou - ble an - y - where?
3. Are we weak and heav - y - la - den, Cum - bered with a load of care?

What a priv - i - lege to car - ry Ev - ery-thing to God in prayer!
We should nev - er be dis - cour - aged, Take it to the Lord in prayer.
Pre - cious Sav - ior, still our ref - uge— Take it to the Lord in prayer.

O what peace we of - ten for - feit, O what need-less pain we bear,
Can we find a friend so faith - ful Who will all our sor - rows share?
Do thy friends de-spise, for-sake thee? Take it to the Lord in prayer;

All be-cause we do not car - ry Ev - ery-thing to God in prayer!
Je - sus knows our ev - ery weak - ness, Take it to the Lord in prayer.
In His arms He'll take and shield thee, Thou wilt find a sol - ace there.

163 I Am Praying for You

He ever liveth to make intercession for them, Heb 7:5

S. O'MALLEY CLOUGH

IRA D. SANKEY

1. I have a Sav - ior, He's plead - ing in glo - ry, A dear, lov - ing
2. I have a Fa - ther; to me He has giv - en A hope for e -
3. I have a peace; it is calm as a riv - er, A peace that the
4. When He has found you, tell oth - ers the sto - ry, That my lov - ing

Sav - ior, tho' earth-friends be few; And now He is watch - ing in
ter - ni - ty, bless - ed and true; And soon He will call me to
friends of this world nev - er knew: My Sav - ior a - lone is its
Sav - ior is your Sav - ior, too; Then pray that your Sav - ior may

ten - der - ness o'er me, But O, that my Sav - ior were your Sav - ior too!
meet Him in heav - en, But O, that He'd let me bring you with me too!
au - thor and giv - er, And O, could I know it was giv - en for you.
bring them to glo - ry, And prayer will be an-swered—'twas an-swered for you!

Refrain

For you I am pray - ing, For you I am pray - ing,

For you I am pray - ing, I'm pray - ing for you.

For in that He Himself hath suffered...He is able to help them...Heb. 2:18

ELISHA A. HOFFMAN   ELISHA A. HOFFMAN

1. I must tell Je - sus all of my tri - als; I can - not bear these
2. I must tell Je - sus all of my trou - bles; He is a kind, com-
3. Tempt-ed and tried, I need a great Sav - ior, One who can help my
4. O how the world to e - vil al - lures me! O how my heart is

bur - dens a - lone; In my dis - tress He kind - ly will help me;
pas - sion - ate Friend; If I but ask Him, He will de - liv - er,
bur - dens to bear; I must tell Je - sus, I must tell Je - sus;
tempt - ed to sin! I must tell Je - sus, and He will help me

Refrain

He ev - er loves and cares for His own.
Make of my trou - bles quick - ly an end.   I must tell Je - sus!
He all my cares and sor - rows will share.
O - ver the world the vic - t'ry to win.

I must tell Je - sus! I can - not bear my bur - dens a - lone; I must tell

Je - sus! I must tell Je - sus! Je - sus can help me, Je - sus a - lone.

165 If My People Will Pray

...I will forgive their sin. II Chron.7:14

CHRONICLES 7:14

JIMMY OWENS

If My peo - ple which are called by My name, Shall

hum - ble them-selves, shall hum - ble them-selves and pray;

If My peo - ple which are called by My name, Shall

seek My face and turn from their wick - ed ways;

Then will I hear from heav - en, Then will I hear from heav - en,

Then will I hear and will for-give, for-give their sin.

If My peo - ple which are called by My name, Shall

hum - ble them-selves, shall hum - ble them-selves and pray;

I will for - give their sin, I will for - give their sin,

I will for - give their sin, And heal their land.

166 Sweet Hour of Prayer

Now Peter and John went up together...at the hour of prayer. Acts 3:1

WILLIAM WALFORD   WILLIAM B. BRADBURY

1. Sweet hour of prayer, sweet hour of prayer, That calls me   from a world of care,
2. Sweet hour of prayer, sweet hour of prayer, Thy wings shall my pe - ti - tion bear,
3. Sweet hour of prayer, sweet hour of prayer, May I   thy con - so - la - tion share,

And bids   me   at   my   Fa-ther's throne Make all   my wants and wish - es known;
To Him   whose truth and faith-ful - ness   En - gage the wait - ing soul to bless;
Till, from Mount Pis-gah's loft - y   height, I   view my home, and take my flight:

In   sea - sons of   dis-tress and grief, My soul has   oft - en found re - lief,
And since He bids   me   seek His face, Be - lieve   His word and trust His grace,
This robe   of   flesh I'll   drop, and rise   To seize the   ev - er - last - ing prize;

And   oft   es-caped the tempt - er's snare, By   thy   re - turn, sweet hour of prayer.
I'll   cast   on Him my   ev - ery care, And wait for thee, sweet hour of prayer.
And shout, while pass-ing through the air, Fare-well, fare-well, sweet hour of prayer!

Teach Me to Pray, Lord 167

Lord, teach us to pray...Luke 11:1

ALBERT S. REITZ   ALBERT S. REITZ

1. Teach me to pray, Lord, teach me to pray; This is my heart-cry day unto day; I long to know Thy will and Thy way; Teach me to pray, Lord, teach me to pray.

2. Pow-er in prayer, Lord, pow-er in prayer, Here 'mid earth's sin and sor-row and care; Men lost and dy-ing, souls in de-spair; O give me pow-er, pow-er in prayer!

3. My weak-ened will, Lord, Thou canst re-new; My sin-ful na-ture Thou canst sub-due; Fill me just now with pow-er a-new, Pow-er to pray and pow-er to do!

4. Teach me to pray, Lord, teach me to pray; Thou art my pat-tern, day unto day; Thou art my sure-ty, now and for aye; Teach me to pray, Lord, teach me to pray.

Refrain

Liv-ing in Thee, Lord, and Thou in me; Con-stant a-bid-ing, this is my plea; Grant me Thy pow-er, bound-less and free: Pow-er with men and pow-er with Thee.

168 The Lord's Prayer

And when thou hast shut thy door, pray to the Father...Matt. 6:6

MATTHEW 6:9-13

ALBERT HAY MALOTTE
ARR. DONALD P. HUSTAD

Unison

Our Fa - ther, which art in heav - en, Hal - low - ed

be Thy name. Thy king - dom come,

Thy will be done on earth as it is in heav -

en. Give us this day our dai - ly bread, And for - give us our

may be omitted

debts, as we for-give our debt-ors. And

lead us not in-to temp-ta-tion but de-liv-er us from e-vil; For

Thine is the king-dom, and the pow-er, and the glo-ry, For-

ev-er, A-men. A-men.

169 I Need Thee Every Hour

Bow down Thine ear, O Lord, and hear me: for I am poor and needy. Psa. 86:1

ANNIE S. HAWKS

ROBERT LOWRY

1. I need Thee ev-ery hour, Most gra-cious Lord; No ten-der voice like
2. I need Thee ev-ery hour, Stay Thou near by; Temp-ta-tions lose their
3. I need Thee ev-ery hour In joy or pain; Come quick-ly and a-
4. I need Thee ev-ery hour, Most Ho-ly One; O make me Thine in-

Refrain

Thine Can peace af-ford.
pow'r When Thou art nigh.
bide Or life is vain.
deed, Thou bless-ed Son!

I need Thee, O I need Thee; Ev-ery hour I

need Thee; O bless me now, my Sav-ior, I come to Thee!

170 Jesus, the Very Thought of Thee

In whom, though now ye see Him not...ye rejoice. I Pet. 1:8

ATTR. BERNARD OF CLAIRVAUX
TR. EDWARD CASWALL

JOHN B. DYKES

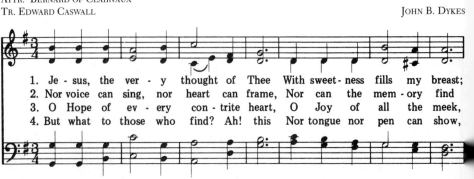

1. Je-sus, the ver-y thought of Thee With sweet-ness fills my breast;
2. Nor voice can sing, nor heart can frame, Nor can the mem-ory find
3. O Hope of ev-ery con-trite heart, O Joy of all the meek,
4. But what to those who find? Ah! this Nor tongue nor pen can show,

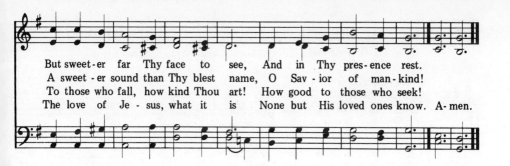

But sweet-er far Thy face to see, And in Thy pres-ence rest.
A sweet-er sound than Thy blest name, O Sav-ior of man-kind!
To those who fall, how kind Thou art! How good to those who seek!
The love of Je-sus, what it is None but His loved ones know. A-men.

Take Time to Be Holy 171

Follow peace with all men, and holiness...Heb. 12:14

WILLIAM D. LONGSTAFF   GEORGE C. STEBBINS

1. Take time to be ho-ly, Speak oft with thy Lord; A-bide in Him
2. Take time to be ho-ly, The world rush-es on; Spend much time in
3. Take time to be ho-ly, Let Him be thy guide, And run not be-
4. Take time to be ho-ly, Be calm in thy soul; Each thought and each

al-ways, And feed on His Word. Make friends of God's chil-dren; Help
se-cret With Je-sus a-lone; By look-ing to Je-sus, Like
fore Him What-ev-er be-tide; In joy or in sor-row Still
mo-tive Be-neath His con-trol; Thus led by His Spir-it To

those who are weak; For-get-ting in noth-ing His bless-ing to seek.
Him thou shalt be; Thy friends in thy con-duct His like-ness shall see.
fol-low thy Lord, And, look-ing to Je-sus, Still trust in His Word.
foun-tains of love, Thou soon shalt be fit-ted For ser-vice a-bove.

172 Lord, Listen to Your Children Praying

The effectual fervent prayer of a righteous man availeth much. James 5:16

KEN MEDEMA

KEN MEDEMA

Refrain - parts

Lord, lis - ten to your chil - dren pray - ing, Lord, send your

Spir - it in this place; Lord, lis - ten to your chil - dren

Fine

pray - ing, Send us love, send us pow'r, send us grace.

Unison

1. Some-thing's gon - na hap - pen like the world has nev - er known, When the
2. ℣ He's gon-na take o - ver, He's gon-na take con-trol, When the
3. ℣ You're gon - na know it when the Lord stretch-es out His hand, When the

peo - ple of the Lord get down to pray;
peo - ple of the Lord get down to pray;
peo - ple of the Lord get down to pray;

A door's gon-na swing o - pen, and the walls come a-tum-bl-ing
He's gon-na move the moun-tain He's gon-na make the wa - ters
There's gon-na be a brand new song of vic - t'ry in this

D.C.

down, When the peo-ple of the Lord get down to pray.
roll, When the peo-ple of the Lord get down to pray.
land, When the peo-ple of the Lord get down to pray.

Greater Is He That Is in Me 173

Greater is He that is in you, than he that is in the world. I John 4:4

LANNY WOLFE   LANNY WOLFE

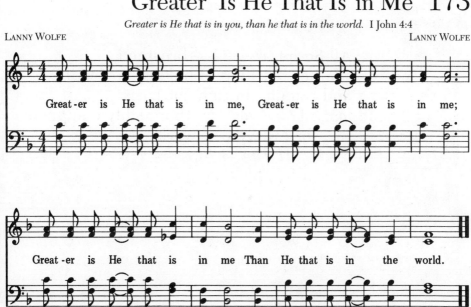

Great-er is He that is in me, Great-er is He that is in me;

Great-er is He that is in me Than He that is in the world.

The Scripture

All Scripture is God-breathed
and is useful for teaching, rebuking, correcting
and training in righteousness,
so that the man of God may be thoroughly equipped
for every good work.
II Tim. 3:16,17

Open My Eyes, That I May See 174

Open Thou mine eyes, that I may behold wondrous things out of Thy law. Psa. 119:18

CLARA H. SCOTT   CLARA H. SCOTT

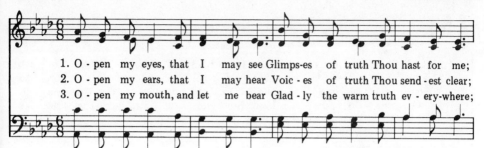

1. O-pen my eyes, that I may see Glimps-es of truth Thou hast for me;
2. O-pen my ears, that I may hear Voic-es of truth Thou send-est clear;
3. O-pen my mouth, and let me bear Glad-ly the warm truth ev-ery-where;

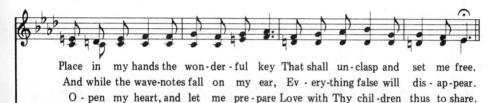

Place in my hands the won-der-ful key That shall un-clasp and set me free.
And while the wave-notes fall on my ear, Ev-ery-thing false will dis-ap-pear.
O-pen my heart, and let me pre-pare Love with Thy chil-dren thus to share.

Refrain

Si-lent-ly now I wait for Thee, Read-y, my God, Thy will to see;

O-pen my eyes, il-lu-mine me, Spir-it di-vine!
O-pen my ears, il-lu-mine me, Spir-it di-vine!
O-pen my heart, il-lu-mine me, Spir-it di-vine!   A-men.

175 Break Thou the Bread of Life

He looked up to heaven, and blessed, and broke the loaves...Mark 6:41

MARY A. LATHBURY

WILLIAM F. SHERWIN

1. Break Thou the bread of life, Dear Lord, to me, As Thou didst
2. Bless Thou the truth, dear Lord, To me, to me, As Thou didst
3. Thou art the bread of life, O Lord, to me, Thy ho-ly
4. O send Thy Spir-it, Lord, Now un-to me, That He may

break the loaves Be-side the sea; Be-yond the sa-cred page
bless the bread By Gal-i-lee; Then shall all bond-age cease,
Word the truth That sav-eth me; Give me to eat and live
touch my eyes And make me see: Show me the truth con-cealed

I seek Thee, Lord, My spir-it pants for Thee, O liv-ing Word.
All fet-ters fall; And I shall find my peace, My All in all.
With Thee a-bove; Teach me to love Thy truth, For Thou art love.
With-in Thy Word, And in Thy Book re-vealed I see the Lord. A-men.

176 Holy Bible, Book Divine

O how I love Thy law! It is my meditation all the day! Psa. 119:97

JOHN BURTON

WILLIAM B. BRADBURY

1. Ho-ly Bi-ble, book di-vine, Pre-cious treas-ure, thou art mine;
2. Mine to chide me when I rove; Mine to show a Sav-ior's love;
3. Mine to com-fort in dis-tress, Suf-f'ring in this wil-der-ness;
4. Mine to tell of joys to come, And the reb-el sin-ner's doom;

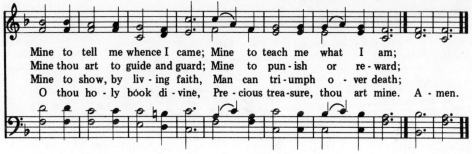

Mine to tell me whence I came; Mine to teach me what I am;
Mine thou art to guide and guard; Mine to pun-ish or re-ward;
Mine to show, by liv-ing faith, Man can tri-umph o-ver death;
O thou ho-ly book di-vine, Pre-cious trea-sure, thou art mine. A-men.

Wonderful Words of Life 177

You have the words of eternal life. John 6:68

PHILIP P. BLISS   PHILIP P. BLISS

1. Sing them o-ver a-gain to me, Won-der-ful words of Life;
2. Christ, the bless-ed One, gives to all Won-der-ful words of Life;
3. Sweet-ly ech-o the gos-pel call, Won-der-ful words of Life;

Let me more of their beau-ty see, Won-der-ful words of Life.
Sin-ner, list to the lov-ing call, Won-der-ful words of Life.
Of-fer par-don and peace to all, Won-der-ful words of Life.

Words of life and beau-ty, Teach me faith and du-ty:
All so free-ly giv-en, Woo-ing us to Heav-en:
Je-sus, on-ly Sav-ior, Sanc-ti-fy for-ev-er:

Refrain

Beau-ti-ful words, won-der-ful words, Won-der-ful words of Life. Life.

178 Thy Word

Thy Word is a lamp unto my feet. Psa. 119:11

MICHAEL W. SMITH
AND AMY GRANT

MICHAEL W. SMITH
AND AMY GRANT

Unison

Thy Word is a lamp un-to my feet and a

light un-to my path.

Repeat after each verse (Fine)

1. When I feel a-fraid, think I've lost my way,
2. I will not for-get Your love for me, and yet my

Still You're there right be-side me. And noth-ing will I fear as
heart for-ev-er is wan-der-ing. Je-sus, be my guide and

D.C.

long as You are near. Please be near me to the end.
hold me to your side; and I will love You to the end.

How Firm a Foundation 179

Heaven and earth shall pass away; but My words shall not...Luke 21:33

RIPPON'S SELECTION OF HYMNS

TRADITIONAL AMERICAN MELODY

1. How firm a foun - da - tion, ye saints of the Lord,
2. "Fear not, I am with thee; O be not dis - mayed,
3. "When through the deep wa - ters I call thee to go,
4. "When through fier - y tri - als thy path - way shall lie,
5. "The soul that on Je - sus hath leaned for re - pose,

Is laid for your faith in His ex - cel - lent Word!
For I am thy God, and will still give thee aid;
The riv - ers of sor - row shall not o - ver - flow;
My grace, all suf - fi - cient, shall be thy sup - ply:
I will not, I will not de - sert to his foes;

What more can He say than to you He hath said,
I'll strength - en thee, help thee, and cause thee to stand,
For I will be with thee, thy trou - bles to bless,
The flame shall not hurt thee; I on - ly de - sign
That soul, though all hell should en - deav - or to shake,

To you who for ref - uge to Je - sus have fled?
Up - held by my right - eous, om - nip - o - tent hand.
And sanc - ti - fy to thee thy deep - est dis - tress.
Thy dross to con - sume, and thy gold to re - fine.
I'll nev - er, no, nev - er, no, nev - er for - sake!" A - men.

180 O Word of God Incarnate

The entrance of Thy words giveth light...Psa. 119:130

WILLIAM W. HOW

ARR. FELIX MENDELSSOHN

1. O Word of God in-car-nate, O Wis-dom from on high,
2. The Church from her dear Mas-ter Re-ceived the gift di-vine,
3. It float-eth like a ban-ner Be-fore God's host un-furled;
4. O make Thy Church, dear Sav-ior, A lamp of pur-est gold,

O Truth un-changed, un-chang-ing, O Light of our dark sky;
And still that light she lift-eth O'er all the earth to shine.
It shin-eth like a bea-con A-bove the dark-ling world.
To bear be-fore the na-tions Thy true light as of old.

We praise Thee for the ra-diance That from the hal-lowed page,
It is the gold-en cas-ket Where gems of truth are stored;
It is the chart and com-pass That o'er life's surg-ing sea,
O teach Thy wan-d'ring pil-grims By this their path to trace,

A lan-tern to our foot-steps, Shines on from age to age.
It is the heav'n-drawn pic-ture Of Christ, the liv-ing Word.
'Mid mists and rocks and quick-sands, Still guides, O Christ, to Thee.
Till, clouds and dark-ness end-ed, They see Thee face to face. A-men.

Standing on the Promises 181

Whereby are given unto us exceeding great and precious promises... II Pet. 1:4

R. KELSO CARTER

R. KELSO CARTER

1. Stand-ing on the prom-is-es of Christ my King, Thro' e-ter-nal a-ges
2. Stand-ing on the prom-is-es that can-not fail, When the howl-ing storms of
3. Stand-ing on the prom-is-es of Christ the Lord, Bound to Him e-ter-nal-
4. Stand-ing on the prom-is-es I can-not fall, List'ning ev-ery mo-ment

let His prais-es ring; Glo-ry in the high-est, I will shout and sing,
doubt and fear as-sail, By the liv-ing Word of God I shall pre-vail,
ly by love's strong cord, O-ver-com-ing dai-ly with the Spir-it's sword,
to the Spir-it's call, Rest-ing in my Sav-ior as my all in all,

Refrain

Stand-ing on the prom-is-es of God. Stand-ing, stand - ing,
stand-ing on the prom-is-es,

Stand - ing on the prom-is-es of God my Sav-ior; Stand-ing,

stand - ing, I'm stand-ing on the prom-is-es of God.
stand-ing on the prom-is-es,

182 More About Jesus

But grow in grace, and in the knowledge of our Lord and Savior Jesus Christ. II Pet. 3:18

ELIZA E. HEWITT

JOHN R. SWENEY

1. More a - bout Je - sus would I know, More of His grace to oth - ers show;
2. More a - bout Je - sus let me learn, More of His ho - ly will dis - cern;
3. More a - bout Je - sus; in His Word, Hold-ing com-mun-ion with my Lord;
4. More a - bout Je - sus on His throne, Rich-es in glo - ry all His own;

More of His sav - ing ful - ness see, More of His love who died for me.
Spir - it of God, my teach - er be, Show-ing the things of Christ to me.
Hear - ing His voice in ev - ery line, Mak-ing each faith - ful say - ing mine.
More of His king-dom's sure in-crease; More of His com-ing, Prince of Peace.

Refrain

More, more a - bout Je - sus, More, more a - bout Je - sus;

More of His sav - ing ful - ness see, More of His love who died for me.

Christmas

Behold, a virgin shall be with child,
and shall bring forth a son,
and they shall call his name Emmanuel,
which being interpreted is,
God with us.
Matt. 1:23

183   Come Let Us Adore Him: Christmas

John 1: 1-16   (NIV)

Leader: Come! Let us adore Him!

People: **In the beginning was the Word,**
and the Word was with God,
and the Word was God.
He was with God in the beginning.

Leader: Through him all things were made;
without him nothing was made that has been made.
In him was life, and that life was the light of men.

All: **Come! Let us adore Him!**

Leader: The light shines in the darkness,
but the darkness has not understood it.

People: **He was in the world,**
and though the world was made through him,
the world did not recognize him.

Leader: He came to that which was his own,
but his own did not receive him.

All: **Come! Let us adore Him!**
Let us adore Him!

Leader: The Word became flesh and made his dwelling among us.

People: **We have seen his glory, the glory of the One and Only,**
who came from the Father, full of grace and truth.

All: **Come! Let us adore Him!**

Leader: From the fullness of his grace we have all received
one blessing after another. Come! Let us adore Him!

People: **Let us adore Him!**

All: **Come! Let us adore Him!**

Simeon's Declaration 184

Luke 2: 29-31

Lord, you now have set your servant free
to go in peace as you have promised.
For these eyes of mine have seen the Savior,
whom you have prepared for all the world to see:
A Light to enlighten the nations,
and the glory of your people Israel.

Emmanuel 185

Call His name Emmanuel...God with us. Matt. 1:23

BOB MCGEE

BOB MCGEE

Unison

Em-man - u - el, Em-man - u - el,

His name is called Em-man - u - el;

God with us, re-vealed in us;

His name is called Em-man - u - el.

186 O Come, O Come, Emmanuel

Behold a virgin shall...bear a son, and shall call His name Immanuel. Isa. 7:14

LATIN HYMN
VERSE 6, VANN O. TRAPP

THOMAS HELMORE

1. O come, O come, Em-man-u-el, And ran-som cap-tive Is-ra-el, That mourns in lone-ly ex-ile here Un-til the Son of God ap-pear. Re-joice! re-joice! Em-man-u-el Shall come to thee, O Is-ra-el!

2. O come, Thou Rod of Jes-se, free Thine own from Sa-tan's tyr-an-ny; From depths of hell Thy peo-ple save And give them vic-t'ry o'er the grave. Re-joice! re-joice! Em-man-u-el Shall come to thee, O Is-ra-el!

3. O come, Thou Day-spring, come and cheer Our spir-its by Thine ad-vent here; And drive a-way the shades of night, And pierce the clouds and bring us light! Re-joice! re-joice! Em-man-u-el Shall come to thee, O Is-ra-el!

4. O come, Thou Key of Da-vid, come, And o-pen wide our heav'n-ly home; Make safe the way that leads on high, And close the path to mis-er-y. Re-joice! re-joice! Em-man-u-el Shall come to thee, O Is-ra-el!

5. *O come, Mes-si-ah, come a-gain, And rid the world of death and sin. Re-turn, thou ris-en Sav-ior and King, That heav'n and earth at last may sing. Re-joice, re-joice; Em-man-u-el Has come to thee, O Is-ra-el! A-men.*

Come, Thou Long Expected Jesus 187

The desire of all nations shall come...Haggai 2:7

ROWLAND H. PRICHARD
HARM. RALPH VAUGHAN WILLIAMS

CHARLES WESLEY

1. Come, Thou long ex-pect-ed Je-sus, Born to set Thy peo-ple free;
2. Born Thy peo-ple to de-liv-er, Born a child and yet a king.

From our fears and sins re-lease us; Let us find our rest in Thee.
Born to reign in us for-ev-er, Now Thy gra-cious king-dom bring.

Is-rael's strength and con-so-la-tion, Hope of all the earth Thou art;
By Thine own e-ter-nal Spir-it Rule in all our hearts a-lone;

Dear De-sire of ev-ery na-tion, Joy of ev-ery long-ing heart.
By Thine all suf-fi-cient mer-it, Raise us to Thy glo-rious throne.

188 O Come, All Ye Faithful

Let us now go even unto Bethlehem...Luke 2:15

LATIN HYMN

JOHN F. WADE

1. O come, all ye faith - ful, joy - ful and tri - um - phant,
2. God of God, and Light of Light be - got - ten,
3. Sing, choirs of an - gels, sing in ex - ul - ta - tion!
4. Yea, Lord, we greet Thee, born this hap - py morn - ing,

O come ye, O come ye to Beth - le - hem!
Lo, He ab - hors not the Vir - gin's womb;
O sing, all ye cit - i - zens of heav'n a - bove;
Je - sus, to Thee be all glo - ry giv'n;

Come and be - hold Him, born the King of an - gels;
Ver - y God, be - got - ten, not cre - a - ted;
Glo - ry to God, all glo - ry in the high - est;
Word of the Fa - ther, now in flesh ap - pear - ing;

Refrain

O come, let us a - dore Him, O come, let us a - dore Him,

O come, let us a - dore Him, Christ the Lord. A - men.

Silent Night! Holy Night! 189

And they...found Mary, and Joseph, and the babe lying in a manger. Luke 2:16

JOSEPH MOHR

FRANZ GRÜBER

1. Si - lent night! ho - ly night! All is calm, all is bright
2. Si - lent night! ho - ly night! Shep - herds quake at the sight,
3. Si - lent night! ho - ly night! Son of God, love's pure light,

'Round yon vir - gin moth - er and Child, Ho - ly In - fant so ten - der and mild,
Glo - ries stream from heav - en a - far, Heav'n - ly hosts sing Al - le - lu - ia;
Ra - diant beams from Thy ho - ly face, With the dawn of re - deem - ing grace,

Sleep in heav - en - ly peace, Sleep in heav - en - ly peace.
Christ the Sav - ior is born, Christ the Sav - ior is born.
Je - sus, Lord, at Thy birth, Je - sus, Lord, at Thy birth. A - men.

I Sing the Birth 190

ing the birth, was born tonight,
e Author both of life and light;
  The angels so did sound it,
d like the ravished shepherds said,
ho saw the light and were afraid,
  Yet searched, and true they found it.

e Son of God, the Eternal King,
at did us all salvation bring,
  And freed the soul from danger;
whom the whole world could not take,
e Word, which heaven and earth did make,
  Was now laid in a manger.

The Father's wisdom willed it so,
The Son's obedience knew no No,
  Both wills were in one stature;
And as that wisdom had decreed,
The Word was now made flesh indeed
  And took on Him our nature.

What comfort by Him do we win?
Who made Himself the Prince of sin
  To make us heirs of glory?
To see this Babe, all innocence;
A Martyr born in our defense;
  Can man forget this story?

Ben Jonson

191 Hark! the Herald Angels Sing

And suddenly there was...a multitude of the heavenly host praising God...Luke 2:13

CHARLES WESLEY

FELIX MENDELSSOHN
ARR. WILLIAM H. CUMMINGS

1. Hark! the her-ald an-gels sing, "Glo-ry to the new-born King:
2. Christ, by high-est heav'n a-dored; Christ, the ev-er-last-ing Lord!
3. Hail the heav'n-born Prince of Peace! Hail the Sun of Right-eous-ness!

Peace on earth, and mer-cy mild, God and sin-ners rec-on-ciled!"
Late in time be-hold Him come, Off-spring of the Vir-gin's womb:
Light and life to all He brings, Ris'n with heal-ing in His wings.

Joy-ful, all ye na-tions, rise, Join the tri-umph of the skies;
Veiled in flesh the God-head see; Hail th'in-car-nate De-i-ty,
Mild He lays His glo-ry by, Born that man no more may die,

With th'an-gel-ic host pro-claim, "Christ is born in Beth-le-hem!"
Pleased as man with men to dwell, Je-sus, our Em-man-u-el.
Born to raise the sons of earth, Born to give them sec-ond birth.

Hark! the her-ald an-gels sing, "Glo-ry to the new-born King." A-men.

How Great Our Joy   192

Therefore with joy shall they draw water out of the wells of salvation... Isa. 12:3

TRADITIONAL GERMAN CAROL   TRADITIONAL GERMAN MELODY

1. While by the sheep we watched at night, Glad tid-ings brought an
2. There shall be born, so he did say, In Beth-le-hem a
3. There shall the Child lie in a stall, This Child who shall re-
4. This gift of God we'll cher-ish well, That ev-er joy our

an - gel bright. How great our joy! Great our joy!
Child to - day. How great our joy! Great our joy!
deem us all. How great our joy! Great our joy!
hearts shall fill. How great our joy! Great our joy!

Joy, joy, joy! Joy, joy, joy! Praise we the Lord in
Joy, joy, joy! Joy, joy, joy! Praise we the Lord in
Joy, joy, joy! Joy, joy, joy! Praise we the Lord in
Joy, joy, joy! Joy, joy, joy! Praise we the Lord in

heav'n on high! Praise we the Lord in heav'n on high!
heav'n on high! Praise we the Lord in heav'n on high!
heav'n on high! Praise we the Lord in heav'n on high!
heav'n on high! Praise we the Lord in heav'n on high!

193 Of the Father's Love Begotten

In the beginning was the Word...and the Word was God. John 1:1

AURELIUS C. PRUDENTIUS
TR. JOHN M. NEALE AND HENRY BAKER

ANCIENT PLAINSONG
ARR. PAUL WOHLGEMUTH

1. Of the Fa-ther's love be-got-ten, Ere the worlds be-gan to be,
2. O that birth for-ev-er bless-ed, When the vir-gin, full of grace,
3. O ye heights of heav'n a-dore Him; An-gel hosts, His prais-es sing;
4. Christ, to Thee with God the Fa-ther, And, O Ho-ly Ghost to Thee,

He is Al-pha and O-me-ga, He the source, the end-ing He,
By the Ho-ly Ghost con-ceiv-ing, Bare the Sav-ior of our race;
Pow'rs, do-min-ions, bow be-fore Him, And ex-tol our God and King;
Hymn and chant and high thanks-giv-ing And un-wear-ied prais-es be:

Of the things that are, that have been, And that fu-ture
And the Babe, the world's Re-deem - er, First re-vealed His
Let no tongue on earth be si - lent, Ev-ery voice in
Hon-or, maj-es-ty, do-min - ion, And e-ter-nal

years shall see, Ev-er-more and ev-er-more!
sa-cred face, Ev-er-more and ev-er-more!
con-cert ring, Ev-er-more and ev-er-more!
vic-to-ry, Ev-er-more and ev-er-more!

Joy to the World! 194

Make a joyful noise unto the Lord, all the earth...Psa. 98:4

ISAAC WATTS

GEORGE FREDERICK HANDEL
ARR. LOWELL MASON

1. Joy to the world! the Lord is come; Let earth re-
2. Joy to the earth! the Sav-ior reigns; Let men their
3. No more let sins and sor-rows grow, Nor thorns in-
4. He rules the world with truth and grace, And makes the

ceive her King; Let ev-ery heart pre-pare Him room,
songs em-ploy; While fields and floods, rocks, hills, and plains
fest the ground; He comes to make His bless-ings flow
na-tions prove The glo-ries of His right-eous-ness,

And heav'n and na-ture sing, And heav'n and na-ture
Re-peat the sound-ing joy, Re-peat the sound-ing
Far as the curse is found, Far as the curse is
And won-ders of His love, And won-ders of His

1. And heav'n and na-ture sing,

1. And

sing, And heav'n, and heav'n and na-ture sing.
joy, Re-peat, re-peat the sound-ing joy.
found, Far as, far as the curse is found.
love, And won-ders, won-ders of His love.

195 O Holy Night

The Desire of all nations shall come. Hag. 2:7

JOHN S. DWIGHT

ADOLPHE C. ADAM

Instrument
(Repeat first time)

1. O ho-ly night, the stars are bright-ly
2. Led by the light of Faith se-rene-ly
3. Tru-ly He taught us to love one an-

shin-ing, It is the night of the dear Sav-ior's birth;
beam-ing, With glow-ing hearts by His cra-dle we stand;
oth-er; His law is love, and His gos-pel is peace;

Long lay the world in sin and er-ror pin-ing, Till He ap-
So led by light of a star sweet-ly gleam-ing, Here came the
Chains shall He break, for the slave is our broth-er, And in His

peared and the soul felt its worth. A thrill of hope the
wise men from the o-rient land. The King of kings lay
Name all op-pres-sion shall cease. Sweet hymns of joy in

wea - ry world re - joic - es, For yon-der breaks a new and glo-rious morn!
thus in low - ly man - ger, In all our tri - als born to be our friend;
grate - ful cho - rus raise we; Let all with-in us praise His ho - ly Name!

Fall on your knees! O hear the an - gel voic - es; O night di -
He knows our need, He guards us from all dan - ger; Be - hold your
Christ is the Lord! O praise His Name for - ev - er! His pow'r and

1,2

vine! O night when Christ was born! O night di - vine! O
King! Be - fore Him low - ly bend! Be - hold your King; be -
glo - ry ev - er - more pro - claim! His pow'r and

D. C.   3   2   2

night, O night di - vine!   glo - ry ev - er - more pro - claim!
fore Him low - ly bend!

196 Lo! How a Rose E'er Blooming

I am the rose of Sharon, the lily of the valley. Song of Sol. 2:1

GERMAN CAROL

GEISTLICHE KIRCHENGESANG
HARM. MICHAEL PRAETORIUS

1. Lo! how a rose e'er bloom - ing From ten - der stem hath
2. I - sa - iah 'twas fore - told it, The rose I have in
3. This flower, whose fra - grance ten - der With sweet - ness fills the

sprung! Of Jes - se's lin - eage com - ing As men of old have
mind; With Mar - y we be - hold it, The vir - gin moth - er
air, Dis - pels with glo - rious splen - dor The dark - ness ev - ery -

sung. It came, a flow - eret bright, A - mid the
kind. To show God's love a - right She bore to
where. True man, yet ver - y God, From sin and

cold of win - ter, When half - spent was the night.
men a Sav - ior, When half - spent was the night.
death He saves us And light - ens ev - ery load.

While Shepherds Watched Their Flocks 197

There were shepherds abiding in the fields, keeping watch over their flocks...Luke 2:8

NAHUM TATE   GEORGE FREDERICK HANDEL

1. While shep-herds watched their flocks by night, All seat-ed on the
2. "Fear not!" said he; for might-y dread Had seized their troub-led
3. "To you, in Da-vid's town this day, Is born of Da-vid's
4. "The heav'n-ly Babe you there shall find To hu-man view dis-
5. "All glo-ry be to God on high, And to the earth be

ground, The an-gel of the Lord came down, And glo-ry shone a-round.
mind, "Glad ti-dings of great joy I bring To you and all man-kind, To
line, The Sav-ior who is Christ the Lord, And this shall be the sign: And
played, All mean-ly wrapped in swath-ing bands, And in a man-ger laid; And
peace: Good will hence-forth from heav'n to men, Be-gin and nev-er cease, Be-

glo-ry shone a-round, And glo-ry shone a-round.
you and all man-kind, To you and all man-kind.
this shall be the sign: And this shall be the sign:
in a man-ger laid; And in a man-ger laid.
gin and nev-er cease, Be-gin and nev-er cease." A-men.

The Gift 198

Gift better than Himself God doth not know—
Gift better than his God no man can see;
This Gift doth here the Giver given bestow,
Gift to this Gift let each receiver be:
God is my Gift, Himself He freely gave me;
God's gift am I, and none but God shall have me.

Robert Southwell

199 It Came upon the Midnight Clear

Glory to God in the highest, and on earth peace...Luke 2:14

EDMUND H. SEARS

RICHARD S. WILLIS

1. It came up - on the mid - night clear, That glo-rious song of old,
2. Still through the clo - ven skies they come, With peace-ful wings un - furled,
3. And ye, be - neath life's crush-ing load, Whose forms are bend - ing low,
4. For lo, the days are has-tening on, By proph-et seen of old,

From an - gels bend-ing near the earth To touch their harps of gold:
And still their heav'n-ly mu - sic floats O'er all the wea - ry world:
Who toil a - long the climb-ing way With pain-ful steps and slow,
When, with the ev - er - cir-cling years, Shall come the time fore - told,

"Peace on the earth, good-will to men, From heav'n's all-gra - cious King": The
A - bove its sad and low - ly plains They bend on hov-ering wing: And
Look now! for glad and gold-en hours Come swift-ly on the wing: O
When the new heav'n and earth shall own The Prince of Peace their King, And

world in sol - emn still - ness lay To hear the an - gels sing.
ev - er o'er its Ba - bel sounds The bless - ed an - gels sing.
rest be - side the wea - ry road, And hear the an - gels sing.
the whole world send back the song Which now the an - gels sing.

O Little Town of Bethlehem 200

Thou, Bethlehem...though thou be little...out of thee shall He come. Micah 5:2

PHILLIPS BROOKS   LEWIS H. REDNER

1. O lit - tle town of Beth - le - hem, How still we see thee lie!
2. For Christ is born of Ma - ry, And gath - ered all a - bove,
3. How si - lent - ly, how si - lent - ly The won - drous gift is giv'n!
4. O ho - ly Child of Beth - le - hem! De - scend to us, we pray;

A - bove thy deep and dream-less sleep The si - lent stars go by.
While mor - tals sleep, the an - gels keep Their watch of won - d'ring love,
So God im - parts to hu - man hearts The bless - ings of His heav'n.
Cast out our sin, and en - ter in; Be born in us to - day.

Yet in thy dark streets shin - eth The ev - er - last - ing Light;
O morn - ing stars, to - geth - er Pro - claim the ho - ly birth!
No ear may hear His com - ing, But in this world of sin,
We hear the Christ - mas an - gels The great glad ti - dings tell;

The hopes and fears of all the years Are met in thee to - night.
And prais - es sing to God the King, And peace to men on earth.
Where meek souls will re - ceive Him still The dear Christ en - ters in.
O come to us, a - bide with us, Our Lord Em - man - u - el. A - men.

201 The Star Carol

When they saw the star, they rejoiced...Matt 2:10

WIHLA HUTSON   ALFRED S. BURT

1. Long years a - go   on a deep win - ter night,
2. Je - sus, the Lord,   was that Ba - by so   small,
3. Dear Ba - by Je - sus,   How   ti - ny Thou art,

High   in   the heavens a   star   shone bright,
Laid   down to   sleep   in a hum - ble stall;
I'll   make a   place   for Thee in my   heart,

While   in   a   man - ger a   wee Ba - by lay,
Then   came the star   and it stood o - ver - head,
And   when the stars   in the heav - ens I   see,

Sweet - ly   a - sleep   on a bed   of hay.
Shed - ding   its light 'round His lit - tle bed.
Ev - er and al - ways I'll think of Thee.

What Child Is This? 202

Where is He that is born King of the Jews? Matt. 2:2

WILLIAM C. DIX

TRADITIONAL ENGLISH MELODY

1. What Child is this, who, laid to rest, On Ma-ry's lap is sleep-ing?
2. Why lies He in such mean es-tate Where ox and ass are feed-ing?
3. So bring Him in-cense, gold and myrrh, Come, peas-ant, king, to own Him;

Whom an-gels greet with an-thems sweet, While shep-herds watch are keep-ing?
Good Chris-tian, fear; for sin-ners here The si-lent Word is plead-ing.
The King of kings sal-va-tion brings, Let lov-ing hearts en-throne Him.

Refrain

This, this is Christ the King, Whom shep-herds guard and an-gels sing:

This, this is Christ the King, The babe, the Son of Ma-ry.

203 Ring the Bells

The Father sent the Son to be the savior of the world. I John 4:14

HARRY BOLLBACK

HARRY BOLLBACK

Ring the bells, ring the bells; Let the whole world know: Christ was born in

Beth - le - hem man - y years a - go. Born to die that man might live,

Came to earth new life to give; Born of Ma - ry, born so low, Man - y years a-

go. God the Fa - ther gave His Son, Gave His own be - lov - ed One

To this wick - ed sin - ful earth To bring man-kind His love, new birth.

Ring the bells, ring the bells; Let the whole world know:

Christ the Sav - ior lives to - day As He did so long a - go!

Come Christ!   204

A Short Service of Congregational Praise

Mt. 11:2; Micah 5:2; John 4:25-26, 29; Mt. 25: 31-34; Rev. 20: 17-20

Leader: Praise to Christ! Praise to Him who comes, who has come,
who is coming, who will come again!

People: **Are you he who is to come, or should we look for another?**

Leader: But you, Bethlehem Ephrathah,
out of you will come for me one who will be ruler over Israel,
whose origins are from of old, from ancient times.

People: **The woman said to him, "I know that Messiah is coming;
when he comes, he will explain everything to us."**

Leader: Jesus said to her, "I who speak to you am he."

People: **"Come, see a man who told me everything I ever did!"**

Leader: When the Son of man comes in his glory, and all the angels with him,
he will sit on his throne in heavenly glory. Then the King will say to those
on his right, "Come, you who are blessed of my Father; take your
inheritance, the kingdom prepared for you since the creation of the world."

People: **This is He who comes, who has come, who is coming, who will come again!**

Leader: The Spirit and the bride say, "Come!"

People: **And let him who hears say, "Come!"**

All: **Give Praise! Praise to Him who comes, who has come,
who is coming, who will come again. Come Lord Jesus! Come!**

205 The First Noel

And there were in the same country shepherds abiding in the field...Luke 2:8

W. SANDYS' CHRISTMAS CAROL
ARR. JOHN STAINER
TRADITIONAL ENGLISH CAROL

1. The first No - el, the an-gel did say, Was to cer-tain poor shepherds in
2. They look - ed up and saw a star Shin-ing in the east, be -
3. And by the light of that same star Three wise men came from
4. This star drew nigh to the north-west, O'er Beth - le - hem it
5. Then en - tered in those wise men three, Full rev - 'rent - ly up -
6. Then let us all with one ac - cord Sing prais - es to our

fields as they lay; In fields where they lay keep-ing their sheep, On a
yond them far, And to the earth it gave great light, And
coun - try far; To seek for a king was their in - tent, And to
took its rest, And there it did both stop and stay, Right
on their knee, And of - fered there in His pres - ence Their
heav'n - ly Lord, That hath made heav'n and earth of naught, And

Refrain

cold win-ter's night that was so deep.
so it con - tin - ued both day and night.
fol - low the star wher - ev - er it went. No - el, No - el, No-
o - ver the place where Je - sus lay.
gold, and myrrh, and frank - in -cense.
with His blood man - kind hath bought.

el, No - el, Born is the King of Is - ra - el.

Angels We Have Heard on High 206

Glory to God in the highest and on earth peace...Luke 2:14

TRADITIONAL FRENCH CAROL   TRADITIONAL FRENCH MELODY

1. An - gels we have heard on high, Sweet - ly sing - ing o'er the plains,
2. Shepherds, why this ju - bi - lee? Why your joy - ous strains pro - long?
3. Come to Beth - le - hem, and see Him whose birth the an - gels sing;
4. See with - in a man - ger laid Je - sus, Lord of heav'n and earth!

And the moun-tains in re - ply Ech - o back their joy - ous strains.
Say what may the ti - dings be, Which in - spire your heav'n - ly song?
Come, a - dore on bend - ed knee Christ the Lord, the new - born King.
Ma - ry, Jo - seph, lend your aid, With us sing our Sav - ior's birth.

Refrain

Glo - - - ri - a in ex-cel-sis De - o,

Glo - - - ri - a in ex-cel-sis De - o.

207 Angels from the Realms of Glory

We...are come to worship Him. Matt 2:2

JAMES MONTGOMERY

HENRY T. SMART

1. An - gels from the realms of glo - ry, Wing your flight o'er all the earth;
2. Shep - herds in the fields a - bid - ing, Watch - ing o'er your flocks by night,
3. Sag - es, leave your con - tem - pla - tions, Bright - er vi - sions beam a - far;
4. Saints be - fore the al - tar bend - ing, Watch - ing long in hope and fear,

Ye who sang cre - a - tion's sto - ry, Now pro - claim Mes - si - ah's birth:
God with man is now re - sid - ing, Yon - der shines the in - fant Light:
Seek the great De - sire of na - tions, Ye have seen His na - tal star:
Sud - den - ly the Lord, de - scend - ing, In His tem - ple shall ap - pear:

Refrain

Come and wor - ship, come and wor - ship, Wor - ship Christ, the new - born King. A - men.

208 I Heard the Bells on Christmas Day

And He shall speak peace unto the heathen...Zech 9:10

HENRY W. LONGFELLOW

J. BAPTISTE CALKIN

1. I heard the bells on Christ - mas day Their old fa - mil - iar car - ols play,
2. I thought how, as the day had come, The bel - fries of all Chris - ten - dom
3. And in de - spair I bowed my head: "There is no peace on earth," I said,
4. Then pealed the bells more loud and deep: "God is not dead: nor doth He sleep;
5. Till, ring - ing, sing - ing on its way, The world re - volved from night to day,

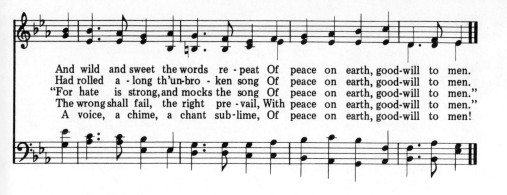

And wild and sweet the words re - peat Of peace on earth, good-will to men.
Had rolled a - long th'un-bro - ken song Of peace on earth, good-will to men.
"For hate is strong, and mocks the song Of peace on earth, good-will to men."
The wrong shall fail, the right pre - vail, With peace on earth, good-will to men."
A voice, a chime, a chant sub-lime, Of peace on earth, good-will to men!

Away in a Manger   209

She brought forth her firstborn son...and laid Him in a manger. Luke 2:7

UNKNOWN

WILLIAM J. KIRKPATRICK

Unison

1. A - way in a man - ger, no crib for a bed, The lit - tle Lord
2. The cat - tle are low - ing, the Ba - by a - wakes, But lit - tle Lord
3. Be near me, Lord Je - sus; I ask Thee to stay Close by me for-

Je - sus laid down His sweet head; The stars in the bright sky looked
Je - sus, no cry - ing He makes. I love Thee, Lord Je - sus, look
ev - er, and love me, I pray. Bless all the dear chil - dren in

down where He lay, The lit - tle Lord Je - sus a - sleep on the hay.
down from the sky, And stay by my cra - dle till morn - ing is nigh.
Thy ten - der care, And fit us for heav - en, to live with Thee there.

210 I Wonder as I Wander

And all they that heard it wondered at those things which were told them...Luke 2:18

APPALACHIAN CAROL
COLLECTED BY JOHN JACOB NILES

JOHN JACOB NILES
ARR. DONALD P. HUSTAD

Unison

1. I won - der as I wan - der, out un - der the sky, How
2. When Ma - ry birthed Je - sus, 'twas in a cow's stall, With
3. If Je - sus had want - ed for an - y wee thing, A
4. I won - der as I wan - der, out un - der the sky, How

Je - sus the Sav - ior did come for to die For
wise men and farm - ers and shep - herds and all. But
star in the sky or a bird on the wing, Or
Je - sus the Sav - ior did come for to die For

poor ord' - nary peo - ple like you and like I; I
high from God's heav - en a star's light did fall, The
all of God's an - gels in heav'n for to sing, He
poor ord' - nary peo - ple like you and like I; I

(Optional Coda)

won - der as I wan - der, out un - der the sky.
prom - ise of a - ges it then did re - call.
sure - ly could have it, 'cause He was the King.
won - der as I wan - der, out un - der the sky. Out un - der the sky.

You will find the babe...lying in a manger. Luke 2:12

<small>TRADITIONAL POLISH CAROL</small>   <small>TRADITIONAL POLISH CAROL</small>

1. In-fant ho-ly, In-fant low-ly, for His bed a cat-tle
2. Flocks were sleep-ing, shep-herds keep-ing vig-il till the morn-ing

stall; Ox-en low-ing, lit-tle know-ing Christ the Babe is Lord of all.
new Saw the glo-ry, heard the sto-ry, tid-ings of a gos-pel true.

Swift are wing-ing an-gels sing-ing, no-els ring-ing, tid-ings bring-ing:
Thus re-joic-ing, free from sor-row, prais-es voic-ing, greet the mor-row:

Christ the Babe is Lord of all, Christ the Babe is Lord of all.
Christ the Babe was born for you. Christ the Babe was born for you.

212 The Birthday of a King

I will raise up a King...who will reign wisely. Jer. 23:5

WILLIAM HAROLD NEIDLINGER   WILLIAM HAROLD NEIDLINGER

1. In the lit - tle vil - lage of Beth - le - hem, there lay a Child one
2. 'Twas a hum - ble birth-place, but oh, how much God gave to us that

day; And the sky was bright with a ho - ly light o'er the
day; From the man - ger bed what a path has led, what a

place where Je - sus lay. *Refrain* Al - le - lu - ia! O how the
per - fect ho - ly way. Al - le - lu - ia! O how the

an - gels sang: Al - le - lu - ia! How it rang! And the

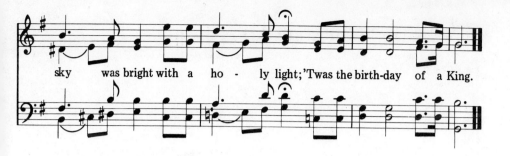

sky was bright with a ho - ly light; 'Twas the birth-day of a King.

Away in a Manger 213

She brought forth her firstborn son...and laid Him in a manger. Luke 2:7

UNKNOWN

JAMES R. MURRAY

Unison or Two-Part

1. A - way in a man - ger, no crib for a bed, The lit - tle Lord
2. The cat - tle are low - ing, the Ba - by a - wakes, But lit - tle Lord
3. Be near me, Lord Je - sus; I ask Thee to stay Close by me for-

Je - sus laid down His sweet head; The stars in the sky looked
Je - sus, no cry - ing He makes; I love Thee, Lord Je - sus, look
ev - er, and love me, I pray. Bless all the dear chil - dren in

down where He lay, The lit - tle Lord Je - sus a - sleep on the hay.
down from the sky, And stay by my cra - dle till morn - ing is nigh.
Thy ten - der care, And fit us for heav - en, to live with Thee there.

214 Good Christian Men, Rejoice

Unto you is born this day...a Savior, which is Christ the Lord. Luke 2:11

LATIN CAROL
TR. JOHN M. NEALE

TRADITIONAL GERMAN MELODY

1. Good Chris-tian men, re - joice With heart and soul and voice!
2. Good Chris-tian men, re - joice With heart and soul and voice!
3. Good Chris-tian men, re - joice With heart and soul and voice!

Give ye heed to what we say: Je - sus Christ is born to - day;
Now ye hear of end - less bliss; Je - sus Christ was born for this!
Now ye need not fear the grave; Je - sus Christ was born to save!

Ox and ass be - fore Him bow, And He is in the man-ger now.
He hath oped the heav'n - ly door, And man is blest for - ev - er - more.
Calls you one and calls you all To gain His ev - er - last - ing hall.

Christ is born to - day! Christ is born to - day!
Christ was born for this! Christ was born for this!
Christ was born to save! Christ was born to save!

O Hearken Ye 215

My soul glorifies the Lord. Luke 1:46

WIHLA HUTSON

ALFRED BURT

1. O heark - en ye who would be - lieve, The gra - cious ti - dings
2. O heark - en ye who long for peace, Your trou - bled search - ing
3. O heark - en ye who long for love And turn your hearts to

now re-ceive: Glo - ri - a, glo - ri - a, In ex - cel - sis De - o. The
now may cease. Glo - ri - a, glo - ri - a, In ex - cel - sis De - o. For
God a - bove. Glo - ri - a, glo - ri - a, In ex - cel - sis De - o. The

might - y Lord of heav'n and earth, To - day is come to hu - man birth.
at his cra - dle you shall find God's heal - ing grace for all man - kind.
an - gels' song the won - der tells: Now Love In - car - nate with us dwells!

Glo - ri - a, glo - ri - a, In ex - cel - sis De - o.

216 Go, Tell It on the Mountain

...They made known abroad the saying...concerning this child. Luke 2:17

JOHN W. WORK

TRADITIONAL SPIRITUAL

Unison

(Ref.) Go, tell it on the moun-tain, O-ver the hills and ev-ery-where;

Fine

Go, tell it on the moun - tain That Je-sus Christ is born.

1. While shep-herds kept their watch-ing O'er si - lent flocks by night, Be-
2. The shep-herds feared and trem-bled When, lo! a-bove the earth Rang
3. Down in a low-ly man-ger Our hum-ble Christ was born, And

D.C.

hold, through-out the heav - ens There shone a ho - ly light.
out the an - gel cho - rus That hailed our Sav - ior's birth.
God sent us sal - va - tion That bless - ed Christ-mas morn.

Once in Royal David's City 217

Unto you is born this day in the city of David a Savior...Luke 2:11

CECIL F. ALEXANDER

HENRY J. GAUNTLETT

1. Once in roy - al Da - vid's cit - y Stood a low - ly cat - tle
2. He came down to earth from heav - en Who is God and Lord of
3. Je - sus is our child-hood's pat - tern, Day by day like us He
4. And our eyes at last shall see Him, Thro' His own re-deem - ing

shed, Where a moth - er laid her ba - by In a
all, And His shel - ter was a sta - ble, And His
grew; He was lit - tle, weak, and help - less, Tears and
love; For that child so dear and gen - tle Is our

man - ger for His bed: Ma - ry was that moth - er
cra - dle was a stall: With the poor, and mean, and
smiles like us He knew: And He feel - eth for our
Lord in heav'n a - bove, And He leads his chil - dren

mild, Je - sus Christ her lit - tle child.
low - ly Lived on earth, our Sav - ior ho - ly.
sad - ness, And He shar - eth in our glad-ness.
on To the place where He is gone.

218 Thou Didst Leave Thy Throne

He came unto His own and His own received Him not. John 1:11

EMILY E.S. ELLIOTT

TIMOTHY R. MATTHEWS

1. Thou didst leave Thy throne and Thy king-ly crown When Thou
2. Heav-en's arch-es rang when the an-gels sang, Pro-
3. The fox-es found rest and the birds their nest In the
4. Thou cam-est, O Lord, with the liv-ing Word That should
5. When the heav-ens shall ring, and the an-gels sing, At Thy

cam-est to earth for me; But in Beth-le-hem's home
claim-ing Thy roy-al de-gree; But in low-ly birth
shade of the for-est tree; But thy couch was the sod,
set Thy peo-ple free; But with mock-ing scorn,
com-ing to vic-to-ry, Let Thy voice call me home,

there was found no room For Thy ho-ly na-tiv-i-ty:
Thou didst come to earth, And in great hu-mil-i-ty:
O Thou Son of God, In the des-ert of Gal-i-lee:
and with crown of thorn, They bore Thee to Cal-va-ry:
say-ing, "Yet there is room, There is room at My side for thee:"

Refrain

1-4. O come to my heart, Lord Je-sus! There is room in my heart for Thee.
5. My heart shall re-joice, Lord Je-sus! When Thou com-est and call-est for me. A-men

As with Gladness Men of Old 219

When they saw the star, they rejoiced.... Matt. 2:10

WILLIAM C. DIX

CONRAD KOCHER

1. As with glad - ness men of old Did the guid - ing
2. As with joy - ful steps they sped To that low - ly
3. As they of - fered gifts most rare At that man - ger
4. Ho - ly Je - sus, ev - ery day Keep us in the

star be - hold; As with joy they hailed its light,
man - ger bed, There to bend the knee be - fore
rude and bare, So may we with ho - ly joy,
nar - row way; And when earth - ly things are past,

Lead - ing on - ward, beam - ing bright, So, most gra - cious
Him whom heav'n and earth a - dore, So, may we with
Pure and free from sin's al - loy, All our cost - liest
Bring our ran - somed souls at last Where they need no

Lord, may we Ev - er more be led to Thee.
will - ing feet Ev - er seek the mer - cy seat.
treas - ures bring, Christ, to Thee our heav'n - ly King.
star to guide, Where no clouds Thy glo - ry hide.

220 We Three Kings of Orient Are

Behold, there came wise men from the east... Matt. 2:1

JOHN H. HOPKINS   JOHN H. HOPKINS

1. We three kings of O - ri - ent are, Bear - ing gifts we
2. Born a King on Beth - le - hem's plain, Gold I bring to
3. Frank - in - cense to of - fer have I, In - cense owns a
4. Myrrh is mine; its bit - ter per - fume Breathes a life of
5. Glo - rious now be - hold Him a - rise, King and God and

trav - erse a - far Field and foun - tain, moor and moun - tain,
crown Him a - gain, King for - ev - er, ceas - ing nev - er
De - i - ty nigh; Prayer and prais - ing, all men rais - ing,
gath - er - ing gloom; Sor - rowing, sigh - ing, bleed - ing, dy - ing,
Sac - ri - fice; Al - le - lu - ia, Al - le - lu - ia!

Refrain

Fol - low - ing yon - der star.
O - ver us all to reign.
Wor - ship Him, God on high. O star of won - der,
Sealed in the stone - cold tomb.
Peals through the earth and skies.

star of night, Star with roy - al beau - ty bright, West - ward

lead - ing, still pro - ceed - ing, Guide us to thy per - fect light.

It gives light to everyone in the house. Matt 5:15

BRYAN JEFFERY LEECH

GERMAN CAROL

1. O Christ-mas tree, O Christ-mas tree, your branch-es are up-lift-ed. You
2. O Christ-mas tree, O Christ-mas tree, you shine like stars a-bove us; And
3. O Christ-mas tree, O Christ-mas tree, in plain-ness you were grow-ing un-

seem to say that on this day our world's su-preme-ly gift-ed. The
with your beau-ty si-lent say, "How great-ly God must love us! You
til we came and brought you here and set your branch-es glow-ing. Your

shin-ing of your can-dles bright, re-minds us Light has come to-night. O
show us Him who with God's face, brought to our hearts the gift of grace. O
liv-ing beau-ty helps us see how clothed with Christ our lives can be. O

Christ-mas tree, O Christ-mas tree, you lift our eyes to heav-en.
Christ-mas tree, O Christ-mas tree, you lift our eyes to heav-en.
Christ-mas tree, O Christ-mas tree, you lift our eyes to heav-en.

222 A Communion Hymn for Christmas

Proclaim the Lord's death till He comes. I Cor. 11:26

MARGARET CLARKSON

TOM FETTKE

Unison

1. Gath - ered round Your ta - ble on this ho - ly eve,
2. Prince of Glo - ry, gra - cing Heav'n ere time be - gan,
3. Beth - lehem's In - car - na - tion, Cal - vary's bit - ter cross,
4. With pro - found - est won - der we Your bo - dy take—
5. Christ - mas Babe so ten - der, Lamb who bore our blame,

View - ing Beth - lehem's sta - ble we re - joice and grieve;
Now for us em - brac - ing death as Son of Man;
Wrought for us sal - va - tion by Your pain and loss;
Laid in man - ger yon - der, bro - ken for our sake;
How shall sin - ners ren - der prais - es due Your name?

Joy to see You ly - ing in Your man - ger bed,
By Your birth so low - ly, by Your love so true,
Now we fall be - fore You in this ho - ly place,
Hushed in ad - o - ra - tion we ap - proach the cup—
Do Your own good plea - sure in the lives we bring;

Weep to see You dy - ing in our sin - ful stead.
By Your cross most ho - ly, Lord, we wor - ship You!
Pros - trate we a - dore You, for Your gift of grace.
Beth - lehem's pure ob - la - tion free - ly of - fered up.
In Your ran - somed trea - sure reign for - ev - er King!

The Life
of
Christ

And Jesus increased in wisdom and stature,
and in favor with God and man.
Luke 2:52

223 Communion Covenant

1 Corinthians 11:23-25

Leader: The Lord Jesus, on the night he was betrayed, took bread, and when he had given thanks, he broke it and said, "Take, eat: This is my Body, which is for you; do this in remembrance of me."

People: **Christ has died.**
Christ is risen.
Christ will come again.

Leader: In the same way, after supper he took the cup, saying, "This cup is the new covenant in my blood; do this, whenever you drink it, in remembrance of me."

People: **We remember his death,**
We proclaim his resurrection,
We await his coming in glory.

Ivory Palaces 224

...Out of the ivory palaces, whereby they have made thee glad. Psa. 45:8

HENRY BARRACLOUGH

HENRY BARRACLOUGH

1. My Lord has gar-ments so won-drous fine, And myrrh their tex-ture fills;
2. His life had al - so its sor-rows sore, For al - oes had a part;
3. His gar-ments too were in cas - sia dipped, With heal-ing in a touch;
4. In gar-ments glo - ri - ous He will come, To o - pen wide the door;

Its fra-grance reached to this heart of mine, With joy my be - ing thrills.
And when I think of the cross He bore, My eyes with tear-drops start.
Each time my feet in some sin have slipped, He took me from its clutch.
And I shall en - ter my heav'n-ly home, To dwell, for - ev - er - more.

Refrain

Out of the i - vo - ry pal - a - ces, In - to a world of woe,

On - ly His great, e - ter - nal love Made my Sav - ior go.

225 One Day

When the fullness of the time was come, God sent forth His Son...Gal. 4:4

J. WILBUR CHAPMAN   CHARLES H. MARSH

1. One day when heav-en was filled with His prais-es, One day when
2. One day they led Him up Cal-va-ry's moun-tain, One day they
3. One day they left Him a-lone in the gar-den, One day He
4. One day the grave could con-ceal Him no long-er, One day the
5. One day the trum-pet will sound for His com-ing, One day the

sin was as black as could be, Je-sus came forth to be
nailed Him to die on the tree; Suf-fer-ing an-guish, de-
rest-ed, from suf-fer-ing free; An-gels came down o'er His
stone rolled a-way from the door; Then He a-rose, o-ver
skies with His glo-ry will shine; Won-der-ful day, my be-

born of a vir-gin, Dwelt a-mong men, my ex-am-ple is He!
spised and re-ject-ed, Bear-ing our sins, my Re-deem-er is He!
tomb to keep vig-il; Hope of the hope-less, my Sav-ior is He!
death He has con-quered; Now is as-cend-ed, my Lord ev-er-more!
lov-ed ones bring-ing; Glo-ri-ous Sav-ior, this Je-sus is mine!

Refrain

Liv-ing, He loved me; dy-ing, He saved me; Bur-ied, He

car-ried my sins far a-way; Ris-ing, He jus-ti-fied

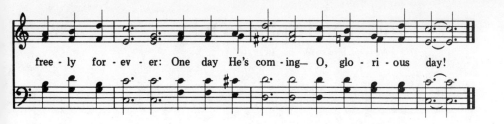

free - ly for - ev - er: One day He's com - ing— O, glo - ri - ous day!

Who Is He in Yonder Stall? 226

He is Lord of lords and King of kings. Rev. 17:14

BENJAMIN R. HANBY

BENJAMIN R. HANBY

1. Who is He in yon - der stall, At whose feet the shep-herds fall?
2. Who is He the peo - ple bless For His words of gen - tle - ness?
3. Who is He that stands and weeps At the grave where Laz - arus sleeps?
4. Lo! at mid - night, who is He Prays in dark Geth - sem - a - ne?
5. Who is He that from the grave Comes to heal and help and save?

Who is He in deep dis - tress, Fast - ing in the wil - der - ness?
Who is He to whom they bring All the sick and sor - row - ing?
Who is He the gath - 'ring throng Greet with loud tri - um - phant song?
Who is He on yon - der tree Dies in grief and ag - o - ny?
Who is He that from His throne Rules through all the world a - lone?

Refrain

'Tis the Lord! O won - drous sto - ry! 'Tis the Lord! the King of

glo - ry! At His feet we hum - bly fall, Crown Him! crown Him, Lord of all!

227 Broken and Spilled Out

This is my body, broken for you. I Cor. 11:24

GLORIA GAITHER

BILL GEORGE

1. Bro-ken and spilled out just for love of You, Je-
2. Bro-ken and spilled out just for love of me, Je-

sus, My most pre-cious treas - ure
sus, God's most pre-cious treas - ure

lav-ished on Thee. Bro-ken and spilled out,
lav-ished on me. Bro-ken and spilled out,

and poured at Your feet, In sweet a -
and poured at my feet, In sweet a -

ban-don, let me be spilled out and used up for Thee.
ban-don, Lord, You were spilled out and used up for me.

I Love You, Lord 228

Love the Lord, all His saints. Psa. 31:23

LAURIE KLEIN   LAURIE KLEIN

I love You, Lord, and I lift my voice to wor-ship

You; O my soul, re-joice! Take joy, my King, in

what You hear; May it be a sweet, sweet sound in Your ear.

229 O How Blessed Are the Poor in Spirit

Blessed are the poor in spirit; for theirs is the kingdom of heaven. Matt. 5:3

RICHARD AVERY AND
DONALD MARSH

RICHARD AVERY AND
DONALD MARSH

Unison

1. O how blessed are the poor in spir - it, Theirs is the
2. O how blessed are the meek and hum - ble, They will in -
3. O how blessed are the mer - cy giv - ers, Such mer - cy
4. O how blessed are the true peace - mak - ers, They will be

King-dom of Heav - en. And how blessed are the sad and
her - it the earth. And how blessed those who hun-ger for
they will re - ceive. And how blessed are the pure in
known as God's chil - dren. And how blessed those who suf - fer for

Refrain

mourn - ful; They'll be con-soled by God.
good - ness, They all will feast with God.
heart, They sure - ly will see God. Blessed and hap-py
jus - tice, They will be hon-ored by God.

we shall be. Lis - ten to the Mas - ter's word!

Soon the King-dom's com-ing—watch and see: the King-dom of the Lord!

*Then cometh Jesus with them unto a place called Gethsemane...*Matt. 26:36

JAMES MONTGOMERY

RICHARD REDHEAD

1. Go to dark Geth - sem - a - ne, Ye that feel the tempt-er's pow'r;
2. Fol - low to the judg - ment hall; View the Lord of life ar-raigned.
3. Cal - v'ry's mourn - ful moun-tain climb; There, a - dor - ing at His feet,
4. Ear - ly has - ten to the tomb Where they laid His breath-less clay;

Your Re - deem - er's con - flict see; Watch with Him one bit - ter hour;
O the worm-wood and the gall! O the pangs His soul sus - tained!
Mark that mir - a - cle of time, God's own sac - ri - fice com - plete:
All is sol - i - tude and gloom, Who hath tak - en Him a - way?

Turn not from His griefs a - way; Learn of Je - sus Christ to pray.
Shun not suf - f'ring, shame, or loss; Learn of Him to bear the cross.
"It is fin - ished!" hear the cry; Learn of Je - sus Christ to die.
Christ is ris'n! He meets our eyes. Sav - ior, teach us so to rise. A-men.

Watching with Christ 231

So, could you not watch with me one hour?

Mt. 26:40

Lord, we would watch with you; we would pray; we would wait.

What do you have to tell us?

What do you have to teach us?

What do you have to show us?

Is there ought we must suffer with you?

Amen.

232 I Walked Today Where Jesus Walked

He said, "Follow me." Matt. 4:19

DANIEL S. TWOHIG

GEOFFREY O'HARA

I walked to-day where Je-sus walked, In days of long a-go; I

wan-dered down each path He knew, With rev-'rent step and slow. Those

lit-tle lanes, they have not changed— A sweet peace fills the

air. I walked to-day where Je-sus walked, And felt His pres-ence

there. My path-way led through Beth-le-hem, Ah! mem-'ries

ev - er sweet; The lit - tle hills of Gal - i - lee, That knew those

child - ish feet; The Mount of Ol - ive's hal - lowed scened That Je - sus

knew be - fore; I saw the might - y Jor - dan roll As in the

days of yore. *mf* (Instruments) I

knelt to - day where Je - sus knelt, Where all a - lone He prayed; The

Gar - den of Geth-sem-a - ne— My heart felt un - a - fraid! I

picked my heav - y bur-den up And with Him by my side, I

climbed the hill of Cal - va-ry, I climbed the hill of Cal - va-ry, I

climbed the hill of Cal - va-ry, Where on the Cross He died! I

walked to - day where Je - sus walked, And felt Him close to me!

Hosanna, Loud Hosanna 233

Hosanna; Blessed is He that cometh in the name of the Lord. Mark 11:9

JENNETTE THRELFALL

WURTEMBERG GESANGBUCH

1. Ho - san - na, loud ho - san - na The lit - tle chil - dren sang;
2. From Ol - i - vet they fol - lowed 'Mid an ex - ult - ant crowd,
3. "Ho - san - na in the high - est!" That an - cient song we sing,

Through pil - lared court and tem - ple The love - ly an - them rang;
The vic - tor palm branch wav - ing, And chant - ing clear and loud;
For Christ is our Re - deem - er, The Lord of heav'n, our King;

To Je - sus, who had blessed them Close fold - ed to His breast,
The Lord of men and an - gels Rode on in low - ly state,
O may we ev - er praise Him With heart and life and voice,

The chil - dren sang their prais - es, The sim - plest and the best.
Nor scorned that lit - tle chil - dren Should on His bid - ding wait.
And in His bliss - ful pres - ence E - ter - nal - ly re - joice!

234 All Glory, Laud and Honor

Blessed is the King of Israel that cometh in the name of the Lord. John 12:13

THEODULPH OF ORLEANS

MELCHIOR TESCHNER

1. All glo - ry, laud and hon - or To Thee, Re - deem - er, King,
2. The com - pa - ny of an - gels Are prais - ing Thee on high,
3. To Thee, be - fore Thy pas - sion, They sang their hymns of praise;

To whom the lips of chil - dren Made sweet ho - san - nas ring:
And mor - tal men and all things Cre - at - ed make re - ply:
To Thee, now high ex - alt - ed, Our mel - o - dy we raise:

Thou art the King of Is - rael, Thou Da - vid's roy - al Son,
The peo - ple of the He - brews With palms be - fore Thee went:
Thou didst ac - cept their prais - es— Ac - cept the praise we bring,

Who in the Lord's name com - est, The King and bless - ed One!
Our praise and prayer and an - thems Be - fore Thee we pre - sent.
Who in all good de - light - est, Thou good and gra - cious King! A - men.

Litany of Praise   235

Psm. 24; John 19:1-22; Rev. 15:3 (NIV)

Leader: Who is this King of glory?

People: **The Lord, strong and mighty, the Lord, mighty in battle. Lift up your heads, O you gates; lift them up, you ancient doors! that the King of glory may come in.**

Leader: And the soldiers mocked him saying, "Hail, king of the Jews!" And the chief priests answered, "We have no king but Caesar!"

People: **And the people shouted, "Crucify him! Crucify him!"**

Leader: And Pilate also wrote a title and put it on the cross; "Jesus of Nazareth, King of the Jews."

People: **And those who had conquered the beast and its image, stood and sang: "Great and marvelous are your deeds, Lord God Almighty. Just and true are your ways, King of the ages."**

Leader: Who is he, this King of glory?

All: **The Lord Almighty—He is the King of glory!**

236 Ride On, Ride On, O Savior King

...Behold, thy King cometh unto thee, meek, and sitting upon a colt...Matt. 2:15

CAROL K. SOLBERG

HENRY S. CUTLER

1. Ride on, ride on, O Sav - ior King, To set the sin - ner free!
2. Ride on, ride on, O Sav - ior King, To claim the hearts of men!
3. Ride on, ride on, O Sav - ior King! Ride on o'er land and sea,

To sin-cursed souls sal - va - tion bring And peace e - ter - nal - ly!
Now death has lost its dread - ful sting And hope is born a - gain.
For You a - lone to man can bring E - ter - nal lib - er - ty.

Ride on to dark Geth - sem - a - ne, To un - told ag - o - ny,
O come, in hu - man hearts to reign; Sup-press the pow'r of sin!
Ride on to sin-bound na - tions, Lord, Un - til each heart shall own

And on the cross of Cal - va - ry Pro - cure our vic - to - ry!
Our own en - deav - or is in vain; Lord, You must help us win!
Your sav - ing, sanc - ti - fy - ing word, And bow be - fore Your throne!

I Will Sing of My Redeemer 237

Jesus Christ; who gave Himself for us, that He might redeem us... Titus 2:13, 14

PHILIP P. BLISS

ROWLAND H. PRICHARD

1. I will sing of my Re - deem-er And His won-drous love to me;
2. I will tell the won-drous sto - ry, How my lost es - tate to save,
3. I will praise my dear Re - deem-er, His tri - umph-ant power I'll tell,
4. I will sing of my Re - deem-er And His heav'n-ly love for me;

On the cru - el cross He suf-fered, From the curse to set me free.
In His bound-less love and mer - cy, He the ran-som free-ly gave.
How the vic - to - ry He giv-eth O - ver sin and death and hell.
He from death to life hath brought me, Son of God, with Him to be.

Refrain

Sing, O sing of my Re - deem-er, With His blood He pur-chased me,

On the cross He sealed my par - don, Paid the debt, and made me free.

The Cross
and
Remembrance

But he was wounded for our transgressions,
he was bruised for our iniquities:
the chastisement of our peace was upon him;
and with his stripes we are healed.
Isa. 53:5

O Sacred Head, Now Wounded 238

When they had platted a crown of thorns, they put it upon His head...Matt. 27:29

ATTR. BERNARD OF CLAIRVAUX
TR. JAMES W. ALEXANDER

HANS LEO HASSLER
ARR. J.S. BACH

1. O sa-cred Head, now wound-ed, With grief and shame weighed down,
2. What Thou, my Lord, hast suf-fered Was all for sin-ners' gain;
3. What lan-guage shall I bor-row To thank Thee, dear-est friend,

Now scorn-ful-ly sur-round-ed With thorns, Thine on-ly crown:
Mine, mine was the trans-gres-sion, But Thine the dead-ly pain.
For this Thy dy-ing sor-row, Thy pit-y with-out end?

O sa-cred Head, what glo-ry, What bliss till now was Thine!
Lo, here I fall, my Sav-ior! 'Tis I de-serve Thy place;
O make me Thine for-ev-er; And should I faint-ing be,

Yet, though de-spised and go-ry, I joy to call Thee mine.
Look on me with Thy fa-vor, Vouch-safe to me Thy grace.
Lord, let me nev-er, nev-er Out-live my love to Thee. A-men.

239 Beneath the Cross of Jesus

Now there stood by the cross of Jesus...John 19:25

ELIZABETH C. CLEPHANE

FREDERICK C. MAKER

1. Be - neath the cross of Je - sus I fain would take my stand—
2. Up - on that cross of Je - sus Mine eye at times can see
3. I take, O cross, thy shad - ow For my a - bid - ing place;

The shad - ow of a might - y Rock With - in a wea - ry land;
The ver - y dy - ing form of One Who suf - fered there for me;
I ask no oth - er sun - shine than The sun - shine of His face;

A home with - in the wil - der - ness, A rest up - on the way,
And from my smit - ten heart with tears Two won - ders I con - fess—
Con - tent to let the world go by, To know no gain nor loss,

From the burn - ing of the noon - tide heat, And the bur - den of the day.
The won - ders of re - deem - ing love And my un - wor - thi - ness.
My sin - ful self my on - ly shame, My glo - ry all the cross. A - men.

He Died for Me 240

Who...bore our sins in His own body on the tree. I Pet. 2:24

JOHN NEWTON

EDWIN O. EXCELL

1. I saw One hang-ing on a tree, In ag-o-ny and blood;
2. Sure, nev-er till my lat-est breath, Can I for-get that look;
3. My con-science felt and owned the guilt, And plunged me in de-spair;
4. A sec-ond look He gave, which said, "I free-ly all for-give:

He fixed His lov-ing eyes on me, As near His cross I stood.
It seemed to charge me with His death, Though not a word He spoke.
I saw my sins His blood had spilt And helped to nail Him there.
This blood is for your ran-som paid, I die that you may live."

Refrain

O, can it be, up-on a tree The Sav-ior died for me?

My soul is thrilled, my heart is filled, To think He died for me!

241 Lamb of Glory

Glory to the Lamb for ever and ever. Rev. 5:13

GREG NELSON AND
PHILL MCHUGH

GREG NELSON AND
PHILL MCHUGH

1. Hear the sto - ry from God's Word that kings and priests and
2. On the cross God loved the world while all the pow'rs of

proph - ets heard; There would be a sac - ri - fice And
hell were hurled; No one there could un - der - stand The

Refrain

blood would flow to pay sin's price.
One they saw was Christ the Lamb. Pre - cious Lamb of

glo - ry, Love's most won - drous sto - ry;

Heart of God's re-demp-tion of man; Wor-ship the Lamb of glo - ry.

Worthy Is the Lamb 242

Worthy is the Lamb who was slain...Rev. 5:12

ROBERT C. CLATTERBUCK

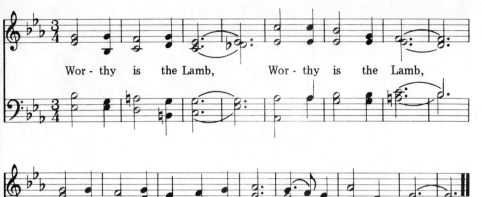

Wor - thy is the Lamb, Wor - thy is the Lamb,

Wor - thy is the Lamb who was slain; Wor - thy is the Lamb.

Praise Song from Revelation 5   243

Verses 11-13 (NIV)

Leader: Then I looked and heard the voice of many
angels, numbering thousands of thousands, and
ten thousand times ten thousand. They
encircled the throne and the living creatures
and the elders. In a loud voice they sang:

People: **"Worthy is the Lamb who was slain, to receive
power and wealth and wisdom and strength
and honor and glory and praise!"**

Leader: Then I heard every creature in heaven and on
earth and under the earth and on the sea, and
all that is in them, singing,

People: **"To him who sits upon the throne and to the
Lamb be praise and honor and glory and power
for ever and ever!"**

All: **Worthy is the Lamb!**

244 Worthy Is the Lamb

Worthy is the Lamb who was slain...Rev. 5:12

REVELATION 5:12; ADAPT. DON WYRTZEN

DON WYRTZEN

Wor-thy is the Lamb that was slain, Wor-thy is the
Lamb that was slain, Wor-thy is the Lamb that was
slain, to re-ceive: Pow-er and rich-es and
wis-dom and strength, Hon-or and glo-ry and bless-ing!
Wor-thy is the Lamb, Wor-thy is the Lamb, Wor-thy is the

Lamb that was slain, Wor - thy is the Lamb!

We Are the Reason 245

While we were still sinners, Christ died for us. Rom. 5:8

DAVID MEECE   DAVID MEECE

Unison

We are the rea - son that He gave His life, We are the rea-

son that He suf-fered and died. To a world that was lost He gave all

He could give, to show us the rea - son to live. live.

246 I Believe in a Hill Called Mount Calvary

It pleased God...to save them that believe. I Cor. 1:21

WILLIAM J. AND GLORIA GAITHER
AND DALE OLDHAM

WILLIAM J. GAITHER

There are things, as we travel this earth's shifting sands,
That transcend all the reason of man;
But the things that matter the most in this world,
They can never be held in our hand.

I believe that the Christ who was slain on that cross
Has the power to change lives today;
For He changed me completely — a new life is mine,
That is why by the cross I will stay.

I believe that this life with its great mysteries
Surely someday will come to an end;
But faith will conquer the darkness and death,
And will lead me at last to my Friend.

I be - lieve in a hill called Mount Cal - v'ry— I'll be - lieve what-
ev - er the cost; And when time has sur - ren - dered and
earth is no more, I'll still cling to that old rug - ged cross.

The Old Rugged Cross 247

Who for the joy that was set before Him endured the cross, despising the shame... Matt. 12:2

GEORGE BENNARD   GEORGE BENNARD

1. On a hill far a - way stood an old rug - ged cross, The em - blem of
2. O that old rug - ged cross, so de-spised by the world, Has a won-drous at-
3. In the old rug - ged cross, stained with blood so di - vine, A won - drous
4. To the old rug - ged cross I will ev - er be true, Its shame and re-

suf-fering and shame; And I love that old cross where the dear - est and best
trac-tion for me; For the dear Lamb of God left His glo - ry a - bove
beau - ty I see; For 'twas on that old cross Je - sus suf - fered and died
proach glad - ly bear; Then He'll call me some day to my home far a - way,

Refrain

For a world of lost sin - ners was slain.
To bear it to dark Cal - va - ry. So I'll cher - ish the old rug - ged
To par - don and sanc - ti - fy me.
Where His glo - ry for - ev - er I'll share. cross, the

cross, Till my tro - phies at last I lay down; I will cling to the
old rug - ged cross,

old rug - ged cross, And ex - change it some day for a crown.
cross, the old rug - ged cross,

248 Blessed Redeemer

They were come to the place called Calvary...Luke 23:33

Avis B. Christiansen

Harry D. Loes

1. Up Cal-vary's moun-tain one dread-ful morn, Walked Christ my Sav - ior,
2. "Fa - ther, for - give them!" thus did He pray, E'en while His life-blood
3. O how I love Him, Sav - ior and Friend, How can my prais - es

wea - ry and worn; Fac - ing for sin - ners death on the cross,
flowed fast a - way; Pray - ing for sin - ners while such woe-
ev - er find end! Thro' years un - num - bered on heav - en's shore,

Refrain

That He might save them from end - less loss.
No one but Je - sus ev - er loved so. Bless - ed Re - deem - er!
My tongue shall praise Him for - ev - er - more.

pre - cious Re-deem - er! Seems now I see Him on Cal - va - ry's tree;

Wound-ed and bleed-ing, for sin-ners plead-ing, Blind and un-heed-ing—dy-ing for me!

Love Was When God Became a Man 249

...And was made in the likeness of men...Phil. 2:7

JOHN E. WALVOORD

DON WYRTZEN

1. Love was when God be-came a man Locked in time and space
   Love was God born of Jew-ish kin, Just a car-pen-ter
2. Love was when God be-came a man Down where I could see
   Love was God dy-ing for my sin— And so trapped was I,

with-out rank or place;
with some fish-er-men. Love was when
love that reached to me;
my whole world caved in. Love was when

Je-sus walked in his-to-ry— Lov-ing-ly He brought
Je-sus rose to walk with me— Lov-ing-ly He brought

a new life that's free; Love was God nailed to
a new life that's free; Love was God— on-ly

bleed and die To reach and love one such as I.
He would try To reach and love one such as I.

250 Wondrous Love

What manner of love the Father hath bestowed upon us... I John 3:1

AMERICAN FOLK HYMN   SOUTHERN HARMONY

1. What won-drous love is this, O my soul, O my soul, What
2. To God and to the Lamb I will sing, I will sing, To
3. And when from death I'm free, I'll sing on, I'll sing on, And

won-drous love is this, O my soul! What won-drous love is
God and to the Lamb I will sing; To God and to the
when from death I'm free, I'll sing on; And when from death I'm

this that caused the Lord of bliss To bear the dread-ful curse for my
Lamb, who is the great "I Am," While mil-lions join the theme, I will
free, I'll sing and joy-ful be, And through e-ter-ni-ty I'll sing

soul, for my soul, To bear the dread-ful curse for my soul!
sing, I will sing, While mil-lions join the theme, I will sing!
on, I'll sing on, And through e-ter-ni-ty I'll sing on!

He Was Wounded for Our Transgressions 251

He was wounded for our transgressions...Isa. 53:5

THOMAS O. CHISHOLM

MERRILL DUNLOP

1. He was wound-ed for our trans - gress - ions, He bore our
2. He was num-bered a - mong trans - gress - ors, We did es-
3. We had wan-dered, we all had wan-dered Far from the
4. Who can num - ber His gen - er - a - tion? Who shall de-

sins in His bod - y on the tree; For our guilt He
teem Him for - sak - en by His God; As our sac - ri-
fold of "the Shep-herd of the sheep;" But He sought us
clare all the tri - umphs of His cross? Mil - lions dead now

gave us peace, From our bond-age gave re - lease, And with His
fice He died, That the law be sat - is - fied, And all our
where we were, On the moun-tains bleak and bare, And brought us
live a - gain, Myr - iads fol - low in His train! Vic - to - rious

stripes, and with His stripes, And with His stripes our souls are healed.
sin, and all our sin, And all our sin' was laid on Him.
home, and brought us home, And brought us safe - ly home to God.
Lord, vic - to - rious Lord, Vic - to - rious Lord and com - ing King!

252 Wounded for Me

...with His stripes we are healed. Isa. 53:5

W.G. OVENS AND GLADYS W. ROBERTS

W.G. OVENS

1. Wound-ed for me, wound-ed for me, There on the cross
2. Dy - ing for me, dy - ing for me, There on the cross
3. Ris - en for me, ris - en for me, Up from the grave
4. Liv - ing for me, liv - ing for me, Up in the skies
5. Com - ing for me, com - ing for me, One day to earth

He was wound - ed for me; Gone my trans - gres - sions, and
He was dy - ing for me; Now in His death my re -
He has ris - en for me; Now ev - er - more from death's
He is liv - ing for me; Dai - ly He's plead - ing and
He is com - ing for me; Then with what joy His dear

now I am free, All be - cause Je - sus was wound-ed for me.
demp- tion I see, All be - cause Je - sus was dy - ing for me.
sting I am free, All be - cause Je - sus has ris - en for me.
pray - ing for me, All be - cause Je - sus is liv - ing for me.
face I shall see, O how I praise Him—He's com - ing for me!

253 When I Survey the Wondrous Cross

What things were gain to me, those I counted loss for Christ. Phil. 3:7

ISAAC WATTS

LOWELL MASON

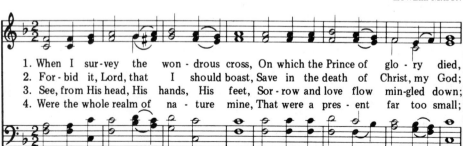

1. When I sur-vey the won - drous cross, On which the Prince of glo - ry died,
2. For - bid it, Lord, that I should boast, Save in the death of Christ, my God;
3. See, from His head, His hands, His feet, Sor - row and love flow min-gled down;
4. Were the whole realm of na - ture mine, That were a pres - ent far too small;

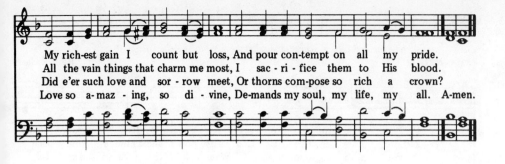

My rich-est gain I count but loss, And pour con-tempt on all my pride.
All the vain things that charm me most, I sac-ri-fice them to His blood.
Did e'er such love and sor-row meet, Or thorns com-pose so rich a crown?
Love so a-maz-ing, so di-vine, De-mands my soul, my life, my all. A-men.

O How He Loves You and Me! 254

Greater love hath no man than this... John 15:13

KURT KAISER

KURT KAISER

1. O how He loves you and me,   O how He loves you and
2. Je-sus to Cal-v'ry did go,   His love for man-kind to

me;   He gave His life—what more could He give? O how He
show;   What He did there bro't hope from de-spair: O how He

loves you,   O how He loves me,   O how He loves you and me!
loves you,   O how He loves me,   O how He loves you and me!

255 Jesus Paid It All

Though your sins be as scarlet, they shall be as white as snow. Isa. 1:18

ELVINA M. HALL   JOHN T. GRAPE

1. I hear the Sav-ior say, "Thy strength in-deed is small, Child of
2. Lord, now in-deed I find Thy pow'r and Thine a-lone Can
3. For noth-ing good have I Where-by Thy grace to claim— I'll
4. And when be-fore the throne I stand in Him com-plete, "Je-sus

Refrain

weak-ness, watch and pray, Find in Me thine all in all."
change the lep-er's spots And melt the heart of stone.
wash my gar-ments white In the blood of Cal-v'ry's Lamb.
died my soul to save," My lips shall still re-peat.

Je-sus paid it all,

All to Him I owe; Sin had left a crim-son stain, He washed it white as snow.

256 In the Cross of Christ I Glory

God forbid that I should glory, save in the cross... Gal. 6:14

JOHN BOWRING   ITHAMAR CONKEY

1. In the cross of Christ I glo-ry, Tow'r-ing o'er the wrecks of time;
2. When the woes of life o'er-take me, Hopes de-ceive, and fears an-noy,
3. When the sun of bliss is beam-ing Light and love up-on my way,
4. Bane and bless-ing, pain and pleas-ure, By the cross are sanc-ti-fied;

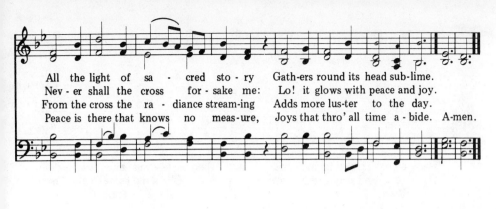

All the light of sa - cred sto - ry Gath-ers round its head sub-lime.
Nev - er shall the cross for - sake me: Lo! it glows with peace and joy.
From the cross the ra - diance stream-ing Adds more lus-ter to the day.
Peace is there that knows no meas-ure, Joys that thro' all time a - bide. A-men.

Near the Cross 257

All those who knew Him stood at a distance, watching. Luke 23:49

FANNY J. CROSBY

WILLIAM H. DOANE

1. Je - sus, keep me near the cross, There a pre - cious foun - tain
2. Near the cross, a trem - bling soul, Love and mer - cy found me;
3. Near the cross! O Lamb of God, Bring its scenes be - fore me;
4. Near the cross I'll watch and wait, Hop - ing, trust - ing ev - er,

Free to all, a heal - ing stream, Flows from Cal - v'ry's moun - tain.
There the Bright and Morn - ing Star Sheds its beams a - round me.
Help me walk from day to day With its shad - ows o'er me.
Till I reach the gold - en strand Just be - yond the riv - er.

Refrain

In the cross, in the cross Be my glo - ry ev - er;

Till my rap - tured soul shall find Rest be - yond the riv - er.

258 We Come as Guests Invited

And the Spirit and the Bride say, Come. Rev. 22:17

TIMOTHY DUDLEY-SMITH

HANS LEO HASSLER
ARR. J. S. BACH

1. We come as guests in - vit - ed When Je - sus bids us dine,
2. We eat and drink, re - ceiv - ing From Christ the grace we need,
3. One bread is ours for shar - ing, One sin - gle, fruit - ful vine,

His friends on earth u - nit - ed To share the bread and wine;
And in our hearts be - liev - ing On Him by faith we feed;
Our fel - low - ship de - clar - ing Re - newed in bread and wine—

The bread of life is bro - ken, The wine is free - ly poured
With won - der and thanks - giv - ing For love that knows no end,
Re - newed, sus - tained and giv - en By to - ken, sign and word,

For us, in sol - emn to - ken Of Christ our dy - ing Lord.
We find in Je - sus liv - ing Our ev - er - pres - ent friend.
The pledge and seal of heav - en, The love of Christ our Lord.

Here, O My Lord, I See Thee 259

The things which are not seen are eternal. II Cor. 4:18

HORATIUS BONAR

FREDERICK C. ATKINSON

1. Here, O my Lord, I see Thee face to face;
2. Here would I feed up - on the bread of God;
3. I have no help but Thine; nor do I need
4. Mine is the sin, but Thine the right - eous - ness;

Here would I touch and han - dle things un - seen,
Here drink with Thee the roy - al wine of heav'n;
An - oth - er arm save Thine to lean up - on;
Mine is the guilt, but Thine the cleans - ing blood.

Here grasp with firm - er hand th'e - ter - nal grace,
Here would I lay a - side each earth - ly load,
It is e - nough, my Lord, e - nough in - deed;
Here is my robe, my ref - uge, and my peace;

And all my wea - ri - ness up - on Thee lean.
Here taste a - fresh the calm of sin for - giv'n.
My strength is in Thy might, Thy might a - lone.
Thy blood, Thy right - eous - ness, O Lord, my God.

260 Come, Share the Lord

Jesus took bread...and said, Take, eat; this is my body. Mark 14:22

BRYAN JEFFERY LEECH   BRYAN JEFFERY LEECH

1. We gath-er here   in   Je - sus' name,   His love   is burn-ing in our
2. He joins us here,   He breaks the bread;   The Lord who pours the cup is
3. We'll gath-er soon where an - gels sing,   We'll see   the glo - ry of our

hearts like liv - ing flame,   For thru the lov - ing Son   the Fa - ther
ris - en from the dead.   The One we love the most   is now our
Lord and com-ing King.   Now we an - tic - i - pate   the feast for

Fine

makes us   one. Come take the bread, come drink the wine, come share the Lord.
gra-cious host. Come take the bread, come drink the wine, come share the Lord.
which we wait. Come take the bread, come drink the wine, come share the Lord.

1. No   one   is   a   stran-ger here,   ev - ery - one   be - longs.
2. We   are now   a   fam - i - ly   of which the Lord is   head.

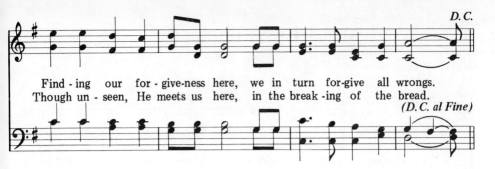

D.C.

Find - ing our for - give-ness here, we in turn for-give all wrongs.
Though un - seen, He meets us here, in the break -ing of the bread.

(D.C. al Fine)

I Know a Fount 261

You were ransomed...with the precious blood of Christ. I Pet. 1:18,19

OLIVER COOKE   OLIVER COOKE

I know a fount where sins are washed a - way,

I know a place where night is turned to day;

Bur - dens are lift - ed, blind eyes made to see, There's a

won - der work- ing pow'r in the blood of Cal - va - ry.

262 My Jesus, I Love Thee

We love Him because He first loved us. I John 4:19

WILLIAM R. FEATHERSTONE

ADONIRAM J. GORDON

1. My Je - sus, I love Thee, I know Thou art mine; For Thee all the
2. I love Thee, be - cause Thou hast first lov - ed me, And pur - chased my
3. I'll love Thee in life, I will love Thee in death, And praise Thee as
4. In man - sions of glo - ry and end - less de - light, I'll ev - er a-

fol - lies of sin I re - sign; My gra - cious Re - deem - er, my Sav - ior art
par - don on Cal - va - ry's tree; I love Thee for wear - ing the thorns on Thy
long as Thou lend - est me breath; And say when the death - dew lies cold on my
dore Thee in heav - en so bright; I'll sing with the glit - ter - ing crown on my

Thou; If ev - er I loved Thee, my Je - sus, 'tis now.
brow; If ev - er I loved Thee, my Je - sus, 'tis now.
brow; If ev - er I loved Thee, my Je - sus, 'tis now.
brow; If ev - er I loved Thee, my Je - sus, 'tis now. A - men.

263 Alas! and Did My Savior Bleed

...He was bruised for our iniquities... Isa. 53:5

ISAAC WATTS

HUGH WILSON

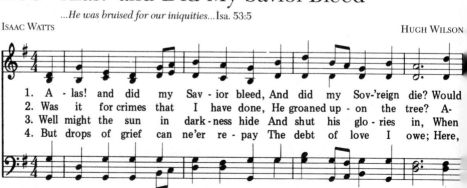

1. A - las! and did my Sav - ior bleed, And did my Sov - 'reign die? Would
2. Was it for crimes that I have done, He groaned up - on the tree? A-
3. Well might the sun in dark - ness hide And shut his glo - ries in, When
4. But drops of grief can ne'er re - pay The debt of love I owe; Here,

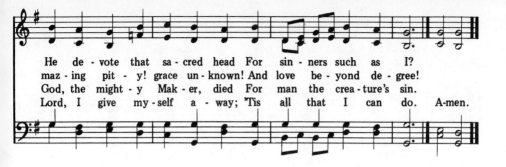

He de - vote that sa - cred head For sin - ners such as I?
maz - ing pit - y! grace un - known! And love be - yond de - gree!
God, the might - y Mak - er, died For man the crea - ture's sin.
Lord, I give my - self a - way; 'Tis all that I can do. A-men.

Nothing But the Blood of Jesus 264

The blood of Jesus Christ His Son cleanseth us from all sin. I John 1:7

ROBERT LOWRY   ROBERT LOWRY

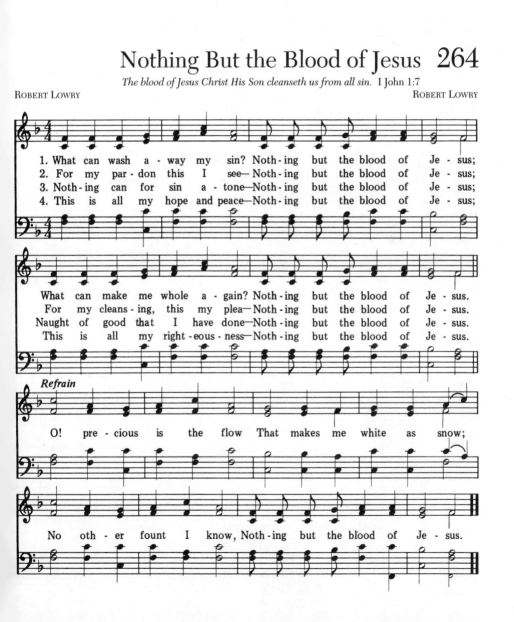

1. What can wash a - way my sin? Noth - ing but the blood of Je - sus;
2. For my par - don this I see— Noth - ing but the blood of Je - sus;
3. Noth - ing can for sin a - tone—Noth - ing but the blood of Je - sus;
4. This is all my hope and peace—Noth - ing but the blood of Je - sus;

What can make me whole a - gain? Noth - ing but the blood of Je - sus.
For my cleans - ing, this my plea— Noth - ing but the blood of Je - sus.
Naught of good that I have done—Noth - ing but the blood of Je - sus.
This is all my right - eous - ness—Noth - ing but the blood of Je - sus.

Refrain

O! pre - cious is the flow That makes me white as snow;

No oth - er fount I know, Noth - ing but the blood of Je - sus.

265 Let Us Break Bread Together

He took bread, and blessed it, and broke, and gave to them. Luke 24:30

TRADITIONAL SPIRITUAL

TRADITIONAL SPIRITUAL

Unison

1. Let us break bread to - geth - er on our knees.
2. Let us drink wine to - geth - er on our knees.
3. Let us praise God to - geth - er on our knees.

Let us break bread to - geth - er on our knees.
Let us drink wine to - geth - er on our knees.
Let us praise God to - geth - er on our knees.

Refrain

When I fall on my knees with my face to the ris - ing sun,

O Lord, have mer - cy on me.

Were You There? 266

It was the third hour, and they crucified Him. Mark 15:25

TRADITIONAL SPIRITUAL

TRADITIONAL SPIRITUAL

1. Were you there when they cru - ci - fied my Lord? Were you
2. Were you there when they nailed Him to the tree? Were you
3. Were you there when they laid Him in the tomb? Were you
4. Were you there when He rose up from the dead? Were you

there when they cru - ci - fied my Lord? O!
there when they nailed Him to the tree? O!
there when they laid Him in the tomb? O!
there when He rose up from the dead? O!

Some - times it caus - es me to trem - ble, trem - ble, trem - ble!
Some - times it caus - es me to trem - ble, trem - ble, trem - ble!
Some - times it caus - es me to trem - ble, trem - ble, trem - ble!
Some - times I feel like shout - ing glo - ry, glo - ry, glo - ry!

Were you there when they cru - ci - fied my Lord?
Were you there when they nailed Him to the tree?
Were you there when they laid Him in the tomb?
Were you there when He rose up from the dead?

Resurrection
and
Ascension

"It is true! The Lord has risen. . ."
Luke 24:34

In the Garden 267

Mary Magdalene came and told the disciples that she had seen the Lord. John 20:18

C. AUSTIN MILES

C. AUSTIN MILES

1. I come to the gar-den a - lone, While the dew is still on the
2. He speaks, and the sound of His voice Is so sweet the birds hush their
3. I'd stay in the gar-den with Him Though the night a-round me be

ros - es; And the voice I hear, fall - ing on my ear, The
sing - ing, And the mel - o - dy that He gave to me With-
fall - ing, But He bids me go; through the voice of woe, His

Refrain

Son of God dis - clos - es.
in my heart is ring - ing. And He walks with me, and He
voice to me is call - ing.

talks with me, And He tells me I am His own, And the

joy we share as we tar - ry there, None oth - er has ev - er known.

268 Christ the Lord Is Risen Today

Now is Christ risen...and become the first fruits of them that slept. I Cor. 15:20

CHARLES WESLEY

ARR. FROM *LYRA DAVIDICA*

1. Christ the Lord is risen to-day, Al - le - lu - ia!
2. Lives a-gain our glo-rious King; Al - le - lu - ia!
3. Love's re-deem-ing work is done, Al - le - lu - ia!
4. Soar we now where Christ has led, Al - le - lu - ia!

Sons of men and an-gels say: Al - le - lu - ia!
Where, O death, is now thy sting? Al - le - lu - ia!
Fought the fight, the bat-tle won; Al - le - lu - ia!
Fol-lowing our ex-alt-ed Head; Al - le - lu - ia!

Raise your joys and tri-umphs high, Al - le - lu - ia!
Dy-ing once, He all doth save: Al - le - lu - ia!
Death in vain for-bids Him rise; Al - le - lu - ia!
Made like Him, like Him we rise; Al - le - lu - ia!

Sing, ye heav'ns, and earth re-ply, Al - le - lu - ia!
Where thy vic-to-ry, O grave? Al - le - lu - ia!
Christ has o-pened Par-a-dise. Al - le - lu - ia!
Ours the cross, the grave, the skies. Al - le - lu - ia! A-men.

Christ Arose! 269

The angel of the Lord...rolled back the stone from the door. Matt. 28:2

ROBERT LOWRY   ROBERT LOWRY

1. Low in the grave He lay—Je-sus my Sav-ior! Wait-ing the com-ing day—
2. Vain-ly they watch His bed—Je-sus my Sav-ior! Vain-ly they seal the dead—
3. Death can-not keep his prey—Je-sus my Sav-ior! He tore the bars a-way—

Refrain

Je-sus my Lord!
Je-sus my Lord! Up from the grave He a-rose, With a
Je-sus my Lord! He a-rose,

might-y tri-umph o'er His foes; He a-rose a vic-tor from the
He a-rose!

dark do-main, And He lives for-ev-er with His saints to reign. He a-

rose! He a-rose!
He a-rose! He a-rose! Hal-le-lu-jah! Christ a-rose!

270 Jesus Christ Is Risen Today

He is not here; for He is risen... Matt. 28:6

LATIN HYMN

ROBERT WILLIAMS

1. Je - sus Christ is ris'n to - day, Al - le - lu - ia!
2. Hymns of praise then let us sing, Al - le - lu - ia!
3. But the pains which He en - dured, Al - le - lu - ia!
4. Sing we to our God a - bove, Al - le - lu - ia!

Our tri - um - phant ho - ly day, Al - le - lu - ia!
Un - to Christ, our heav'n - ly King, Al - le - lu - ia!
Our sal - va - tion have pro - cured; Al - le - lu - ia!
Praise e - ter - nal as His love; Al - le - lu - ia!

Who did once, up - on the cross, Al - le - lu - ia!
Who en - dured the cross and grave, Al - le - lu - ia!
Now a - bove the sky He's King, Al - le - lu - ia!
Praise Him, all ye heav'n - ly host, Al - le - lu - ia!

Suf - fer to re - deem our loss, Al - le - lu - ia!
Sin - ners to re - deem and save, Al - le - lu - ia!
Where the an - gels ev - er sing: Al - le - lu - ia!
Fa - ther, Son, and Ho - ly Ghost, Al - le - lu - ia!

I Know That My Redeemer Liveth 271

...My Redeemer liveth, and...He shall stand at the latter day upon the earth. Job 19:25

JESSIE B. POUNDS   JAMES H. FILLMORE

1. I know that my Re-deem-er liv - eth, And on the earth
2. I know His prom-ise nev-er fail - eth, The word He speaks,
3. I know my man-sion He pre-par - eth, That where He is

1. And on the earth

a - gain shall stand; I know e - ter-nal life He giv - eth, That grace and
it can-not die; Tho' cru - el death my flesh as - sail - eth, Yet I shall
there I may be; O won-drous thought, for me He car - eth, And He at

1. That

Chorus

pow'r are in His hand.
see Him by and by.   I know, I know that Je - sus
last will come for me.   I know, I know
grace and pow'r

liv - eth, And on the earth   a - gain shall stand. I know, I
And on the earth   I

know that life He giv - eth, That grace and pow'r are in His hand.
know, I know

272 Easter Song

He is not here; for He is risen, as He said. Matt 28:6

ANNE HERRING ANNE HERRING

Hear the bells ring-ing, they're sing-ing that we can be born a - gain.

Hear the bells ring-ing, they're sing-ing "Christ is ris-en from the dead." The an - gel up on the tomb-stone said "He is ris-en just as He said.

273 Come, Ye Faithful, Raise the Strain

Thou has ascended on high, Thou has led captivity captive. Psa. 68:18

TR. JOHN M. NEALE

ARTHUR S. SULLIVAN

1. Come, ye faith-ful, raise the strain Of tri-um-phant glad-ness;
2. 'Tis the spring of souls to-day, Christ hath burst His pris-on,
3. "Al-le-lu-ia!" now we cry To our King Im-mor-tal,

God hath brought His peo-ple forth In-to joy from sad-ness.
And from three day's sleep in death As a sun hath ris-en.
Who, tri-um-phant, burst the bars Of the tomb's dark por-tal;

Now re-joice, Je-ru-sa-lem, And with true af-fec-tion
All the win-ter of our sins, Long and dark, is fly-ing
"Al-le-lu-ia!" with the Son, God the Fa-ther prais-ing;

Wel-come in un-wea-ried strains Je-sus' res-ur-rec-tion.
From His light, to whom we give Laud and praise un-dy-ing.
"Al-le-lu-ia!" yet a-gain To the Spir-it rais-ing. A-men.

Morning Has Broken 274

I will awaken the dawn. I will praise you, O Lord. Psa. 57:8,9

ELEANOR FARJEON

ARR. JACK SCHRADER

Unison

1. Morn-ing has bro - ken Like the first morn - ing,
2. Sweet the rain's new fall Sun - lit from heav - en,
3. Mine is the sun - light! Mine is the morn - ing

Black-bird has spo - ken Like the first bird.
Like the first dew - fall On the first grass.
Born of the one light E - den saw play!

Praise for the sing - ing! Praise for the morn - ing!
Praise for the sweet - ness Of the wet gar - den,
Praise with e - la - tion, Praise ev - ery morn - ing,

Praise for them, spring - ing Fresh from the Word!
Sprung in com - plete - ness Where His feet pass.
God's re - cre - a - tion Of the new day!

275 Because He Lives

Because I live, ye shall live also. John 14:19

WILLIAM J. AND GLORIA GAITHER

WILLIAM J. GAITHER

1. God sent His Son, they called Him Je - sus; He came to love,
2. How sweet to hold a new-born ba - by, And feel the pride
3. And then one day I'll cross the riv - er; I'll fight life's fi -

heal, and for - give; He lived and died to buy my
and joy He gives; But great - er still the calm as -
nal war with pain; And then as death gives way to

par - don, An emp - ty grave is there to prove my Sav - ior lives.
sur - ance, This child can face un - cer - tain days be - cause He lives.
vic - tory, I'll see the lights of glo - ry and I'll know He lives.

Refrain

Be - cause He lives I can face to - mor - row; Be - cause He lives

all fear is gone; Be - cause I know He holds the fu - ture,

And life is worth the liv-ing just be-cause He lives.

The Day of Resurrection 276

Jesus met them, saying, All hail. Matt 28:9

Tr. John Neale

Henry T. Smart

1. The day of res-ur-rec-tion! Earth, tell it out a-broad;
2. Our hearts be pure from e-vil, That we may see a-right
3. Now let the heav'ns be joy-ful! Let earth her song be-gin!

The Pass-o-ver of glad-ness, The Pass-o-ver of God.
The Lord in rays e-ter-nal Of res-ur-rec-tion light;
The world re-sound in tri-umph, And all that is there-in;

From death to life e-ter-nal, From earth un-to the sky,
And, lis-t'ning to His ac-cents, May hear, so calm and plain,
Let all things seen and un-seen Their notes of glad-ness blend;

Our Christ hath brought us o-ver With hymns of vic-to-ry.
His own "All hail!" and, hear-ing, May raise the vic-tor strain.
For Christ the Lord hath ris-en, Our Joy that hath no end.

277 Hymn of Promise

Promise of the life that is and is to come. I Tim. 4:8

NATALIE SLEETH

NATALIE SLEETH

Unison

1. In the bulb   there is a flow - er;   In the seed,   an ap - ple tree;
2. There's a song   in ev - ery si - lence, Seek-ing word   and mel - o - dy;
3. In our end   is our be - gin - ning;   In our time,   in - fin - i - ty.

In co-coons, a hid -den prom-ise: But - ter -flies   will soon be free!
There's a dawn in ev - ery dark-ness, Bring-ing hope   to you and me.
In our doubt there is be - liev - ing; In our life,   e - ter - ni - ty.

In the cold   and snow of win - ter There's a spring that waits to be,
From the past   will come the fu - ture; What it holds,   a mys-ter - y,
In our death   a res - ur-rec - tion; At the last,   a vic - to - ry.

Un-re-vealed un-til its sea - son, Some-thing God a-lone can   see.

278

So it is with the resurrection of the dead —
What is sown is perishable/what is raised is imperishable.
It is sown in dishonor/it is raised in glory.
It is sown in weakness/it is raised in power.
It is sown a physical body/it is raised a spiritual body.
We shall not all sleep/but we shall all be changed —
Lo! I tell you a mystery.

From I Cor. 15

My Hope Is in the Lord 279

Christ in you, the hope of glory. Col. 1:27

NORMAN J. CLAYTON

NORMAN J. CLAYTON

1. My hope is in the Lord Who gave Him-self for me,
2. No mer-it of my own His an-ger to sup-press,
3. And now for me He stands Be-fore the Fa-ther's throne,
4. His grace has planned it all, 'Tis mine but to be-lieve,

And paid the price of all my sin at Cal-va-ry.
My on-ly hope is found in Je-sus' right-eous-ness.
He shows His wound-ed hands, and names me as His own.
And rec-og-nize His work of love and Christ re-ceive.

Refrain

For me He died, For me He lives,
For me He died, For me He lives,

And ev-er-last-ing life and light He free-ly gives.

280 The Unveiled Christ

And the veil of the temple was rent in the midst. Luke 23:45

N. B. HERRELL

N. B. HERRELL

1. Once our bless-ed Christ of beau-ty   Was veiled off from hu-man view;
2. Now He is with God the Fa-ther,   In-ter-ced-ing there for you;
3. Ho-ly an-gels bow be-fore Him,   Men of earth give prais-es due;
4. Thro'-out time and end-less a-ges, Heights and depths of love so true;

But thro' suf-f'ring, death and sor-row   He has rent the veil in two.
For He is the might-y con-qu'ror Since He rent the veil in two.
For He is the well-be-lov-ed   Since He rent the veil in two.
He a-lone can be the giv-er   Since He rent the veil in two.

Chorus

O be-hold the Man of Sor-rows, O be-hold Him in plain view;

Lo! He is the might-y con-qu'ror, Since He rent the veil in two.

Lo! He is the might-y con-qu'ror, Since He rent the veil in two.

Thine Is the Glory, Risen Conquering Son 281

O grave, where is thy victory? I Cor. 15:55

Tr. Richard B. Hoyle

George Frederick Handel

1. Thine is the glo - ry, Ris - en, con-qu'ring Son; End - less is the
2. Lo! Je - sus meets us, Ris - en, from the tomb; Lov - ing - ly He
3. No more we doubt Thee, Glo -rious Prince of Life! Life is naught with-

vic - t'ry Thou o'er death hast won. An - gels in bright rai - ment
greets us, Scat - ters fear and gloom; Let His church with glad - ness
out Thee; Aid us in our strife; Make us more than con-qu'rors,

Rolled the stone a - way, Kept the fold - ed grave - clothes
Hymns of tri - umph sing, For her Lord now liv - eth;
Through Thy death - less love; Bring us safe through Jor - dan

Refrain

Where Thy bod - y lay. Thine is the glo - ry, Ris - en, con-qu'ring Son;
Death hath lost its sting.
To Thy home a - bove.

End - less is the vic - t'ry Thou o'er death hast won. A - men.

282 Rejoice, the Lord Is King

But we see Jesus...crowned with glory and honor. Heb. 2:9

CHARLES WESLEY

JOHN DARWALL

1. Re - joice, the Lord is King: Your Lord and King a - dore! Re-
2. Je - sus the Sav - ior reigns, The God of truth and love; When
3. His king - dom can - not fail, He rules o'er earth and heav'n; The
4. Re - joice in glo - rious hope! Our Lord the Judge shall come, And

joice, give thanks, and sing, And tri - umph ev - er - more: Lift up your
He had purged our stains He took His seat a - bove: Lift up your
keys of death and hell Are to our Je - sus giv'n: Lift up your
take his serv - ants up To their e - ter - nal home. Lift up your

heart, lift up your voice! Re - joice, a - gain I say, re - joice!
heart, lift up your voice! Re - joice, a - gain I say, re - joice!
heart, lift up your voice! Re - joice, a - gain I say, re - joice!
heart, lift up your voice! Re - joice, a - gain I say, re - joice! A - men.

283 Hallelujah! What a Savior!

A man of sorrows and acquainted with grief... Isa. 53:3

PHILIP P. BLISS

PHILIP P. BLISS

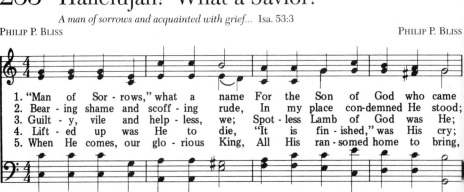

1. "Man of Sor - rows," what a name For the Son of God who came
2. Bear - ing shame and scoff - ing rude, In my place con - demned He stood;
3. Guilt - y, vile and help - less, we; Spot - less Lamb of God was He;
4. Lift - ed up was He to die, "It is fin - ished," was His cry;
5. When He comes, our glo - rious King, All His ran - somed home to bring,

Ru - ined sin - ners to re - claim! Hal - le - lu - jah! what a Sav - ior!
Sealed my par - don with His blood; Hal - le - lu - jah! what a Sav - ior!
"Full a - tone - ment" can it be? Hal - le - lu - jah! what a Sav - ior!
Now in heav'n ex - alt - ed high; Hal - le - lu - jah! what a Sav - ior!
Then a - new this song we'll sing: Hal - le - lu - jah! what a Sav - ior!

Look, Ye Saints! the Sight Is Glorious 284

God hath made that same Jesus...both Lord and Christ. Acts 2:36

THOMAS KELLY

HENRY T. SMART

1. Look, ye saints! the sight is glo - rious: See the Man of Sor - rows now;
2. Crown the Sav - ior! an - gels crown Him! Rich the tro - phies Je - sus brings;
3. Sin - ners in de - ri - sion crowned Him, Mocking thus the Sav - ior's claim;
4. Hark, those bursts of ac - cla - ma - tion! Hark, those loud tri - um - phant chords!

From the fight re - turned vic - to - rious, Ev - ery knee to Him shall bow:
In the seat of power en - throne Him, While the vault of heav - en rings:
Saints and an - gels crowd a - round Him, Own His ti - tle, praise His name:
Je - sus takes the high - est sta - tion, O, what joy the sight af - fords:

Crown Him! crown Him! crown Him! crown Him! Crowns be - come the Vic - tor's brow.
Crown Him! crown Him! crown Him! crown Him! Crown the Sav - ior King of kings.
Crown Him! crown Him! crown Him! crown Him! Spread a - broad the Vic - tor's fame.
Crown Him! crown Him! crown Him! crown Him! King of kings, and Lord of lords.

285 He Lives

...That I may know Him, and the power of His resurrection. Phil. 3:10

ALFRED H. ACKLEY   ALFRED H. ACKLEY

1. I serve a ris-en Sav-ior, He's in the world to-day; I know that He is
2. In all the world a-round me I see His lov-ing care, And tho' my heart grows
3. Re-joice, re-joice, O Christ-ian, lift up your voice and sing E-ter-nal hal-le-

liv-ing, what-ev-er men may say; I see His hand of mer-cy, I
wea-ry, I nev-er will de-spair; I know that He is lead-ing thro'
lu-jahs to Je-sus Christ the King! The Hope of all who seek Him, the

hear His voice of cheer, And just the time I need Him He's al-ways near.
all the storm-y blast, The day of His ap-pear-ing will come at last.
Help of all who find, None oth-er is so lov-ing, so good and kind.

Refrain

He lives, He lives, Christ Je-sus lives to-day! He walks with me and
He lives, He lives,

talks with me a-long life's nar-row way. He lives, He lives, sal-
He lives, He lives,

va-tion to im - part! You ask me how I know He lives? He lives within my heart.

Rise, Heart 286

Rise heart; thy Lord is risen. Sing his praise
Without delays,
Who takes thee by the hand, that thou likewise
With Him mayst rise . . .

George Herbert

I Am Not Skilled to Understand 287

Him hath God exalted with His right hand to be a...Savior. Acts. 5:31

DORA GREENWELL

WILLIAM J. KIRKPATRICK

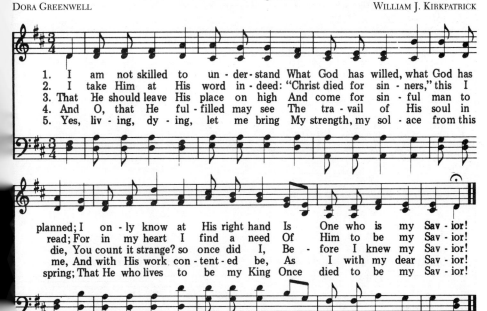

1. I am not skilled to un - der-stand What God has willed, what God has
2. I take Him at His word in - deed: "Christ died for sin - ners," this I
3. That He should leave His place on high And come for sin - ful man to
4. And O, that He ful - filled may see The tra - vail of His soul in
5. Yes, liv - ing, dy - ing, let me bring My strength, my sol - ace from this

planned; I on - ly know at His right hand Is One who is my Sav - ior!
read; For in my heart I find a need Of Him to be my Sav - ior!
die, You count it strange? so once did I, Be - fore I knew my Sav - ior!
me, And with His work con - tent - ed be, As I with my dear Sav - ior!
spring; That He who lives to be my King Once died to be my Sav - ior!

288 Jesus Lives and So Shall I

O Death, where is thy sting? I Cor. 15:55

CHRISTIAN F. GELLERT

JOHANN CRÜGER

1. Je - sus lives, and so shall I. Death! thy sting is
2. Je - sus lives and reigns su - preme; And, His king - dom
3. Je - sus lives, I know full well, Naught from Him my
4. Je - sus lives, and death is now But my en - trance

gone for - ev - er. He who deigned for me to die,
still re - main - ing; I shall al - so be with Him,
heart can sev - er: Life nor death nor pow'rs of hell,
in - to glo - ry. Cour - age, then, my soul for thou

Lives, the bands of death to sev - er. He shall raise me
Ev - er liv - ing, ev - er reign - ing. God has prom - ised:
Joy nor grief, hence - forth for - ev - er. None of all His
Hast a crown of life be - fore thee; Thou shalt find thy

with the just: Je - sus is my Hope and Trust.
be it must; Je - sus is my Hope and Trust.
saints is lost; Je - sus is my Hope and Trust.
hopes were just; Je - sus is the Christ - ian's Trust. A - men.

We Come, O Christ, to You 289

I am the way, the truth, and the life...John 14:6

Margaret Clarkson

John Darwall

1. We come, O Christ, to You, True Son of God and man, By Whom all things con - sist, In Whom all life be - gan: In You a - lone we live and move, And have our be - ing in Your love.

2. You are the Way to God, Your blood our ran - som paid; In You we face our Judge And Mak - er un - a - fraid. Be - fore the throne ab - solved we stand, Your love has met Your law's de - mand.

3. You are the liv - ing Truth! All wis - dom dwells in You, The Source of ev - ery skill, The One E - ter - nal, true! O great I AM! In You we rest, Sure an - swer to our ev - ery quest.

4. You on - ly are true Life, To know You is to live The more a - bun - dant life That earth can nev - er give: O ris - en Lord! We live in You, in us each day Your life re - new!

5. We wor - ship You, Lord Christ, Our Sav - ior and our King, To You our youth and strength A - dor - ing - ly we bring: So fill our hearts, that all may view Your life in us, and turn to You! A - men.

290 Our God Reigns

Good news... Your God reigns. Isa. 52:7

LEONARD W. SMITH

LEONARD W. SMITH

1. How love-ly on the moun-tains are the feet of him
2. He had no state-ly form, He had no maj - es - ty,
3. Out from the tomb He came with grace and maj - es - ty,

who brings good news, good news An-nounc-ing
That we should be drawn to Him. He was de-
He is a - live, He is a - live. God loves us

peace, pro - claim - ing news of hap - pi - ness. Our God
spised and we took no ac - count of Him, Yet now He
so, see here His hands, His feet, His side. Yes, we

Refrain

reigns, Our God reigns! Our God reigns! Our God
reigns with the Most High. Our God reigns! Our God
know, He is a - live.

reigns!   Our God reigns!   Our God reigns!

King of Kings 291

The King of kings and Lord of lords. I Tim. 6:15

SOPHIE CONTY AND
NAOMI BATYA

ANCIENT HEBREW FOLK SONG

Unison

King of Kings and Lord of Lords, glo-ry, hal-le-lu-jah! King of Kings and

Lord of Lords, glo-ry, hal-le-lu-jah! Je - sus, Prince of Peace,

glo-ry, hal-le-lu-jah! Je - sus, Prince of Peace, glo-ry, hal-le-lu-jah!

292 Behold the Lamb

Behold the Lamb of God. John 1:36

DOTTIE RAMBO   DOTTIE RAMBO

Be- hold the Lamb, be - hold the Lamb, slain from the foun-

da- tion of the world. For sin-ners cru - ci -fied, O ho - ly

Fine

sac - ri -fice, be-hold the Lamb of God, be-hold the Lamb.

More movement

play cued notes
first time only

Crown   Him,   crown   Him,   wor - thy   is the   Lamb.

D. S. al Fine

Praise   Him,   praise   Him. Heav'n and earth re - sound.   Be -

A Perfect Heart 293

A new heart will I give you. Ezek. 36:26

DONY McGUIRE AND
REBA RAMBO

DONY McGUIRE AND
REBA RAMBO

Bless the Lord (bless the Lord) who reigns in beau - ty;

Bless the Lord (bless the Lord) who reigns in wis - dom and with pow'r.

Bless the Lord (bless the Lord) who reigns my

life with so much love, He can make a per - fect heart.

Testimony

O give thanks unto the Lord, for he is good:
for his mercy endureth for ever.
Let the redeemed of the Lord say so,
whom he hath redeemed
from the hand of the enemy.
Psm. 107:1,2

I'd Rather Have Jesus 294

*...I count all things but loss for the excellency of the knowledge of Christ Jesus...*Phil. 3:8

RHEA F. MILLER

GEORGE BEVERLY SHEA

1. I'd rath - er have Je - sus than sil - ver or gold, I'd rath - er be
2. I'd rath - er have Je - sus than men's ap - plause, I'd rath - er be
3. He's fair - er than lil - ies of rar - est bloom, He's sweet - er than

His than have rich - es un - told; I'd rath - er have Je - sus than
faith - ful to His dear cause; I'd rath - er have Je - sus than
hon - ey from out the comb; He's all that my hun - ger - ing

hous - es or lands, I'd rath - er be led by His nail-pierced hand
world - wide fame, I'd rath - er be true to His ho - ly name
spir - it needs, I'd rath - er have Je - sus and let Him lead

Than to be the king of a vast do - main Or be held in sin's dread sway; I'd

rath - er have Je - sus than an - y - thing This world af - fords to - day.

295 Blessed Assurance

I will sing praises unto my God while I have my being. Psa. 146:2

FANNY J. CROSBY

PHOEBE P. KNAPP

1. Bless - ed as - sur - ance, Je - sus is mine! O, what a fore-taste of
2. Per - fect sub - mis - sion, per - fect de - light, Vi - sions of rap - ture now
3. Per - fect sub - mis - sion, all is at rest, I in my Sav - ior am

glo - ry di - vine! Heir of sal - va - tion, pur - chase of God,
burst on my sight; An - gels de - scend - ing, bring from a - bove
hap - py and blest; Watch - ing and wait - ing, look - ing a - bove,

Refrain

Born of His Spir - it, washed in His blood.
Ech - oes of mer - cy, whis-pers of love. This is my sto - ry, this is my
Filled with His good-ness, lost in His love.

song, Prais - ing my Sav - ior all the day long; This is my sto - ry,

this is my song, Prais - ing my Sav - ior all the day long.

Jesus Is the Sweetest Name I Know 296

Far above...every name that is named... Eph. 1:21

LELA B. LONG   LELA B. LONG

1. There have been names that I have loved to hear, But nev-er has there
2. There is no name in earth or heav'n a-bove, That we should give such
3. And some day I shall see Him face to face To thank and praise Him

been a name so dear To this heart of mine, as the name di-vine, The
hon-or and such love As the bless-ed name, let us all ac-claim, That
for His won-drous grace, Which He gave to me, when He made me free, The

Chorus

pre-cious, pre-cious name of Je-sus.
won-drous, glo-rious name of Je-sus. Je-sus is the sweet-est name I
bless-ed Son of God called Je-sus.

know, And He's just the same as His love-ly name, And that's the rea-son

why I love Him so; Oh, Je-sus is the sweet-est name I know.

297 Heaven Came Down and Glory Filled My Soul

If any man be in Christ, he is a new creature. II Cor. 5:17

JOHN W. PETERSON

JOHN W. PETERSON

1. O what a won-der-ful, won-der-ful day— Day I will
2. Born of the Spir-it with life from a-bove In-to God's
3. Now I've a hope that will sure-ly en-dure Aft-er the

nev-er for-get; Aft-er I'd wan-dered in dark-ness a-way,
fam-i-ly di-vine, Jus-ti-fied ful-ly thro' Cal-va-ry's love,
pass-ing of time; I have a fu-ture in heav-en for sure,

Je-sus my Sav-ior I met. O what a ten-der, com-pas-sion-ate friend—
O what a stand-ing is mine! And the trans-ac-tion so quick-ly was made
There in those man-sions sub-lime. And it's be-cause of that won-der-ful day

He met the need of my heart; Shad-ows dis-pel-ling, With
When as a sin-ner I came, Took of the of-fer Of
When at the cross I be-lieved; Rich-es e-ter-nal And

joy I am tell - ing, He made all the dark - ness de - part!
grace He did prof - fer— He saved me, O praise His dear name!
bless - ings su - per - nal From His pre - cious hand I re - ceived.

Refrain

Heav - en came down and glo - ry filled my soul, (filled my soul,)

When at the cross the Sav - ior made me whole; (made me whole;) My

sins were washed a - way And my night was turned to day—

Heav - en came down and glo - ry filled my soul! (filled my soul!)

298 The Blood Will Never Lose Its Power

Thou...has redeemed us to God by Thy blood...Rev. 5:9

ANDRAÉ CROUCH

ANDRAÉ CROUCH

1. The blood that Je - sus shed for me, 'Way back on
2. It soothes my doubts and calms my fears, And it dries

Cal - va - ry; The blood that gives me strength from day to
all my tears; The blood that gives me strength from day to

day, It will nev - er lose its power.
day, It will nev - er lose its power.

Refrain

It reach - es to the high - est moun - tain. It flows to the

low - est val - ley. The blood that gives me strength from

day to day, It will nev - er lose its power.

Amazing Grace! 299

*God is able to make all grace abound toward you...*II Cor. 9:8

TRADITIONAL AMERICAN MELODY

JOHN NEWTON

ARR. EDWIN O. EXCELL

1. A - maz - ing grace! how sweet · the sound That saved a wretch like me!
2. 'Twas grace that taught my heart to fear, And grace my fears re - lieved;
3. Through man - y dan - gers, toils and snares, I have al - read - y come;
4. When we've been there ten thou-sand years, Bright shin - ing as the sun,

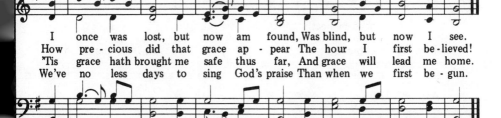

I once was lost, but now am found, Was blind, but now I see.
How pre - cious did that grace ap - pear The hour I first be - lieved!
'Tis grace hath brought me safe thus far, And grace will lead me home.
We've no less days to sing God's praise Than when we first be - gun.

300 There Is a Fountain Filled with Blood

In that day there shall be a fountain opened...for sin and for uncleanness. Zech. 13:1

WILLIAM COWPER

TRADITIONAL AMERICAN MELODY
ARR. LOWELL MASON

1. There is a foun-tain filled with blood Drawn from Im - man-uel's veins;
2. The dy - ing thief re-joiced to see That foun-tain in his day;
3. Dear dy - ing Lamb, Thy pre-cious blood Shall nev - er lose its pow'r,
4. E'er since by faith I saw the stream Thy flow-ing wounds sup - ply,
5. When this poor lisp - ing, stamm'ring tongue Lies si - lent in the grave,

And sin - ners, plunged be-neath that flood, Lose all their guilt - y stains:
And there may I, though vile as he, Wash all my sins a - way:
Till all the ran-somed Church of God Be saved, to sin no more:
Re - deem - ing love has been my theme, And shall be till I die:
Then in a no - bler, sweet - er song, I'll sing Thy pow'r to save:

Lose all their guilt - y stains, Lose all their guilt - y stains; And
Wash all my sins a - way, Wash all my sins a - way; And
Be saved, to sin no more, Be saved, to sin no more; Till
And shall be till I die, And shall be till I die; Re -
I'll sing Thy pow'r to save, I'll sing Thy pow'r to save; Then

sin - ners, plunged be-neath that flood, Lose all their guilt - y stains.
there may I, though vile as he, Wash all my sins a - way.
all the ran-somed Church of God Be saved, to sin no more.
deem - ing love has been my theme, And shall be till I die.
in a no - bler, sweet-er song I'll sing Thy pow'r to save. A-men.

At the Cross 301

Surely He hath borne our griefs, and carried our sorrows. Isa. 53:4

ISAAC WATTS

RALPH E. HUDSON

1. A - las! and did my Sav - ior bleed? And did my Sov -'reign die?
2. Was it for crimes that I have done He groaned up - on the tree?
3. Well might the sun in dark - ness hide, And shut his glo - ries in,
4. But drops of grief can ne'er re - pay The debt of love I owe:

Would He de - vote that sa - cred head For sin - ners such as I?
A - maz - ing pit - y! grace un - known! And love be - yond de - gree!
When Christ, the might - y Mak - er, died For man the crea - ture's sin.
Here, Lord, I give my - self a - way, 'Tis all that I can do!

Refrain

At the cross, at the cross where I first saw the light, And the

bur - den of my heart rolled a - way, (rolled a - way,) It was there by faith

I re - ceived my sight, And now I am hap - py all the day!

302 Calvary Covers It All

Blessed is he whose...sin is covered. Psa. 32:1

MRS. WALTER G. TAYLOR

MRS. WALTER G. TAYLOR

1. Far dear - er than all that the world can im - part Was the mes - sage that
2. The stripes that He bore and the thorns that He wore Told His mer - cy and
3. How match-less the grace, when I looked on the face Of this Je - sus, my
4. How bless - ed the thought, that my soul by Him bought, Shall be His in the

came to my heart; How that Je - sus a - lone for my sin did a - tone,
love ev - er - more; And my heart bowed in shame as I called on His name,
cru - ci - fied Lord; My re - demp-tion com-plete I then found at His feet,
glo - ry on high; Where with glad-ness and song I'll be one of the throng,

Chorus

And Cal - va - ry cov - ers it all. Cal - va - ry cov - ers it

all, My past with its sin and stain; My guilt and de - spair Je - sus

took on Him there, And Cal - va - ry cov - ers it all.

It Took a Miracle 303

Greater love hath no man than this...John 15:13

JOHN W. PETERSON

JOHN W. PETERSON

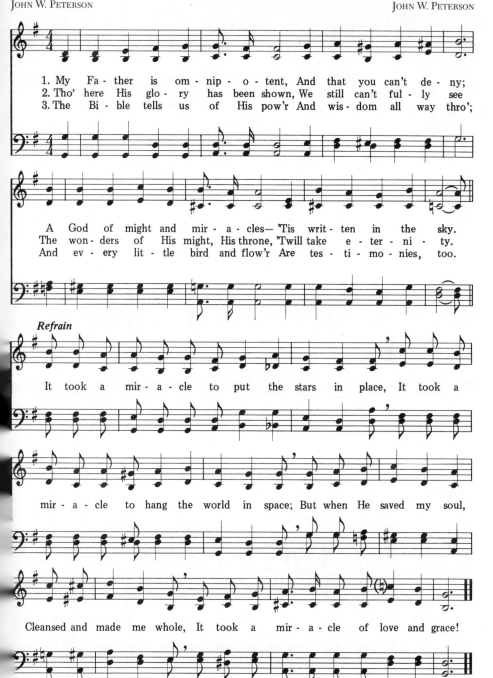

1. My Father is om-nip-o-tent, And that you can't de-ny;
2. Tho' here His glo-ry has been shown, We still can't ful-ly see
3. The Bi-ble tells us of His pow'r And wis-dom all way thro';

A God of might and mir-a-cles— 'Tis writ-ten in the sky.
The won-ders of His might, His throne, 'Twill take e-ter-ni-ty.
And ev-ery lit-tle bird and flow'r Are tes-ti-mo-nies, too.

Refrain

It took a mir-a-cle to put the stars in place, It took a

mir-a-cle to hang the world in space; But when He saved my soul,

Cleansed and made me whole, It took a mir-a-cle of love and grace!

304 Through It All

All things work together for good to them that love God...Rom 8:28

ANDRAÉ CROUCH   ANDRAÉ CROUCH

1. I've had man - y tears and sor - rows, I've had ques - tions
2. I've been to lots of plac - es, And I've seen a
3. I thank God for the moun - tains, And I thank Him

for to - mor - row, There've been times I did - n't know right from
lot of fac - es, There've been times I felt so all a -
for the val - leys, I thank Him for the storms He brought me

wrong; But in ev - ery sit - u - a - tion God gave
lone; But in my lone - ly hours, Yes, those
through; For if I'd nev - er had a prob - lem, I

bless - ed con - so - la - tion That my tri - als come to
pre - cious lone - ly hours, Je - sus let me know that
would - n't know that He could solve them, I'd nev - er know what

Refrain

on - ly make me strong.
I was His own.
faith in God could do.

Through it all,

Through it all, I've learned to trust in Je - sus, I've

learned to trust in God; Through it all, Through it all,

I've learned to de - pend up - on His Word.

305 The Love of God

Behold, what manner of love the Father hath bestowed upon us...I John 3:1

FREDERICK M. LEHMAN

ARR. CLAUDIA LEHMAN MAYS

FREDERICK M. LEHMAN

1. The love of God is great-er far Than tongue or pen can
2. When hoar-y time shall pass a-way, And earth-ly thrones and
3. Could we with ink the o-cean fill, And were the skies of

ev-er tell, It goes be-yond the high-est star, And reach-es
king-doms fall; When men who here re-fuse to pray, On rocks and
parch-ment made, Were ev-ery stalk on earth a quill And ev-ery

to the low-est hell; The guilt-y pair, bowed down with care,
hills and moun-tains call; God's love, so sure, shall still en-dure,
man a scribe by trade; To write the love of God a-bove

God gave His Son to win; His err-ing child He rec-on-ciled,
All meas-ure-less and strong; Re-deem-ing grace to Ad-am's race—
Would drain the o-cean dry; Nor could the scroll con-tain the whole,

Chorus

And par-doned from his sin.
The saints' and an-gels' song. Oh love of God, how rich and
Tho' stretched from sky to sky.

pure! How meas-ure-less and strong! It shall for-ev-er-more en-dure, The saints' and an-gels' song.

Psalm 136

306

Leader: Let us with a gladsome mind
Praise the Lord for He is kind:
People: **For His mercies aye endure, ever faithful, ever sure.**
Leader: Let us blaze His Name abroad,
For of gods He is the God:
People: **For His mercies aye endure, ever faithful, ever sure.**
Leader: He, with all-commanding might,
Filled the new-made world with light:
People: **For his mercies aye endure, ever faithful, ever sure.**
Leader: He the golden-tressed sun
Caused all day his course to run;
People: **For His mercies aye endure, ever faithful, ever sure.**
Leader: And the moon to shine by night,
'Mid her spangled sisters bright:
People: **For His mercies aye endure, ever faithful, ever sure.**
Leader: All things living He doth feed;
His full hand supplies their need:
People: **For His mercies aye endure, ever faithful, ever sure.**
Leader: Let us therefore warble forth
His high majesty and worth:
People: **For His mercies aye endure, ever faithful, ever sure.**

Adapted from John Milton

307 And Can It Be That I Should Gain?

While we were yet sinners, Christ died for us. Rom. 5:8

CHARLES WESLEY   THOMAS CAMPBELL

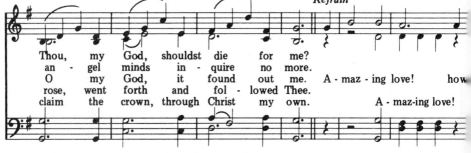

1. And can it be that I should gain An in-t'rest in the
2. 'Tis mys-tery all! Th'Im-mor-tal dies! Who can ex-plore His
3. He left His Fa-ther's throne a-bove, So free, so in-fi-
4. Long my im-pris-oned spir-it lay Fast bound in sin and
5. No con-dem-na-tion now I dread; Je-sus, and all in

Sav-ior's blood? Died He for me, who caused His pain? For me, who
strange de-sign? In vain the first-born ser-aph tries To sound the
nite His grace; Emp-tied Him-self of all but love, And bled for
na-ture's night; Thine eye dif-fused a quick-'ning ray, I woke, the
Him, is mine! A-live in Him, my liv-ing Head, And clothed in

Him to death pur-sued? A-maz-ing love! how can it be That
depths of love di-vine! 'Tis mer-cy all! let earth a-dore, Let
Ad-am's help-less race; 'Tis mer-cy all, im-mense and free; For,
dun-geon flamed with light; My chains fell off, my heart was free; I
right-eous-ness di-vine, Bold I ap-proach th'e-ter-nal throne, And

Refrain

Thou, my God, shouldst die for me?
an-gel minds in-quire no more.
O my God, it found out me. A-maz-ing love! how
rose, went forth and fol-lowed Thee.
claim the crown, through Christ my own. A-maz-ing love!

can it be   That Thou,   my   God, shouldst die for me. A - men.
How can it be   That Thou, my God,

No Other Plea 308

While we were yet sinners, Christ died for us. Rom 5:8

André Grétry
Arr. William J. Kirkpatrick

Lidie H. Edmunds

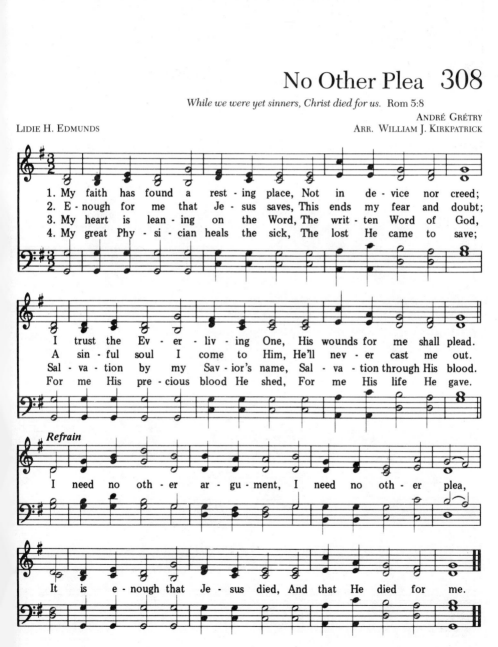

1. My faith has found a rest - ing place, Not in de - vice nor creed;
2. E - nough for me that Je - sus saves, This ends my fear and doubt;
3. My heart is lean - ing on the Word, The writ - ten Word of God,
4. My great Phy - si - cian heals the sick, The lost He came to save;

I trust the Ev - er - liv - ing One, His wounds for me shall plead.
A sin - ful soul I come to Him, He'll nev - er cast me out.
Sal - va - tion by my Sav - ior's name, Sal - va - tion through His blood.
For me His pre - cious blood He shed, For me His life He gave.

Refrain

I need no oth - er ar - gu - ment, I need no oth - er plea,

It is e - nough that Je - sus died, And that He died for me.

309 Redeemed

In whom we have redemption through His blood...Eph. 1:7

FANNY J. CROSBY

WILLIAM J. KIRKPATRICK

1. Redeemed, how I love to pro-claim it! Redeemed by the blood of the Lamb;
2. Redeemed and so hap-py in Je-sus, No lan-guage my rap-ture can tell;
3. I think of my bless-ed Re-deem-er, I think of Him all the day long;
4. I know I shall see in His beau-ty The King in whose law I de-light;

Redeemed thro' His in-fi-nite mer-cy, His child, and for-ev-er, I am.
I know that the light of His pres-ence With me doth con-tin-ual-ly dwell.
I sing, for I can-not be si-lent; His love is the theme of my song.
Who lov-ing-ly guardeth my foot-steps, And giv-eth me songs in the night.

Chorus

Re-deemed, re-deemed, Redeemed by the blood of the Lamb;
re-deemed, re-deemed,

Re-deemed, re-deemed, His child, and for-ev-er, I am.
re-deemed, re-deemed,

I Know Whom I Have Believed 310

*For I know whom I have believed...*II Tim. 1:12

DANIEL W. WHITTLE

JAMES McGRANAHAN

1. I know not why God's won-drous grace To me He hath made known,
2. I know not how this sav - ing faith To me He did im - part,
3. I know not how the Spir - it moves, Con-vinc - ing men of sin,
4. I know not when my Lord may come, At night or noon-day fair,

Nor why, un - wor - thy, Christ in love Re-deemed me for His own.
Nor how be - liev - ing in His Word Wrought peace with-in my heart.
Re - veal - ing Je - sus through the Word, Cre - at - ing faith in Him.
Nor if I'll walk the vale with Him, Or "meet Him in the air."

Refrain

But "I know whom I have be - liev - ed, And am per - suad - ed that He is

a - ble To keep that which I've com-mit - ted Un-to Him a-gainst that day."

311 He Giveth More Grace

God is able to make all grace abound toward you... II Cor. 9:8

ANNIE JOHNSON FLINT   HUBERT MITCHELL

1. He giv-eth more grace when the bur-dens grow great-er; He send-eth more
2. When we have ex-haust-ed our store of en-dur-ance, When our strength has

strength when the la-bors in-crease. To add-ed af-flic-tion He
failed ere the day is half done, When we reach the end of our

add-eth His mer-cy; To mul-ti-plied tri-als, His mul-ti-plied peace.
hoard-ed re-sourc-es, Our Fa-ther's full giv-ing is on-ly be-gun.

Refrain

His love has no lim-it; His grace has no meas-ure; His pow'r has no

bound-a-ry known un-to men. For out of His in-fi-nite

rich-es in Je-sus, He giv-eth, and giv-eth, and giv-eth a-gain!

Something Beautiful 312

If any man be in Christ, he is a new creature. II Cor. 5:17

GLORIA GAITHER

WILLIAM J. GAITHER

Some-thing beau-ti-ful, some-thing good; All my con-fu-sion

He un-der-stood; All I had to of-fer Him was bro-ken-ness and

strife, But He made some-thing beau-ti-ful of my life.

313 At Calvary

And when they were come to...Calvary, there they crucified Him. Luke 23:33

WILLIAM R. NEWELL

DANIEL B. TOWNER

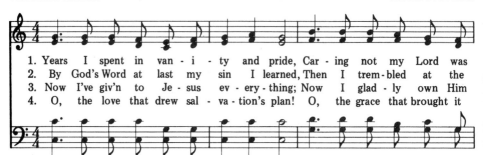

1. Years I spent in van - i - ty and pride, Car - ing not my Lord was
2. By God's Word at last my sin I learned, Then I trem - bled at the
3. Now I've giv'n to Je - sus ev - ery - thing; Now I glad - ly own Him
4. O, the love that drew sal - va - tion's plan! O, the grace that brought it

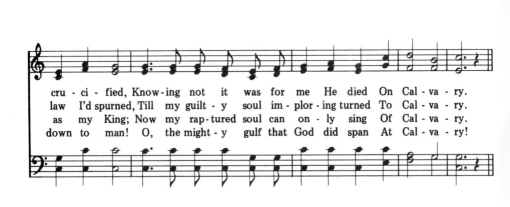

cru - ci - fied, Know-ing not it was for me He died On Cal - va - ry.
law I'd spurned, Till my guilt - y soul im - plor - ing turned To Cal - va - ry.
as my King; Now my rap - tured soul can on - ly sing Of Cal - va - ry.
down to man! O, the might - y gulf that God did span At Cal - va - ry!

Refrain

Mer - cy there was great, and grace was free; Par - don there was mul - ti -

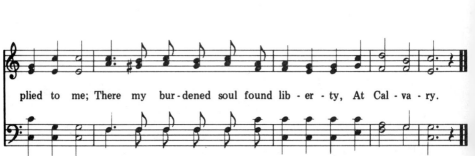

plied to me; There my bur - dened soul found lib - er - ty, At Cal - va - ry.

He Touched Me 314

Jesus put forth His hand and touched him, saying, I will; be thou clean. Matt 8:3

WILLIAM J. GAITHER

WILLIAM J. GAITHER

1. Shack - led by a heav - y bur - den, 'Neath a load of
2. Since I met this bless - ed Sav - ior, Since He cleansed and

guilt and shame; Then the hand of Je - sus touched me,
made me whole; I will nev - er cease to praise Him,

Refrain

And now I am no long - er the same. He touched me, O, He
I'll shout it while e - ter - ni - ty rolls.

touched me, And O, the joy that floods my soul; Some-thing

hap - pened, and now I know, He touched me and made me whole.

315 The Solid Rock

Other foundation can no man lay than that is laid, which is Jesus Christ. I Cor. 3:11

EDWARD MOTE

WILLIAM B. BRADBURY

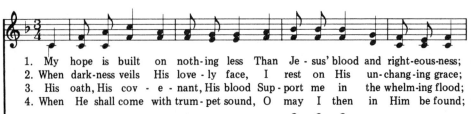

1. My hope is built on noth-ing less Than Je-sus' blood and right-eous-ness;
2. When dark-ness veils His love-ly face, I rest on His un-chang-ing grace;
3. His oath, His cov-e-nant, His blood Sup-port me in the whelm-ing flood;
4. When He shall come with trum-pet sound, O may I then in Him be found;

I dare not trust the sweet-est frame, But whol-ly lean on Je-sus' name.
In ev-ery high and storm-y gale, My an-chor holds with-in the veil.
When all a-round my soul gives way He then is all my hope and stay.
Dressed in His right-eous-ness a-lone, Fault-less to stand be-fore the throne.

Refrain

On Christ the sol-id Rock I stand; All oth-er ground

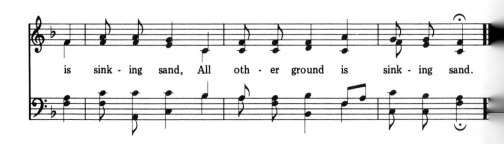

is sink-ing sand, All oth-er ground is sink-ing sand.

A Shelter in the Time of Storm 316

A man shall be...like the shadow of a great rock in a weary land. Isa. 32:2

ADAPTED BY IRA D. SANKEY

IRA D. SANKEY

1. The Lord's our rock, in Him we hide, A shel-ter in the time of storm;
2. A shade by day, de-fense by night, A shel-ter in the time of storm;
3. The rag-ing storms may round us beat, A shel-ter in the time of storm;
4. O Rock di-vine, O Ref-uge dear, A shel-ter in the time of storm;

Se-cure what-ev-er ill be-tide, A shel-ter in the time of storm.
No fears a-larm, no foes af-fright, A shel-ter in the time of storm.
We'll nev-er leave our safe re-treat, A shel-ter in the time of storm.
Be Thou our help-er ev-er near, A shel-ter in the time of storm.

Refrain

O, Je-sus is a rock in a wea-ry land, A wea-ry land, a wea-ry land;

O, Je-sus is a rock in a wea-ry land, A shel-ter in the time of storm.

317 Love Lifted Me

And Jesus took him by the hand, and lifted him up. Mark 9:27

JAMES ROWE

HOWARD E. SMITH

1. I was sink-ing deep in sin, Far from the peace-ful shore, Ver-y deep-ly
2. All my heart to Him I give, Ev-er to Him I'll cling, In His bless-ed
3. Souls in dan-ger, look a-bove, Je-sus com-plete-ly saves; He will lift you

stained with-in, Sink-ing to rise no more; But the Mas-ter of the sea
pres-ence live, Ev-er His prais-es sing. Love so might-y and so true
by His love Out of the an-gry waves. He's the Mas-ter of the sea,

Heard my des-pair-ing cry, From the wa-ters lift-ed me, Now safe am I.
Mer-its my soul's best songs; Faith-ful, lov-ing serv-ice too To Him be-longs.
Bil-lows His will o-bey; He your Sav-ior wants to be— Be saved to-day.

Chorus

Love lift-ed me! Love lift-ed me! When noth-ing
e-ven me! e-ven me!

else could help, Love lift-ed me. Love lift-ed me!
e-ven me!

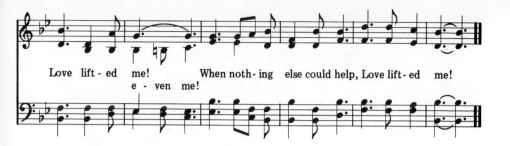

Love lift - ed me! When noth - ing else could help, Love lift - ed me!
e - ven me!

He Lifted Me 318

He brought me up also out of an horrible pit...Psa. 40:2

CHARLES H. GABRIEL

CHARLES H. GABRIEL

1. In lov - ing kind - ness Je - sus came My soul in mer - cy to re - claim,
2. He called me long be - fore I heard, Be - fore my sin - ful heart was stirred,
3. His brow was pierced with man - y a thorn, His hands by cru - el nails were torn,
4. Now on a high - er plane I dwell, And with my soul I know 'tis well;

And from the depths of sin and shame Thro' grace He lift - ed me.
But when I took Him at His word, For - giv'n He lift - ed me.
When from my guilt and grief, for - lorn, In love He lift - ed me.
Yet how or why, I can - not tell, He should have lift - ed me.

(He lift-ed me.)

Refrain

From sink - ing sand He lift - ed me, With ten - der hand He lift - ed me,

From shades of night to plains of light, O praise His name, He lift - ed me!

319 Wonderful Grace of Jesus

For ye know the grace of our Lord Jesus Christ...II Cor. 8:9

HALDOR LILLENAS   HALDOR LILLENAS

1. Won - der - ful grace of Je - sus, Great - er than all my sin;
2. Won - der - ful grace of Je - sus, Reach - ing to all the lost,
3. Won - der - ful grace of Je - sus, Reach - ing the most de - filed,

How shall my tongue de - scribe it, Where shall its praise be - gin?
By it I have been par - doned, Saved to the ut - ter - most;
By its trans - form - ing pow - er Mak - ing him God's dear child,

Tak - ing a - way my bur - den, Set - ting my spir - it free,
Chains have been torn a - sun - der, Giv - ing me lib - er - ty,
Pur - chas - ing peace and heav - en For all e - ter - ni - ty—

For the won - der - ful grace of Je - sus reach - es me.
For the won - der - ful grace of Je - sus reach - es me.
And the won - der - ful grace of Je - sus reach - es me.

Refrain

Won - der - ful the match-less grace of Je - sus, the match-less grace of Je - sus, Deep - er than the

320 The Wonder of It All

What is man that Thou art mindful of him? Psa. 8:4

GEORGE BEVERLY SHEA

GEORGE BEVERLY SHEA

1. There's the won-der of sun-set at eve-ning, The won-der as
2. There's the won-der of spring-time and har-vest, The sky, the

sun-rise I see; But the won-der of won-ders that thrills my soul
stars, the sun; But the won-der of won-ders that thrills my soul

Is the won-der that God loves me. O, the won-der of it all! The

won-der of it all! Just to think that God loves me. O, the won-der of it

all! The won-der of it all! Just to think that God loves me.

Why Do I Sing About Jesus? 321

Therefore, my heart greatly rejoiceth; and with my song will I praise Him. Psa. 28:7

ALBERT A. KETCHUM

ALBERT A. KETCHUM

1. Deep in my heart there's a glad - ness, Je - sus has saved me from
2. On - ly a glimpse of His good - ness, That was suf - fi - cient for
3. He is the fair - est of fair ones, He is the Lil - y, the

sin! Praise to His name—what a Sav - ior! Cleans - ing with-
me; On - ly one look at the Sav - ior, Then was my
Rose; Riv - ers of mer - cy sur - round Him, Grace, love and

Refrain — Unison or Two Parts

out and with - in. Why do I sing a - bout Je - sus?
spir - it set free. Why do I sing a - bout Je - sus?
pit - y He shows.

Why is He pre - cious to me? He is my Lord and my

Sav - ior, Dy - ing! He set me free!
(set me free!)

322 I Love to Tell the Story

And they sang a new song saying, Thou art worthy...Rev. 5:9

A.CATHERINE HANKEY

WILLIAM G FISCHER

1. I love to tell the story Of un-seen things a-bove, Of Je-sus and His glo-ry, Of Je-sus and His love. I love to tell the sto-ry Be-cause I know 'tis true; It sat-is-fies my long-ings As noth-ing else can do.

2. I love to tell the story, More won-der-ful it seems Than all the gold-en fan-cies Of all our gold-en dreams. I love to tell the sto-ry, It did so much for me; And that is just the rea-son I tell it now to thee.

3. I love to tell the story, 'Tis pleas-ant to re-peat What seems, each time I tell it, More won-der-ful-ly sweet. I love to tell the sto-ry, For some have nev-er heard The mes-sage of sal-va-tion From God's own Ho-ly Word.

4. I love to tell the story, For those who know it best Seem hun-ger-ing and thirst-ing To hear it like the rest. And when, in scenes of glo-ry, I sing the new, new song, 'Twill be the old, old sto-ry That I have loved so long.

Refrain

I love to tell the sto-ry, 'Twill be my theme in glo-ry,

To tell the old, old sto-ry Of Je-sus and His love.

Satisfied 323

He satisfieth the longing soul, and filleth the hungry soul with goodness, Psa. 107:9

CLARA T. WILLIAMS   RALPH E. HUDSON

1. All my life long I had pant-ed For a drink from some cool spring
2. Feed-ing on the husks a-round me Till my strength was al-most gone,
3. Poor I was, and sought for rich-es, Some-thing that would sat-is-fy;
4. Well of wa-ter, ev-er spring-ing, Bread of life, so rich and free,

That I hoped would quench the burn-ing Of the thirst I felt with-in.
Longed my soul for some-thing bet-ter, On-ly still to hun-ger on.
But the dust I gath-ered round me On-ly mocked my soul's sad cry.
Un-told wealth that nev-er fail-eth, My Re-deem-er is to me.

Refrain

Hal - le - lu - jah! I have found Him—Whom my soul so long has craved!

Je - sus sat - is - fies my long - ings; Thro' His blood I now am saved.

324 My Redeemer

Jesus Christ, who gave Himself for us, that He might redeem us. Titus 2:13,14

PHILIP P. BLISS

JAMES McGRANAHAN

1. I will sing of my Re-deem - er, And His won - drous love to me;
2. I will tell the won-drous sto - ry, How my lost es - tate to save,
3. I will praise my dear Re-deem - er, His tri - um - phant pow'r I'll tell,
4. I will sing of my Re-deem - er, And His heav'n - ly love to me;

On the cru - el cross He suf - fered, From the curse to set me free.
In His bound-less love and mer - cy, He the ran - som free - ly gave.
How the vic - to - ry He giv - eth O - ver sin, and death, and hell.
He from death to life hath bro't me, Son of God with Him to be.

Chorus

Sing, oh, sing of my Re-deem - er,
of my Re-deem - er, Sing, oh, sing of my Re-deem - er,

With His blood He pur-chased me,
He pur-chased me, With His blood He pur-chased me,

On the cross He sealed my par - don,
He sealed my par - don, On the cross He sealed my par - don,

Paid the debt, and made me free.
and made me free, and made me free.

Jesus, Thy Blood and Righteousness 325

He hath clothed me with the garments of salvation...Isa. 61:10

NIKOLAUS VON ZINZENDORF
TR. JOHN WESLEY

WILLIAM GARDINER'S
SACRED MELODIES

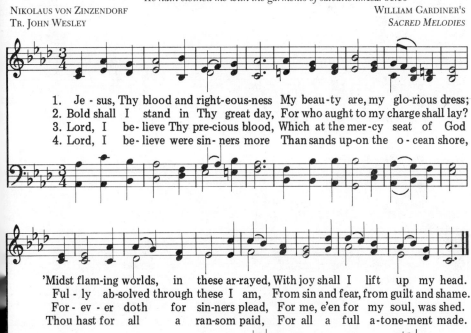

1. Je - sus, Thy blood and right-eous-ness My beau-ty are, my glo-rious dress;
2. Bold shall I stand in Thy great day, For who aught to my charge shall lay?
3. Lord, I be-lieve Thy pre-cious blood, Which at the mer-cy seat of God
4. Lord, I be-lieve were sin-ners more Than sands up-on the o - cean shore,

'Midst flam-ing worlds, in these ar-rayed, With joy shall I lift up my head.
Ful - ly ab-solved through these I am, From sin and fear, from guilt and shame.
For - ev - er doth for sin-ners plead, For me, e'en for my soul, was shed.
Thou hast for all a ran-som paid, For all a full a-tone-ment made.

326 I'll Tell the World That I'm a Christian

Tell them how great things the Lord hath done for thee. Mark 5:19

BAYNARD L. FOX

BAYNARD L. FOX

1. I'll tell the world that I'm a Christ-ian— I'm not a-shamed
2. I'll tell the world that He is com-ing— It may be near

His name to bear; I'll tell the world that I'm a Christ-ian—
or far a - way; But we must live as if His com-ing

I'll take Him with me an - y - where. I'll tell the world
Would be to - mor - row or to - day. For when He comes

how Je - sus saved me, And how He gave me a life brand-new;
and life is o - ver, For those who love Him, there's more to be;

And I know that if you trust Him That all He gave me
Eyes have nev - er seen the won - ders That He's pre -par - ing

He'll give to you. I'll tell the world that He's my Sav - ior,
for you and me. O tell the world that you're a Christ - ian,

No oth - er one could love me so; My life, my all
Be not a - shamed His name to bear; O tell the world

is His for - ev - er, And where He leads me I will go.
that you're a Christ - ian, And take Him with you ev - ery -where.

327 Jesus Has Lifted Me

I will extol Thee, O Lord; for Thou hast lifted me up. Psa. 30:1

AVIS B. CHRISTIANSEN

HALDOR LILLENAS

1. Out of the depths to the glo - ry a - bove, I have been
2. Out of the world in - to heav - en - ly rest, In - to the
3. Out of my - self in - to Him I a - dore, There to a -

lift - ed in won - der - ful love; From ev - ery fet - ter my
land of the ran - somed and blest; There in the glo - ry with
bide in His love ev - er - more; Thro' end - less a - ges His

spir - it is free— For Je - sus has lift - ed me!
Him I shall be— For Je - sus has lift - ed me!
glo - ry to see— My Je - sus has lift - ed me!

Refrain

Je - sus has lift - ed me! Je - sus has lift - ed me!
lift - ed me! lift - ed me!

Out of the night in - to glo - ri - ous light, Yes, Je - sus has lift - ed me!
lift - ed me!

I Will Sing the Wondrous Story   328

And they sing the song...of the Lamb, saying, great and marvelous are Thy works. Rev. 15:3

FRANCIS H. ROWLEY   PETER P. BILHORN

1. I will sing the won-drous sto - ry Of the Christ who died for me,
2. I was lost but Je - sus found me, Found the sheep that went a - stray,
3. I was bruised but Je - sus healed me; Faint was I from man - y a fall;
4. Days of dark - ness still come o'er me, Sor-row's paths I oft - en tread,

How He left His home in glo - ry For the cross of Cal - va - ry.
Threw His lov - ing arms a - round me, Drew me back in - to His way.
Sight was gone, and fears pos-sessed me, But He freed me from them all.
But the Sav - ior still is with me; By His hand I'm safe - ly led.

Refrain

Yes, I'll sing the won-drous sto - ry Of the
Yes, I'll sing the won-drous sto - ry

Christ who died for me, Sing it with the saints in
Of the Christ who died for me, Sing it with

glo - ry Gath-ered by the crys-tal sea.
the saints in glo - ry, Gath-ered by the crys-tal sea.

329 I Will Sing the Wondrous Story

I will sing of the mercies of the Lord forever. Psa. 89:1

Francis H. Rowley

Folk Song
Arr. Jack Schrader

1. I will sing the won-drous sto-ry of the Christ who died for me,
2. I was lost but Je-sus found me, found the sheep that went a-stray;
3. Days of dark-ness still come o'er me, sor-row's paths I oft-en tread,

How he left his home in glo-ry for the cross of Cal-va-ry.
Threw his lov-ing arms a-round me, drew me back in-to his way.
But the Sav-ior still is with me; by his hand I'm safe-ly led.

Refrain

Yes, I'll sing, I'll sing the won-drous sto-ry Of the Christ who

died for me; Yes, I'll sing it with the saints in

glo - ry Gath-ered by the crys - tal sea.

Jesus, Lord to Me 330

Jesus Christ is Lord. Phil. 2:11

GARY MCSPADDEN AND
GREG NELSON

GARY MCSPADDEN AND
GREG NELSON

Je - sus, Je - sus, Lord to me; Mas - ter,

Sav - ior, Prince of Peace; Rul - er of my

heart to - day; Je - sus, Lord to me.

331 In Tenderness He Sought Me

Rejoice with me; for I have found my sheep which was lost. Luke 15:6

W. SPENCER WALTON

ADONIRAM J. GORDON

1. In ten-der-ness He sought me, Wea-ry and sick with sin,
2. He washed the bleed-ing sin-wounds And poured in oil and wine;
3. He point-ed to the nail-prints, For me His blood was shed,
4. I'm sit-ting in His pres-ence, The sun-shine of His face,
5. So while the hours are pass-ing All now is per-fect rest;

And on His shoul-ders brought me Back to His fold a-gain. While
He whis-pered to as-sure me, "I've found thee, thou art Mine;" I
A mock-ing crown so thorn-y Was placed up-on His head: I
While with a-dor-ing won-der His bless-ings I re-trace: It
I'm wait-ing for the morn-ing, The bright-est and the best, When

an-gels in His pres-ence sang Un-til the courts of heav-en rang.
nev-er heard a sweet-er voice; It made my ach-ing heart re-joice!
won-dered what He saw in me To suf-fer such deep ag-o-ny.
seems as if e-ter-nal days Are far too short to sound His praise.
He will call us to His side, To be with Him, His spot-less bride.

Refrain

O the love that sought me! O the blood that bought me! O the grace that

brought me to the fold, Won-drous grace that brought me to the fold!

I Heard the Voice of Jesus Say 332

Come unto Me, all ye that labor...and I will give you rest. Matt. 11:28

HORATIUS BONAR

JOHN B. DYKES

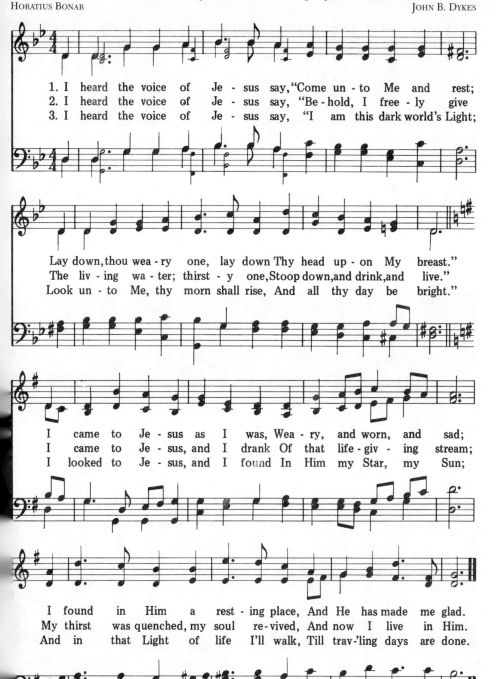

1. I heard the voice of Je - sus say, "Come un - to Me and rest;
2. I heard the voice of Je - sus say, "Be - hold, I free - ly give
3. I heard the voice of Je - sus say, "I am this dark world's Light;

Lay down, thou wea - ry one, lay down Thy head up - on My breast."
The liv - ing wa - ter; thirst - y one, Stoop down, and drink, and live."
Look un - to Me, thy morn shall rise, And all thy day be bright."

I came to Je - sus as I was, Wea - ry, and worn, and sad;
I came to Je - sus, and I drank Of that life - giv - ing stream;
I looked to Je - sus, and I found In Him my Star, my Sun;

I found in Him a rest - ing place, And He has made me glad.
My thirst was quenched, my soul re - vived, And now I live in Him.
And in that Light of life I'll walk, Till trav - 'ling days are done.

333 Only a Sinner

For by grace are ye saved through faith...Eph. 2:8

JAMES M. GRAY

DANIEL B. TOWNER

1. Naught have I got-ten but what I re-ceived; Grace hath be-stowed it since
2. Once I was fool-ish, and sin ruled my heart, Caus-ing my foot-steps from
3. Tears un - a - vail - ing, no mer - it had I; Mer - cy had saved me, or
4. Suf - fer a sin - ner whose heart o - ver-flows, Lov - ing his Sav - ior to

I have be - lieved; Boast - ing ex - clud - ed, pride I a - base; I'm
God to de - part; Je - sus hath found me, hap - py my case; I
else I must die; Sin had a - larmed me, fear - ing God's face; But
tell what he knows; Once more to tell it would I em - brace — I'm

Refrain

on - ly a sin - ner saved by grace!
now am a sin - ner saved by grace!
now I'm a sin - ner saved by grace! On - ly a sin - ner saved by grace!
on - ly a sin - ner saved by grace!

On - ly a sin - ner saved by grace! This is my sto - ry, to

God be the glo - ry— I'm on - ly a sin - ner saved by grace!

There Is Power in the Blood 334

In whom we have redemption through His blood...Col. 1:14

Lewis E. Jones

Lewis E. Jones

1. Would you be free from the bur-den of sin? There's pow'r in the blood,
2. Would you be free from your pas-sion and pride? There's pow'r in the blood,
3. Would you be whit-er, much whit-er than snow? There's pow'r in the blood,
4. Would you do serv-ice for Je-sus your King? There's pow'r in the blood,

pow'r in the blood; Would you o'er e-vil a vic-to-ry win? There's
pow'r in the blood; Come for a cleans-ing to Cal-va-ry's tide? There's
pow'r in the blood; Sin-stains are lost in its life-giv-ing flow; There's
pow'r in the blood; Would you live dai-ly His prais-es to sing? There's

Chorus

won-der-ful pow'r in the blood. There is pow'r, pow'r, won-der-work-ing pow'r
there is

In the blood of the Lamb; There is pow'r, pow'r,
In the blood of the Lamb; there is

won-der-work-ing pow'r In the pre-cious blood of the Lamb.

335 Since I Have Been Redeemed

Let the redeemed of the Lord say so...Psa. 107:2

EDWIN O. EXCELL   EDWIN O. EXCELL

1. I have a song I love to sing, Since I have been re-deemed,
2. I have a Christ who sat-is-fies, Since I have been re-deemed;
3. I have a wit-ness bright and clear, Since I have been re-deemed,
4. I have a home pre-pared for me, Since I have been re-deemed,

Of my Re-deem-er, Sav-ior, King, Since I have been re-deemed.
To do His will my high-est prize, Since I have been re-deemed.
Dis-pel-ling ev-ery doubt and fear, Since I have been re-deemed.
Where I shall dwell e-ter-nal-ly, Since I have been re-deemed.

Refrain

Since I have been re-deemed, Since I have been re-
Since I have been re-deemed, Since I have been re-deemed,

deemed, I will glo-ry in His name; Since I have been re-
Since I have been re-deemed, Since

deemed, I will glo-ry in my Sav-ior's name.
I have been re-deemed,

Jesus Loves Even Me 336

I will love him, and will manifest myself to him. John 14:21

PHILIP P. BLISS

PHILIP P. BLISS

1. I am so glad that our Fa - ther in heav'n Tells of His
2. Though I for - get Him and wan - der a - way, Still He doth
3. Oh, if there's on - ly one song I can sing, When in His

love in the Book He has giv'n; Won - der - ful things · in the
love me wher - ev - er I stray; Back to His dear lov - ing
beau - ty I see the great King, This shall my song in e -

Bi - ble I see— This is the dear - est, that Je - sus loves me.
arms would I flee, When I re - mem - ber that Je - sus loves me.
ter - ni - ty be: "Oh, what a won - der that Je - sus loves me!"

Chorus

I am so glad that Je - sus loves me, Je - sus loves me, Je - sus loves me;

I am so glad that Je - sus loves me, Je - sus loves e - ven me.

337 In My Heart There Rings a Melody

Singing and making melody in your heart to the Lord. Eph. 5:19

ELTON M. ROTH   ELTON M. ROTH

1. I have a song that Je - sus gave me, It was sent from
2. I love the Christ who died on Cal - v'ry, For He washed my
3. 'Twill be my end - less theme in glo - ry, With the an - gels

heav'n a - bove; There nev - er was a sweet - er mel - o - dy, 'Tis a
sins a - way; He put with - in my heart a mel - o - dy, And I
I will sing; 'Twill be a song with glo - rious har - mo - ny, When the

Refrain

mel - o - dy of love.
know it's there to stay.   In my heart there rings a mel - o - dy, There
courts of heav - en ring.

rings a mel - o - dy with heav - en's har - mo - ny; In my heart there

rings a mel - o - dy; There rings a mel - o - dy of love.

My Savior's Love 338

God, who is rich in mercy, for His great love wherewith He loved us...Eph. 2:4

CHARLES H. GABRIEL   CHARLES H. GABRIEL

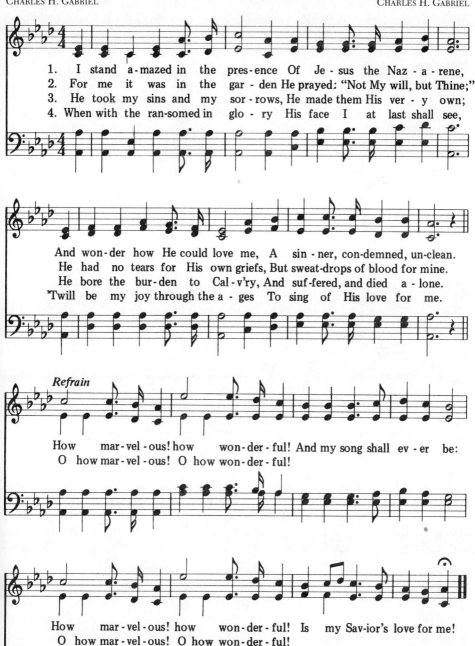

1. I stand a-mazed in the pres-ence Of Je-sus the Naz-a-rene,
2. For me it was in the gar-den He prayed: "Not My will, but Thine;"
3. He took my sins and my sor-rows, He made them His ver-y own;
4. When with the ran-somed in glo-ry His face I at last shall see,

And won-der how He could love me, A sin-ner, con-demned, un-clean.
He had no tears for His own griefs, But sweat-drops of blood for mine.
He bore the bur-den to Cal-v'ry, And suf-fered, and died a-lone.
'Twill be my joy through the a-ges To sing of His love for me.

Refrain

How mar-vel-ous! how won-der-ful! And my song shall ev-er be:
O how mar-vel-ous! O how won-der-ful!

How mar-vel-ous! how won-der-ful! Is my Sav-ior's love for me!
O how mar-vel-ous! O how won-der-ful!

339 Common Prayers for Our Children

A

Almighty God, heavenly Father, you have blessed us with the joy and care of children. As we bring them up, give us calm strength and patient wisdom, that we may teach them to love whatever is just and true and good, following the example of our Savior Jesus Christ. Amen.

B

God our father, you see your children growing up in an uncertain and confusing world. Show them that your ways give more life than the ways of the world, and that following you is better than chasing after selfish goals. Help them to take failure, not as a measure of their worth, but as an opportunity for a new start. Give them strength to hold their faith in you and to keep alive their joy in your creation, through Jesus Christ our Lord. Amen.

340 Jesus Loves the Little Children

Let the little children come to me, do not hinder them. Matt 19:14

UNKNOWN

GEORGE F. ROOT

1. Je - sus loves the lit - tle chil - dren, All the chil-dren of the world. Red and yel - low, black and white, They are pre-cious in His sight— Je - sus loves the lit - tle chil - dren of the world.

2. Je - sus died for all the chil - dren, All the chil-dren of the world. Red and yel - low, black and white, They are pre-cious in His sight— Je - sus died for all the chil - dren of the world.

Jesus Loves Me 341

Who shall separate us from the love of Christ? Rom. 8:35

ANNA B. WARNER

WILLIAM B. BRADBURY

1. Je - sus loves me! this I know, For the Bi - ble
2. Je - sus loves me! He who died Heav - en's gate to
3. Je - sus loves me! He will stay Close be - side me

tells me so; Lit - tle ones to Him be - long, They are weak but
o - pen wide; He will wash a - way my sin, Let His lit - tle
all the way; Thou hast bled and died for me, I will hence-forth

Chorus

He is strong. Yes, Je - sus loves me! Yes, Je - sus
child come in.
live for Thee.

loves me! Yes, Je - sus loves me! The Bi - ble tells me so.

342 Jesus Is All the World to Me

I have called you friends. John 15:15

WILL L. THOMPSON

WILL L. THOMPSON

1. Je-sus is all the world to me, My life, my joy, my all;
2. Je-sus is all the world to me, My Friend in tri-als sore;
3. Je-sus is all the world to me, And true to Him I'll be;
4. Je-sus is all the world to me, I want no bet-ter friend;

He is my strength from day to day, With-out Him I would fall.
I go to Him for bless-ings, and He gives them o'er and o'er.
O, how could I this Friend de-ny, When He's so true to me?
I trust Him now, I'll trust Him when Life's fleet-ing days shall end.

When I am sad to Him I go, No oth-er one can cheer me so;
He sends the sun-shine and the rain, He sends the har-vest's gold-en grain;
Fol-low-ing Him I know I'm right, He watch-es o'er me day and night;
Beau-ti-ful life with such a Friend; Beau-ti-ful life that has no end;

When I am sad He makes me glad, He's my Friend.
Sun-shine and rain, har-vest of grain, He's my Friend.
Fol-low-ing Him by day and night, He's my Friend.
E-ter-nal life, e-ter-nal joy, He's my Friend.

Tell Me the Story of Jesus 343

He expounded unto them...the things concerning Himself. Luke 24:27

FANNY J. CROSBY

JOHN R. SWENEY

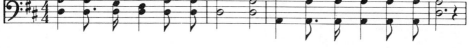

1. Tell me the sto - ry of Je - sus, Write on my heart ev - ery word;
2. Fast - ing a - lone in the des - ert, Tell of the days that are past,
3. Tell of the cross where they nailed Him, Writhing in an - guish and pain;
Ref. Tell me the sto - ry of Je - sus, Write on my heart ev - ery word;

Fine

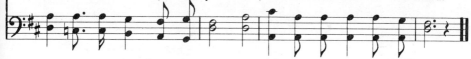

Tell me the sto - ry most pre - cious, Sweet-est that ev - er was heard.
How for our sins He was tempt - ed, Yet was tri - um-phant at last.
Tell of the grave where they laid Him, Tell how He liv - eth a - gain.
Tell me the sto - ry most pre - cious, Sweet-est that ev - er was heard.

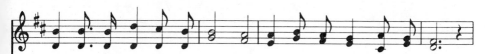

Tell how the an - gels in cho - rus Sang as they wel-comed His birth,
Tell of the years of His la - bor, Tell of the sor - row He bore,
Love in that sto - ry so ten - der Clear-er than ev - er I see:

D.C. for Refrain

"Glo - ry to God in the high - est! Peace and good ti - dings to earth."
He was de-spised and af - flict - ed, Home-less, re - ject - ed and poor.
Stay, let me weep while you whis - per, Love paid the ran - som for me.

344 Yesterday, Today and Tomorrow

Christ died for our sins according to the scriptures...I Cor. 15:3

JACK WYRTZEN

DON WYRTZEN

Yes-ter-day He died for me, yes-ter-day, yes-ter-day, Yes-ter-day He

died for me, yes-ter-day, Yes-ter-day He died for me, died for me—

This is his-to-ry. To-day He lives for me, to-day,

to-day, To-day He lives for me, to-day, To-day He

lives for me, lives for me— This is vic-to-ry.

To - mor-row He comes for me, He comes, He comes, To-mor-row He comes for me, He comes, To - mor-row He comes for me, comes for me— This is mys-ter - y. O friend, do you know Him? know Him? know Him? O friend, do you know Him? know Him? O friend, do you know Him, do you know Him? Je - sus Christ the Lord. Je - sus Christ the Lord. Je - sus Christ the Lord.

345 Saved, Saved!

He is able also to save them to the uttermost...Heb. 7:25

JACK P. SCHOLFIELD   JACK P. SCHOLFIELD

1. I've found a friend who is all to me, His
2. He saves me from ev - ery sin and harm, Se -
3. When poor and need - y and all a - lone, In

love is ev - er true; I love to tell how He
cures my soul each day; I'm lean - ing strong on His
love He said to me, "Come un - to me and I'll

lift - ed me, And what His grace can do for you.
might - y arm; I know He'll guide me all the way.
lead you home, To live with me e - ter - nal - ly."

Chorus

Saved by His pow'r di - vine, Saved to new life sub - lime!
Saved by His pow'r, Saved to new life,

Life now is sweet and my joy is com-plete, For I'm saved, saved, saved!

Now I Belong to Jesus 346

Whether we live, therefore, or die, we are the Lord's. Rom. 14:8

NORMAN J. CLAYTON   NORMAN J. CLAYTON

1. Je - sus my Lord will love me for - ev - er, From Him no pow'r of e - vil can
2. Once I was lost in sin's deg - ra - da - tion, Je - sus came down to bring me sal -
3. Joy floods my soul for Je - sus has saved me, Freed me from sin that long had en -

sev - er, He gave His life to ran - som my soul, Now I be - long to Him;
va - tion, Lift - ed me up from sor - row and shame, Now I be - long to Him;
slaved me, His pre - cious blood He gave to re - deem, Now I be - long to Him;

Refrain

Now I be - long to Je - sus, Je - sus be - longs to me,

Not for the years of time a - lone, But for e - ter - ni - ty.

347 No One Ever Cared for Me Like Jesus

Cast all your cares on Him; He cares for you. I Pet. 5:7

C. F. WEIGLE

C. F. WEIGLE

1. I would love to tell you what I think of Je - sus
2. All my life was full of sin when Je - sus found me,
3. Ev - 'ry day He comes to me with new as - sur - ance,

Since I found in Him a friend so strong and true; I would
All my heart was full of mis - er - y and' woe; Je - sus
More and more I un - der - stand His words of love; But I'll

tell you how He chang'd my life com - plete - ly— He did some-thing
placed His strong and lov - ing arms a - round me, And He led me
nev - er know just why He came to save me, Till some day I

Refrain

that no oth - er friend could do.
in the way I ought to go.   No one ev - er cared for me like
see His bless - ed face a - bove.

Je - sus, There's no oth-er friend so kind as He; No one else could take the sin and dark-ness from me— O how much He cared for me!

Prayer

Grant us, O most loving Lord,
to rest in You above all creatures,
above all glory and honour, above all power and dignity,
above all knowledge and subtilty,
above all riches and art, above all fame and praise,
above all sweetness and comfort, above all hope and promise,
above all gifts and favors that You can give and impart to us . . .
It is too small and unsatisfying, whatever
You bestow on us apart from You,
or reveal to us, or promise,
if You are not seen, and not fully obtained.
For surely our hearts cannot truly rest,
nor be entirely contented, unless they rest in Thee—Amen.

Thomas 'a Kempis

349 Saved!

For there is none other name under heaven...whereby we must be saved. Acts 4:12

OSWALD J. SMITH

ROGER M. HICKMAN

1. Saved! saved! saved! my sins are all for - giv'n; Christ is
2. Saved! saved! saved! by grace and grace a - lone; O, what
3. Saved! saved! saved! O, joy be - yond com - pare! Christ my

mine! I'm on my way to heav'n; Once a guilt - y
won - drous love to me was shown, In my stead Christ
life and I His con - stant care; Yield - ing all and

sin - ner, lost, un - done, Now a child of God, saved thro' His Son.
Je - sus bled and died, Bore my sins, for me was cru - ci - fied.
trust - ing Him a - lone, Liv - ing now each mo-ment as His own.

Refrain - parts

Saved! I'm saved thro' Christ, my all in all; Saved! I'm saved, what-
my all in all;

ev - er may be - fall, He died up - on the cross for me, He bore the aw - ful

pen - al - ty; And now I'm saved e - ter - nal - ly—I'm saved! saved! saved!

O Happy Day 350

*This day is salvation come to this house...*Luke 19:9

PHILIP DODDRIDGE   EDWARD F. RIMBAULT

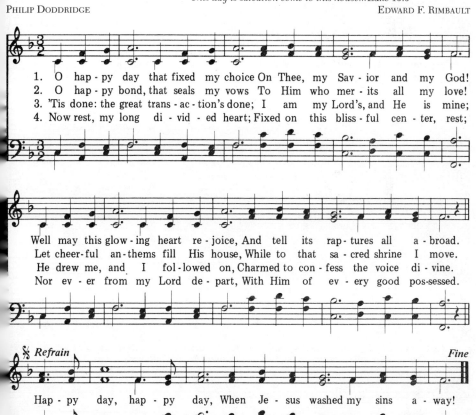

1. O hap - py day that fixed my choice On Thee, my Sav - ior and my God!
2. O hap - py bond, that seals my vows To Him who mer - its all my love!
3. 'Tis done: the great trans - ac - tion's done; I am my Lord's, and He is mine;
4. Now rest, my long di - vid - ed heart; Fixed on this bliss - ful cen - ter, rest;

Well may this glow - ing heart re - joice, And tell its rap - tures all a - broad.
Let cheer - ful an - thems fill His house, While to that sa - cred shrine I move.
He drew me, and I fol - lowed on, Charmed to con - fess the voice di - vine.
Nor ev - er from my Lord de - part, With Him of ev - ery good pos - sessed.

Refrain   *Fine*

Hap - py day, hap - py day, When Je - sus washed my sins a - way!

D.S.

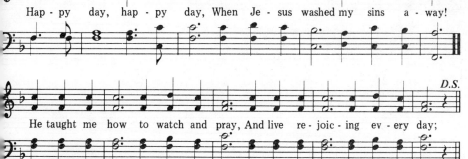

He taught me how to watch and pray, And live re - joic - ing ev - ery day;

351 Since Jesus Came into My Heart

If any man be in Christ, he is a new creature... II Cor. 5:17

RUFUS H. McDANIEL

CHARLES H. GABRIEL

1. What a won-der-ful change in my life has been wrought Since Je-sus came
2. I have ceased from my wand-'ring and go - ing a - stray, Since Je-sus came
3. There's a light in the val - ley of death now for me, Since Je-sus came
4. I shall go there to dwell in that Cit - y, I know, Since Je-sus came

in - to my heart! I have light in my soul for which long I have sought,
in - to my heart! And my sins, which were man - y, are all washed a - way,
in - to my heart! And the gates of the Cit - y be - yond I can see,
in - to my heart! And I'm hap - py, so hap - py, as on - ward I go,

Refrain

Since Je - sus came in - to my heart! Since Je - sus came in - to my
Since Je - sus came in, came

heart, Since Je - sus came in-to my heart, Floods of joy o'er my
in - to my heart, Since Je-sus came in, came in - to my heart,

soul like the sea bil - lows roll, Since Je - sus came in - to my heart.

He Hideth My Soul 352

I will put thee in a cleft of the rock, and will cover thee with My hand. Exo. 33:22

FANNY J. CROSBY

WILLIAM J. KIRKPATRICK

1. A won-der-ful Sav-ior is Je-sus my Lord, A won-der-ful
2. A won-der-ful Sav-ior is Je-sus my Lord, He tak-eth my
3. With num-ber-less bless-ings each mo-ment He crowns, And, filled with His
4. When clothed in His bright-ness, trans-port-ed I rise To meet Him in

Sav-ior to me; He hid-eth my soul in the cleft of the rock, Where
bur-den a-way; He hold-eth me up, and I shall not be moved, He
full-ness di-vine, I sing in my rap-ture, O glo-ry to God For
clouds of the sky, His per-fect sal-va-tion, His won-der-ful love, I'll

Refrain

riv-ers of pleas-ure I see.
giv-eth me strength as my day.
such a Re-deem-er as mine!
shout with the mil-lions on high.

He hid-eth my soul in the cleft of the rock

That shad-ows a dry, thirst-y land; He hid-eth my life in the depths of His love,

And cov-ers me there with His hand, And cov-ers me there with His hand.

353 Constantly Abiding

I will never leave thee, nor forsake thee. Heb. 13:5

ANNE S. MURPHY   ANNE S. MURPHY

1. There's a peace in my heart that the world nev - er gave, A peace it can
2. All the world seemed to sing of a Sav - ior and King, When peace sweetly
3. This treas - ure I have in a tem - ple of clay, While here on His

not take a - way; Tho' the tri - als of life may sur-round like a cloud,
came to my heart; Troub-les all fled a - way and my night turned to day,
foot-stool I roam: But He's com - ing to take me some glo - ri - ous day,

Refrain

I've a peace that has come there to stay! Con - stant-ly a -
Bless-ed Je - sus, how glorious Thou art! Con-stant-ly a - bid - ing,
O - ver there to my heav-en - ly home!

bid - ing, Je - sus is mine;
con-stant-ly a - bid - ing, Je - sus is mine, yes, Je - sus is mine;

Con - stant-ly a - bid - ing, rap - ture di -
Con-stant-ly a - bid - ing, con-stant-ly a - bid-ing, rap-ture di-vine, O

vine;   He   nev - er leaves me lone   -   ly, whis-pers,
rap-ture di-vine;   He nev - er leaves   me,   nev - er leaves me lone-ly, whis-pers,

O   so   kind: "I will nev - er leave   thee,"   Je - sus is   mine.
whis-pers, O so kind: nev -er leave thee, Je-sus, Je-sus is mine.

John 15

354

Verses 1-18

I am the true vine, and my Father is the gardener.
I am the vine; you are the branches.
Remain in me and I will remain in you.

If you remain in me, you will:
    bear much fruit:
If you remain in me and my words remain in you,
    ask whatever you wish, and it will be given you.
If you obey my commands,
    you will remain in my love.
If you do what I command,
    you are my friends.
If the world hates you,
    keep in mind that it hated me first.

Remain in me and I will remain in you.

355 Christ Liveth in Me

Nevertheless I live; yet not I, but Christ liveth in me... Gal. 2:20

DANIEL W. WHITTLE

JAMES MCGRANAHAN

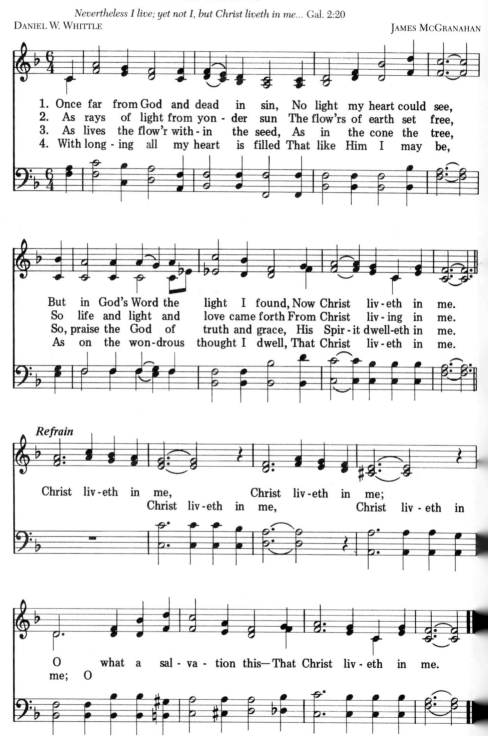

1. Once far from God and dead in sin, No light my heart could see,
2. As rays of light from yon - der sun The flow'rs of earth set free,
3. As lives the flow'r with - in the seed, As in the cone the tree,
4. With long - ing all my heart is filled That like Him I may be,

But in God's Word the light I found, Now Christ liv - eth in me.
So life and light and love came forth From Christ liv - ing in me.
So, praise the God of truth and grace, His Spir - it dwell - eth in me.
As on the won - drous thought I dwell, That Christ liv - eth in me.

Refrain

Christ liv - eth in me, Christ liv - eth in me;
Christ liv - eth in me, Christ liv - eth in
me; O

O what a sal - va - tion this—That Christ liv - eth in me.

A Child of the King 356

We are the children of God; and if children, then heirs. Rom. 8:16,17

HARRIET E. BUELL

JOHN B. SUMNER

1. My Fa - ther is rich in hous - es and lands, He hold - eth the
2. My Fa - ther's own Son, the Sav - ior of men, Once wan - dered on
3. I once was an out - cast stran - ger on earth, A sin - ner by
4. A tent or a cot - tage, why should I care? They're build-ing a

wealth of the world in His hands! Of ru - bies and dia -monds, of
earth as the poor - est of them; But now He is reign - ing for-
choice, and an al - ien by birth; But I've been a - dopt - ed, my
pal - ace for me o - ver there; Though ex - iled from home, yet

sil - ver and gold, His cof - fers are full, He has rich - es un -told.
ev - er on high, And will give me a home in heav'n by and by.
name's writ - ten down, An heir to a man-sion, a robe, and a crown.
still I may sing: All glo - ry to God, I'm a child of the King.

Refrain

I'm a child of the King, A child of the King:

With Je - sus my Sav - ior, I'm a child of the King.

357 He's Everything to Me

When I consider Thy heavens...what is man, that Thou art mindful of him? Psa. 8:3,4

RALPH CARMICHAEL

RALPH CARMICHAEL

1. In the stars His hand-i-work I see, On the wind He speaks in maj-es-ty,
2. I will cel - e - brate na - tiv - i - ty For it has a place in his-to-ry,

Though He ruleth o - ver land and sea, What is that to me? What is that to
Sure, He came to set His people free,

me? Till by faith I met Him face to face, And I felt the won-der of His grace,

Then I knew that He was more than just a God who did-n't care, who lived a-way out

there, And now He walks be-side me day by day, Ev-er watch-ing o'er me lest I stray,

Helping me to find that narrow way, He's everything to me.

'Tis So Sweet to Trust in Jesus 358

That we should be to the praise of His glory, who first trusted in Christ. Eph. 1:12

LOUISA M. R. STEAD

WILLIAM J. KIRKPATRICK

1. 'Tis so sweet to trust in Jesus, Just to take Him at His word;
2. O how sweet to trust in Jesus, Just to trust His cleansing blood;
3. Yes, 'tis sweet to trust in Jesus, Just from sin and self to cease;
4. I'm so glad I learned to trust Thee, Precious Jesus, Savior, Friend;

1. Just to rest upon His promise; Just to know, "Thus saith the Lord."
2. Just in simple faith to plunge me 'Neath the healing, cleansing flood!
3. Just from Jesus simply taking Life and rest, and joy and peace.
4. And I know that Thou art with me, Wilt be with me to the end.

Refrain

Jesus, Jesus, how I trust Him! How I've proved Him o'er and o'er!

Jesus, Jesus, precious Jesus! O for grace to trust Him more!

359 He Keeps Me Singing

We know that we have passed from death to life...I John 3:14

LUTHER B. BRIDGERS   LUTHER B. BRIDGER

1. There's with-in my heart a mel - o - dy, Je - sus whis-pers sweet and low,
2. All my life was wrecked by sin and strife, Dis-cord filled my heart with pain,
3. Feast-ing on the rich - es of His grace, Rest-ing 'neath His sheltering wing,
4. Tho' some-times He leads thro' wa - ters deep, Tri - als fall a - cross my way,
5. Soon He's com - ing back to wel- come me Far be-yond the star - ry sky;

"Fear not, I am with thee, peace, be still," In all of life's ebb and flow.
Je - sus swept a - cross the bro - ken strings, Stirred the slum-b'ring chords a-gain.
Al - ways look-ing on His smil - ing face, That is why I shout and sing.
Tho' some-times the path seems rough and steep, See His foot-prints all the way.
I shall wing my flight to worlds un-known, I shall reign with Him on high.

Refrain

Je - sus, Je - sus, Je - sus— Sweet - est name I know,

Fills my ev - ery long - ing, Keeps me sing - ing as I go.

Peace Like a River 360

The fruit of the Spirit is love, joy, peace... Gal. 5:22

TRADITIONAL

TRADITIONAL

1. I've got peace like a river, I've got peace like a
2. I've got love like an o - cean, I've got love like an
3. I've got joy like a foun - tain, I've got joy like a

riv - er, I've got peace like a riv - er in my soul, I've got
o - cean, I've got love like an o - cean in my soul, I've got
foun - tain, I've got joy like a foun - tain in my soul, I've got

peace like a riv - er, I've got peace like a riv - er,
love like an o - cean, I've got love like an o - cean,
joy like a foun - tain, I've got joy like a foun - tain,

I've got peace like a riv - er in my soul. (my soul)
I've got love like an o - cean in my soul. (my soul)
I've got joy like a foun - tain in my soul. (my soul)

Invitation

Come to me,
all you who are weary and burdened,
and I will give you rest.
Matt. 11:28

Only Trust Him 361

He is able also to save them to the uttermost...Heb. 7:25

JOHN H. STOCKTON   JOHN H. STOCKTON

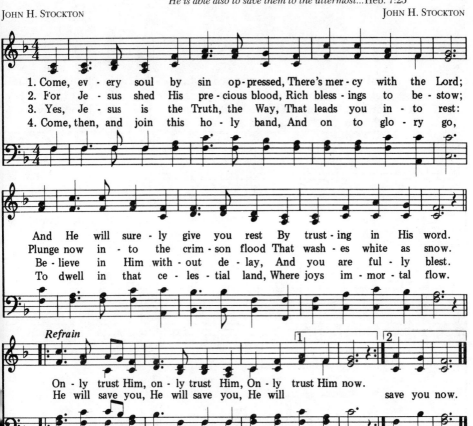

1. Come, ev - ery soul by sin op - pressed, There's mer - cy with the Lord;
2. For Je - sus shed His pre - cious blood, Rich bless - ings to be - stow;
3. Yes, Je - sus is the Truth, the Way, That leads you in - to rest:
4. Come, then, and join this ho - ly band, And on to glo - ry go,

And He will sure - ly give you rest By trust - ing in His word.
Plunge now in - to the crim - son flood That wash - es white as snow.
Be - lieve in Him with - out de - lay, And you are ful - ly blest.
To dwell in that ce - les - tial land, Where joys im - mor - tal flow.

Refrain

On - ly trust Him, on - ly trust Him, On - ly trust Him now.
He will save you, He will save you, He will save you now.

Invitation 362

Isaiah 55:1-2; Matthew 11:28-29; John 6:37

Come, all you who are thirsty, come to the waters;
and you who have no money, come, buy and eat!
Come, buy wine and milk without money and without cost.
Why spend money on what is not bread,
and your labor on what does not satisfy?

Come to me, all you who are weary and burdened,
and I will give you rest.
Take my yoke upon you and learn from me,
for I am gentle and humble in heart,
and you will find rest for your souls.
For my yoke is easy and my burden is light.

All that the Father gives me will come to me;
and him who comes to me I will never drive away.

363 Turn Your Eyes Upon Jesus

Look unto Me, and be ye saved, all the ends of the earth. Isa. 45:22

HELEN H. LEMMEL

HELEN H. LEMMEL

1. O soul, are you wea-ry and troub-led? No light in the
2. Through death in-to life ev-er-last-ing He passed, and we
3. His word shall not fail you— He prom-ised; Be-lieve Him and

dark-ness you see? There's light for a look at the Sav-ior,
fol-low Him there; O-ver us sin no more hath do-min-ion—
all will be well: Then go to a world that is dy-ing,

Refrain

And life more a-bun-dant and free!
For more than con-qu'rors we are! Turn your eyes up-on Je-
His per-fect sal-va-tion to tell!

sus, Look full in His won-der-ful face; And the things of

earth will grow strange-ly dim In the light of His glo-ry and grace.

The Savior Is Waiting 364

Behold, I stand at the door, and knock...Rev. 3:20

RALPH CARMICHAEL

RALPH CARMICHAEL

1. The Sav-ior is wait-ing to en-ter your heart, Why don't you
2. If you'll take one step t'ward the Sav-ior, my friend, You'll find His

let Him come in? There's noth-ing in this world to keep you a-part,
arms o-pen wide; Re-ceive Him, and all of your dark-ness will end,

Refrain

What is your an-swer to Him?
With-in your heart He'll a-bide. Time af-ter time He has

wait-ed be-fore, And now He is wait-ing a-gain To

see if you're will-ing to o-pen the door, O, how He wants to come in.

365 No One Understands Like Jesus

He has borne our griefs and carried our sorrow. Isa. 53:4

JOHN W. PETERSON

JOHN W. PETERSON

1. No one un-der-stands like Je-sus, He's a friend be-yond com-pare;
2. No one un-der-stands like Je-sus, Ev-ery woe He sees and feels;
3. No one un-der-stands like Je-sus, When the foes of life as-sail;
4. No one un-der-stands like Je-sus, When you falt-er on the way;

Meet Him at the throne of mer-cy, He is wait-ing for you there.
Ten-der-ly He whis-pers com-fort, And the bro-ken heart He heals.
You should nev-er be dis-cour-aged, Je-sus cares and will not fail.
Tho' you fail Him, sad-ly fail Him, He will par-don you to-day.

Chorus

No one un-der-stands like Je-sus, When the days are dark and grim;

No one is so near, so dear as Je-sus, Cast your ev-ery care on Him.

Give Me Jesus 366

What good is it for a man to gain the whole world, yet forfeit his soul? Mark 8:36

FANNY J. CROSBY

JOHN R. SWENEY

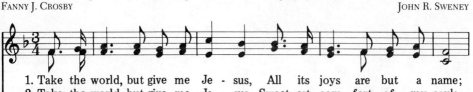

1. Take the world, but give me Je - sus, All its joys are but a name;
2. Take the world, but give me Je - sus, Sweet-est com - fort of my soul;
3. Take the world, but give me Je - sus, Let me view His con-stant smile;
4. Take the world, but give me Je - sus, In His cross my trust shall be;

But His love a - bid - eth ev - er, Thru e - ter - nal years the same.
With my Sav - ior watch-ing o'er me, I can sing tho bil - lows roll.
Then thru - out my pil - grim jour - ney Light will cheer me all the while.
Till, with clear - er, bright - er vi - sion, Face to face my Lord I see.

Refrain

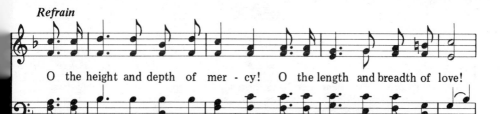

O the height and depth of mer - cy! O the length and breadth of love!

O the full - ness of re - demp - tion, Pledge of end - less life a - bove!

367 Fill My Cup, Lord

Whosoever drinketh of the water that I shall give him shall never thirst. John 4:14

RICHARD BLANCHARD

RICHARD BLANCHARD
ARR. EUGENE CLARK

1. Like the wom-an at the well I was seek-ing For things that could not
2. There are mil-lions in this world who are crav-ing The pleas-ure earth-ly
3. So, my broth-er, if the things this world gave you Leave hun-gers that won't

sat-is-fy. And then I heard my Sav-ior speak-ing: "Draw from my
things af-ford. But none can match the won-drous treas-ure That I
pass a-way. My bless-ed Lord will come and save you If you

Chorus

well that nev-er shall run dry." Fill my cup, Lord, I lift it
find in Je-sus Christ, my Lord.
kneel to Him and hum-bly pray.

up, Lord. Come and quench this thirst-ing of my soul. Bread of heav-en,

feed me till I want no more; Fill my cup, fill it up and make me whole.

Whiter Than Snow 368

Wash me, and I shall be whiter than snow. Psa. 51:7

JAMES L. NICHOLSON

WILLIAM G. FISCHER

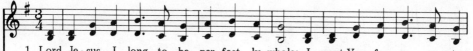

1. Lord Je - sus, I long to be per - fect - ly whole; I want You for - ev - er to
2. Lord Je - sus, look down from Your throne in the skies, And help me to make a com-
3. Lord Je - sus, for this I most hum - bly en - treat, I wait, bless-ed Lord, at Your
4. Lord Je - sus, You see that I pa - tient - ly wait, Come now, and with - in me a

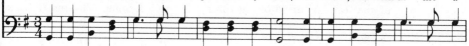

live in my soul, Break down ev - ery i - dol, cast out ev - ery foe;
plete sac - ri - fice; I give up my - self, and what - ev - er I know,
cru - ci - fied feet; By faith, for my cleans - ing I see Your blood flow,
new heart cre - ate; To those who have sought You, You nev - er said "No,"

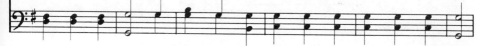

Refrain

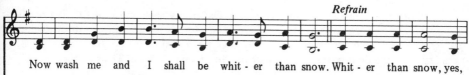

Now wash me and I shall be whit - er than snow. Whit - er than snow, yes,

whit - er than snow; Now wash me, and I shall be whit - er than snow.

369 Jesus, I Come

He hath sent Me...to proclaim liberty to the captives...Isa. 61:1

WILLIAM T. SLEEPER

GEORGE C. STEBBINS

1. Out of my bond-age, sor-row and night, Je - sus, I come, Je - sus, I come;
2. Out of my shame-ful fail-ure and loss, Je - sus, I come, Je - sus, I come;
3. Out of un-rest and ar - ro-gant pride, Je - sus, I come, Je - sus, I come;
4. Out of the fear and dread of the tomb, Je - sus, I come, Je - sus, I come;

In - to Thy free-dom, glad-ness and light, Je - sus, I come to Thee.
In - to the glo-rious gain of Thy cross, Je - sus, I come to Thee.
In - to Thy bless-ed will to a - bide, Je - sus, I come to Thee.
In - to the joy and light of Thy home, Je - sus, I come to Thee.

Out of my sick-ness in - to Thy health, Out of my want and in - to Thy wealth,
Out of earth's sor-rows in - to Thy balm, Out of life's storms and in - to Thy calm,
Out of my-self to dwell in Thy love, Out of de-spair in-to rap-tures a - bove,
Out of the depths of ru - in un-told, In - to the peace of Thy shel-ter-ing fold,

Out of my sin and in - to Thy-self, Je - sus, I come to Thee.
Out of dis-tress to ju - bi-lant psalm, Je - sus, I come to Thee.
Up-ward for aye on wings like a dove, Je - sus, I come to Thee.
Ev - er Thy glo-rious face to be-hold, Je - sus, I come to Thee.

Pass Me Not 370

Lord, I believe; help Thou mine unbelief. Mark 9:24

FANNY J. CROSBY

WILLIAM H. DOANE

1. Pass me not, O gen - tle Sav - ior— Hear my hum - ble cry!
2. Let me at a throne of mer - cy Find a sweet re - lief;
3. Trust - ing on - ly in Thy mer - it, Would I seek Thy face;
4. Thou the spring of all my com - fort, More than life to me!

While on oth - ers Thou art call - ing, Do not pass me by.
Kneel - ing there in deep con - tri - tion, Help my un - be - lief.
Heal my wound-ed, bro - ken spir - it, Save me by Thy grace.
Whom have I on earth be - side Thee? Whom in heav'n but Thee?

Chorus

Sav - ior, Sav - ior, Hear my hum - ble cry!

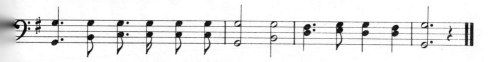

While on oth - ers Thou art call - ing, Do not pass me by.

371 Reach Out to Jesus

In the time of trouble...Thou wilt answer me. Psa. 86:7

RALPH CARMICHAEL   RALPH CARMICHAEL

1. Is your bur - den heav - y as you bear it all a - lone?
2. Is the life you're liv - ing filled with sor - row and de - spair?

Does the road you trav - el har - bor dan - ger yet un - known?
Does the fu - ture press you with its wor - ry and its care?

Are you grow - ing wea - ry in the strug - gle of it all?
Are you tired and friend-less, have you al - most lost your way?

Je - sus will help you when on His name you call.
Je - sus will help you, just come to Him to - day.

Chorus

He is al-ways there, hear-ing ev-ery prayer, faith-ful and true;

Walk-ing by our side, in His love we hide all the day through.

When you get dis-cour-aged, just re-mem-ber what to do—

Reach out to Je-sus, He's reach-ing out to you.

372 Burdens Are Lifted at Calvary

Cast thy burden upon the Lord, and He shall sustain thee. Psa. 55:22

JOHN M. MOORE

JOHN M. MOORE

1. Days are filled with sor-row and care, Hearts are lone-ly and drear;
2. Cast your care on Je-sus to-day, Leave your wor-ry and fear;
3. Trou-bled soul, the Sav-ior can see Ev-ery heart-ache and tear;

Bur-dens are lift-ed at Cal-va-ry, Je-sus is ver-y near.
Bur-dens are lift-ed at Cal-va-ry, Je-sus is ver-y near.
Bur-dens are lift-ed at Cal-va-ry, Je-sus is ver-y near.

Refrain

Bur-dens are lift-ed at Cal-va-ry, Cal-va-ry, Cal-va-ry;

Bur-dens are lift-ed at Cal-va-ry, Je-sus is ver-y near.

The Light of the World Is Jesus 373

I am the light of the world...John 8:12

PHILIP P. BLISS   PHILIP P. BLISS

1. The whole world was lost in the dark-ness of sin; The Light of the
2. No dark-ness have we who in Je-sus a-bide, The Light of the
3. Ye dwell-ers in dark-ness with sin-blind-ed eyes, The Light of the
4. No need of the sun-light in heav-en, we're told, The Light of the

world is Je-sus; Like sun-shine at noon-day His glo-ry shone in,
world is Je-sus; We walk in the Light when we fol-low our Guide,
world is Je-sus; Go wash at His bid-ding and light will a-rise,
world is Je-sus; The Lamb is the Light in the Cit-y of Gold,

Refrain

The Light of the world is Je-sus. Come to the Light, 'tis

shin-ing for thee; Sweet-ly the Light has dawned up-on me;

Once I was blind, but now I can see; The Light of the world is Je-sus.

374 The Way of the Cross Leads Home

The preaching of the cross...is the power of God. I Cor. 1:18

JESSIE B. POUNDS

CHARLES H. GABRIEL

1. I must needs go home by the way of the cross, There's no oth - er
2. I must needs go on in the blood-sprin-kled way, The path that the
3. Then I bid fare - well to the way of the world, To walk in it

way but this; I shall ne'er get sight of the Gates of Light,
Sav - ior trod; If I ev - er climb to the heights sub - lime,
nev - er more; For my Lord says "Come," and I seek my home,

Chorus

If the way of the cross I miss.
Where the soul is at home with God.   The way of the cross leads
Where He waits at the o - pen door.

home,   The way of the cross leads home;   It is
leads home,   leads home;

sweet to know as I on - ward go, The way of the cross leads home.

Jesus Is Calling 375

Today if ye will hear His voice, harden not your hearts...Heb. 3:15

FANNY J. CROSBY

GEORGE C. STEBBINS

1. Je - sus is ten - der - ly call - ing you home, Call - ing to - day,
2. Je - sus is call - ing the wea - ry to rest, Call - ing to - day,
3. Je - sus is wait - ing, O come to Him now, Wait - ing to - day,
4. Je - sus is plead - ing, O list to His voice: Hear Him to - day,

call - ing to - day, Why from the sun - shine of love will you roam
call - ing to - day, Bring Him your bur - den and you shall be blest;
wait - ing to - day, Come with your sins, at His feet low - ly bow;
hear Him to - day, They who be - lieve on His name shall re - joice;

Chorus

Far - ther and far - ther a - way? Call - ing to - day,
He will not turn you a - way.
Come, and no long - er de - lay.
Quick - ly a - rise and a - way. Call - ing, call - ing to - day, to - day,

Call - ing to - day, Je - sus is
Call - ing, call - ing to - day, to - day, Je - sus is ten - der - ly

call - ing, Is ten - der - ly call - ing to - day.
call - ing to - day,

376 Are You Washed in the Blood?

Wash me, and I shall be whiter than snow. Psa. 51:7

ELISHA A. HOFFMAN   ELISHA A. HOFFMAN

1. Have you been to Je-sus for the cleans-ing pow'r? Are you
2. Are you walk-ing dai-ly by the Sav-ior's side? Are you
3. When the Bride-groom com-eth, will your robes be white? Are you
4. Lay a-side the gar-ments that are stained with sin, And be

washed in the blood of the Lamb? Are you ful-ly trust-ing in His
washed in the blood of the Lamb? Do you rest each mo-ment in the
washed in the blood of the Lamb? Will your soul be read-y for the
washed in the blood of the Lamb;There's a foun-tain flow-ing for the

grace this hour? Are you washed in the blood of the Lamb?
Cru-ci-fied? Are you washed in the blood of the Lamb?
man-sions bright, And be washed in the blood of the Lamb?
soul un-clean, O be washed in the blood of the Lamb?

Chorus

Are you washed in the blood, In the
Are you washed in the blood,

soul-cleans-ing blood of the Lamb? Are your gar-ments
of the Lamb?

spot-less? Are they white as snow? Are you washed in the blood of the Lamb?

Lord, I'm Coming Home 377

I will arise and go to my father...Luke 15:18

WILLIAM J. KIRKPATRICK

WILLIAM J. KIRKPATRICK

1. I've wan-dered far a - way from God, Now I'm com - ing home;
2. I've wast - ed man - y pre - cious years, Now I'm com - ing home;
3. I've tired of sin and stray - ing, Lord, Now I'm com - ing home;
4. My soul is sick, my heart is sore, Now I'm com - ing home;

The paths of sin too long I've trod, Lord, I'm com - ing home.
I now re - pent with bit - ter tears, Lord, I'm com - ing home.
I'll trust Thy love, be - lieve Thy word, Lord, I'm com - ing home.
My strength re - new, my hope re - store, Lord, I'm com - ing home.

Chorus

Com - ing home, com - ing home, Nev - er more to roam,

O - pen wide Thine arms of love, Lord, I'm com - ing home.

378 Tell Me the Old, Old Story

Tell them how great things the Lord hath done for thee...Mark 5:19

A. CATHERINE HANKEY

WILLIAM H. DOANE

1. Tell me the Old, Old Sto - ry, Of un - seen things a -
2. Tell me the sto - ry slow - ly, That I may take it
3. Tell me the sto - ry soft - ly, With ear - nest tones and
4. Tell me the same old sto - ry, When you have cause to

bove, Of Je - sus and His glo - ry, Of Je - sus and His love;
in— That won - der - ful re - demp - tion, God's rem - e - dy for sin;
grave; Re - mem - ber I'm the sin - ner Whom Je - sus came to save;
fear That this world's emp - ty glo - ry Is cost - ing me too dear;

Tell me the sto - ry sim - ply, As to a lit - tle child, For
Tell me the sto - ry oft - en, For I for - get so soon, The
Tell me the sto - ry al - ways, If you would real - ly be, In
Yes, and when that world's glo - ry Is dawn - ing on my soul, Tell

I am weak and wea - ry, And help - less and de - filed.
"ear - ly dew" of morn - ing Has passed a - way at noon.
an - y time of troub - le, A com - fort - er to me.
me the Old, Old Sto - ry: "Christ Je - sus makes thee whole."

Chorus

Tell me the Old, Old Sto - ry, Tell me the Old, Old Sto - ry,

Tell me the Old, Old Sto - ry Of Je - sus and His love.

There's a Wideness in God's Mercy 379

Thou, O Lord, art a God...plenteous in mercy and truth. Psa. 86:15

FREDERICK W. FABER

LIZZIE S. TOURJÉE

1. There's a wide - ness in God's mer - cy Like the wide - ness of the sea;
2. There is wel - come for the sin - ner And more grac - es for the good;
3. For the love of God is broad - er Than the meas - ure of man's mind;
4. If our love were but more sim - ple We should take Him at His word,

There's a kind - ness in His jus - tice Which is more than lib - er - ty.
There is mer - cy with the Sav - ior; There is heal - ing in His blood.
And the heart of the E - ter - nal Is most won - der - ful - ly kind.
And our lives would be all sun-shine In the sweet - ness of our Lord. A-men.

380 God So Loved the World

God has given to us eternal life, and this life is in His Son. I John 5:11

JOHN 3:16,17   JOHN STAINER

God so loved the world, God so loved the world,

that He gave His on - ly be - got - ten Son, that who- so be -

liev - eth, be - liev - eth in Him should not per - ish, should not

per - ish but have ev - er - last - ing life. For God sent not His

Son in-to the world to con-demn the world, God sent not His

Son in-to the world to con-demn the world; But that the world through

Him might be sav - ed. life, ev - er - last - ing life, ev - er-

last - ing, ev - er - last - ing life. God so loved the

world, God so loved the world, God so loved the world.

381 Room at the Cross for You

The Lord... is longsuffering...that all should come to repentance. II Pet. 3:9

IRA F. STANPHILL

IRA F. STANPHILL

1. The cross up-on which Je-sus died Is a shel-ter in
2. Tho' mil-lions have found Him a friend And have turned from the
3. The hand of my Sav-ior is strong, And the love of my

which we can hide; And its grace so free is suf-
sins they have sinned, The Sav-ior still waits to
Sav-ior is long; Through sun-shine or rain, through

fi-cient for me, And deep is its foun-tain— as wide as the sea.
o-pen the gates And wel-come a sin-ner be-fore it's too late.
loss or in gain, The blood flows from Cal-v'ry to cleanse ev-ery stain.

Chorus

There's room at the cross for you, There's room at the cross for you; Tho'

mil-lions have come, there's still room for one—Yes, there's room at the cross for you.

Glory to His Name 382

...Having made peace by the blood of His cross. Col. 1:20

ELISHA A. HOFFMAN

JOHN H. STOCKTON

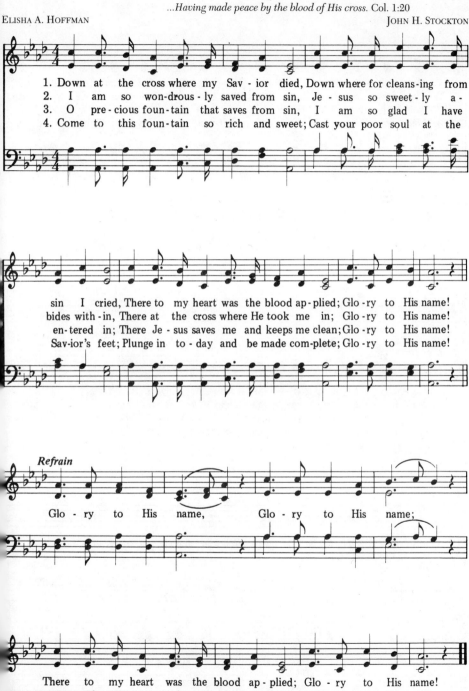

1. Down at the cross where my Sav - ior died, Down where for cleans-ing from
2. I am so won-drous-ly saved from sin, Je - sus so sweet-ly a -
3. O pre-cious foun-tain that saves from sin, I am so glad I have
4. Come to this foun-tain so rich and sweet; Cast your poor soul at the

sin I cried, There to my heart was the blood ap-plied; Glo-ry to His name!
bides with-in, There at the cross where He took me in; Glo-ry to His name!
en-tered in; There Je-sus saves me and keeps me clean; Glo-ry to His name!
Sav-ior's feet; Plunge in to-day and be made com-plete; Glo-ry to His name!

Refrain

Glo - ry to His name, Glo - ry to His name;

There to my heart was the blood ap-plied; Glo - ry to His name!

383 Grace Greater Than Our Sin

Where sin abounded, grace did much more abound. Rom. 5:20

JULIA H. JOHNSTON

DANIEL B. TOWNER

1. Mar - vel - ous grace of our lov - ing Lord, Grace that ex - ceeds our
2. Sin and de - spair like the sea waves cold, Threat - en the soul with
3. Dark is the stain that we can - not hide, What can a - vail to
4. Mar - vel - ous, in - fi - nite, match - less grace, Free - ly be - stowed on

sin and our guilt, Yon - der on Cal - va - ry's mount out - poured,
in - fi - nite loss; Grace that is great - er, yes, grace un - told,
wash it a - way? Look! there is flow - ing a crim - son tide;
all who be - lieve; All who are long - ing to see His face,

Refrain

There where the blood of the Lamb was spilt.
Points to the ref - uge, 'the might - y cross. Grace, grace,
Whit - er than snow you may be to - day. Mar - vel - ous grace,
Will you this mo - ment His grace re - ceive?

God's grace, Grace that will par - don and cleanse with - in; Grace,
in - fi - nite grace, Mar - vel - ous

grace, God's grace, Grace that is great - er than all our sin.
grace, in - fi - nite grace,

Trust in the Lord 384

Trust in the Lord with all thine heart... Prov. 3:5

Thomas O. Chisholm

Wendell P. Loveless

1. Trust in the Lord with all your heart, This is God's gra-cious com-mand;
2. Trust in the Lord who rul - eth all, See - eth all things as they are,
3. Trust in the Lord—His eye will guide All thro' your path-way a - head,

In all your ways ac- knowl-edge Him, So shall you dwell in the land.
Be it a bird - ling in its nest, Or yon - der ut - ter - most star.
He hath re-deemed and He will keep, Trust Him and be not a - fraid.

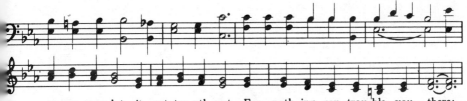

Refrain

Trust in the Lord, O trou-bled soul, Rest in the arms of His care; What-
care, of His care;

ev - er your lot, it mat-ter-eth not, For noth-ing can trou-ble you there;

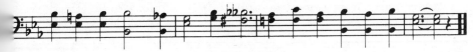

Trust in the Lord, O trou-bled soul, Noth-ing can trou-ble you there.

385 Almost Persuaded

Almost thou persuadest me to be a Christian. Acts. 26:28

PHILIP P. BLISS

PHILIP P. BLISS

1. "Al - most per - suad - ed," now to be - lieve;
2. "Al - most per - suad - ed," come, come to - day;
3. "Al - most per - suad - ed," har - vest is past!

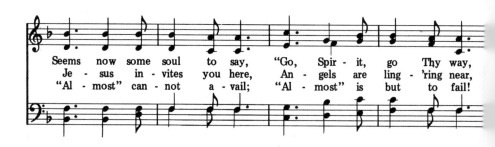

"Al - most per - suad - ed," Christ to re - ceive;
"Al - most per - suad - ed," turn not a - way;
"Al - most per - suad - ed," doom comes at last!

Seems now some soul to say, "Go, Spir - it, go Thy way,
Je - sus in - vites you here, An - gels are ling - 'ring near,
"Al - most" can - not a - vail; "Al - most" is but to fail!

Some more con - ven - ient day On Thee I'll call."
Prayers rise from hearts so dear, O wan - d'rer, come.
Sad, sad, that bit - ter wail, "Al - most," but lost.

Have You Any Room for Jesus? 386

Today if ye will hear His voice, harden not your hearts...Heb. 3:15

SOURCE UNKNOWN
ADAPTED BY DANIEL W. WHITTLE

C.C. WILLIAMS

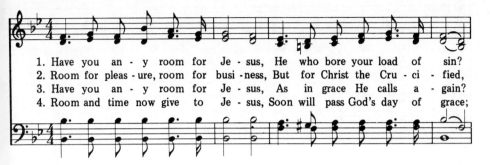

1. Have you an-y room for Je-sus, He who bore your load of sin?
2. Room for pleas-ure, room for busi-ness, But for Christ the Cru-ci-fied,
3. Have you an-y room for Je-sus, As in grace He calls a-gain?
4. Room and time now give to Je-sus, Soon will pass God's day of grace;

As He knocks and asks ad-mis-sion, Sin-ner, will you let Him in?
Not a place that He can en-ter, In the heart for which He died?
O, to-day is time ac-cept-ed, You will nev-er call in vain.
Soon your heart left cold and si-lent, And the Sav-ior's plead-ing cease.

Refrain

Room for Je-sus, King of glo-ry! Has-ten now, His word o-bey;

Swing the heart's door wide-ly o-pen, Bid Him en-ter while you may.

387   Just As I Am, Without One Plea

Him that cometh to Me I will in no wise cast out. John 6:37

CHARLOTTE ELLIOTT

WILLIAM B. BRADBURY

1. Just as I am, with-out one plea But that Thy blood was
2. Just as I am, and wait-ing not To rid my soul of
3. Just as I am, though tossed a-bout With man-y a con-flict,
4. Just as I am, poor, wretch-ed, blind; Sight, rich-es, heal-ing
5. Just as I am, Thou wilt re-ceive, Wilt wel-come, par-don,

shed for me, And that Thou bidd'st me come to Thee, O
one dark blot, To Thee whose blood can cleanse each spot, O
man-y a doubt, Fight-ings and fears with-in, with-out, O
of the mind, Yea, all I need, in Thee I find, O
cleanse, re-lieve; Be-cause Thy prom-ise I be-lieve, O

Coda (after last stanza)

Lamb of God, I come! I come!
Lamb of God, I come! I come!
Lamb of God, I come! I come!
Lamb of God, I come! I come!
Lamb of God, I come! I come! O Lamb of God, I come. A-men.

388   I Come

These are they which have washed their robes, and made them white in the blood of the Lamb. He who sits on the throne will spread his tent over them. Never again will they hunger; never again will they thirst. The sun will not beat on them, nor any scorching heat. For the Lamb will be their shepherd; he will lead them to springs of living water. And God will wipe away every tear from their eyes.

The Spirit and the bride say, "Come!"
Whoever is thirsty, let him come;
and whoever wishes,
let him take the free gift of the water of life.

From The Revelation

Softly and Tenderly Jesus Is Calling 389

Come unto Me, all ye that labor and are heavy laden...Matt. 11:28

WILL L. THOMPSON   WILL L. THOMPSON

1. Soft - ly and ten - der - ly Je - sus is call - ing, Call - ing for
2. Why should we tar - ry when Je - sus is plead - ing, Plead - ing for
3. Time is now fleet - ing, the mo - ments are pass - ing, Pass - ing from
4. O for the won - der - ful love He has prom - ised, Prom - ised for

you and for me; See, on the por - tals He's wait - ing and watch - ing,
you and for me? Why should we lin - ger and heed not His mer - cies,
you and from me; Shad - ows are gath - er - ing, death's night is com - ing,
you and for me! Though we have sinned, He has mer - cy and par - don,

Refrain

Watch - ing for you and for me.
Mer - cies for you and for me?   Come home,   come home,
Com - ing for you and for me.   Come home,   come home,
Par - don for you and for me.

Ye who are wea - ry, come home; Ear - nest - ly, ten - der - ly,

Je - sus is call - ing, Call - ing, O sin - ner, come home!

390 Let Jesus Come into Your Heart

Behold, now is the accepted time...now is the day of salvation. II Cor. 6:2

LELIA N. MORRIS

LELIA N. MORRIS

1. If you are tired of the load of your sin, Let Je - sus come in - to your heart; If you de - sire a new life to be - gin,
2. If 'tis for pu - ri - ty now that you sigh, Let Je - sus come in - to your heart; Foun - tains for cleans-ing are flow-ing near by,
3. If there's a tem-pest your voice can - not still, Let Je - sus come in - to your heart; If there's a void this world nev - er can fill,
4. If you would join the glad songs of the blest, Let Je - sus come in - to your heart; If you would en - ter the man-sions of rest,

Let Je - sus come in - to your heart.

Chorus

Just now your doubt-ings give o'er; Just now re - ject Him no more; Just now throw o - pen the door; Let Je - sus come in - to your heart.

Into My Heart 391

If any man...open the door, I will come in...Rev. 3:20

Harry D. Clarke

Harry D. Clarke

In - to my heart, in - to my heart, Come in - to my heart, Lord Je - sus;

Come in to - day, come in to stay, Come in - to my heart, Lord Je - sus.

Only Believe 392

Everything is possible for him who believes. Mark 9:23

Paul Rader

Paul Rader

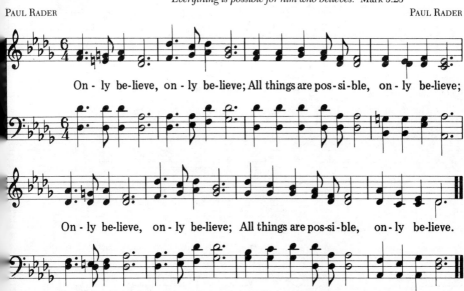

On - ly be - lieve, on - ly be - lieve; All things are pos - si - ble, on - ly be - lieve;

On - ly be - lieve, on - ly be - lieve; All things are pos-si-ble, on - ly be - lieve.

393 Without Him

The Son of man is come to save that which was lost. Matt. 18:11

MYLON R. LeFEVRE

MYLON R. LeFEVRE

1. With - out Him I could do noth - ing, With - out Him
2. With - out Him I could be dy - ing, With - out Him

I'd sure - ly fail; With - out Him I would be drift - ing
I'd be en - slaved; With - out Him life would be hope - less,

Chorus

Like a ship with - out a sail. Je - sus, O Je - sus,
But with Je - sus, thank God, I'm saved.

Do you know Him to - day? You can't turn Him a - way. O

Je - sus, O Je - sus, With - out him, How lost I would be.

Just a Closer Walk with Thee 394

As you have received Christ Jesus, so walk in Him. Col. 2:6

UNKNOWN UNKNOWN

1. I am weak, but Thou art strong; Je - sus,
2. Thru this world of toil and snares, If I
3. When my fee - ble life is o'er, Time for
Refrain: Just a clos - er walk with Thee, Grant it,

keep me from all wrong; I'll be sat - is - fied as
fal - ter, Lord, who cares? Who with me my bur - den
me will be no more; Guide me gent - ly, safe - ly
Je - sus, is my plea; Dai - ly walk-ing close to

long As I walk, let me walk close to Thee.
shares? None but Thee, dear Lord, none but Thee.
o'er To Thy king - dom shore, to Thy shore.
Thee, Let it be, dear Lord, let it be.

God in Me 395

God to enfold me, God to surround me, God in my speaking, God in my thinking.
God in my sleeping, God in my waking, God in my watching, God in my hoping.
God in my life, God in my lips, God in my soul, God in my heart.
God in my sufficing, God in my slumber, God in my living soul, God in mine eternity.

Celtic Prayer

Consecration

You are a people holy to the Lord your God.
Out of all the peoples on the face of the earth,
the Lord has chosen you
to be His treasured possession.
Deut. 14:2

O for a Heart to Praise My God 396

I will praise Thee, O Lord, with my whole heart. Psa. 9:1

CHARLES WESLEY

CARL G. GLÄSER
ARR. LOWELL MASON

1. O for a heart to praise my God, A heart from sin set free,
2. A hum-ble, low-ly, con-trite heart, Be-liev-ing, true and clean;
3. A heart in ev-ery thought re-newed, And full of love di-vine;
4. Thy na-ture, gra-cious Lord, im-part; Come quick-ly from a-bove,

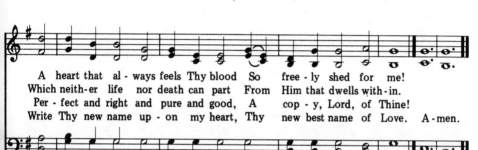

A heart that al-ways feels Thy blood So free-ly shed for me!
Which neith-er life nor death can part From Him that dwells with-in.
Per-fect and right and pure and good, A cop-y, Lord, of Thine!
Write Thy new name up-on my heart, Thy new best name of Love. A-men.

A New Heart 397

Then will I sprinkle clean water upon you, and ye shall be clean: from all your filthiness, and from all your idols, will I cleanse you.

A new heart also will I give you, and a new spirit will I put within you: and I will take away the stony heart out of your flesh, and I will give you a heart of flesh.

And I will put my Spirit within you, and cause you to walk in my statutes, and ye shall keep my judgments, and do *them.*

And ye shall dwell in the land that I gave to your fathers; and ye shall be my people, and I will be your God.

Ezekiel 36:25-28

398 Cleanse Me

Search me, O God, and know my heart...Psa. 139:23

CHARLES WESLEY   EDWARD J. HOPKINS

1. Search me, O God, and know my heart to-day;
2. I praise Thee, Lord, for cleans-ing me from sin;
3. Lord, take my life and make it whol-ly Thine;
4. O Ho-ly Ghost, re-viv-al comes from Thee;

Try me O Sav-ior, know my thoughts, I pray.
Ful-fill Thy Word and make me pure with-in.
Fill my poor heart with Thy great love di-vine.
Send a re-viv-al, Start the work in me.

See if there be some wick-ed way in me;
Fill me with fire where once I burned with shame;
Take all my will, my pas-sion, self, and pride;
Thy Word de-clares Thou wilt sup-ply our need;

cleanse me from ev-ery sin and set me free.
Grant my de-sire to mag-ni-fy Thy name.
I now sur-ren-der; Lord, in me a-bide.
For bless-ings now, O Lord, I hum-bly plead. A-men.

Jesus Is Lord 399

Jesus Christ is Lord. Phil. 2:11

Ed Seabough

Otis Skillings

With my heart I be-lieve Je-sus Christ is Lord, And that Je-sus rose a-gain, Je-sus Christ is Lord. With my lips I con-fess Je-sus Christ is Lord, And I, too, shall live a-gain, Je-sus Christ is Lord.

Je-sus is Lord, Lord of my life; Je-sus is Lord, Lord of my life.

Je-sus is Lord, Lord of my life; Je-sus is Lord!

400 Be Thou My Vision

Jesus Christ is all. Col. 3:11

IRISH HYMN
TR. MARY BYRNE; ED. ELEANOR HULL

TRADITIONAL IRISH MELODY
ARR. JACK SCHRADER

1. Be Thou my Vi - sion, O Lord of my heart;
2. Be Thou my Wis - dom, and Thou my true Word;
3. Rich - es I need not, nor man's emp - ty praise,
4. High King of heav - en, my vic - to - ry won,

Naught be all else to me, save that Thou art—
I ev - er with Thee and Thou with me, Lord;
Thou mine in - her - i - tance, now and al - ways;
May I reach heav - en's joys, O bright heav'n's Sun!

Thou my best thought by day or by night,
Thou my great Fa - ther, and I thy true son,
Thou and Thou on - ly be first in my heart,
Heart of my own heart, what - ev - er be - fall,

Wak - ing or sleep - ing, Thy pres - ence my light.
Thou in me dwell - ing, and I with Thee one.
High King of heav - en, my Treas - ure Thou art.
Still be my Vi - sion, O Rul - er of all.

Your attitude should be the same as
  that of Christ Jesus:
Who, being in very nature God,
  did not consider equality with God
    something to be grasped,
but made himself nothing,
  taking the very nature of a servant,
  being made in human likeness.
And being found in appearance as a
  man,
  he humbled himself
  and became obedient to death—
    even death on a cross!

Therefore God exalted him to the
  highest place
  and gave him the name that is
    above every name,
that at the name of Jesus every knee
  should bow,
  in heaven and on earth and under
    the earth,
and every tongue confess that Jesus
  Christ is Lord,
  to the glory of God the Father.

From Philippians 2 (NIV)

May the Mind of Christ My Savior 402

Let this mind be in you which was also in Christ Jesus. Phil 2:5

KATE B. WILKINSON

A. CYRIL BARHAM-GOULD

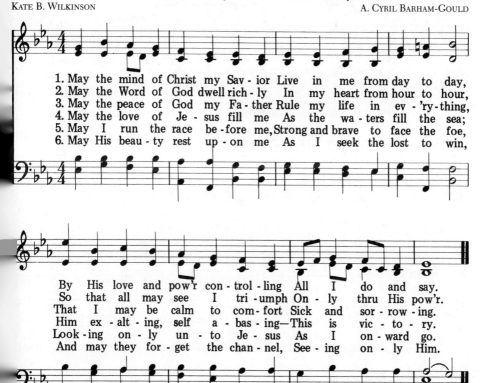

1. May the mind of Christ my Sav-ior Live in me from day to day,
2. May the Word of God dwell rich-ly In my heart from hour to hour,
3. May the peace of God my Fa-ther Rule my life in ev-'ry-thing,
4. May the love of Je-sus fill me As the wa-ters fill the sea;
5. May I run the race be-fore me, Strong and brave to face the foe,
6. May His beau-ty rest up-on me As I seek the lost to win,

By His love and pow'r con-trol-ling All I do and say.
So that all may see I tri-umph On-ly thru His pow'r.
That I may be calm to com-fort Sick and sor-row-ing.
Him ex-alt-ing, self a-bas-ing—This is vic-to-ry.
Look-ing on-ly un-to Je-sus As I on-ward go.
And may they for-get the chan-nel, See-ing on-ly Him.

403 O to Be Like Thee!

...to be conformed to the image of His Son. Rom. 8:29

THOMAS O. CHISHOLM

WILLIAM J. KIRKPATRICK

1. O to be like Thee! bless-ed Re-deem-er, This is my con-stant
2. O to be like Thee! full of com-pas-sion, Lov-ing, for-giv-ing,
3. O to be like Thee! low-ly in spir-it, Ho-ly and harm-less,
4. O to be like Thee! while I am plead-ing, Pour out Thy Spir-it,

long-ing and prayer. Glad-ly I'll for-feit all of earth's treas-ures,
ten-der and kind, Help-ing the help-less, cheer-ing the faint-ing,
pa-tient and brave; Meek-ly en-dur-ing cru-el re-proach-es,
fill with Thy love; Make me a tem-ple meet for Thy dwell-ing,

Refrain

Je-sus, Thy per-fect like-ness to wear.
Seek-ing the wan-d'ring sin-ner to find.
Will-ing to suf-fer 'oth-ers to save.
Fit me for life and heav-en a-bove.

O to be like Thee!

O to be like Thee, Bless-ed Re-deem-er, pure as Thou art! Come in Thy

sweet-ness, come in Thy full-ness; Stamp Thine own im-age deep on my heart.

Prayer of Cleansing

Almighty God,
to whom all hearts are open,
all desires known,
and from whom no secrets are hidden:
cleanse the thoughts of our hearts
by the inspiration of Your Holy Spirit,
that we may perfectly love You,
and worthily magnify Your holy name;
through Christ our Lord. *Amen.*

Channels Only   405

A vessel unto honor... and fit for the Master's use... II Tim. 2:21

MARY E. MAXWELL

ADA R. GIBBS

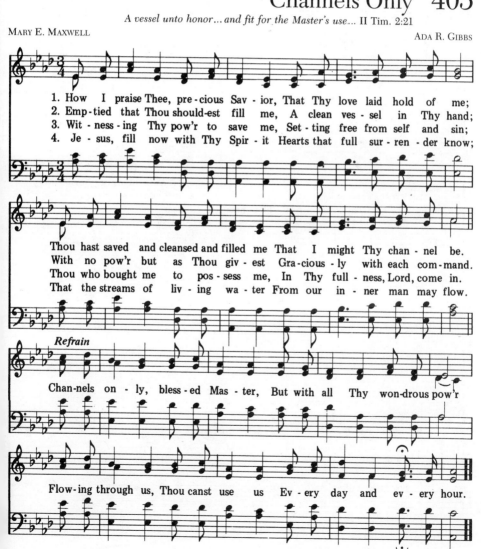

1. How I praise Thee, pre-cious Sav-ior, That Thy love laid hold of me;
2. Emp-tied that Thou should-est fill me, A clean ves-sel in Thy hand;
3. Wit-ness-ing Thy pow'r to save me, Set-ting free from self and sin;
4. Je-sus, fill now with Thy Spir-it Hearts that full sur-ren-der know;

Thou hast saved and cleansed and filled me That I might Thy chan-nel be.
With no pow'r but as Thou giv-est Gra-cious-ly with each com-mand.
Thou who bought me to pos-sess me, In Thy full-ness, Lord, come in.
That the streams of liv-ing wa-ter From our in-ner man may flow.

Refrain

Chan-nels on-ly, bless-ed Mas-ter, But with all Thy won-drous pow'r

Flow-ing through us, Thou canst use us Ev-ery day and ev-ery hour.

406 Bring Back the Springtime

Lo, the winter is past...the time of the singing of birds is come. Song of Sol. 2:11,12

KURT KAISER

KURT KAISER

1. When in the spring the flow'rs are bloom-ing bright and fair Aft-er the
2. Lord, make me like that stream that flows so cool and clear Down from the

gray of win-ter's gone, Once a-gain the lark be-gins its
moun-tains high a-bove; I will tell the world the won-drous

tun-ing Back in the mead-ows of my home.
sto-ry Of the pre-cious stream filled with your love.

Refrain

Lord, to my heart bring back the spring-time, Take a-way the

cold and dark of sin; O re-turn to me, sweet Ho-ly

Spir - it, May I warm and ten - der be a - gain.

Close to Thee 407

Surely, I am with you always...Matt. 28:20

FANNY J. CROSBY   SILAS J. VAIL

1. Thou, my ev - er - last - ing por - tion, More than friend or life to me;
2. Not for ease or world - ly pleas - ure, Nor for fame my prayer shall be;
3. Lead me thro' the vale of shad - ows, Bear me o'er life's fit - ful sea;

All a - long my pil - grim jour - ney, Sav - ior, let me walk with Thee.
Glad - ly will I toil and suf - fer, On - ly let me walk with Thee.
Then the gate of life e - ter - nal May I en - ter, Lord, with Thee.

Chorus

Close to Thee, close to Thee, Close to Thee, close to Thee;

All a - long my pil - grim jour - ney, Sav - ior, let me walk with Thee.
Glad - ly will I toil and suf - fer, On - ly let me walk with Thee.
Then the gate of life e - ter - nal May I en - ter, Lord, with Thee.

408 I Surrender All

Lo, we have left all, and have followed Thee. Mark 10:28

JUDSON W. VAN DE VENTER

WINFIELD S. WEEDEN

1. All to Je - sus I sur - ren - der, All to Him I free - ly give;
2. All to Je - sus I sur - ren - der, Hum - bly at His feet I bow,
3. All to Je - sus I sur - ren - der, Make me, Sav - ior, whol - ly Thine;
4. All to Je - sus I sur - ren - der, Lord, I give my - self to Thee;

I will ev - er love and trust Him, In His pres - ence dai - ly live.
World - ly pleas - ures all for - sak - en, Take me, Je - sus, take me now.
May Thy Ho - ly Spir - it fill me, May I know Thy pow'r di - vine.
Fill me with Thy love and pow - er, Let Thy bless - ing fall on me.

Refrain

I sur - ren - der all, I sur - ren - der all.
I sur - ren - der all, I sur - ren - der all.

All to Thee, my bless - ed Sav - ior, I sur - ren - der all.

Make Me a Captive, Lord 409

...He that loseth his life for My sake shall find it. Matt. 10:39

GEORGE MATHESON

DONALD P. HUSTAD

1. Make me a cap-tive, Lord, And then I shall be free;
2. My heart is weak and poor Un-til it mas-ter find;
3. My pow'r is faint and low Till I have learned to serve;
4. My will is not my own Till Thou hast made it Thine;

Force me to ren-der up my sword, And I shall con-queror be;
It has no spring of ac-tion sure— It var-ies with the wind;
It wants the need-ed fire to glow, It wants the breeze to nerve;
If it would reach the mon-arch's throne It must its crown re-sign:

I sink in life's a-larms When by my-self I stand;
It can-not free-ly move Till Thou hast wrought its chain;
It can-not drive the world Un-til it-self be driv'n;
It on-ly stands un-bent, A-mid the clash-ing strife,

Im-pris-on me with-in Thine arms, And strong shall be my hand.
En-slave it with Thy match-less love, And death-less it shall reign.
Its flag can on-ly be un-furled When Thou shalt breathe from heav'n.
When on Thy bos-om it has leaned, And found in Thee its life.

410 Cleanse Me

Search me, O God, and know my heart...Psa. 139:23

J. EDWIN ORR

TRADITIONAL MAORI MELODY

1. Search me, O God, and know my heart to-day; Try me, O
2. I praise Thee, Lord, for cleans-ing me from sin; Ful-fill Thy
3. Lord, take my life and make it whol-ly Thine; Fill my poor
4. O Ho-ly Spir-it, re-viv-al comes from Thee; Send a re-

Sav-ior, know my thoughts, I pray. See if there be some wick-ed
Word and make me pure with-in. Fill me with fire where once I
heart with Thy great love di-vine. Take all my will, my pas-sion,
viv-al— start the work in me. Thy Word de-clares Thou wilt sup-

way in me; Cleanse me from ev-ery sin and set me free.
burned with shame; Grant my de-sire to mag-ni-fy Thy name.
self and pride; I now sur-ren-der, Lord— in me a-bide.
ply our need; For bless-ings now, O Lord, I hum-bly plead.

411   The Heart-Search

The heart is deceitful above all things
and beyond cure.
Who can understand it?

"I the Lord search the heart
and examine the mind,
to reward a man according to his
conduct,
according to what his deeds
deserve."

Jeremiah 17:9, 10 (NIV)

Draw Me Nearer 412

Let us draw near with a true heart ... Heb. 10:22

FANNY J. CROSBY   WILLIAM H. DOANE

1. I am Thine, O Lord, I have heard Thy voice, And it
2. Con - se - crate me now to Thy serv - ice, Lord, By the
3. O, the pure de - light of a sin - gle hour That be -
4. There are depths of love that I can - not know Till I

told Thy love to me; But I long to rise in the arms of faith,
pow'r of grace di - vine; Let my soul look up with a stead - fast hope,
fore Thy throne I spend, When I kneel in prayer, and with Thee, my God,
cross the nar - row sea; There are heights of joy that I may not reach

Refrain

And be clos - er drawn to Thee.
And my will be lost in Thine.
I com - mune as friend with friend!   Draw me near - er,
Till I rest in peace with Thee.

near - er, bless - ed Lord, To the cross where Thou hast died; Draw me

near - er, near - er, near - er, bless - ed Lord, To Thy pre - cious, bleed - ing side.

413 Living for Jesus

That ye might walk worthy of the Lord...Col. 1:10

THOMAS O. CHISHOLM

C. HAROLD LOWDEN

1. Liv-ing for Je-sus a life that is true, Striv-ing to please Him in
2. Liv-ing for Je-sus who died in my place, Bear-ing on Cal-v'ry my
3. Liv-ing for Je-sus wher-ev-er I am, Do-ing each du-ty in
4. Liv-ing for Je-sus through earth's lit-tle while, My dear-est treas-ure, the

all that I do; Yield-ing al-le-giance, glad-heart-ed and free,
sin and dis-grace; Such love con-strains me to an-swer His call,
His ho-ly name; Will-ing to suf-fer af-flic-tion and loss,
light of His smile; Seek-ing the lost ones He died to re-deem,

Refrain

This is the path-way of bless-ing for me.
Fol-low His lead-ing and give Him my all.   O Je-sus, Lord and
Deem-ing each tri-al a part of my cross.
Bring-ing the wea-ry to find rest in Him.

Sav-ior, I give my-self to Thee, For Thou, in Thy a-tone-ment, Didst

give Thy-self for me; I own no oth-er Mas-ter, My heart shall be Thy

throne; My life I give, hence-forth to live, O Christ, for Thee a-lone.

Have Thine Own Way, Lord 414

We are the clay, and Thou our potter...Isa. 64:8

ADELAIDE A. POLLARD

GEORGE C. STEBBINS

1. Have Thine own way, Lord! Have Thine own way! Thou art the
Pot - ter, I am the clay. Mold me and make me aft - er Thy
will, While I am wait - ing yield - ed and still.

2. Have Thine own way, Lord! Have Thine own way! Search me and
try me, Mas - ter, to - day! Whit - er than snow, Lord, wash me just
now, As in Thy pres - ence hum - bly I bow.

3. Have Thine own way, Lord! Have Thine own way! Wound - ed and
wea - ry, help me, I pray! Pow - er— all pow - er— sure - ly is
Thine! Touch me and heal me, Sav - ior di - vine!

4. Have Thine own way, Lord! Have Thine own way! Hold o'er my
be - ing ab - so - lute sway! Fill with Thy Spir - it till all shall
see Christ on - ly, al - ways, liv - ing in me! A - men.

415 Make Me a Servant

By love serve one another Gal. 5:13

KELLY WILLARD   KELLY WILLARD

Make me a ser-vant, hum-ble and meek; Lord, let me

lift up those who are weak. And may the prayer of my

heart al-ways be: Make me a ser-vant, make me a

ser-vant, make me a ser-vant to-day.

416   The Servant *Adapted from John 13 (NIV)*

It was just before the Passover Feast. Jesus knew that His time had come. Having loved His own, He now showed them the full extent of His love.

While the evening meal was being served, Jesus rose, wrapped a towel around His waist, and began washing His disciples' feet. When He had finished, He returned to His place.

"Do you understand what I have done for you?" He asked them. Now that I, your Lord and Teacher, have washed your feet . . . I have set you an example. This is the truth: No servant is greater than his master, nor is a messenger greater than the one who sent him.

Now that you know these things, you will be blessed if you do them.

Let the Words of My Mouth 417

...And my heart's meditation be acceptable, O Lord. Psa. 19:14

BASED ON PSALM 19:14

WARREN W. WIERSBE

Let the words of my mouth, and my heart's med-i-ta-tion Be ac-

cept-a-ble to Thee, O Lord (O Lord). Lord (O Lord). In Thy

sight (in Thy sight), In Thy sight (in Thy sight), May my heart's med-i-

ta-tion be right (be right). Let the words of my mouth, and my

heart's med-i-ta-tion Be ac-cept-a-ble to Thee, O Lord (O Lord).

418 Dear Lord and Father of Mankind

...Sitting at the feet of Jesus, clothed, and in his right mind. Luke 8:35

JOHN G. WHITTIER

FREDERICK C. MAKER

1. Dear Lord and Fa - ther of man - kind, For - give our fool - ish
2. In sim - ple trust like theirs who heard, Be - side the Syr - ian
3. Drop Thy still dews of qui - et - ness, Till all our striv - ings
4. Breathe through the heats of our de - sire Thy cool - ness and Thy

ways! Re - clothe us in our right - ful mind; In pur - er
Sea, The gra - cious call - ing of the Lord, Let us, like
cease; Take from our souls the strain and stress, And let our
balm; Let sense be dumb, let flesh re - tire; Speak through the

lives Thy serv - ice find, In deep - er rev - 'rence, praise.
them, with - out a word, Rise up and fol - low Thee.
or - dered lives con - fess The beau - ty of Thy peace.
earth - quake, wind, and fire, O still small voice of calm! A-men.

419 I Am Trusting Thee, Lord Jesus

Trust ye in the Lord forever... Isa. 26:4

FRANCES R. HAVERGAL

ETHELBERT W. BULLINGER

1. I am trust - ing Thee, Lord Je - sus, Trust - ing on - ly Thee;
2. I am trust - ing Thee to guide me; Thou a - lone shalt lead,
3. I am trust - ing Thee for pow - er: Thine can nev - er fail;
4. I am trust - ing Thee, Lord Je - sus; Nev - er let me fall;

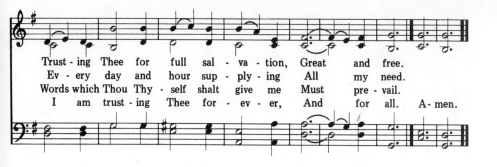

Trust - ing Thee for full sal - va - tion, Great and free.
Ev - ery day and hour sup - ply - ing All my need.
Words which Thou Thy - self shalt give me Must pre - vail.
I am trust - ing Thee for - ev - er, And for all. A - men.

Teach Me Thy Will, O Lord 420

Teach me to do Thy will; for Thou art my God. Psa. 143:10

KATHERINE A. GRIMES   WILLIAM M. RUNYAN

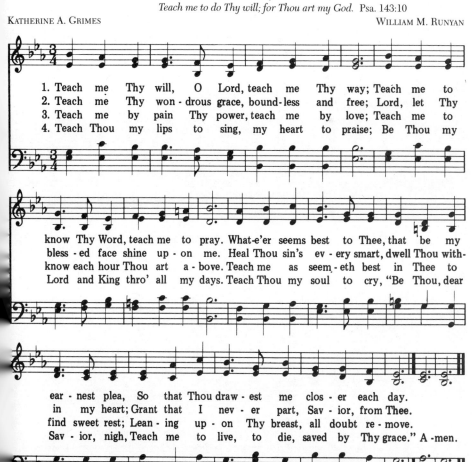

1. Teach me Thy will, O Lord, teach me Thy way; Teach me to
2. Teach me Thy won - drous grace, bound-less and free; Lord, let Thy
3. Teach me by pain Thy power, teach me by love; Teach me to
4. Teach Thou my lips to sing, my heart to praise; Be Thou my

know Thy Word, teach me to pray. What-e'er seems best to Thee, that be my
bless - ed face shine up - on me. Heal Thou sin's ev - ery smart, dwell Thou with-
know each hour Thou art a - bove. Teach me as seem - eth best in Thee to
Lord and King thro' all my days. Teach Thou my soul to cry, "Be Thou, dear

ear - nest plea, So that Thou draw - est me clos - er each day.
in my heart; Grant that I nev - er part, Sav - ior, from Thee.
find sweet rest; Lean - ing up - on Thy breast, all doubt re - move.
Sav - ior, nigh, Teach me to live, to die, saved by Thy grace." A - men.

421 All for Jesus

Offer your bodies as living sacrifices...to God—this is your spiritual...worship. Rom. 12:1

MARY D. JAMES   UNKNOWN

1. All   for Je - sus, all   for Je - sus! All   my   be-ing's ran-somed pow'rs:
2. Let   my hands per-form His   bid - ding, Let   my feet run   in   His ways;
3. Since my eyes were fixed on   Je - sus, I've lost sight of   all   be - side;
4. Oh,   what won-der! how a -maz - ing! Je - sus, glo-rious King of kings,

All   my tho'ts and words and do - ings, All   my days and   all   my hours.
Let   my eyes see Je - sus on - ly, Let   my lips speak forth His praise.
So   en-chained my spir- it's vi - sion, Look-ing   at   the Cru - ci - fied.
Deigns to call me His be -lov - ed, Let's me rest be - neath His wings.

Refrain

All   for Je - sus! all   for Je - sus! All   my   days and all   my hours;
All   for Je - sus! all   for Je - sus! Let   my   lips speak forth His praise;
All   for Je - sus! all   for Je - sus! Look-ing   at   the Cru - ci - fied;
All   for Je - sus! all   for Je - sus! Rest - ing now be -neath His wings;

All   for Je - sus! all   for Je - sus! All   my days and   all   my hours.
All   for Je - sus! all   for Je - sus! Let   my lips speak forth His praise.
All   for Je - sus! all   for Je - sus! Look-ing   at   the Cru - ci - fied.
All   for Je - sus! all   for Je - sus! Rest - ing now be -neath His wings.

Give of Your Best to the Master 422

Unto whomsoever much is given, of him shall much be required. Luke 12:48

HOWARD B. GROSE

CHARLOTTE A. BARNARD

1. Give of your best to the Mas-ter, Give of the strength of your youth;
2. Give of your best to the Mas-ter, Give Him first place in your heart;
3. Give of your best to the Mas-ter, Naught else is wor-thy His love;
Ch. Give of your best to the Mas-ter, Give of the strength of your youth;

Fine

Throw your soul's fresh, glow-ing ar - dor In-to the bat-tle for truth.
Give Him first place in your serv-ice, Con-se-crate ev - ery part.
He gave Him-self for your ran-som, Gave up His glo-ry a - bove;
Clad in sal - va-tion's full ar - mor, Join in the bat-tle for truth.

Je - sus has set the ex - am - ple—Daunt-less was He, young and brave;
Give, and to you shall be giv - en— God His be - lov - ed Son gave;
Laid down His life with-out mur - mur, You from sin's ru - in to save;

D. C. Chorus

Give Him your loy - al de - vo - tion, Give Him the best that you have.
Grate-ful - ly seek-ing to serve Him, Give Him the best that you have.
Give Him your heart's ad-o - ra - tion, Give Him the best that you have.

423 Fill All My Vision

They saw no man, save Jesus only. Matt. 17:8

AVIS B. CHRISTIANSEN

HOMER HAMMONTREE

1. Fill all my vi - sion, Sav - ior, I pray, Let me see on - ly
2. Fill all my vi - sion, ev - ery de - sire Keep for Thy glo - ry;
3. Fill all my vi - sion, let naught of sin Shad - ow the bright - ness

Je - sus to - day; Though thro' the val - ley Thou lead - est me,
my soul in - spire With Thy per - fec - tion, Thy ho - ly love
shin - ing with - in. Let me see on - ly Thy bless - ed face,

Refrain

Give me Thy glo - ry and beau - ty to see.
Flood - ing my path - way with light from a - bove. Fill all my vi - sion,
Feast - ing my soul on Thy in - fi - nite grace.

Sav - ior di - vine, Till with Thy glo - ry my spir - it shall shine. Fill all my

vi - sion, that all may see Thy ho - ly im - age re - flect - ed in me.

Teach Me Thy Way, O Lord 424

Teach me Thy way, O Lord, and lead me in a plain path. Psa. 27:11

B. MANSELL RAMSEY   B. MANSELL RAMSEY

1. Teach me Thy way, O Lord, Teach me Thy way! Thy guid-ing grace af-ford—
2. When I am sad at heart, Teach me Thy way! When earth-ly joys de-part,
3. When doubts and fears a-rise, Teach me Thy way! When storms o'er-spread the skies,
4. Long as my life shall last, Teach me Thy way! Wher-e'er my lot be cast,

Teach me Thy way! Help me to walk a-right, More by faith,
Teach me Thy way! In hours of lone-li-ness, In times of
Teach me Thy way! Shine thro' the cloud and rain, Thro' sor-row,
Teach me Thy way! Un-til the race is run, Un-til the

less by sight; Lead me with heav'n-ly light, Teach me Thy way!
dire dis-tress, In fail-ure or suc-cess, Teach me Thy way!
toil and pain; Make Thou my path-way plain, Teach me Thy way!
jour-ney's done, Un-til the crown is won, Teach me Thy way! A-men.

Christ, My Every Need 425

Lord, Jesus Christ,
you are for me medicine when I am sick;
you are my strength when I need help;
you are life itself when I fear death;
you are the way when I long for heaven;
you are light when all is dark;
you are my food when I need nourishment.

Ambrose

426 Lead Me to Calvary

Consider Him that endured such contradiction of sinners against Himself. Heb. 12:3

JENNIE E. HUSSEY

WILLIAM J. KIRKPATRICK

1. King of my life, I crown Thee now, Thine shall the glo - ry be;
2. Show me the tomb where Thou wast laid, Ten - der - ly mourned and wept;
3. Let me, like Ma - ry thro' the gloom, Come with a gift to Thee;
4. May I be will - ing, Lord, to bear Dai - ly my cross for Thee;

Lest I for - get Thy thorn-crowned brow, Lead me to Cal - va - ry.
An - gels in robes of light ar - rayed Guard - ed Thee whilst Thou slept.
Show to me now the emp - ty tomb, Lead me to Cal - va - ry.
E - ven Thy cup of grief to share, Thou hast borne all for me.

Refrain

Lest I for - get Geth - sem - a - ne; Lest I for - get Thine ag - o - ny;

Lest I for - get Thy love for me, Lead me to Cal - va - ry.

427 I Have Decided to Follow Jesus

Master, I will follow Thee whithersoever Thou goest. Matt. 8:19

UNKNOWN

FOLK MELODY FROM INDIA

Unison

1. I have de - cid - ed to fol - low Je - sus, I have de - cid - ed to fol - low
2. The world be-hind me, the cross be-fore me; The world be-hind me, the cross be-
3. Tho' none go with me, I still will fol - low, Tho' none go with me, I still will
4. Will you de - cide now to fol - low Je - sus? Will you de - cide now to fol - low

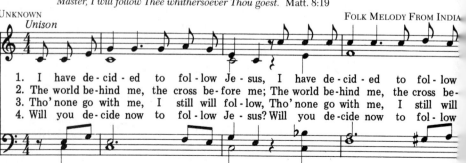

Je-sus, I have de-cid-ed to fol-low Je-sus, No turn-ing back, no turn-ing back.
fore me; The world be-hind me, the cross be-fore me, No turn-ing back, no turn-ing back.
fol-low, Tho' none go with me, I still will fol-low, No turn-ing back, no turn-ing back.
Je-sus, Will you de-cide now to fol-low Je-sus? No turn-ing back, no turn-ing back.

More Love to Thee 428

This I pray, that your love may abound yet more and more. Phil. 1:9

ELIZABETH P. PRENTISS   WILLIAM H. DOANE

1. More love to Thee, O Christ, More love to Thee! Hear Thou the
2. Once earth-ly joy I craved, Sought peace and rest; Now Thee a-
3. Let sor-row do its work, Send grief and pain; Sweet are Thy
4. Then shall my lat-est breath Whis-per Thy praise; This be the

prayer I make On bend-ed knee; This is my ear-nest plea:
lone I seek, Give what is best; This all my prayer shall be:
mes-sen-gers, Sweet their re-frain, When they can sing with me:
part-ing cry My heart shall raise; This still its prayer shall be:

More love, O Christ, to Thee, More love to Thee, More love to Thee! A-men.

429 Jesus Is Lord of All

For he is Lord of lords, and King of kings...Rev. 17:14

WILLIAM J. AND GLORIA GAITHER

WILLIAM J. GAITHER

1. All my to-mor-rows, all my past, Je-sus is Lord of
2. All of my con-flicts, all my thoughts, Je-sus is Lord of
3. All of my long-ings, all my dreams, Je-sus is Lord of

all. I've quit my strug-gles, con-tent-ment at last,
all. His love wins the bat-tles I could not have fought,
all. All of my fail-ures His pow-er re-deems,

Chorus

Je-sus is Lord of all.
Je-sus is Lord of all. King of kings, Lord of lords,
Je-sus is Lord of all.

Je-sus is Lord of all; All my pos-sess-ions and

all my life, Je-sus is Lord of all.

All That Thrills My Soul 430

My Beloved is ... the chiefest among ten thousand. S. of Sol. 5:10

THORO HARRIS   THORO HARRIS

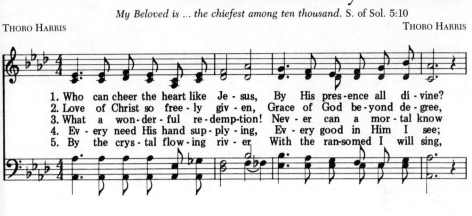

1. Who can cheer the heart like Je - sus, By His pres - ence all di - vine?
2. Love of Christ so free - ly giv - en, Grace of God be - yond de - gree,
3. What a won - der - ful re - demp - tion! Nev - er can a mor - tal know
4. Ev - ery need His hand sup - ply - ing, Ev - ery good in Him I see;
5. By the crys - tal flow - ing riv - er With the ran - somed I will sing,

True and ten - der, pure and pre - cious, O how blest to call Him mine!
Mer - cy high - er than the heav - en, Deep - er than the deep - est sea.
How my sin, tho' red like crim - son, Can be whit - er than the snow.
On His strength di - vine re - ly - ing, He is all in all to me.
And for - ev - er and for - ev - er, Praise and glo - ri - fy the King.

Chorus

All that thrills my soul is Je - sus, He is more than life to me. (to me);

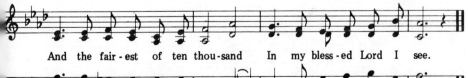

And the fair - est of ten thou - sand In my bless - ed Lord I see.

431 I Would Be Like Jesus

We...are changed into the same image from glory to glory. II Cor. 3:18

JAMES ROWE

BENTLEY D. ACKLEY

1. Earth-ly pleas-ures vain-ly call me, I would be like Je - sus;
2. He has bro-ken ev-ery fet-ter, I would be like Je - sus;
3. All the way from earth to glo-ry, I would be like Je - sus;
4. That in heav-en He may meet me, I would be like Je - sus;
    would be like Je - sus;

Noth-ing world-ly shall en-thrall me, I would be like Je - sus.
That my soul may serve Him bet-ter, I would be like Je - sus.
Tell-ing o'er and o'er the sto-ry, I would be like Je - sus.
That His words "Well done" may greet me, I would be like Je - sus.
    would be like Je - sus.

Refrain

Be like Je-sus, this my song, In the home and in the throng

Be like Je-sus, all day long! I would be like Je - sus.

I Would Be True 432

Be thou an example of the believers ... I Tim. 4:12

HOWARD A. WALTER

JOSEPH Y. PEEK

1. I would be true, for there are those who trust me; I would be
pure, for there are those who care: I would be strong, for there is
much to suf - fer; I would be brave, for there is much to
dare; I would be brave, for there is much to dare.

2. I would be friend of all— the foe, the friend - less; I would be
giv - ing, and for - get the gift; I would be hum - ble, for I
know my weak - ness; I would look up, and laugh, and love, and
lift; I would look up, and laugh, and love, and lift.

3. I would be learn - ing day by day the les - sons My heav'n - ly
Fa - ther gives me in His Word; I would be quick to hear His
light - est whis - per, And prompt and glad to do the things I've
heard; And prompt and glad to do the things I've heard.

4. I would be prayer - ful through each bus - y mo - ment; I would be
con - stant - ly in touch with God; I would be tuned to hear His
slight - est whis - per, I would have faith to keep the path Christ
trod; I would have faith to keep the path Christ trod. A - men.

433 Near to the Heart of God

Draw nigh to God, and He will draw nigh to you. James 4:8

CLELAND B. MCAFEE

CLELAND B. MCAFEE

1. There is a place of qui - et rest Near to the heart of God,
2. There is a place of com - fort sweet Near to the heart of God,
3. There is a place of full re - lease Near to the heart of God,

A place where sin can - not mo - lest, Near to the heart of God.
A place where we our Sav - ior meet, Near to the heart of God.
A place where all is joy and peace, Near to the heart of God.

Refrain

O Je - sus, blest Re - deem - er Sent from the heart of God,

Hold us who wait be - fore Thee Near to the heart of God.

434 Our Dwelling Place

I love, my God, but with no love of mine,
  For I have none to give;
I love Thee, Lord, but all the Love is Thine,
  For by Thy life I live.
I am as nothing, and rejoice to be
Emptied and lost and swallowed up in Thee.
Thou, Lord, alone art all Thy children need,
  And there is none beside;
From Thee the streams of blessedness proceed;
  In Thee the blest abide,
Fountain of life, and all-abounding grace,
Our source, our center, and our dwelling place!

Madame Jeanne Marie Guyon

Moment by Moment 435

Who are kept by the power of God through faith unto salvation. I Pet. 1:5

DANIEL W. WHITTLE   MAY W. MOODY

1. Dy - ing with Je - sus, by death reck-oned mine; Liv - ing with Je - sus a
2. Nev - er a tri - al that He is not there, Nev - er a bur - den that
3. Nev - er a heart-ache and nev - er a groan, Nev - er a tear-drop and
4. Nev - er a weak-ness that He doth not feel, Nev - er a sick-ness that

new life di - vine; Look-ing to Je - sus till glo - ry doth shine, Mo-ment by
He doth not bear, Nev - er a sor - row that He doth not share, Mo-ment by
nev - er a moan; Nev - er a dan - ger, but there on the throne, Mo-ment by
He can - not heal; Mo-ment by mo-ment, in woe or in weal, Je - sus my

Refrain

mo - ment, O Lord, I am Thine.
mo - ment, I'm un - der His care.   Mo-ment by mo-ment I'm kept in His love;
mo - ment, He thinks of His own.
Sav - ior a - bides with me still.

Mo - ment by mo-ment I've life from a - bove; Look-ing to Je - sus till

glo - ry doth shine; Mo - ment by mo - ment, O Lord, I am Thine.

436 Take My Life and Let It Be

Ye are bought with a price; therefore glorify God in your body...I Cor. 6:20

FRANCES R. HAVERGAL

HENRI A. CÉSAR MALAN

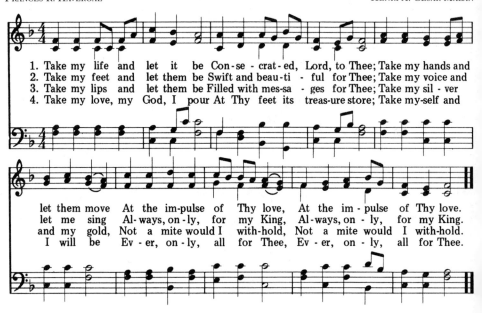

1. Take my life and let it be Con-se-crat-ed, Lord, to Thee; Take my hands and
2. Take my feet and let them be Swift and beau-ti-ful for Thee; Take my voice and
3. Take my lips and let them be Filled with mes-sa-ges for Thee; Take my sil-ver
4. Take my love, my God, I pour At Thy feet its treas-ure store; Take my-self and

let them move At the im-pulse of Thy love, At the im-pulse of Thy love.
let me sing Al-ways, on-ly, for my King, Al-ways, on-ly, for my King.
and my gold, Not a mite would I with-hold, Not a mite would I with-hold.
I will be Ev-er, on-ly, all for Thee, Ev-er, on-ly, all for Thee.

437 Nearer, My God, to Thee

It is good for me to draw near to God...Psa. 73:28

SARAH F. ADAMS

LOWELL MASON

1. Near-er, my God, to Thee, Near-er to Thee! E'en though it
2. Though like the wan-der-er, The sun gone down, Dark-ness be
3. There let the way ap-pear Steps un-to heav'n; All that Thou
4. Then, with my wak-ing thoughts Bright with Thy praise, Out of my
5. Or if on joy-ful wing, Cleav-ing the sky, Sun, moon, and

be a cross That rais-eth me; Still all my song shall be, Near-er, my
o-ver me, My rest a stone; Yet in my dreams I'd be Near-er, my
send-est me In mer-cy giv'n; An-gels to beck-on me Near-er, my
ston-y griefs, Beth-el I'll raise; So by my woes to be Near-er, my
stars for-got, Up-ward I fly, Still all my song shall be Near-er, my

God, to Thee, Near-er, my God, to Thee, Near-er to Thee. A-men.

Nearer, Still Nearer 438

For to me to live is Christ, and to die is gain. Phil. 1:21

LELIA N. MORRIS   LELIA N. MORRIS

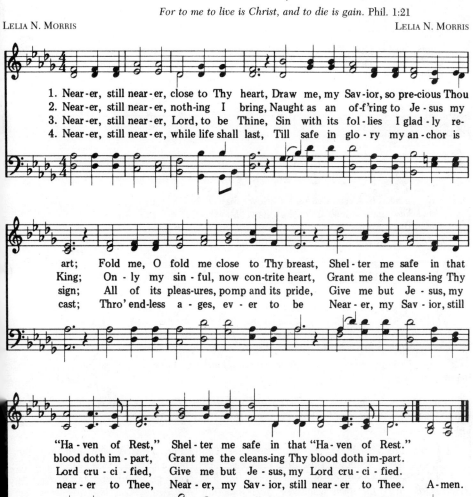

1. Near-er, still near-er, close to Thy heart, Draw me, my Sav-ior, so pre-cious Thou
2. Near-er, still near-er, noth-ing I bring, Naught as an of-f'ring to Je-sus my
3. Near-er, still near-er, Lord, to be Thine, Sin with its fol-lies I glad-ly re-
4. Near-er, still near-er, while life shall last, Till safe in glo-ry my an-chor is

art;   Fold me, O fold me close to Thy breast, Shel-ter me safe in that
King;   On-ly my sin-ful, now con-trite heart, Grant me the cleans-ing Thy
sign;   All of its pleas-ures, pomp and its pride, Give me but Je-sus, my
cast;   Thro' end-less a-ges, ev-er to be Near-er, my Sav-ior, still

"Ha-ven of Rest,"   Shel-ter me safe in that "Ha-ven of Rest."
blood doth im-part,   Grant me the cleans-ing Thy blood doth im-part.
Lord cru-ci-fied,   Give me but Je-sus, my Lord cru-ci-fied.
near-er to Thee,   Near-er, my Sav-ior, still near-er to Thee. A-men.

439 O Love That Will Not Let Me Go

The Lord hath appeared..saying, Yea, I have loved thee with an everlasting love. Jer. 31:3

GEORGE MATHESON   ALBERT L. PEACE

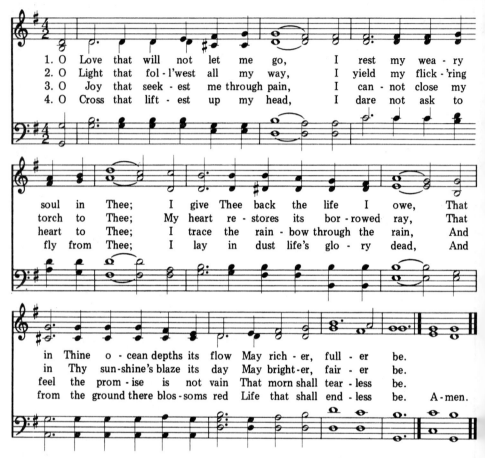

1. O Love that will not let me go, I rest my wea - ry soul in Thee; I give Thee back the life I owe, That in Thine o - cean depths its flow May rich - er, full - er be.
2. O Light that fol - l'west all my way, I yield my flick - 'ring torch to Thee; My heart re - stores its bor - rowed ray, That in Thy sun - shine's blaze its day May bright - er, fair - er be.
3. O Joy that seek - est me through pain, I can - not close my heart to Thee; I trace the rain - bow through the rain, And feel the prom - ise is not vain That morn shall tear - less be.
4. O Cross that lift - est up my head, I dare not ask to fly from Thee; I lay in dust life's glo - ry dead, And from the ground there blos - soms red Life that shall end - less be. A - men.

440 I'll Live for Him

That they might live...unto Him which died for them. II Cor. 5:15

RALPH E. HUDSON   C.R. DUNBAR

1. My life, my love I give to Thee, Thou Lamb of God who died for me;
2. I now be - lieve Thou dost re - ceive, For Thou hast died that I might live;
3. O Thou who died on Cal - va - ry, To save my soul and make me free,
Ref. – I'll live for Him who died for me, How hap - py then my life shall be!

O may I ev - er faith - ful be, My Sav - ior and my God!
And now hence - forth I'll trust in Thee, My Sav - ior and my God!
I'll con - se - crate my life to Thee, My Sav - ior and my God!
I'll live for Him who died for me, My Sav - ior and my God!

Something for Jesus 441

...Faith which worketh by love. Gal. 5:6

SYLVANUS D. PHELPS

ROBERT LOWRY

1. Sav - ior, Thy dy - ing love Thou gav - est me, Nor should I
2. At the blest mer - cy - seat Plead - ing for me, My fee - ble
3. Give me a faith - ful heart, Like - ness to Thee, That each de -
4. All that I am and have— Thy gifts so free— In joy, in

aught with-hold, Dear Lord, from Thee: In love my soul would bow, My heart ful-
faith looks up, Je - sus, to Thee: Help me the cross to bear, Thy won-drous
part - ing day Henceforth may see Some work of love be - gun, Some deed of
grief, thro' life, Dear Lord, for Thee! And when Thy face I see, My ran-somed

fill its vow, Some of - fering bring Thee now, Some - thing for Thee.
love de - clare, Some song to raise, or prayer, Some - thing for Thee.
kind - ness done, Some wan - d'rer sought and won, Some - thing for Thee.
soul shall be Through all e - ter - ni - ty, Some - thing for Thee. A - men.

Guidance

I will instruct thee and teach thee
in the way which thou shalt go:
I will guide thee with mine eye.
Psalm 32:8

Guide Me, O Thou Great Jehovah 442

This God is our God...He will be our guide even unto death. Psa. 48:14

WILLIAM WILLIAMS   JOHN HUGHES

1. Guide me, O Thou great Je - ho - vah, Pil - grim through this bar - ren land;
2. O - pen now the crys - tal foun - tain, Whence the healing stream doth flow;
3. When I tread the verge of Jor - dan, Bid my anx - ious fears sub - side;

I am weak, but Thou art might - y; Hold me with Thy pow'r - ful hand;
Let the fire and cloud - y pil - lar Lead me all my jour - ney through;
Death of death, and hell's de - struc - tion, Land me safe on Ca - naan's side;

Bread of heav - en, Bread of heav - en, Feed me till I want no
Strong De - liv - erer, strong De - liv - erer, Be Thou still my strength and
Songs of prais - es, songs of prais - es I will ev - er give to

more, (want no more,) Feed me till I want no more.
shield, (strength and shield,) Be Thou still my strength and shield.
Thee, (give to Thee,) I will ev - er give to Thee. A - men.

443 The New 23rd

The Lord is my shepherd, I shall not want. Psa. 23:1

RALPH CARMICHAEL

RALPH CARMICHAEL

Unison

Be - cause the Lord is my Shep - herd, I have ev - ery - thing that I

need. He lets me rest in mead - ows green and leads me be - side the

qui - et stream. He keeps on giv - ing life to me, and helps me to

do what hon - ors Him the most. E - ven when walk - ing thro' the dark

val - ley of death, val - ley of death, I will nev - er

be a-fraid, for He is close be - side me. Guard-ing, guid - ing all the

way, He spreads a feast be - fore me in the pres - ence of my

en - e - mies. He wel-comes me as His spe - cial guest with bless-ing ev - er

flow - ing, His good-ness and un - fail - ing kind-ness shall be with me all of my

life, And af - ter-wards I shall live with Him for - ev - er, for - ev - er

in His home, for - ev - er in His home. For - ev - er in His home.

444 The Lord's My Shepherd

The Lord is my shepherd, I shall not want. Psa. 23:1

SCOTTISH PSALTER

JESSIE S. IRVINE

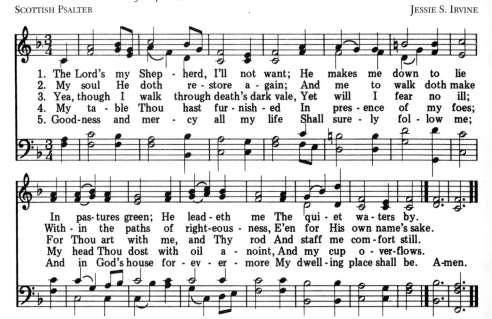

1. The Lord's my Shep - herd, I'll not want; He makes me down to lie
2. My soul He doth re - store a - gain; And me to walk doth make
3. Yea, though I walk through death's dark vale, Yet will I fear no ill;
4. My ta - ble Thou hast fur - nish - ed In pres - ence of my foes;
5. Good-ness and mer - cy all my life Shall sure - ly fol - low me;

In pas - tures green; He lead - eth me The qui - et wa - ters by.
With - in the paths of right-eous - ness, E'en for His own name's sake.
For Thou art with me, and Thy rod And staff me com - fort still.
My head Thou dost with oil a - noint, And my cup o - ver-flows.
And in God's house for - ev - er - more My dwell-ing place shall be. A-men.

445 Psalm 23

A Psalm of David.

The Lord is my shepherd; I shall not want.

He maketh me to lie down in green pastures: he leadeth me beside the still waters.

He restoreth my soul: he leadeth me in the paths of righteousness for his name's sake.

Yea, though I walk through the valley of the shadow of death, I will fear no evil: for thou art with me; thy rod and thy staff they comfort me.

Thou preparest a table before me in the presence of mine enemies: thou anointest my head with oil; my cup runneth over.

Surely goodness and mercy shall follow me all the days of my life: and I will dwell in the house of the Lord for ever.

Shepherd of Love 446

Our Lord Jesus, that great shepherd of the sheep ... Heb. 13:20

JOHN W. PETERSON

JOHN W. PETERSON

1. Shep - herd of love, You knew I had lost my way;
2. Shep - herd of love— Sav - ior and Lord and Guide,

Shep - herd of love, You cared that I'd gone a - stray.
Shep - herd of love, For - ev - er I'll stay by your side.

You sought and found me, placed a - round me

Strong arms that car - ried me home; No foe can harm me

D.C. al Fine

or a - larm me, Nev - er a - gain will I roam.

447 He Leadeth Me

I am the Lord thy God...which leadeth thee...Isa. 48:17

JOSEPH H. GILMORE   WILLIAM B. BRADBURY

1. He lead - eth me, O bless - ed thought! O words with heav'n - ly
2. Some-times 'mid scenes of deep - est gloom, Some-times where E - den's
3. Lord, I would clasp Thy hand in mine, Nor ev - er mur - mur
4. And when my task on earth is done, When by Thy grace the

com - fort fraught! What - e'er I do, wher - e'er I be, Still
bow - ers bloom, By wa - ters still, o'er trou - bled sea, Still
nor re - pine; Con - tent, what - ev - er lot I see, Since
vic - t'ry's won, E'en death's cold wave I will not flee, Since

Refrain

'tis God's hand that lead - eth me.
'tis His hand that lead - eth me.   He lead - eth me, He
'tis my God that lead - eth me.
God through Jor - dan lead - eth me.

lead - eth me! By His own hand He lead - eth me! His

faith - ful fol - l'wer I would be, For by His hand He lead-eth me.

Higher Ground 448

I press toward the mark for the prize... Phil. 3:14

JOHNSON OATMAN, JR.

CHARLES H. GABRIEL

1. I'm press-ing on the up-ward way, New heights I'm gain-ing ev-ery
2. My heart has no de-sire to stay Where doubts a-rise and fears dis-
3. I want to live a-bove the world, Though Sa-tan's darts at me are
4. I want to scale the ut-most height, And catch a gleam of glo-ry

day; Still pray-ing as I'm on-ward bound, "Lord, plant my
may; Though some may dwell where these a-bound, My prayer, my
hurled; For faith has caught the joy-ful sound, The song of
bright; But still I'll pray till heav'n I've found, "Lord, lead me

Refrain

feet on high-er ground."
aim is high-er ground. Lord, lift me up and let me stand
saints on high-er ground.
on to high-er ground."

By faith on heav-en's ta-ble-land, A high-er plane

than I have found; Lord, plant my feet on high-er ground.

449 Savior, Like a Shepherd Lead Us

When He putteth forth His own sheep, He goeth before them. John 10:4

ATTR. DOROTHY A. THRUPP

WILLIAM B. BRADBURY

1. Sav - ior, like a shep-herd lead us, Much we need Thy ten-der care;
2. We are Thine, do Thou be-friend us, Be the guard-ian of our way;
3. Thou hast prom-ised to re-ceive us, Poor and sin-ful though we be;
4. Ear - ly let us seek Thy fa - vor, Ear - ly let us do Thy will;

In Thy pleas-ant pas-tures feed us, For our use Thy folds pre-pare;
Keep Thy flock, from sin de - fend us, Seek us when we go a-stray:
Thou hast mer - cy to re - lieve us, Grace to cleanse, and pow'r to free:
Bless - ed Lord and on - ly Sav - ior, With Thy love our bos-oms fill:

Bless - ed Je - sus, bless - ed Je - sus, Thou hast bought us, Thine we are;
Bless - ed Je - sus, bless - ed Je - sus, Hear, O hear us when we pray;
Bless - ed Je - sus, bless - ed Je - sus, Ear - ly let us turn to Thee;
Bless - ed Je - sus, bless - ed Je - sus, Thou hast loved us, love us still;

Bless - ed Je - sus, bless - ed Je - sus, Thou hast bought us, Thine we are.
Bless - ed Je - sus, bless - ed Je - sus, Hear, O hear us when we pray.
Bless - ed Je - sus, bless - ed Je - sus, Ear - ly let us turn to Thee.
Bless - ed Je - sus, bless - ed Je - sus, Thou hast loved us, love us still.

Gentle Shepherd 450

He shall feed His flock like a shepherd. Isa. 40:11

GLORIA GAITHER

WILLIAM J. GAITHER

Gen-tle Shep-herd, come and lead us, For we need You to
help us find our way. Gen-tle Shep-herd, come and feed us,
For we need Your strength from day to day. There's no oth-er
we can turn to Who can help us face an-oth-er day; Gen-tle
Shep-herd, come and lead us, For we need You to help us find our way.

451 Like a River Glorious

Then had Thy peace been as a river...Isa. 48:18

FRANCES R. HAVERGAL

JAMES MOUNTAIN

1. Like a riv-er glo-rious Is God's per-fect peace, O-ver all vic-to-rious
2. Hid-den in the hol-low Of His bless-ed hand, Nev-er foe can fol-low,
3. Ev-ery joy or tri-al Fall-eth from a-bove, Traced up-on our di-al

In its bright in-crease: Per-fect, yet it flow-eth Full-er ev-ery day,
Nev-er trai-tor stand; Not a surge of wor-ry, Not a shade of care,
By the Sun of Love. We may trust Him ful-ly All for us to do;

Refrain

Per-fect, yet it grow-eth Deep-er all the way.
Not a blast of hur-ry Touch the spir-it there. Stayed up-on Je-ho-vah,
They who trust Him whol-ly Find Him whol-ly true.

Hearts are ful-ly blest; Find-ing, as He prom-ised, Per-fect peace and rest.

452 Christ's Peace

Peace I leave with you;
My peace I give you.
I do not give to you as the world gives.
Do not let your hearts be troubled
and do not be afraid.

I have told you these things,
so that in me you may have peace.
In this world you will have trouble.
But take heart!
I have overcome the world.
From the Gospel of John

It Is Well with My Soul 453

Blessed is the one who perseveres under trial. James 1:12

HORATIO G. SPAFFORD

PHILIP P. BLISS

1. When peace like a riv - er at - tend - eth my way, When sor - rows like
2. Though Sa - tan should buf - fet, tho' tri - als should come, Let this blest as -
3. My sin— O, the bliss of this glo - ri - ous thought, My sin— not in
4. And, Lord, haste the day when the faith shall be sight, The clouds be rolled

sea - bil - lows roll; What - ev - er my lot, Thou hast taught me to say,
sur - ance con - trol, That Christ has re - gard - ed my help - less es - tate,
part but the whole, Is nailed to the cross and I bear it no more,
back as a scroll, The trump shall re - sound and the Lord shall de - scend,

Refrain

"It is well, it is well with my soul."
And hath shed His own blood for my soul. It is well with my
Praise the Lord, praise the Lord, O my soul! It is well
"E - ven so"— it is well with my soul.

soul, It is well, it is well with my soul.
with my soul,

454 He Is Our Peace

The God of peace be with you all. Rom. 15:33

KANDELA GROVES

KANDELA GROVES

He is our peace, who has bro-ken down ev - ery wall;

He is our peace, He is our peace. peace.

Cast all your cares on Him, for He cares for you;

He is our peace, He is our peace. peace.

In Heavenly Love Abiding 455

If you obey my commands, you will remain in my love. John 15:10

ANNA L. WARING

FELIX MENDELSSOHN

1. In heav'n-ly love a-bid - ing, No change my heart shall fear;
2. Wher-ev - er He may guide me, No want shall turn me back;
3. Green pas-tures are be-fore me, Which yet I have not seen;

And safe is such con-fid - ing, For noth-ing chan - ges here.
My Shep-herd is be-side me, And noth-ing can I lack.
Bright skies will soon be o'er me, Where dark-est clouds have been.

The storm may roar with-out me, My heart may low be laid,
His wis - dom ev-er wak - eth; His sight is nev-er dim.
My hope I can-not meas - ure; My path to life is free;

But God is round a-bout me, And can I be dis-mayed?
He knows the way He tak - eth, And I will walk with Him.
My Sav-ior has my treas - ure, And He will walk with me.

456 Unto the Hills

I will lift up mine eyes unto the hills. Psa 121:1

JOHN D.S. CAMPBELL
BASED ON PSALM 121

CHARLES H. PURDAY

1. Un - to the hills a - round do I lift up My long - ing eyes;
2. He will not suf - fer that thy foot be moved: Safe shalt thou be.
3. Je - ho - vah is Him - self thy keep - er true, Thy change - less shade;
4. From ev - ery e - vil shall He keep thy soul, From ev - ery sin;

O whence for me shall my sal - va - tion come, From whence a - rise?
No care - less slum - ber shall His eye - lids close, Who keep - eth thee.
Je - ho - vah thy de - fense on thy right hand Him - self hath made.
Je - ho - vah shall pre - serve thy go - ing out, Thy com - ing in.

From God the Lord doth come my cer - tain aid,
Be - hold our God the Lord, He slum - bereth ne'er,
And thee no sun by day shall ev - er smite;
A - bove thee watch - ing, He whom we a - dore

From God the Lord who heav'n and earth hath made.
Who keep - eth Is - rael in His ho - ly care.
No moon shall harm thee in the si - lent night.
Shall keep thee hence - forth, yea, for - ev - er - more. A-men.

Be Still, My Soul 457

Be still, and know that I am God. Psa. 46:10

KATHARINE A. VON SCHLEGEL
TR. JANE L. BORTHWICK

JEAN SIBELIUS

1. Be still, my soul! the Lord is on thy side: Bear pa-tient-ly the
2. Be still, my soul! thy God doth un-der-take To guide the fu-ture
3. Be still, my soul! the hour is has-t'ning on When we shall be for-

cross of grief or pain; Leave to thy God to or-der and pro-vide;
as He has the past. Thy hope, thy con-fi-dence let noth-ing shake;
ev-er with the Lord, When dis-ap-point-ment, grief and fear are gone,

In ev-ery change He faith-ful will re-main. Be still, my soul! thy
All now mys-te-rious shall be bright at last. Be still, my soul! the
Sor-row for-got, love's pur-est joys re-stored. Be still, my soul! when

best, thy heav'n-ly Friend Thro' thorn-y ways leads to a joy-ful end.
waves and winds still know His voice who ruled them while He dwelt be-low.
change and tears are past, All safe and bless-ed we shall meet at last.

458 Give to the Winds Your Fears

Commit thy way unto the Lord...and He shall bring it to pass. Psa. 37:5

PAUL GERHARDT
TR. JOHN WESLEY

GEORGE J. ELVEY

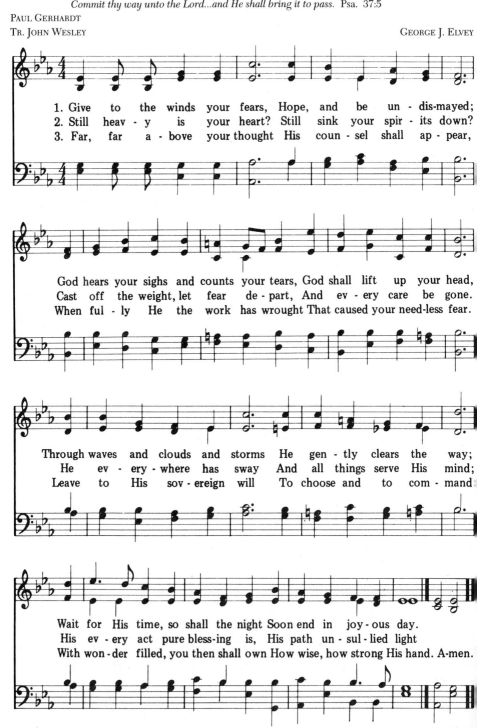

1. Give to the winds your fears, Hope, and be un - dis-mayed;
2. Still heav - y is your heart? Still sink your spir - its down?
3. Far, far a - bove your thought His coun - sel shall ap - pear,

God hears your sighs and counts your tears, God shall lift up your head,
Cast off the weight, let fear de - part, And ev - ery care be gone.
When ful - ly He the work has wrought That caused your need-less fear.

Through waves and clouds and storms He gen - tly clears the way;
He ev - ery - where has sway And all things serve His mind;
Leave to His sov - ereign will To choose and to com - mand;

Wait for His time, so shall the night Soon end in joy - ous day.
His ev - ery act pure bless-ing is, His path un - sul - lied light
With won - der filled, you then shall own How wise, how strong His hand. A-men.

Eternal Father, Strong to Save   459

He guided them to their desired haven.   Psa. 107:30

WILLIAM WHITING AND
ROBERT N. SPENCER

JOHN B. DYKES

1. E - ter - nal Fa - ther, strong to save, Whose arm hath bound the
2. O Christ, the Lord of hill and plain O'er which our traf - fic
3. O Spir - it, whom the Fa - ther sent To spread a - broad the
4. O Trin - i - ty of love and power, Our breth - ren shield in

rest - less wave, Who bids the might - y o - cean deep Its
runs a - main By moun - tain pass or val - ley low: Wher-
fir - ma - ment: O Wind of heav - en, by Thy might Save
dan - ger's hour; From rock and tem - pest, fire and foe, Pro -

own ap - point - ed lim - its keep: O hear us when we
ev - er, Lord, our breth - ren go, Pro - tect them by Thy
all who dare the ea - gle's flight, And keep them by Thy
tect them where - so - e'er they go; Thus ev - er - more shall

cry to Thee For those in per - il on the sea.
guard - ing hand From ev - ery per - il on the land.
watch - ful care From ev - ery per - il in the air.
rise to Thee Glad praise from air and land and sea. A - men.

460 Alleluia!

Alleluia; salvation, and glory, and honor and power unto the Lord our God. Rev. 19:1

JERRY SINCLAIR

JERRY SINCLAIR

1. Al - le - lu - ia, al - le - lu - ia, al - le - lu - ia, al - le - lu - ia! Al - le - lu - ia, al - le - lu - ia, al - le - lu - ia, al - le - lu - ia!
2. He's my Sav - ior, al - le - lu - ia, He's my Sav - ior, al - le - lu - ia; He's my Sav - ior, al - le - lu - ia, He's my Sav - ior, al - le - lu - ia.
3. I will praise Him, al - le - lu - ia, I will praise Him, al - le - lu - ia; I will praise Him, al - le - lu - ia, I will praise Him, al - le - lu - ia.
4. He is wor - thy, al - le - lu - ia, He is wor - thy, al - le - lu - ia; He is wor - thy, al - le - lu - ia, He is wor - thy, al - le - lu - ia.

461 How Sweet the Name of Jesus Sounds

*Unto you therefore which believe He is precious...*I Pet. 2:7

JOHN NEWTON

ALEXANDER R. REINAGLE

1. How sweet the name of Je - sus sounds In a be - liev - er's ear!
2. Dear name! the rock on which I build, My shield and hid - ing - place
3. Je - sus, my Shep-herd, Broth - er, Friend, My Proph - et, Priest, and King
4. Weak is the ef - fort of my heart, And cold my warm-est thought
5. Till then I would Thy love pro - claim With ev - ery fleet - ing breath

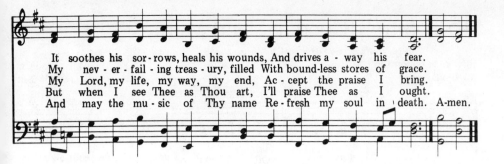

It soothes his sor-rows, heals his wounds, And drives a-way his fear.
My nev-er-fail-ing treas-ury, filled With bound-less stores of grace.
My Lord, my life, my way, my end, Ac-cept the praise I bring.
But when I see Thee as Thou art, I'll praise Thee as I ought.
And may the mu-sic of Thy name Re-fresh my soul in death. A-men.

My Faith Looks Up to Thee 462

Looking unto Jesus the author and finisher of our faith. Heb 12:2

RAY PALMER

LOWELL MASON

1. My faith looks up to Thee, Thou Lamb of Cal-va-ry,
2. May Thy rich grace im-part Strength to my faint-ing heart,
3. While life's dark maze I tread, And griefs a-round me spread,
4. When ends life's tran-sient dream, When death's cold, sul-len stream

Sav-ior di-vine! Now hear me while I pray, Take all my
My zeal in-spire; As Thou hast died for me, O may my
Be Thou my guide; Bid dark-ness turn to day, Wipe sor-row's
Shall o'er me roll; Blest Sav-ior, then, in love, Fear and dis-

guilt a-way, O let me from this day Be whol-ly Thine!
love to Thee Pure, warm, and change-less be, A liv-ing fire!
tears a-way, Nor let me ev-er stray From Thee a-side.
trust re-move; O bear me safe a-bove, A ran-somed soul! A-men.

463 Surely Goodness and Mercy

Surely goodness and mercy shall follow me all the days of my life. Psa. 23:6

JOHN W. PETERSON AND
ALFRED B. SMITH

JOHN W. PETERSON AND
ALFRED B. SMITH

1. A pil-grim was I and a-wan-d'ring, In the cold night of sin I did roam, When Je-sus the kind Shep-herd found me, And now I am on my way home.

2. He re-stor-eth my soul when I'm wea-ry, He giv-eth me strength day by day; He leads me be-side the still wa-ters, He guards me each step of the way.

3. When I walk thro' the dark lone-some val-ley, My Sav-ior will walk with me there; And safe-ly His great hand will lead me To the man-sions He's gone to pre-pare.

Refrain

Sure-ly good-ness and mer-cy shall fol-low me All the days, all the days of my life; Sure-ly good-ness and mer-cy shall fol-low me All the days, all the days of my life.

Coda

And I shall dwell in the house of the Lord for - ev - er, And I shall feast at the

ta - ble spread for me; Sure - ly good-ness and mer - cy shall fol - low me

All the days, all the days of my life, All the days, all the days of my life.

God's Goodness 464

O give thanks unto the Lord, for he is good;
for his mercy endureth forever.
Let the redeemed of the Lord say so,
whom he hath redeemed from the hand of the enemy;

O, that men would praise the Lord for his goodness,
and for his wonderful works to the children of men!
For he satisfieth the longing soul,
and filleth the hungry soul with goodness.

O, that men would praise the Lord for his goodness,
and for his wonderful works to the children of men!
And let them sacrifice the sacrifices of thanksgiving,
and declare his works with rejoicing.

O, that men would praise the Lord for his goodness,
and for his wonderful works to the children of men!
Let them exalt him also in the congregation of the people,
and praise him in the assembly of the elders.

O give thanks unto the Lord, for he is good;
for his mercy endureth forever.

From Psalm 107

465 I Need Jesus

One thing is needful and Mary hath chosen that good part...Luke 10:42

GEORGE O. WEBSTER

CHARLES H. GABRIEL

1. I need Je-sus, my need I now con-fess; No friend like Him in
2. I need Je-sus, I need a friend like Him, A friend to guide when
3. I need Je-sus, I need Him to the end; No one like Him, He

times of deep dis-tress; I need Je-sus, the need I glad-ly own; Tho'
paths of life are dim; I need Je-sus, when foes my soul as-sail; A-
is the sin-ner's Friend; I need Je-sus, no oth-er friend will do; So

some may bear their load a-lone, Yet I need Je-sus.
lone I know I can but fail, So I need Je-sus.
con-stant, kind, so strong and true, Yes, I need Je-sus.

Chorus

I need Je-sus, I need Je-sus, I need Je-sus ev-ery
I need Je-sus with me, I need Je-sus al-ways,

day; Need Him in the sun-shine hour, Need Him when the
ev-ery day;

storm-clouds low'r; Ev - ery day a - long my way, Yes, I need Je - sus.

O Jesus, I Have Promised 466

If any man serve Me, let him follow Me...John 12:26

JOHN E. BODE

ARTHUR H. MANN

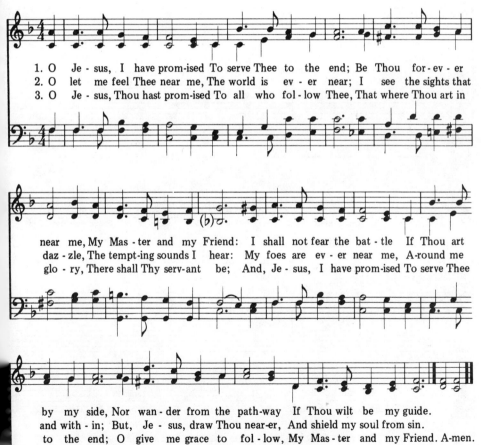

1. O Je - sus, I have prom-ised To serve Thee to the end; Be Thou for - ev - er
2. O let me feel Thee near me, The world is ev - er near; I see the sights that
3. O Je - sus, Thou hast prom-ised To all who fol - low Thee, That where Thou art in

near me, My Mas - ter and my Friend: I shall not fear the bat - tle If Thou art
daz - zle, The tempt-ing sounds I hear: My foes are ev - er near me, A-round me
glo - ry, There shall Thy serv-ant be; And, Je - sus, I have prom-ised To serve Thee

by my side, Nor wan - der from the path-way If Thou wilt be my guide.
and with - in; But, Je - sus, draw Thou near-er, And shield my soul from sin.
to the end; O give me grace to fol - low, My Mas - ter and my Friend. A-men.

467 Footprints of Jesus

And when the people had heard...they followed Him on foot...Matt. 14:33

MARY B.C. SLADE

ASA B. EVERETT

1. Sweet - ly, Lord, have we heard Thee call - ing, "Come, fol - low
2. Tho' they lead o'er the cold, dark moun - tains, Seek - ing His
3. If they lead thro' the tem - ple ho - ly, Preach - ing the
4. Then at last, when on high He sees us, Our jour - ney

Me!" And we see where Thy foot - prints fall - ing
sheep, Or a - long by Si - lo - am's foun - tains,
Word, Or in homes of the poor and low - ly,
done, We will rest where the steps of Je - sus

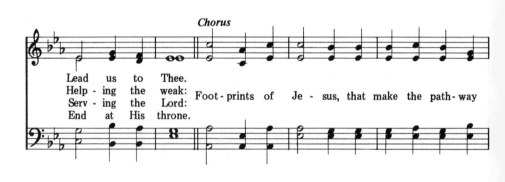

Chorus

Lead us to Thee.
Help - ing the weak:
Serv - ing the Lord:
End at His throne.

Foot - prints of Je - sus, that make the path - way

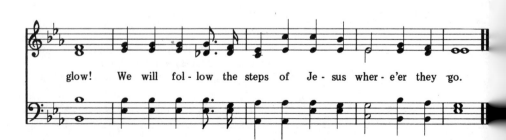

glow! We will fol - low the steps of Je - sus wher - e'er they go.

Anywhere with Jesus 468

Lo, I am with you always...Matt. 28:20

JESSIE B. POUNDS AND
HELEN C. DIXON

DANIEL B. TOWNER

1. An - y - where with Je - sus I can safe - ly go; An - y - where He
2. An - y - where with Je - sus I am not a - lone, Oth - er friends may
3. An - y - where with Je - sus o - ver land and sea, Tell - ing souls in

leads me in this world be - low; An - y - where with - out Him dear - est
fail me, He is still my own; Though His hand may lead me o - ver
dark - ness of sal - va - tion free; Read - y as He sum - mons me to

joys would fade; An - y - where with Je - sus I am not a - fraid.
drear - y ways, An - y - where with Je - sus is a house of praise.
go or stay, An - y - where with Je - sus when He points the way.

Refrain

An - y - where! an - y - where! Fear I can - not know;

An - y - where with Je - sus I can safe - ly go.

469 Trust and Obey

If ye continue in My word, then are ye My disciples indeed. John 8:31

JOHN H. SAMMIS

DANIEL B. TOWNER

1. When we walk with the Lord in the light of His Word,
2. Not a shad - ow can rise, not a cloud in the skies,
3. Not a bur - den we bear, not a sor - row we share,
4. But we nev - er can prove the de - lights of His love
5. Then in fel - low-ship sweet we will sit at His feet,

What a glo - ry He sheds on our way! While we do His good
But His smile quick - ly drives it a - way; Not a doubt nor a
But our toil He doth rich - ly re - pay; Not a grief nor a
Un - til all on the al - tar we lay; For the fa - vor He
Or we'll walk by His side in the way; What He says we will

will He a - bides with us still, And with all who will
fear, not a sigh nor a tear, Can a - bide while we
loss, not a frown nor a cross, But is blest if we
shows and the joy He be - stows Are for them who will
do, where He sends we will go— Nev - er fear, on - ly

Refrain

trust and o - bey. Trust and o - bey, for there's no oth - er

way To be hap - py in Je - sus, But to trust and o - bey.

Take the Name of Jesus with You 470

...Do all in the name of the Lord Jesus. Col. 3:17

LYDIA BAXTER

WILLIAM H. DOANE

1. Take the name of Je - sus with you, Child of sor - row and of
2. Take the name of Je - sus ev - er, As a shield from ev - ery
3. O the pre - cious name of Je - sus! How it thrills our souls with
4. At the name of Je - sus bow - ing, Fall - ing pros - trate at His

woe; It will joy and com - fort give you, Take it,
snare; If temp - ta - tions 'round you gath - er, Breathe that
joy, When His lov - ing arms re - ceive us, And His
feet, King of kings in heav'n we'll crown Him, When our

Refrain

then, wher - e'er you go.
ho - ly name in prayer. Pre - cious name, O how
songs our tongues em - ploy. Pre - cious name,
jour - ney is com - plete.

sweet! Hope of earth and joy of heav'n; Pre - cious
O how sweet!

name, O how sweet! Hope of earth and joy of heav'n.
Pre - cious name, O how sweet, how sweet!

471 All Your Anxiety

Cast all your anxiety on Him because He cares for you. I Pet. 5:7

EDWARD HENRY JOY   EDWARD HENRY JOY

1. Is there a heart o'er-bound by sor - row? Is there a
2. No oth - er friend so keen to help you, No oth - er
3. Come then at once— de - lay no long - er! Heed His en-

life weighed down by care? Come to the cross— each
friend so quick to hear; No oth - er place to
treat - y kind and sweet; You need not fear a

bur - den bear - ing, All your anx - i - e - ty—leave it there.
leave your bur - den, No oth - er one to hear your prayer.
dis - ap - point-ment— You shall find peace at the mer - cy seat.

Refrain

All your anx - i - e - ty, all your care, Bring to the

mer - cy seat—leave it there; Nev - er a bur - den He

can - not bear, Nev - er a friend like Je - sus!

In His Time 472

He has made everything beautiful in its time. Eccl. 3:11

DIANE BALL   DIANE BALL

1. In His time, in His time; He makes all things beau-ti-ful
2. In your time, in your time; You make all things beau-ti-ful

in His time. Lord, please show me ev-ery day, as You're
in your time. Lord, my life to You I bring; may each

teach-ing me your way, that You do just what You say in your time.
song I have to sing be to You a love-ly thing in your time.

473 Jesus Never Fails

I will never leave thee nor forsake thee. Heb. 13:5

ARTHUR A. LUTHER

ARTHUR A. LUTHER

1. Earth - ly friends may prove un - true, Doubts and fears as - sail;
2. Though the sky be dark and drear, Fierce and strong the gale,
3. In life's dark and bit - ter hour Love will still pre - vail;

One still loves and cares for you, One who will not fail.
Just re - mem - ber He is near, And He will not fail.
Trust His ev - er - last - ing pow'r— Je - sus will not fail.

Chorus

Je - sus nev - er fails, Je - sus nev - er fails;

Heav'n and earth may pass a - way, But Je - sus nev - er fails.

I Am His, and He Is Mine 474

I am persuaded that nothing shall separate us from the love of God. Rom. 8:38,39

GEORGE W. ROBINSON

JAMES MOUNTAIN

1. Loved with ev-er-last-ing love, Led by grace that love to know;
2. Heav'n a-bove is soft-er blue, Earth a-round is sweet-er green!
3. Things that once were wild a-larms Can-not now dis-turb my rest;
4. His for-ev-er, on-ly His; Who the Lord and me shall part?

Gra-cious Spir-it from a-bove, Thou hast taught me it is so!
Some-thing lives in ev-ery hue Christ-less eyes have nev-er seen:
Closed in ev-er-last-ing arms, Pil-lowed on the lov-ing breast.
Ah, with what a rest of bliss Christ can fill the lov-ing heart!

O, this full and per-fect peace! O, this trans-port all di-vine!
Birds with glad-der songs o'er-flow, Flow'rs with deep-er beau-ties shine,
O, to lie for-ev-er here, Doubt and care and self re-sign,
Heav'n and earth may fade and flee, First-born light in gloom de-cline;

In a love which can-not cease, I am His, and He is mine. mine.
Since I know, as now I know, I am His, and He is mine. mine.
While He whis-pers in my ear, I am His, and He is mine. mine.
But while God and I shall be, I am His, and He is mine. mine.

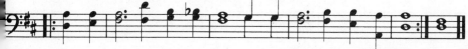

475 Jesus, Lover of My Soul

Thou hast been...a refuge from the storm...Isa. 25.4

CHARLES WESLEY   JOSEPH PARRY

1. Je - sus, Lov - er of my soul, Let me to Thy bos - om fly,
2. Oth - er ref - uge have I none; Hangs my help - less soul on Thee;
3. Thou, O Christ, art all I want; More than all in Thee I find;
4. Plen - teous grace with Thee is found, Grace to cov - er all my sin;

While the near - er wa - ters roll, While the tem - pest still is high;
Leave, ah! leave me not a - lone, Still sup - port and com - fort me.
Raise the fall - en, cheer the faint, Heal the sick, and lead the blind.
Let the heal - ing streams a - bound; Make and keep me pure with - in.

Hide me, O my Sav - ior, hide, Till the storm of life is past;
All my trust on Thee is stayed, All my help from Thee I bring;
Just and ho - ly is Thy name, I am all un - right - eous - ness;
Thou of life the foun - tain art, Free - ly let me take of Thee;

Safe in - to the ha - ven guide; O re - ceive my soul at last!
Cov - er my de - fense - less head With the shad - ow of Thy wing.
False and full of sin I am, Thou art full of truth and grace.
Spring Thou up with - in my heart, Rise to all e - ter - ni - ty.

Just When I Need Him Most 476

God is our refuge and strength, a very present help in trouble. Psa. 46:1

WILLIAM C. POOLE

CHARLES H. GABRIEL

1. Just when I need Him Je - sus is near, Just when I fal - ter,
2. Just when I need Him Je - sus is true, Nev - er for - sak - ing
3. Just when I need Him Je - sus is strong, Bear - ing my bur - dens
4. Just when I need Him He is my all, An - swer - ing when up -

just when I fear; Read - y to help me, read - y to cheer,
all the way through; Giv - ing for bur - dens pleas - ures a - new,
all the day long; For all my sor - row giv - ing a song,
on Him I call; Ten - der - ly watch - ing lest I should fall,

Refrain

Just when I need Him most. Just when I need Him most,

Just when I need Him most; Je - sus is near to

com - fort and cheer, Just when I need Him most.

477 No, Not One!

There is friend that sticketh closer than a brother. Prov. 18:24

JOHNSON OATMAN, JR.   GEORGE C. HUGG

1. There's not   a friend like the low - ly   Je - sus,   No, not one!   no, not one!
2.   No friend like Him   is   so high and ho - ly,   No, not one!   no, not one!
3. There's not   an hour that He   is   not near us,   No, not one!   no, not one!
4.   Did ev - er saint find this friend for-sake him? No, not one!   no, not one!
5.   Was e'er   a   gift like the Sav - ior giv - en? No, not one!   no, not one!

None else could heal all   our soul's dis - eas - es,   No, not one!   no, not one!
And yet no friend is   so   meek and low - ly,   No, not one!   no, not one!
No night so dark but His   love can cheer us,   No, not one!   no, not one!
Or sin - ner find that He would not take him?   No, not one!   no, not one!
Will He   re - fuse us   a   home in heav - en?   No, not one!   no, not one!

Refrain

Je - sus knows all a - bout our strug-gles,   He will guide till the day is done;

There's not   a friend like the low - ly   Je - sus,   No, not one!   no, not one!

I've Found a Friend 478

Greater love hath no man than this, that a man lay down his life for his friends. John 15:13

JAMES G. SMALL · GEORGE C. STEBBINS

1. I've found a Friend, O such a Friend! He loved me ere I knew Him;
2. I've found a Friend, O such a Friend! He bled, He died to save me;
3. I've found a Friend, O such a Friend! So kind and true and ten-der,

He drew me with the cords of love, And thus He bound me to Him.
And not a-lone the gift of life, But His own self He gave me.
So wise a Coun-sel-or and Guide, So might-y a De-fend-er!

And round my heart still close-ly twine Those ties which naught can sev-er,
Naught that I have my own I call, I hold it for the Giv-er;
From Him who loves me now so well, What pow'r my soul can sev-er?

For I am His and He is mine, For-ev-er and for-ev-er.
My heart, my strength, my life, my all Are His, and His for-ev-er.
Shall life or death, or earth or hell? No! I am His for-ev-er.

479 God Leads Us Along

When you pass through the waters, I will be with you. Isa. 43:2

G.A. YOUNG

G.A. YOUNG

1. In shad - y, green pas - tures, so rich and so sweet, God
2. Some-times on the mount where the sun shines so bright, God
3. Tho' sor - rows be - fall us and Sa - tan op - pose, God
4. A - way from the mire and a - way from the clay, God

leads His dear chil-dren a - long; Where the wa - ter's cool flow bathes the
leads His dear chil-dren a - long; Some - times in the val - ley, in
leads His dear chil-dren a - long; Thru grace we can con - quer, de-
leads His dear chil-dren a - long; A - way up in glo - ry, e-

Refrain

wea - ry one's feet, God leads His dear chil-dren a long.
dark - est of night, God leads His dear chil-dren a long.
feat all our foes, God leads His dear chil-dren a long.   Some thru the wa - ters,
ter - ni - ty's day, God leads His dear chil-dren a long.

some thru the flood, Some thru the fire, but all thru the blood: Some thru great

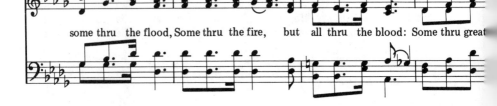

sor-row, but God gives a song, In the night sea-son and all the day long.

I Want Jesus to Walk with Me   480

I am with thee, and will keep thee...whither thou goest. Gen. 28:15

TRADITIONAL SPIRITUAL

TRADITIONAL SPIRITUAL

Unison

1. I want Je - sus to walk with me; I want
2. In my tri - als, Lord, walk with me; In my
3. When I'm in trou - ble, Lord, walk with me; When I'm in

Je - sus to walk with me; All a - long my
tri - als, Lord, walk with me; When my heart is
trou - ble, Lord, walk with me; When my head is

pil - grim jour - ney, Lord, I want Je - sus to walk with me.
al - most break - ing, Lord, I want Je - sus to walk with me.
bowed in sor - row, Lord, I want Je - sus to walk with me.

481 All the Way My Savior Leads Me

I will guide thee with mine eye. Psa. 32:8

FANNY J. CROSBY

ROBERT LOWRY

1. All the way my Sav-ior leads me; What have I to ask be-side?
2. All the way my Sav-ior leads me; Cheers each wind-ing path I tread;
3. All the way my Sav-ior leads me; O the full-ness of His love!

Can I doubt His ten-der mer-cy, Who thru life has been my guide?
Gives me grace for ev-ery tri-al, Feeds me with the liv-ing bread;
Per-fect rest to me is prom-ised In my Fa-ther's house a-bove;

Heav'n-ly peace, di-vin-est com-fort, Here by faith in Him to dwell!
Though my wea-ry steps may fal-ter, And my soul a-thirst may be,
When my spir-it, clothed im-mor-tal, Wings its flight to realms of day,

For I know, what-e'er be-fall me, Je-sus do-eth all things well; well.
Gush-ing from the rock be-fore me, Lo! a spring of joy I see, see.
This my song thru end-less a-ges, Je-sus led me all the way. way.

Like a Lamb Who Needs the Shepherd 482

He will gather the lambs with his arm. Isa. 50:11

RALPH CARMICHAEL

RALPH CARMICHAEL

1. Where He leads me I must fol-low, With-out Him I'd lose my way.
2. Life is like a wind-ing path-way, Who can tell what lies a-head?
3. Tho' you walk thro' dark-est val-leys And the sky is cold and gray,

I will see a bright to-mor-row If I fol-low Him to-day.
Will it lead to shad-y pas-tures, Or to wil-der-ness in-stead?
Tho' you climb the steep-est moun-tains, He will nev-er let you stray.

Like a lamb who needs the Shep-herd, At His side I'll al-ways stay.
Like a lamb who needs the Shep-herd, When in-to the night I go,
Like a lamb who needs the Shep-herd, By your side He'll al-ways stay.

Thro' the night His strength I'll bor-row, Then I'll see an-oth-er day.
Help me find the path that's nar-row, While I trav-el here be-low.
Till the end of life's long jour-ney, He will lead you all the way.

483 Jesus, I Am Resting, Resting

Looking unto Jesus the author and finisher of our faith. Heb 12:2

JEAN S. PIGOTT

JAMES MOUNTAIN

1. Je - sus, I am rest - ing, rest - ing In the joy of what Thou art;
2. O, how great Thy lov - ing kind - ness, Vast - er, broad - er than the sea!
3. Sim - ply trust - ing Thee, Lord Je - sus, I be - hold Thee as Thou art,
4. Ev - er lift Thy face up - on me As I work and wait for Thee;
(Ref.) Je - sus, I am rest - ing, rest - ing In the joy of what Thou art;

Fine

I am find - ing out the great - ness Of Thy lov - ing heart.
O, how mar - vel - ous Thy good - ness, Lav - ished all on me!
And Thy love, so pure, so change - less, Sat - is - fies my heart;
Rest - ing 'neath Thy smile, Lord Je - sus, Earth's dark shad - ows flee.
I am find - ing out the great - ness Of Thy lov - ing heart.

Thou hast bid me gaze up - on Thee, And Thy beau - ty fills my soul,
Yes, I rest in Thee, Be - lov - ed, Know what wealth of grace is Thine,
Sat - is - fies its deep - est long - ings, Meets, sup - plies its ev - ery need,
Bright-ness of my Fa - ther's glo - ry, Sun - shine of my Fa - ther's face,

D.C. Refrain

For by Thy trans - form - ing pow - er, Thou hast made me whole.
Know Thy cer - tain - ty of prom - ise, And have made it mine.
Com - pass - eth me round with bless - ings: Thine is love in - deed!
Keep me ev - er trust - ing, rest - ing, Fill me with Thy grace.

Under His Wings I Am Safely Abiding 484

Under His wings shalt thou trust. Psa. 91:4

WILLIAM O. CUSHING

IRA D. SANKEY

1. Un - der His wings I am safe - ly a - bid - ing; Though the night
2. Un - der His wings, what a ref - uge in sor - row! How the heart
3. Un - der His wings, O what pre - cious en - joy - ment! There will I

deep - ens and tem - pests are wild, Still I can trust Him— I
yearn - ing - ly turns to His rest! Oft - en when earth has no
hide till life's tri - als are o'er; Shel - tered, pro - tect - ed, no

know He will keep me; He has re - deemed me and I am His child.
balm for my heal - ing, There I find com - fort and there I am blest.
e - vil can harm me; Rest - ing in Je - sus I'm safe ev - er - more.

Refrain

Un - der His wings, un - der His wings, Who from His love can sev - er?

Un - der His wings my soul shall a - bide, Safe - ly a - bide for - ev - er.

485 God Will Take Care of You

Casting all your care on Him; for He careth for you. I Pet 5:7

CIVILLA D. MARTIN

W. STILLMAN MARTIN

1. Be not dis-mayed what-e'er be-tide, God will take care of you;
2. Thro' days of toil when heart doth fail, God will take care of you;
3. All you may need He will pro-vide, God will take care of you;
4. No mat-ter what may be the test, God will take care of you;

Be - neath His wings of love a - bide, God will take care of you.
When dan - gers fierce your path as - sail, God will take care of you.
Noth - ing you ask will be de - nied, God will take care of you.
Lean, wea - ry one, up - on His breast, God will take care of you.

Refrain

God will take care of you, Thro' ev - ery day, o'er all the way;

He will take care of you, God will take care of you.

Day by Day 486

As thy days, so shall thy strength be. Deut. 33:25

Carolina Sandell Berg
Tr. A.L. Skoog

Oscar Ahnfelt

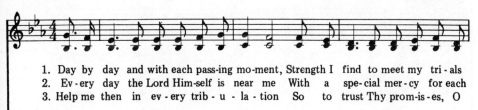

1. Day by day and with each pass-ing mo-ment, Strength I find to meet my tri - als
2. Ev - ery day the Lord Him-self is near me With a spe- cial mer - cy for each
3. Help me then in ev - ery trib - u - la - tion So to trust Thy prom-is - es, O

here; Trust-ing in my Fa-ther's wise be-stow-ment, I've no cause for wor - ry or for
hour; All my cares He fain would bear, and cheer me, He whose name is Coun-sel-lor and
Lord, That I lose not faith's sweet con-so-la-tion Of-fered me with-in Thy ho - ly

fear. He whose heart is kind be-yond all meas-ure Gives un - to each day what He deems
Pow'r. The pro-tec - tion of His child and treas-ure Is a charge that on Him-self He
Word. Help me, Lord, when toil and trouble meeting, E'er to take, as from a fa-ther's

best—Lov-ing -ly, its part of pain and pleas-ure, Min-gling toil with peace and rest.
laid; "As your days, your strength shall be in meas-ure," This the pledge to me He made.
hand, One by one, the days, the mo-ments fleeting, Till I reach the prom-ised land.

487 Sunshine in My Soul

For God, who commanded the light to shine out of darkness, hath shined in our hearts... II Cor. 4:6

ELIZA E. HEWITT   JOHN R. SWENEY

1. There is sun - shine in my soul to - day, More glo - ri - ous and bright
2. There is mu - sic in my soul to - day, A car - ol to my King,
3. There is spring - time in my soul to - day, For when the Lord is near
4. There is glad - ness in my soul to - day, And hope and praise and love,

Than glows in an - y earth - ly sky, For Je - sus is my light.
And Je - sus, lis - ten - ing can hear The songs I can - not sing.
The dove of peace sings in my heart, The flow'rs of grace ap - pear.
For bless - ings which He gives me now, For joys "laid up a - bove."

Refrain

O there's sun - shine, bless - ed sun - shine, When the peace - ful, hap - py mo - ments

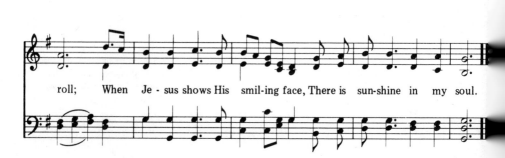

roll; When Je - sus shows His smil - ing face, There is sun - shine in my soul.

Heavenly Sunlight 488

He that followeth Me shall not walk in darkness...John 8:12

HENRY J. ZELLEY

GEORGE H. COOK

1. Walk-ing in sun-light all of my jour-ney, O-ver the moun-tains,
2. Shad-ows a-round me, shad-ows a-bove me Nev-er con-ceal my
3. In the bright sun-light, ev-er re-joic-ing, Press-ing my way to

through the deep vale; Je-sus has said, "I'll nev-er for-sake thee,"
Sav-ior and Guide; He is the Light, in Him is no dark-ness;
man-sions a-bove; Sing-ing His prais-es glad-ly I'm walk-ing,

Prom-ise di-vine that nev-er can fail.
Ev-er I'm walk-ing close to His side.   Heav-en-ly sun-light,
Walk-ing in sun-light, sun-light of love.

Refrain

heav-en-ly sun-light, Flood-ing my soul with glo-ry di-vine; Hal-le-

lu-jah! I am re-joic-ing, Sing-ing His prais-es, Je-sus is mine.

489 The Haven of Rest

This hope we have as an anchor of the soul, sure and steadfast. Heb. 6:19

HENRY L. GILMOUR

GEORGE D. MOORE

1. My soul in sad ex - ile was out on life's sea, So bur - dened with
2. I yield - ed my - self to His ten - der em - brace, And faith tak - ing
3. The song of my soul, since the Lord made me whole, Has been the old
4. How pre - cious the thought that we all may re - cline, Like John the be -
5. Oh, come to the Sav - ior, He pa - tient - ly waits To save by His

sin and dis - trest, Till I heard a sweet voice say - ing, "Make me your
hold of the Word, My fet - ters fell off, and I an - chored my
sto - ry so blest, Of Je - sus, who'll save who - so - ev - er will
lov - ed and blest, On Je - sus' strong arm, where no tem - pest can
pow - er di - vine; Come, an - chor your soul in the "Ha - ven of

Refrain

choice;" And I en - tered the "Ha - ven of Rest!"
soul; The "Ha - ven of Rest" is the Lord.
have A home in the "Ha - ven of Rest!" I've an - chored my
harm, Se - cure in the "Ha - ven of Rest!"
Rest," And say, "My Be - lov - ed is mine."

soul in the "Ha - ven of Rest," I'll sail the wide seas no more; The

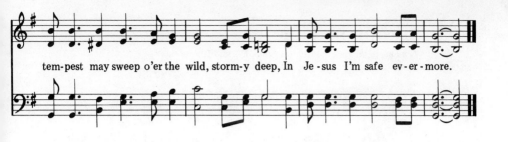

tem-pest may sweep o'er the wild, storm-y deep, In Je-sus I'm safe ev-er-more.

Rock of Ages 490

I will put thee in a cleft of the rock, and will cover thee...Ex. 33:22

AUGUSTUS M. TOPLADY   THOMAS HASTINGS

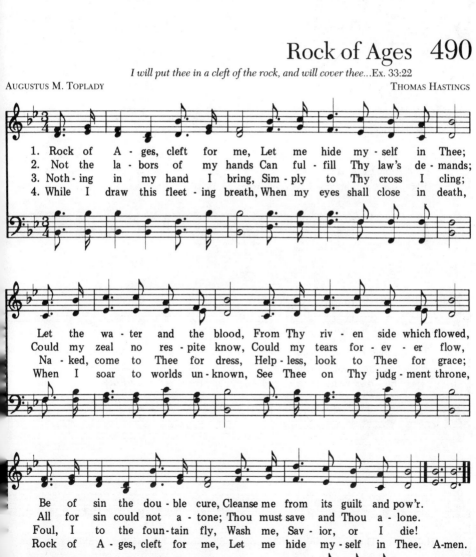

1. Rock of A - ges, cleft for me, Let me hide my - self in Thee;
2. Not the la - bors of my hands Can ful - fill Thy law's de - mands;
3. Noth - ing in my hand I bring, Sim - ply to Thy cross I cling;
4. While I draw this fleet - ing breath, When my eyes shall close in death,

Let the wa - ter and the blood, From Thy riv - en side which flowed,
Could my zeal no res - pite know, Could my tears for - ev - er flow,
Na - ked, come to Thee for dress, Help - less, look to Thee for grace;
When I soar to worlds un - known, See Thee on Thy judg - ment throne,

Be of sin the dou - ble cure, Cleanse me from its guilt and pow'r.
All for sin could not a - tone; Thou must save and Thou a - lone.
Foul, I to the foun-tain fly, Wash me, Sav - ior, or I die!
Rock of A - ges, cleft for me, Let me hide my - self in Thee. A-men.

491 Hiding in Thee

Lead me to the rock that is higher than I. Psa. 61:2

WILLIAM O. CUSHING

IRA D. SANKEY

1. O safe to the Rock that is high - er than I, My soul in its
2. In the calm of the noon-tide, in sor-row's lone hour, In times when temp-
3. How oft in the con-flict, when pressed by the foe, I have fled to my

con - flicts and sor - rows would fly; So sin - ful, so wea - ry, Thine,
ta - tion casts o'er me its pow'r; In the tem - pests of life, on its
Ref - uge and breathed out my woe; How oft - en, when tri - als like

Thine would I be; Thou blest Rock of A - ges, I'm hid - ing in Thee.
wide, heav - ing sea, Thou blest Rock of A - ges, I'm hid - ing in Thee.
sea - bil - lows roll, Have I hid - den in Thee, O Thou Rock of my soul.

Refrain

Hid - ing in Thee, Hid - ing in Thee, Thou blest Rock of A-ges, I'm hid - ing in Thee.

Leaning on the Everlasting Arms 492

The eternal God is thy refuge, and underneath are the everlasting arms. Deut. 33:27

ELISHA A. HOFFMAN   ANTHONY J. SHOWALTER

1. What a fel - low - ship, what a joy di - vine, Lean - ing on the ev - er-
2. O how sweet to walk in this pil - grim way, Lean - ing on the ev - er-
3. What have I to dread, what have I to fear, Lean - ing on the ev - er-

last - ing arms; What a bless - ed - ness, what a peace is mine,
last - ing arms; O, how bright the path grows from day to day,
last - ing arms? I have bless - ed peace with my Lord so near,

Refrain

Lean - ing on the ev - er - last - ing arms. Lean - ing,
Lean - ing on the ev - er - last - ing arms. Lean - ing on Je - sus,
Lean - ing on the ev - er - last - ing arms.

lean - ing, Safe and se - cure from all a - larms; Lean -
lean - ing on Je - sus, Lean - ing on

ing, lean - ing, Lean - ing on the ev - er - last - ing arms.
Je - sus, lean - ing on Je - sus,

493 We'll Understand It Better By and By

Faith is the substance of things hoped for, the evidence of things not seen. Heb. 11:1

CHARLES A. TINDLEY

CHARLES A. TINDLEY
ARR. B.B. McKINNEY

1. Tri-als dark on ev-ery hand, and we can-not un-der-stand
2. Oft our cher-ished plans have failed, dis-ap-point-ments have pre-vailed,
3. Temp-ta-tions, hid-den snares of-ten take us un-a-wares,

All the ways that God would lead us to that bless-ed Prom-ised Land;
And we've wan-dered in the dark-ness, heav-y heart-ed and a-lone;
And our hearts are made to bleed for some tho't-less word or deed,

But He'll guide us with His eye, and we'll fol-low till we die; We will
But we're trust-ing in the Lord, and, ac-cord-ing to His Word, We will
And we won-der why the test when we try to do our best, But we'll

Refrain

un-der-stand it bet-ter by and by. By and by, when the morn-ing comes,

When the saints of God are gath-ered home, We will tell the sto-ry

how we've o-ver-come; We will un-der-stand it bet-ter by and by.

Precious Lord, Take My Hand 494

...And lead me in the way everlasting. Psa. 139:24

GEORGE N. ALLEN

THOMAS A. DORSEY

ADAPTED BY THOMAS A. DORSEY

1. Pre-cious Lord, take my hand, Lead me on, help me stand— I am
2. When my way grows drear, Pre-cious Lord, lin-ger near— When my

tired, I am weak, I am worn; Thro' the storm, thro' the night, Lead me
life is al-most gone; Hear my cry, hear my call, Hold my

on to the light— Take my hand, pre-cious Lord, lead me home.
hand lest I fall— Take my hand, pre-cious Lord, lead me home.

495 I Know Who Holds Tomorrow

Ye know not what shall be on the morrow. James 4:14

IRA STANPHILL

IRA STANPHILL

1. I don't know a-bout to-mor-row, I just live from day to day. I don't bor-row from its sun-shine, For its skies may turn to gray. I don't wor-ry o'er the fu-ture, For I know what Je-sus said, And to-day I'll walk be-side Him, For He knows what is a-head.

2. Ev-ery step is get-ting bright-er, As the gold-en stairs I climb; Ev-ery bur-den's get-ting light-er; Ev-ery cloud is sil-ver lined. There the sun is al-ways shin-ing, There no tear will dim the eye, At the end-ing of the rain-bow, Where the moun-tains touch the sky.

3. I don't know a-bout to-mor-row, It may bring me pov-er-ty; But the one who feeds the spar-row, Is the one who stands by me. And the path that be my por-tion, May be through the flame or flood, But His pres-ence goes be-fore me, And I'm cov-ered with His blood.

Man-y things a-bout to-mor-row, I don't seem to un-der-stand; But I know who holds to-mor-row, And I know who holds my hand.

I Asked . . . God Answered 496

I asked God for strength, that I
  might achieve;

  I was made weak, that I might
    learn humbly to obey.

I asked for health, that I might
  do greater things;

  I was given infirmity, that I might
    do better things.

I asked for riches, that I might
  be happy;

  I was given poverty, that I
    might be wise.

I asked for power, that I might
  have the praise of men;

  I was given weakness, that I
    might feel the need of God.

I asked for all things, that I
  might enjoy life;

  I was given life, that I might
    enjoy all things.

I got nothing that I asked for—
  but everything I had hoped for.

  Almost despite myself, my un-
    spoken prayers were answered.

I am, among all men, most richly blessed.

An Unknown Confederate Soldier

497 If You Will Only Let God Guide You

Cast your burden upon the Lord and He will sustain you. Psa. 55:22

GEORG NEUMARK
TR. CATHERINE WINKWORTH

GEORG NEUMARK

1. If you will on - ly let God guide you, And hope in Him thro'
2. On - ly be still, and wait His lei - sure In cheer - ful hope, with
3. Sing, pray, and swerve not from His ways, But do your part in

all your ways, What - ev - er comes, He'll stand be - side you,
heart con - tent To take what - e'er the Fa - ther's plea - sure
con - science true; Trust His rich prom - is - es of grace,

To bear you thro' the e - vil days; Who trusts in God's un -
And all dis - cern - ing love have sent; Nor doubt our in - mos
So shall they be ful - filled in you; God hears the call of

chang - ing love Builds on the rock that can - not move.
wants are known To Him who chose us for His own.
those in need, The souls that trust in Him in - deed.

Trusting Jesus 498

Commit thy way unto the Lord; trust also in Him...Psa. 37:5

EDGAR P. STITES   IRA D. SANKEY

1. Sim - ply trust - ing ev - ery day, Trust - ing through a storm - y way;
2. Bright - ly doth His Spir - it shine In - to this poor heart of mine;
3. Sing - ing if my way is clear, Pray - ing if the path be drear;
4. Trust - ing Him while life shall last, Trust - ing Him till earth be past;

E - ven when my faith is small, Trust - ing Je - sus—that is all.
While He leads I can - not fall, Trust - ing Je - sus—that is all.
If in dan - ger, for Him call, Trust - ing Je - sus—that is all.
Till with - in the jas - per wall, Trust - ing Je - sus—that is all.

Refrain

Trust - ing as the mo - ments fly, Trust - ing as the days go by;

Trust - ing Him what-e'er be - fall, Trust - ing Je - sus—that is all.

Activity
and
Service

He died for all, that those who live in Him
should no longer live for themselves,
but for Him who died for them and rose again.
II Cor. 5:15

I Will Serve Thee 499

It is the Lord Christ you are serving. Col. 3:24

WILLIAM J. AND GLORIA GAITHER

WILLIAM J. GAITHER

I will serve Thee be-cause I love Thee, You have giv - en

life to me; I was noth-ing be-fore You found me,

You have giv - en life to me. Heart-aches, bro-ken

piec - es, Ru-ined lives are why You died on Cal - vary; Your touch

was what I longed for, You have giv - en life to me.

500 The Longer I Serve Him

Ye serve the Lord Christ. Col. 3:24

WILLIAM J. GAITHER

WILLIAM J. GAITHER

1. Since I start-ed for the King-dom, Since my life He con-
2. Ev-ery need He is sup-ply-ing, Plen-teous grace He be-

trols, Since I gave my heart to Je-sus; The long-er I
stows; Ev-ery day my way gets bright-er, The long-er I

Refrain

serve Him, the sweet-er He grows.
serve Him, the sweet-er He grows. The long-er I serve Him, the

sweet - er He grows; The more that I love Him, mor

love He be-stows. Each day is like heav-en, my heart o-ver-

flows; The long-er I serve Him, the sweet-er He grows.

Faithful Men 501

The things you have heard...commit to faithful men. II Tim. 2:2

TWILA PARIS   TWILA PARIS

1. Come and join the reap-ers; All the King-dom seek-ers;
2. Come and share the har-vest; Help to light the dark-ness,

1

2

Lay-ing down your life to find it in the end.
For the Lord is call-ing faith-ful men.

502 The Master Has Come

And he said unto them, "Follow Me." Matt. 4:19

SARAH DOUDNEY

TRADITIONAL WELSH MELODY

1. The Mas - ter has come, and He calls us to
2. The Mas - ter has called us— the road may be
3. The Mas - ter has called us in life's ear - ly

fol - low The track of the foot - prints He leaves on our way;
drear - y, And dan - gers and sor - rows are strewn on the track;
morn - ing, With spir - its as fresh as the dew on the sod;

Far o - ver the moun - tain and thru the deep
But God's Ho - ly Spir - it shall com - fort the
We turn from the world with its smiles and its

hol - low The path leads us on to the man - sions of day.
wear - y— We fol - low the Sav - ior and can - not turn back.
scorn - ing To cast in our lot with the peo - ple of God.

The Mas-ter has called us, the chil-dren who fear Him, Who
The Mas-ter has called us— tho' doubt and temp-ta-tion May
The Mas-ter has called us, His sons and His daugh-ters, We

march 'neath Christ's ban-ner, His own lit-tle band:
com-pass our jour-ney, we cheer-ful-ly sing:
plead for His bless-ing and trust in His love:

We love Him and seek Him, we long to be
"Press on-ward, look up ward"— thru much trib-u-
And thru the green past-ures, be-side the still

near Him, And rest in the light of His beau-ti-ful land.
la-tion The chil-dren of Zi-on must fol-low their King.
wa-ters, He'll lead us at last to His king-dom a-bove.

503 Pass It On

Since God loved us so, we ought to love one another. I John 4:11

KURT KAISER   KURT KAISER

Unison

1. It on - ly takes a spark to get a fire go - ing,
2. What a won - drous time is spring when all the trees are bud - ding,
3. I wish for you, my friend, this hap - pi-ness that I've found,

And soon all those a-round can warm up in its glow-ing.
The birds be-gin to sing, the flow - ers start their bloom-ing,
You can de-pend on Him, it mat - ters not where you're bound.

That's how it is with God's love once you've ex-pe-ri-enced it;
That's how it is with God's love once you've ex-pe-ri-enced it;
I'll shout it from the moun-tain top— I want my world to know;

You spread His love to ev - ery one; You want to pass it on.
You want to sing, it's fresh like spring, You want to pass it on.
The Lord of love has come to me, I want to pass it on.

Rescue the Perishing 504

The Son of man is come to seek and to save that which was lost. Luke 19:10

FANNY J. CROSBY   WILLIAM H. DOANE

1. Res-cue the per-ish-ing, care for the dy-ing, Snatch them in pit-y from
2. Though they are slight-ing Him, still He is wait-ing, Wait-ing the pen-i-tent
3. Down in the hu-man heart, crushed by the tempt-er, Feel-ings lie bur-ied that
4. Res-cue the per-ish-ing, du-ty de-mands it; Strength for thy la-bor the

sin and the grave; Weep o'er the err-ing one, lift up the fall-en,
child to re-ceive; Plead with them ear-nest-ly, plead with them gen-tly,
grace can re-store; Touched by a lov-ing heart, wak-ened by kind-ness,
Lord will pro-vide; Back to the nar-row way pa-tient-ly win them;

Refrain

Tell them of Je-sus the might-y to save.
He will for-give if they on-ly be-lieve.
Cords that are bro-ken will vi-brate once more. Res-cue the per-ish-ing,
Tell the poor wan-d'rer a Sav-ior has died.

care for the dy-ing; Je-sus is mer-ci-ful, Je-sus will save.

505 Reach Out and Touch

And Jesus put forth His hand and touched him...Matt 8:3

CHARLES F. BROWN   CHARLES F. BROWN

Unison

1. Reach out and touch a soul that is hun-gry; Reach out and touch a
2. Reach out and touch a friend who is wea-ry; Reach out and touch a

spir - it in de - spair; Reach out and touch a life torn and
seek - er un - a - ware; Reach out and touch, tho' touch - ing means

dirt-y, A man who is lone-ly— If you care! Reach out and
los-ing A part of your own self— If you dare! Reach out and

touch that neigh-bor who hates you; Reach out and touch that stran-ger who
give your love to the love-less; Reach out and make a home for the

meets you; Reach out and touch the broth-er who needs you; Reach out and
home-less; Reach out and shed God's light in the dark-ness; Reach out and

let the smile of God touch thro' you.

you.

Lead Me to Some Soul Today 506

Now that we are ambassadors for Christ...II Cor. 5:20

WILL H. HOUGHTON

WENDELL P. LOVELESS

Lead me to some soul to-day, O teach me, Lord, just what to say;

Friends of mine are lost in sin, And can-not find their way.

Few there are who seem to care, And few there are who pray;
who pray;

Melt my heart and fill my life, Give me one soul to-day.

507 "Are Ye Able," Said the Master

Jesus said...Can ye drink of the cup that I drink of? Mark 10:38

EARL MARLATT   HARRY S. MASON

1. "Are ye a - ble," said the Mas - ter, "To be cru - ci - fied with me?"
2. "Are ye a - ble," to re - mem - ber, When a thief lifts up his eyes,
3. "Are ye a - ble," when the shad-ows Close a - round you with the sod,
4. "Are ye a - ble?" still the Mas - ter Whis - pers down e - ter - ni - ty,

"Yea," the stur - dy dream - ers an-swered, "To the death we fol - low Thee."
That his par-doned soul is wor - thy Of a place in par - a - dise?
To be - lieve that spir - it tri - umphs, To com-mend your soul to God?
And he - ro - ic spir - its an - swer Now, as then in Gal - i - lee.

Refrain

"Lord, we are a - ble," our spir - its are Thine. Re - mold them,

make us like Thee, di - vine: Thy guid - ing ra - diance a - bove us shall

be A bea - con to God, To love and loy - al - ty. A - men.

Joy in Serving Jesus 508

Serve the Lord with gladness; come before His presence with singing. Psa. 100:2

OSWALD J. SMITH

BENTLEY D. ACKLEY

1. There is joy in serv-ing Je-sus, As I jour-ney on my way,
2. There is joy in serv-ing Je-sus, Joy that tri-umphs o-ver pain;
3. There is joy in serv-ing Je-sus, As I walk a-lone with God;
4. There is joy in serv-ing Je-sus, Joy a-mid the dark-est night,

Joy that fills the heart with prais-es, Ev-ery hour and ev-ery day.
Fills my soul with heav-en's mu-sic, Till I join the glad re-frain.
'Tis the joy of Christ, my Sav-ior, Who the path of suf-fering trod.
For I've learned the won-drous se-cret, And I'm walk-ing in the light.

Refrain

There is joy, joy, Joy in serv-ing Je-sus, Joy that throbs with-in my heart; Ev-ery mo-ment, ev-ery hour, As I draw up-on His pow'r, There is joy, joy, Joy that nev-er shall de-part.

509 Ring the Bells of Heaven

Joy shall be in heaven over one sinner that repenteth...Luke 15:7

WILLIAM O. CUSHING

GEORGE F. ROOT

1. Ring the bells of heav - en! there is joy to - day For a
2. Ring the bells of heav - en! there is joy to - day, For the
3. Ring the bells of heav - en! spread the feast to - day! An - gels,

soul re - turn - ing from the wild! See! the Fa - ther meets him
wan - d'rer now is rec - on - ciled; Yes, a soul is res - cued
swell the glad tri - um - phant strain! Tell the joy - ful ti - dings,

out up - on the way, Wel - com - ing His wea - ry, wan - d'ring child.
from his sin - ful way, And is born a - new a ran - somed child.
bear it far a - way! For a pre - cious soul is born a - gain.

Chorus

Glo - ry! glo - ry! how the an - gels sing; Glory!

glo - ry! how the loud harps ring! 'Tis the ran - somed ar - my,

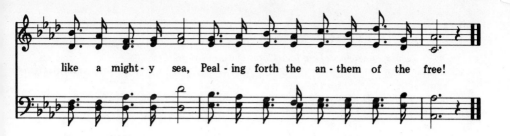

like a might-y sea, Peal-ing forth the an-them of the free!

Stand Up, Stand Up for Jesus 510

Therefore endure hardness as a good soldier of Jesus Christ. II Tim. 2:3

GEORGE DUFFIELD

GEORGE J. WEBB

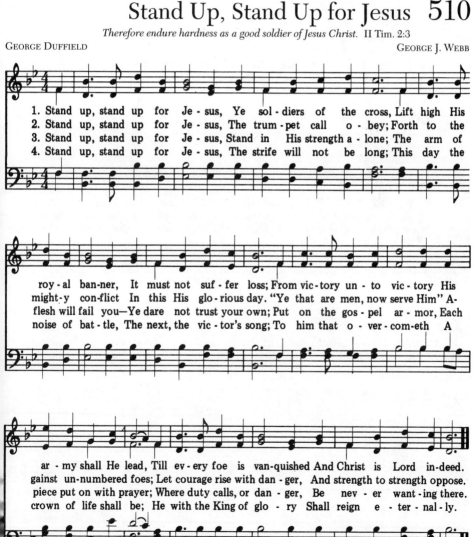

1. Stand up, stand up for Je-sus, Ye sol-diers of the cross, Lift high His
2. Stand up, stand up for Je-sus, The trum-pet call o - bey; Forth to the
3. Stand up, stand up for Je-sus, Stand in His strength a-lone; The arm of
4. Stand up, stand up for Je-sus, The strife will not be long; This day the

roy-al ban-ner, It must not suf-fer loss; From vic-to-ry un - to vic-tory His
might-y con-flict In this His glo-rious day. "Ye that are men, now serve Him" A-
flesh will fail you—Ye dare not trust your own; Put on the gos-pel ar - mor, Each
noise of bat-tle, The next, the vic-tor's song; To him that o - ver-com-eth A

ar - my shall He lead, Till ev-ery foe is van-quished And Christ is Lord in-deed.
gainst un-numbered foes; Let courage rise with dan - ger, And strength to strength oppose.
piece put on with prayer; Where duty calls, or dan - ger, Be nev - er want-ing there.
crown of life shall be; He with the King of glo - ry Shall reign e - ter-nal-ly.

511 Victory in Jesus

Victory...through our Lord Jesus Christ. I Cor. 15:57

EUGENE M. BARTLETT

EUGENE M. BARTLETT

1. I heard an old, old sto - ry, how a Sav - ior came from glo - ry,
2. I heard a - bout His heal - ing, of His cleans - ing pow'r re - veal - ing,
3. I heard a - bout a man - sion He has built for me in glo - ry,

How He gave his life on Cal - va - ry to save a wretch like me;
How He made the lame to walk a - gain and caused the blind to see;
And I heard a - bout the streets of gold be - yond the crys - tal sea;

I heard a - bout His groan - ing, of His pre - cious blood's a - ton - ing,
And then I cried "Dear Je - sus, come and heal my bro - ken spir - it,"
A - bout the an - gels sing - ing, and the old re - demp - tion sto - ry,

Then I re - pent - ed of my sins and won the vic - to - ry.
And some - how Je - sus came and bro't to me the vic - to - ry.
And some sweet day I'll sing up there the song of vic - to - ry.

Refrain

O vic - to - ry in Je - sus, my Sav - ior, for - ev - er, He sought me and

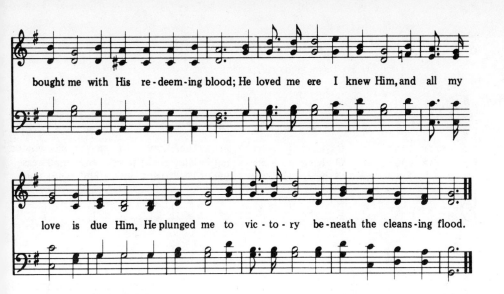

bought me with His re-deem-ing blood; He loved me ere I knew Him, and all my

love is due Him, He plunged me to vic-to-ry be-neath the cleans-ing flood.

Must Jesus Bear the Cross Alone? 512

If any man will come after Me, let him...take up his cross. Matt. 16:24

THOMAS SHEPHERD   GEORGE N. ALLEN

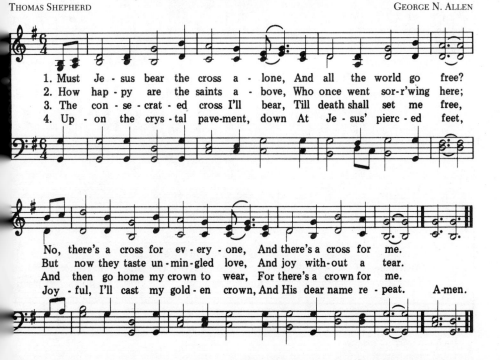

1. Must Je - sus bear the cross a - lone, And all the world go free?
2. How hap - py are the saints a - bove, Who once went sor-r'wing here;
3. The con - se - crat - ed cross I'll bear, Till death shall set me free,
4. Up - on the crys - tal pave-ment, down At Je - sus' pierc - ed feet,

No, there's a cross for ev - ery - one, And there's a cross for me.
But now they taste un - min-gled love, And joy with-out a tear.
And then go home my crown to wear, For there's a crown for me.
Joy - ful, I'll cast my gold - en crown, And His dear name re - peat. A-men.

513 Lead On, O King Eternal

Henceforth there is laid up for me a crown of righteousness…II Tim. 4:8

ERNEST W. SHURTLEFF

HENRY T. SMART

1. Lead on, O King E - ter - nal, The day of march has come;
2. Lead on, O King E - ter - nal, Till sin's fierce war shall cease,
3. Lead on, O King E - ter - nal, We fol - low, not with fears;

Hence - forth in fields of con - quest Your tents shall be our home.
And ho - li - ness shall whis - per The sweet A - men of peace;
For glad - ness breaks like morn - ing Wher - e'er Your face ap - pears;

Through days of prep - a - ra - tion Your grace has made us strong,
For not with swords loud clash - ing, Nor roll of stir - ring drums,
Your cross is lift - ed o'er us; We jour - ney in its light:

And now, O King E - ter - nal, We lift our bat - tle song.
With deeds of love and mer - cy The heav'n - ly king - dom comes.
The crown a - waits the con - quest; Lead on, O God of might. A - men.

God of Grace and God of Glory 514

Be not afraid, for the Lord thy God is with thee. Josh. 1:9

HARRY E. FOSDICK

JOHN HUGHES

1. God of grace and God of glo - ry, On Thy peo - ple
2. Lo! the hosts of e - vil round us Scorn Thy Christ, as -
3. Cure Thy chil - dren's war - ring mad - ness; Bend our pride to
4. Set our feet on loft - y plac - es, Gird our lives that

pour Thy power; Crown Thine an - cient Church - 's sto - ry, Bring her
sail His ways! From the fears that long have bound us, Free our
Thy con - trol; Shame our wan - ton, self - ish glad - ness, Rich in
they may be Ar - mored with all Christ-like grac - es In the

bud to glo - rious flower. Grant us wis - dom, Grant us cour - age, For the
hearts to faith and praise. Grant us wis - dom, Grant us cour - age, For the
things and poor in soul. Grant us wis - dom, Grant us cour - age, Lest we
fight to set men free. Grant us wis - dom, Grant us cour - age, That we

fac - ing of this hour, For the fac - ing of this hour.
liv - ing of these days, For the liv - ing of these days.
miss Thy king-dom's goal, Lest we miss Thy king-dom's goal.
fail not man nor Thee, That we fail not man nor Thee. A - men.

515 The Son of God Goes Forth to War

Can ye drink of the cup that I drink of ?...Mark 10:38

REGINALD HEBER

HENRY S. CUTLER

1. The Son of God goes forth to war, A king-ly crown to gain;
His blood-red ban-ner streams a-far: Who fol-lows in His train?
Who best can drink His cup of woe, Tri-um-phant o-ver pain,
Who pa-tient bears His cross be-low, He fol-lows in His train.

2. The mar-tyr first, whose ea-gle eye Could pierce be-yond the grave,
Who saw his Mas-ter in the sky And called on Him to save.
Like Him, with par-don on his tongue In midst of mor-tal pain,
He prayed for them that did the wrong: Who fol-lows in his train?

3. A glo-rious band, the cho-sen few On whom the Spir-it came,
Twelve val-iant saints, their hope they knew And mocked the cross and flame:
They met the ty-rant's bran-dished steel, The li-on's go-ry mane;
They bowed their necks the death to feel: Who fol-lows in their train?

4. A no-ble ar-my, men and boys, The ma-tron and the maid,
A-round the Sav-ior's throne re-joice, In robes of light ar-rayed.
They climbed the steep as-cent of heav'n Through per-il, toil, and pain;
O God, to us may grace be giv'n To fol-low in their train! A-men.

Soldiers of Christ, Arise 516

Be strong in the Lord...Put on the whole armor of God. Eph. 6:10, 11

CHARLES WESLEY

GEORGE J. ELVEY

1. Sol - diers of Christ, a - rise And put your ar - mor on,
2. Stand then in His great might, With all His strength en - dued,
3. Leave no un - guard - ed place, No weak - ness of the soul;

Strong in the strength which God sup - plies Through His e - ter - nal Son;
And take, to arm you for the fight, The pan - o - ply of God;
Take ev - ery vir - tue, ev - ery grace, And for - ti - fy the whole.

Strong in the Lord of hosts, And in His might - y pow'r, Who
From strength to strength go on, Wres - tle and fight and pray; Tread
That hav - ing all things done, And all your con - flicts past, Ye

in the strength of Je - sus trusts Is more than con - quer - or.
all the pow'rs of dark - ness down, And win the well - fought day.
may o'er - come through Christ a - lone, And stand com - plete at last. A - men.

517 Onward, Christian Soldiers

Thou therefore endure hardness, as a good soldier of Jesus Christ. II Tim. 2:3

SABINE BARING-GOULD

ARTHUR S. SULLIVAN

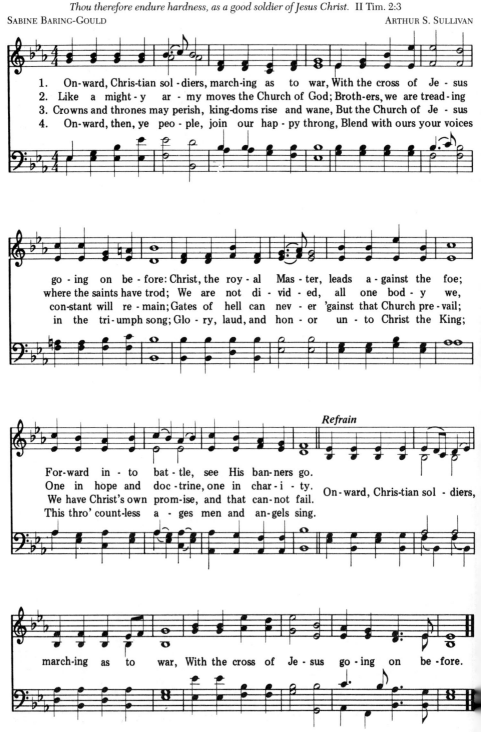

1. On-ward, Chris-tian sol-diers, march-ing as to war, With the cross of Je-sus going on be-fore: Christ, the roy-al Mas-ter, leads a-gainst the foe; For-ward in-to bat-tle, see His ban-ners go.

2. Like a might-y ar-my moves the Church of God; Broth-ers, we are tread-ing where the saints have trod; We are not di-vid-ed, all one bod-y we, One in hope and doc-trine, one in char-i-ty.

3. Crowns and thrones may perish, king-doms rise and wane, But the Church of Je-sus con-stant will re-main; Gates of hell can nev-er 'gainst that Church pre-vail; We have Christ's own prom-ise, and that can-not fail.

4. On-ward, then, ye peo-ple, join our hap-py throng, Blend with ours your voices in the tri-umph song; Glo-ry, laud, and hon-or un-to Christ the King; This thro' count-less a-ges men and an-gels sing.

Refrain

On-ward, Chris-tian sol-diers, march-ing as to war, With the cross of Je-sus go-ing on be-fore.

Who Is on the Lord's Side? 518

Who is on the Lord's side? Ex. 32:26

C. LUISE REICHARDT
ARR. JOHN GOSS

FRANCES. R. HAVERGAL

1. Who is on the Lord's side? Who will serve the King? Who will be His
2. Not for weight of glo - ry, Not for crown and palm, En - ter we the
3. Je - sus, Thou hast bought us, Not with gold or gem, But with Thine own
4. Fierce may be the con - flict, Strong may be the foe, But the King's own

help - ers, Oth - er lives to bring? Who will leave the world's side?
ar - my, Raise the war - rior psalm; But for love that claim - eth
life - blood, For Thy di - a - dem. With Thy bless - ing fill - ing
ar - my None can o - ver - throw. Round His stand - ard rang - ing

Who will face the foe? Who is on the Lord's side? Who for
Lives for whom He died; He whom Je - sus nam - eth Must be
Each who comes to Thee, Thou hast made us will - ing, Thou hast
Vic - t'ry is se - cure; For His truth un - chang - ing Makes the

Him will go? By Thy call of mer - cy, By Thy grace di - vine,
on His side. By Thy love con - strain - ing, By Thy grace di - vine,
made us free. By Thy grand re - demp - tion, By Thy grace di - vine,
tri - umph sure. Joy - ful - ly en - list - ing By Thy grace di - vine,

We are on the Lord's side, Sav - ior, we are Thine. A - men.

519 Faith Is the Victory

This is the victory that overcometh the world, even our faith. I John 5:4

JOHN H. YATES

IRA D. SANKEY

1. En-camped a-long the hills of light, Ye Chris-tian sol-diers, rise,
2. His ban-ner o-ver us is love, Our sword the Word of God;
3. On ev-ery hand the foe we find Drawn up in dread ar-ray;
4. To him that o-ver-comes the foe, White rai-ment shall be giv'n;

And press the bat-tle ere the night Shall veil the glow-ing skies.
We tread the road the saints a-bove With shouts of tri-umph trod.
Let tents of ease be left be-hind, And on-ward to the fray;
Be-fore the an-gels he shall know His name con-fessed in heav'n.

A-gainst the foe in vales be-low Let all our strength be hurled;
By faith they, like a whirl-wind's breath, Swept on o'er ev-ery field;
Sal-va-tion's hel-met on each head, With truth all girt a-bout,
Then on-ward from the hills of light, Our hearts with love a-flame,

Faith is the vic-to-ry, we know, That o-ver-comes the world.
The faith by which they con-quered death Is still our shin-ing shield.
The earth shall trem-ble 'neath our tread, And ech-o with our shout.
We'll van-quish all the hosts of night, In Je-sus' con-quering name.

Refrain

Faith is the vic - to - ry! Faith is the vic - to - ry!

O, glo - ri - ous vic - to - ry, That o - ver - comes the world.

Am I a Soldier of the Cross? 520

...Endure hardness, as a good soldier of Jesus Christ. II Tim. 2:3

ISAAC WATTS

THOMAS A. ARNE

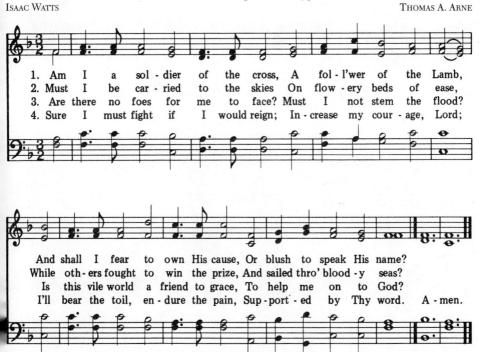

1. Am I a sol - dier of the cross, A fol - l'wer of the Lamb,
2. Must I be car - ried to the skies On flow - ery beds of ease,
3. Are there no foes for me to face? Must I not stem the flood?
4. Sure I must fight if I would reign; In - crease my cour - age, Lord;

And shall I fear to own His cause, Or blush to speak His name?
While oth - ers fought to win the prize, And sailed thro' blood - y seas?
Is this vile world a friend to grace, To help me on to God?
I'll bear the toil, en - dure the pain, Sup - port - ed by Thy word. A - men.

Missions

---

521   ## Send Me

Use me, God, in thy great harvest field,
Which stretcheth far and wide like a wide sea;
The gatherers are so few; I fear the precious yield
Will suffer loss. Oh, find a place for me!
A place where best the strength I have will tell:
It may be one the older toilers shun;
Be it a wide or narrow place, 'tis well
So that the work it holds be only done.
Christina G. Rossetti

O Zion, Haste 522

We declare unto you glad tidings. Act. 13:32

MARY A. THOMSON   JAMES WALCH

1. O Zi - on, haste, your mis-sion high ful - fill - ing, To tell to all the
2. Be - hold how man - y thou-sands still are ly - ing, Bound in the dark-some
3. Pro-claim to ev - ery peo - ple, tongue and na - tion That God, in whom they
4. Give of your sons to bear the mes-sage glo-rious; Give of your wealth to

world that God is Light; That He who made all na - tions is not will - ing
pris - on-house of sin, With none to tell them of the Sav-ior's dy - ing,
live and move, is love: Tell how He stooped to save His lost cre - a - tion,
speed them on their way; Pour out your soul for them in prayer vic - to-rious;

Chorus

One soul should per - ish, lost in shades of night.
Or of the life He died for them to win.
And died on earth that man might live a - bove.   Pub - lish glad ti - dings,
And all your spend-ing Je - sus will re - pay.

ti - dings of peace; Ti - dings of Je - sus, re - demp-tion, and re - lease.

523 Lift High the Cross

I, if I be lifted up from the earth, will draw all men unto Me. John 12:32

GEORGE W. KITCHIN AND
MICHAEL R. NEWBOLT

SYDNEY H. NICHOLSON

(Ref.) Lift high the Cross, the love of Christ pro-claim, Till

all the world a - dore His sa - cred name.

1. Come, breth - ren, fol - low where our Sav - ior trod, Our
2. Led on their way by this tri - um - phant sign, The
3. O Lord, once lift - ed on the glo - rious Tree, As
4. Set up Thy throne, that earth's de - spair may cease Be -
5. For Thy blest Cross which doth for all a - tone, Cre -

King vic - to - rious, Christ, the Son of God.
hosts of God in con-qu'ring ranks com-bine.
Thou hast prom - ised, draw men un - to Thee.
neath the shad - ow of its heal - ing peace.
a - tion's prais - es rise be - fore Thy throne.

We've a Story to Tell to the Nations 524

And this gospel...shall be preached in all the world for a witness unto all nations. Matt. 24:14

H. ERNEST NICHOL

H. ERNEST NICHOL

1. We've a sto - ry to tell to the na - tions That shall
2. We've a song to be sung to the na - tions That shall
3. We've a mes - sage to give to the na - tions That the
4. We've a Sav - ior to show to the na - tions Who the

turn their hearts to the right, A sto - ry of truth and mer - cy,
lift their hearts to the Lord, A song that shall con - quer e - vil
Lord who reign - eth a - bove Hath sent us His Son to save us,
path of sor - row hath trod, That all of the world's great peo - ples

A sto - ry of peace and light, A sto - ry of peace and light.
And shat - ter the spear and sword, And shat - ter the spear and sword.
And show us that God is love, And show us that God is love.
Might come to the truth of God, Might come to the truth of God.

Refrain

For the dark-ness shall turn to dawn-ing, And the dawn-ing to noon-day bright,

And Christ's great king-dom shall come to earth, The king-dom of love and light.

525 Make Me a Blessing

So will I save you and ye shall be a blessing. Zech. 8:13

IRA B. WILSON

GEORGE S. SCHULER

1. Out in the high-ways and by-ways of life, Man-y are wea-ry and sad;
are wea-ry and sad;
2. Tell the sweet sto-ry of Christ and His love, Tell of His pow'r to for-give;
His pow'r to for-give;
3. Give as 'twas giv-en to you in your need, Love as the Mas-ter loved you;
the Mas-ter loved you;

Car-ry the sun-shine where dark-ness is rife, Mak-ing the sor-row-ing glad.
Oth-ers will trust Him if on-ly you prove True, ev-ery mo-ment you live.
Be to the help-less a help-er in-deed, Un-to your mis-sion be true.

Refrain

Make me a bless-ing, make me a bless-ing, Out of my

life may Je-sus shine; Make me a bless-ing, O Sav-ior,
out of my life

I pray,
I pray Thee, my Sav-ior, Make me a bless-ing to some-one to-day.

Lonely Voices 526

I...am as a sparrow alone upon the housetop. Psa. 102:7

BILLIE HANKS, JR.

BILLIE HANKS, JR.

Unison

1. Lone-ly voic-es cry-ing in the cit-y, Lone-ly voic-es
2. Lone-ly fac-es look-ing for the sun-rise, Just to find an-
3. Lone-ly eyes, I see them in the sub-way, Bur-dened by the
4. A-bund-ant life Christ came to tru-ly give them, But so few His

sound-ing like a child. Lone-ly voic-es come from bus-y peo-ple,
oth-er bus-y day. Lone-ly 'fac-es all a-round the cit-y,
wor-ries of the day: Lives of lei-sure, yet they're so un-hap-py,
gift of grace re-ceive. Lone-ly peo-ple live in ev-ery cit-y,

Too dis-turbed to stop a lit-tle while. Lone-ly voic-es
Though a-fraid, they're too a-shamed to pray. Lone-ly fac-es
Tired of fool-ish roles they try to play. Lone-ly peo-ple
Those who face a dark and lone-ly grave. Lone-ly fac-es

fill my dreams, Lone-ly voic-es haunt my mem-o-ry.
do I see, Lone-ly fac-es haunt my mem-o-ry.
do I see, Lone-ly peo-ple haunt my mem-o-ry.
do I see, Lone-ly voic-es call-ing out to me.

527 People Need the Lord

They are scattered, like sheep without a shepherd. Matt 9:36

GREG NELSON AND PHILL McHUGH

GREG NELSON AND PHILL McHUGH

1. Peo - ple need the Lord, peo - ple need the Lord; At the end of
2. Peo - ple need the Lord, peo - ple need the Lord; When will we

bro - ken dreams, He's the o - pen door.
re - al - ize peo - ple need the Lord.

528 Lord, Be Glorified

Let the Lord be glorified. Isa. 66:5

BOB KILPATRICK

BOB KILPATRICK

1. In my life, Lord, be glo - ri - fied, be glo - ri - fied.
2. In your church, Lord, be glo - ri - fied, be glo - ri - fied.

In my life, Lord, be glo - ri - fied to - day.
In your church, Lord, be glo - ri - fied to - day.

Only One Life to Offer 529

But this I say, brethren, the time is short...I Cor. 7:29

Avis B. Christiansen   Merrill Dunlop

1. On - ly one life to of - fer— Je - sus, my Lord and King;
2. On - ly this hour is mine, Lord—May it be used for Thee;
3. On - ly one life to of - fer— Take it, dear Lord, I pray;

On - ly one tongue to praise Thee And of Thy mer - cy sing (for - ev - er);
May ev - ery pass - ing mo - ment Count for e - ter - ni - ty (my Sav - ior);
Noth - ing from Thee with - hold - ing, Thy will I now o - bey (my Je - sus);

On - ly one heart's de - vo - tion—Sav - ior, O may it be Con - se -
Souls all a - bout are dy - ing, Dy - ing in sin and shame; Help me
Thou who hast free - ly giv - en Thine all in all for me, Claim this

crat - ed a - lone to Thy match - less glo - ry, Yield - ed ful - ly to Thee.
bring them the mes - sage of Cal - v'ry's re - demp - tion In Thy glo - ri - ous name.
life for Thine own, to be used, my Sav - ior, Ev - ery mo - ment for Thee.

530 The Vision of a Dying World

Lift up your eyes, and look on the fields; for they are white...John 4:35

ANNE ORTLUND

HENRY S. CUTLER

1. The vi-sion of a dy-ing world Is vast be-fore our eyes;
2. The sav-age hugs his god of stone And fears de-scent of night;
3. To-day, as un-der-stand-ing's bounds Are stretch'd on ev-ery hand,
4. The warn-ing bell of judg-ment tolls, A-bove us looms the cross;

We feel the heart-beat of its need, We hear its fee-ble cries:
The cit-y dwell-er cring-es lone A-mid the gar-ish light:
O clothe Thy Word in bright, new sounds, And speed it o'er the land;
A-round are ev-er-dy-ing souls— How great, how great the loss!

Lord Je-sus Christ, re-vive Thy church In this, her cru-cial hour!
Lord Je-sus Christ, a-rouse Thy church To see their mute dis-tress!
Lord Je-sus Christ, em-pow-er us To preach by ev-ery means!
O Lord, con-strain and move Thy church The glad news to im-part!

Lord Je-sus Christ, a-wake Thy church With Spir-it-giv-en pow'r.
Lord Je-sus Christ, e-quip Thy church With love and ten-der-ness.
Lord Je-sus Christ, em-bold-en us In near and dis-tant scenes.
And Lord, as Thou dost stir Thy church, Be-gin with-in my heart. A-men.

So Send I You—by Grace 531

As My Father hath sent Me, even so send I you. John 20:21

Margaret Clarkson

John W. Peterson

1. So send I you— by grace made strong to tri-umph O'er hosts of hell, o'er dark-ness, death and sin, My name to bear and in that name to con-quer So send I you, My vic-to-ry to win.

2. So send I you— to take to souls in bon-dage The Word of Truth that sets the cap-tive free, To break the bonds of sin, to loose death's fet-ters So send I you, to bring the lost to Me.

3. So send I you— My strength to know in weak-ness, My joy in grief, My per-fect peace in pain, To prove My pow'r, My grace, My prom-ised pres-ence So send I you, e-ter-nal fruit to gain.

4. So send I you— to bear my cross with pa-tience, And then one day with joy to lay it down, To hear My voice, "Well done, My faith-ful ser-vant Come share My throne, My king-dom and My crown."

Refrain (following the final stanza)

"As the Fa-ther hath sent me, So send I you."

532 So Send I You

As My Father hath sent Me, even so send I you. John 20:21

MARGARET CLARKSON

JOHN W. PETERSON

1. So send I you to la-bor un-re-ward-ed, To serve un-
2. So send I you to bind the bruised and bro-ken, O'er wand-'ring
3. So send I you to lone-li-ness and long-ing, With heart a-
4. So send I you to leave your life's am-bi-tion, To die to
5. So send I you to hearts made hard by ha-tred, To eyes made

paid, un-loved, un-sought, un-known, To bear re-buke, to suf-fer
souls to work, to weep, to wake, To bear the bur-dens of a
hung-'ring for the loved and known, For-sak-ing home and kin-dred,
dear de-sire, self-will re-sign, To la-bor long, and love where
blind be-cause they will not see, To spend, though it be blood, to

scorn and scoff-ing— So send I you to toil for Me a-lone.
world a-wea-ry— So send I you to suf-fer for My sake.
friend and dear one— So send I you to know My love a-lone.
men re-vile you— So send I you to lose your life in Mine.
spend and spare not— So send I you to taste of Cal-va-ry.

Refrain (following the final stanza)

"As the Fa-ther hath sent me, So send I you."

Jesus Calls Us; O'er the Tumult 533

He saith unto them, follow me. Matt. 4:19

CECIL F. ALEXANDER

WILLIAM H. JUDE

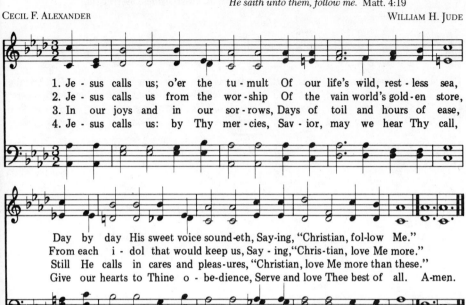

1. Je - sus calls us; o'er the tu - mult Of our life's wild, rest - less sea,
2. Je - sus calls us from the wor - ship Of the vain world's gold - en store,
3. In our joys and in our sor - rows, Days of toil and hours of ease,
4. Je - sus calls us: by Thy mer - cies, Sav - ior, may we hear Thy call,

Day by day His sweet voice sound-eth, Say-ing, "Christian, fol-low Me."
From each i - dol that would keep us, Say - ing, "Chris-tian, love Me more."
Still He calls in cares and pleas-ures, "Christian, love Me more than these."
Give our hearts to Thine o - be-dience, Serve and love Thee best of all. A-men.

Rise Up, O Men of God! 534

Yet a little while, and He...will come, and will not tarry. Heb. 10:37

WILLIAM P. MERRILL

WILLIAM H. WALTER

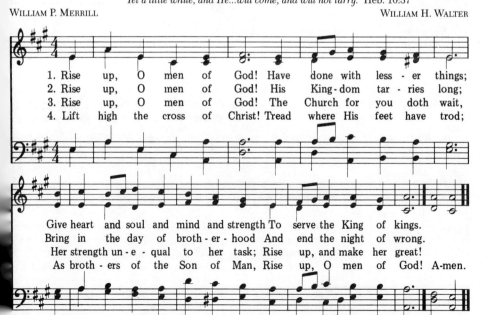

1. Rise up, O men of God! Have done with less - er things;
2. Rise up, O men of God! His King-dom tar - ries long;
3. Rise up, O men of God! The Church for you doth wait,
4. Lift high the cross of Christ! Tread where His feet have trod;

Give heart and soul and mind and strength To serve the King of kings.
Bring in the day of broth - er - hood And end the night of wrong.
Her strength un - e - qual to her task; Rise up, and make her great!
As broth - ers of the Son of Man, Rise up, O men of God! A-men.

535 Lord, Speak to Me, That I May Speak

The things that thou hast heard of Me...commit thou to faithful men. II Tim. 2:2

FRANCES R. HAVERGAL

ROBERT A. SCHUMANN

1. Lord, speak to me, that I may speak In liv-ing ech-oes of Thy tone;
2. O teach me, Lord, that I may teach The pre-cious things Thou dost im-part;
3. O fill me with Thy full-ness, Lord, Un-til my ver-y heart o'er-flow
4. O use me, Lord, use e-ven me, Just as Thou wilt and when and where;

As Thou hast sought, so let me seek Thy err-ing chil-dren lost and lone.
And wing my words, that they may reach The hid-den depths of many a heart.
In kind-ling thought and glow-ing word Thy love to tell, Thy praise to show.
Un-til Thy bless-ed face I see, Thy rest, Thy joy, Thy glo-ry share. A-men.

536 Jesus Shall Reign Where'er the Sun

All kings shall fall down before Him; all nations shall serve Him. Psa. 72:11

ISAAC WATTS

JOHN HATTON

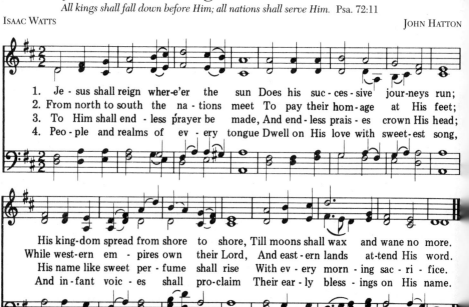

1. Je-sus shall reign wher-e'er the sun Does his suc-ces-sive jour-neys run;
2. From north to south the na-tions meet To pay their hom-age at His feet;
3. To Him shall end-less prayer be made, And end-less prais-es crown His head;
4. Peo-ple and realms of ev-ery tongue Dwell on His love with sweet-est song,

His king-dom spread from shore to shore, Till moons shall wax and wane no more.
While west-ern em-pires own their Lord, And east-ern lands at-tend His word.
His name like sweet per-fume shall rise With ev-ery morn-ing sac-ri-fice.
And in-fant voic-es shall pro-claim Their ear-ly bless-ings on His name.

Go Ye into All the World 537

Go ye into all the world, and preach the gospel...Mark 16:15

JAMES MCGRANAHAN   JAMES MCGRANAHAN

1. Far, far a - way, in death and dark - ness dwell- ing, Mil- lions of souls for-
2. See o'er the world wide o - pen doors in - vit - ing, Sol - diers of Christ, a -
3. "Why will ye die?" the voice of God is call - ing, "Why will ye die?" re-
4. God speed the day, when those of ev - ery na - tion "Glo - ry to God!" tri-

ev - er may be lost; Who, who will go, sal - va - tion's sto - ry tell - ing,
rise and en - ter in! Chris- tians, a - wake! your forc - es all u - nit - ing,
ech - o in His name; Je - sus hath died to save from death ap- pall - ing,
um - phant - ly shall sing; Ran- somed, re- deemed, re - joic - ing in sal - va - tion,

Refrain

Look- ing to Je - sus, mind- ing not the cost?
Send forth the gos - pel, break the chains of sin.   "All pow'r is giv - en un - to Me,
Life and sal - va - tion there- fore go pro- claim.
Shout Hal - le - lu - jah, for the Lord is King.

All pow'r is giv - en un - to Me, Go ye in - to all the world and

preach the gos - pel, And lo, I am with you al - way."

538 I'll Go Where You Want Me to Go

Then said I, Here am I; send me. Isa. 6:8

CHARLES H. GABRIEL

CARRIE E. ROUNSEFELL

1. It may not be on the moun-tain's height, Or o - ver the storm-y
2. Per - haps to - day there are lov - ing words Which Je - sus would have me
3. There's sure - ly some-where a low - ly place In earth's har - vest-fields so

sea; It may not be at the bat - tle's front My
speak; There may be now, in the paths of sin, Some
wide, Where I may la - bor thro' life's short day For

Lord will have need of me; But if by a still, small
wan - d'rer whom I should seek. O Sav - ior, if Thou wilt
Je - sus, the Cru - ci - fied. So, trust - ing my all un -

voice He calls To paths I do not know, I'll
be my Guide, Tho' dark and rug - ged the way, My
to Thy care, I know Thou lov - est me! I'll

an - swer, dear Lord, with my hand in Thine, I'll go where you
voice shall ech - o the mes - sage sweet, I'll say what you
do Thy will with a heart sin - cere, I'll be what you

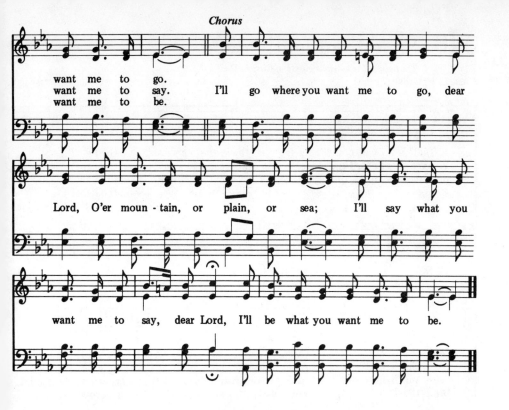

Chorus

want me to go.
want me to say.   I'll go where you want me to go, dear
want me to be.

Lord, O'er moun - tain, or plain, or sea;   I'll say what you

want me to say, dear Lord, I'll be what you want me to be.

Where He Leads Me   539

Master, I will follow Thee whithersoever Thou goest.   Matt. 8:19

E.W. BLANDY   JOHN S. NORRIS

1. I   can hear my Sav - ior call - ing,   I   can hear my Sav - ior call - ing,
2. I'll   go with Him thro' the gar - den, I'll   go with Him thro' the gar - den,
3. I'll   go with Him thro' the judg - ment, I'll   go with Him thro' the judg - ment,
4. He will give me grace and glo - ry, He will give me grace and glo - ry,
Ref. – Where He leads me I will fol - low, Where He leads me I will fol - low,

D.C. Refrain

I   can hear my Sav - ior call - ing, "Take thy cross and fol - low, fol - low Me."
I'll   go with Him thro' the gar - den, I'll   go with Him, with Him all the way.
I'll   go with Him thro' the judg - ment, I'll   go with Him, with Him all the way.
He will give me grace and glo - ry, And go with me, with me all the way.
Where He leads me I will fol - low, I'll go with Him, with Him all the way.

540 Send the Light!

The light of the glorious gospel of Christ...II Cor. 4:4

Charles H. Gabriel   Charles H. Gabriel

1. There's a call comes ring-ing o'er the rest-less wave,"Send the light!
2. We have heard the Mac - e - do - nian call to - day, "Send the light!
3. Let us pray that grace may ev-ery-where a-bound, Send the light!
4. Let us not grow wea - ry in the work of love, Send the light!

Send the light!

Send the light!"   There are souls to res - cue, there are souls to save,
Send the light!"   And a gold - en off'ring at the cross we lay,
Send the light!   And a Christ-like spir - it ev - ery-where be found,
Send the light!   Let us gath - er jew - els for a crown a - bove,
Send the light!

Chorus

Send the light!   Send the light!   Send the light,   the
Send the light!   Send the light!   Send the light,

bless - ed gos - pel light; Let it shine   from shore to
the   bless - ed gos - pel light;   Let it shine

shore!   shine   for - ev - er - more!

from shore to shore!   Let   it shine   for - ev - er - more!

Jesus said,   **541**
"I am the Light of the world.
Whoever follows me will never walk in darkness,
But will have the Light of Life."

John 8:12

O Master, Let Me Walk with Thee   542

He appeared...unto two of them, as they walked...Mark 16:12

WASHINGTON GLADDEN   H. PERCY SMITH

1. O Mas-ter, let me walk with Thee In low-ly paths of ser-vice free;
2. Help me the slow of heart to move By some clear, win-ning word of love;
3. Teach me Thy pa-tience! still with Thee In clos-er, dear-er com-pa-ny,
4. In hope that sends a shin-ing ray Far down the fu-ture's broad-'ning way,

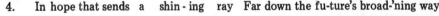

Tell me Thy se-cret; help me bear The strain of toil, the fret of care.
Teach me the way-ward feet to stay, And guide them in the home-ward way.
In work that keeps faith sweet and strong, In trust that tri-umphs o-ver wrong;
In peace that on-ly Thou canst give, With Thee, O Mas-ter, let me live.

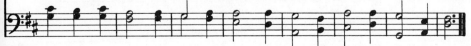

543 Wherever He Leads I'll Go

Whosoever will come after Me, let him...take up his cross and follow Me. Mark 8:34

B.B. McKinney

B.B. McKinney

1. "Take up thy cross and fol-low Me," I heard my Mas-ter say;
2. He drew me clos-er to His side, I sought His will to know,
3. It may be through the shad-ows dim, Or o'er the storm-y sea,
4. My heart, my life, my all I bring To Christ who loves me so;

"I gave My life to ran-som thee, Sur-ren-der your all to-day."
And in that will I now a-bide, Wher-ev-er He leads I'll go.
I take my cross and fol-low Him, Wher-ev-er He lead-eth me.
He is my Mas-ter, Lord, and King, Wher-ev-er He leads I'll go.

Refrain

Wher-ev-er He leads I'll go, Wher-ev-er He leads I'll go,

I'll fol-low my Christ who loves me so, Wher-ev-er He leads I'll go.

Hark, the Voice of Jesus Calling 544

The harvest truly is great, but the laborers are few...Luke 10:2

DANIEL MARCH

ATTR. WOLFGANG A. MOZART

1. Hark, the voice of Je - sus call - ing, "Who will go and work to - day?
2. If you can - not be the watch - man Stand - ing high on Zi - on's wall,
3. Let none hear you i - dly say - ing, "There is noth - ing I can do,"

Fields are white, and har - vests wait - ing, Who will bear the sheaves a - way?"
Point - ing out the path to heav - en, Off - 'ring life and peace to all,
While the souls of men are dy - ing, And the Mas - ter calls for you:

Loud and long the Mas - ter call - eth, Rich re - ward He of - fers free;
If you can - not speak like an - gels, If you can - not preach like Paul,
Take the task He gives you glad - ly; Let His work your pleas - ure be;

Who will an - swer, glad - ly say - ing, "Here am I; send me, send me"?
You can tell the love of Je - sus, You can say, "He died for all."
An - swer quick - ly when He call - eth, "Here am I; send me, send me." A - men.

545 Christ for the World We Sing

Go ye into all the world and preach the gospel. Mark 16:15

SAMUEL WOLCOTT

FELICE DE GIARDINI

1. Christ for the world we sing; The world to
2. Christ for the world we sing; The world to
3. Christ for the world we sing; The world to
4. Christ for the world we sing; The world to

Christ we bring With lov - ing zeal—
Christ we bring With fer - vent prayer—
Christ we bring With one ac - cord—
Christ we bring With joy - ful song—

The poor and them that mourn, The faint and o - ver - borne,
The way - ward and the lost, By rest - less pas - sions tossed,
With us the work to share, With us re - proach to dare,
The new - born souls whose days, Re - claimed from er - ror's ways,

Sin - sick and sor - row - worn, For Christ to heal.
Re - deemed at count - less cost From dark de - spair.
With us the cross to bear, For Christ our Lord.
In - spired with hope and praise, To Christ be - long.

Jesus Saves! 546

Tell of His salvation from day to day. Declare His glory...Psa. 96:2,3

PRISCILLA J. OWENS

WILLIAM J. KIRKPATRICK

1. We have heard the joy - ful sound: Je - sus saves! Je - sus saves!
2. Waft it on the roll - ing tide; Je - sus saves! Je - sus saves!
3. Sing a - bove the bat - tle strife, Je - sus saves! Je - sus saves!
4. Give the winds a might - y voice, Je - sus saves! Je - sus saves!

Spread the ti - dings all a - round: Je - sus saves! Je - sus saves!
Tell to sin - ners far and wide: Je - sus saves! Je - sus saves!
By His death and end - less life, Je - sus saves! Je - sus saves!
Let the na - tions now re - joice— Je - sus saves! Je - sus saves!

Bear the news to ev - ery land, Climb the steeps and cross the waves;
Sing, ye is - lands of the sea; Ech - o back, ye o - cean caves;
Sing it soft - ly through the gloom, When the heart for mer - cy craves;
Shout sal - va - tion full and free, High - est hills and deep - est caves;

On - ward! 'tis our Lord's com - mand; Je - sus saves! Je - sus saves!
Earth shall keep her ju - bi - lee: Je - sus saves! Je - sus saves!
Sing in tri - umph o'er the tomb— Je - sus saves! Je - sus saves!
This our song of vic - to - ry— Je - sus saves! Je - sus saves!

Second Coming
and
Eternal Life

547   Then I saw a new heaven and a new earth,
for the first heaven and the first earth had passed away,
and there was no longer any sea.
I saw the Holy City, the new Jerusalem,
coming down out of heaven from God,
prepared as a bride beautifully dressed for her husband.
And I heard a loud voice from the throne saying,
"Now the dwelling of God is with men,
and he will live with them.
They will be his people,
and God himself will be with them and be their God.
He will wipe every tear from their eyes.
There will be no more death or mourning
or crying or pain,
for the old order of things has passed away."
Revelation 21:1-4 (NIV)

For All the Saints 548

These all died in faith. Heb. 11:13

WILLIAM W. HOW

RALPH VAUGHAN WILLIAMS

1. For all the saints who from their la - bors rest, Who
2. Thou wast their rock, their for - tress, and their might, Thou
3. O may Thy sol - diers, faith - ful, true, and bold, Fight
4. O blest com - mun - ion, fel - low-ship di - vine! We
5. But lo! there breaks a yet more glo - rious day; The
6. From earth's wide bounds, from o - cean's far - thest coast, Through

Thee by faith be - fore the world con - fessed, Thy
Lord, their cap - tain in the well-fought fight;
Fight as the saints who no - bly fought of old, And
We fee - bly strug - gle, they in glo - ry shine; Yet
saints tri - um - phant rise in bright ar - ray; The
gates of pearl stream in the count - less host,

name, O Je - sus, be for - ev - er blest:
Thou, in the dark - ness drear, their one true light:
win with them the vic - tor's crown of gold:
all are one in Thee, for all are Thine;
King of glo - ry pass - es on His way:
Sing - ing to Fa - ther, Son, and Ho - ly Ghost:

Al - le - lu - ia! Al - le - lu - ia!

549 What If It Were Today?

*The Lord Himself shall descend from heaven with a shout...*I Thess. 4:16

LELIA N. MORRIS   LELIA N. MORRIS

1. Je - sus is com - ing to earth a - gain, What if it were to - day?
2. Sa - tan's do - min - ion will soon be o'er, O, that it were to - day!
3. Faith - ful and true would He find us here, If He should come to - day?

Com - ing in pow - er and love to reign, What if it were to - day?
Sor - row and sigh - ing shall be no more, O, that it were to - day!
Watch - ing in glad - ness and not in fear, If He should come to - day?

Com - ing to claim His cho - sen Bride, All the re - deemed and pu - ri - fied,
Then shall the dead in Christ a - rise, Caught up to meet Him in the skies,
Signs of His com - ing mul - ti - ply, Morn-ing light breaks in east - ern sky,

O - ver this whole earth scat-tered wide, What if it were to - day?
When shall these glo - ries meet our eyes? What if it were to - day?
Watch, for that time is draw - ing nigh, What if it were to - day?

Refrain

Glo - ry, glo - ry! Joy to my heart 'twill bring; Glo - ry,
Joy to my heart 'twill bring;

glo - ry! When we shall crown Him King; Glo - ry, glo - ry!
When we shall crown Him King;

Haste to pre-pare the way; Glo - ry, glo - ry! Je-sus will come some day.
Haste to pre-pare the way;

Lift Up the Trumpet 550

He which testifieth...saith, Surely I come quickly. Rev. 22:20

GEORGE E. LEE

JESSIE E. STROUT

ARR. ELDON BURKWALL

1. Lift up the trum-pet and loud let it ring: Je - sus is com-ing a - gain!
2. Na - tions are an - gry— by this do we know: Je - sus is com-ing a - gain!
3. Fierce fires and earth-quakes con-firm to the throng: Je - sus is com-ing a - gain!
4. Shout from the hill - tops the joy - ful re - frain: Je - sus is com-ing a - gain!

Take heart, ye pil - grims, re - joice now and sing: Je - sus is com-ing a - gain!
Knowl-edge in - creas - es, men run to and fro: Je - sus is com-ing a - gain!
Tem-pests and whirl-winds the an - them pro - long: Je - sus is com-ing a - gain!
Com - ing in glo - ry the Lamb that was slain: Je - sus is com-ing a - gain!

Com - ing a-gain, com - ing a-gain, Je - sus is com-ing a - gain!

551 The King Is Coming

Till they see the Son of man coming in His kingdom. Matt. 16:28

WILLIAM J. AND GLORIA GAITHER
AND CHARLES MILHUFF

WILLIAM J. GAITHER

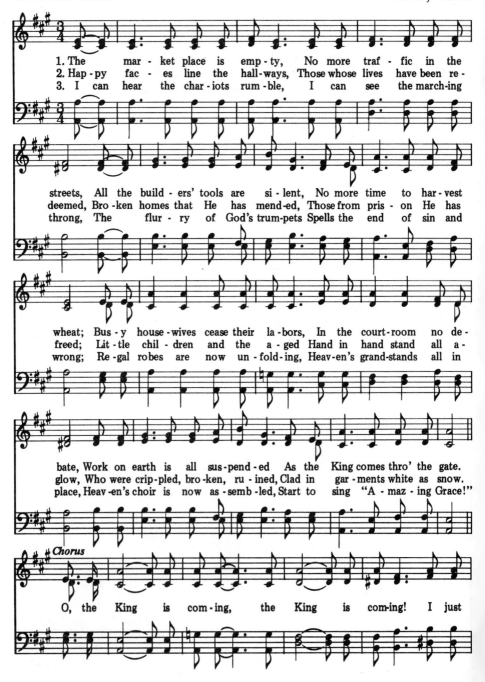

1. The mar - ket place is emp - ty, No more traf - fic in the
2. Hap - py fac - es line the hall - ways, Those whose lives have been re -
3. I can hear the char - iots rum - ble, I can see the march - ing

streets, All the build - ers' tools are si - lent, No more time to har - vest
deemed, Bro - ken homes that He has mend - ed, Those from pris - on He has
throng, The flur - ry of God's trum - pets Spells the end of sin and

wheat; Bus - y house - wives cease their la - bors, In the court - room no de -
freed; Lit - tle chil - dren and the a - ged Hand in hand stand all a -
wrong; Re - gal robes are now un - fold - ing, Heav - en's grand - stands all in

bate, Work on earth is all sus - pend - ed As the King comes thro' the gate.
glow, Who were crip - pled, bro - ken, ru - ined, Clad in gar - ments white as snow.
place, Heav - en's choir is now as - semb - led, Start to sing "A - maz - ing Grace!"

Chorus

O, the King is com - ing, the King is com - ing! I just

heard the trum-pets sound-ing, And now His face I see; O the King is

com-ing, the King is com-ing! Praise God, He's com-ing for me!

When He Shall Come 552

And they shall walk with me in white. Rev. 3:4

ALMEDA J. PEARCE

ALMEDA J. PEARCE

1. When He shall come, re - splen-dent in His glo - ry, To take His
2. When I shall stand with - in the court of heav - en Where white-robed
3. When He shall call, from earth's re - mot-est cor - ners, All who have

own from out this vale of night, O may I know the
pil - grims pass be - fore my sight— Earth's mar-tyred saints and
stood tri - um-phant in His might, O to be wor - thy

joy at His ap - pear-ing— On - ly at morn to walk with Him in white!
blood-washed o - ver - com-ers—These then are they who walk with Him in white!
then to stand be - side them, And in that morn to walk with Him in white!

553 Behold a Host

Lo, a great multitude...clothed with white robes. Rev. 7:9

HANS ADOLPH BRORSON
TR. GRACIA GRINDAL

TRADITIONAL NORSE MELODY
HARM. EDVARD GRIEG

1. Be - hold a host ar - rayed in white Like thou - sand
2. On earth their work was not thought wise, But see them
3. O bless - ed saints, now take your rest; A thou - sand

snow - clad moun - tains bright. They stand with palms And
now in heav - en's eyes; Be - fore God's throne Of
times shall you be blest For keep - ing faith Firm

sing their psalms Be - fore the throne of light. These are the
pre - cious stone They shout their vic - t'ry cries. On earth they
un - to death And scorn - ing world - ly trust. For now you

saints who kept God's Word; They are the hon - ored
wept through bit - ter years; Now God has wiped a -
live at home with God; You har - vest seeds once

of the Lord. He is their Prince Who drowned their sins,
way their tears, Trans-formed their strife To heav'n - ly life,
cast a - broad In tears and sighs. See with new eyes

So they were cleansed, re - stored. They now serve God both
And freed them from their fears. For now they have the
The pat - tern in the seed. The myr - iad an - gels

day and night; They sing their songs in end - less light. Their
best at last; They keep their sweet e - ter - nal feast. At
raise their song. O saints, sing with that hap - py throng; Lift

an - thems ring When they all sing With an - gels shin - ing bright.
God's right hand Our Lord com-mands; He is both host and guest.
up one voice; Let heav'n re - joice In our Re - deem - er's song.

554 Ten Thousand Times Ten Thousand

Behold, the Lord cometh with ten thousands of His saints. Jude 14

HENRY ALFORD

JOHN B. DYKES

1. Ten thou-sand times ten thou-sand In spark-ling rai-ment bright,
2. What rush of al-le-lu-ias Fills all the earth and sky!
3. O then what rap-tured greet-ings On Ca-naan's hap-py shore!
4. Bring near Thy great sal-va-tion, Thou Lamb for sin-ners slain;

The ar-mies of the ran-somed saints Throng up the steeps of light:
What ring-ing of a thou-sand harps Be-speaks the tri-umph nigh!
What knit-ting sev-ered friend-ships up, Where part-ings are no more!
Fill up the roll of Thine e-lect, Then take Thy pow'r and reign:

Tis fin-ished, all is fin-ished, Their fight with death and sin:
O day, for which cre-a-tion And all its tribes were made;
Then eyes with joy shall spar-kle That brimmed with tears of late,
Ap-pear, De-sire of na-tions, Thine ex-iles long for home;

Fling o-pen wide the gold-en gates, And let the vic-tors in.
O joy, for all its for-mer woes A thou-sand-fold re-paid!
Or-phans no lon-ger fa-ther-less, Nor wid-ows des-o-late.
Show in the heav'ns Thy prom-ised sign; Thou Prince and Sav-ior, come. A-men.

When We All Get to Heaven 555

...At Thy right hand there are pleasures for evermore. Psa. 16:11

ELIZA E. HEWITT

EMILY D. WILSON

1. Sing the won-drous love of Je - sus, Sing His mer - cy
2. While we walk the pil - grim path - way Clouds will o - ver -
3. Let us then be true and faith - ful, Trust - ing, serv - ing
4. On - ward to the prize be - fore us! Soon His beau - ty

and His grace; In the man - sions bright and bless - ed He'll pre -
spread the sky; But when trav - 'ling days are o - ver, Not a
ev - ery day; Just one glimpse of Him in glo - ry Will the
we'll be - hold; Soon the pearl - y gates will o - pen, We shall

Refrain

pare for us a place.
sha - dow, not a sigh. When we all get to heav - en,
toils of life re - pay. When we all
tread the streets of gold.

What a day of re - joic - ing that will be! When we
What a day of re - joic - ing that will be!

all see Je - sus, We'll sing and shout the vic - to - ry.
When we all and shout the vic - to - ry.

556 When the Roll Is Called Up Yonder

I...heard behind me a great voice, as of a trumpet. Rev. 1:10

JAMES M. BLACK   JAMES M. BLACK

1. When the trum - pet of the Lord shall sound, and
2. On that bright and cloud - less morn - ing when the
3. Let us la - bor for the Mas - ter from the

time shall be no more, And the morn-ing breaks, e - ter - nal, bright and
dead in Christ shall rise, And the glo - ry of His res - ur - rec - tion
dawn till set - ting sun, Let us talk of all His won-drous love and

fair; When the saved of earth shall gath - er o - ver
share; When His cho - sen ones shall gath - er to their
care; Then when all of life is o - ver, and our

on the oth - er shore, And the roll is called up yon - der, I'll be there.
home be-yond the skies, And the roll is called up yon - der, I'll be there.
work on earth is done, And the roll is called up yon - der, I'll be there.

Chorus

When the roll is called up
When the roll is called up

yon - der, When the roll is called up
yon - der, I'll be there, When the roll is called up

yon - der, When the roll is called up
yon - der, I'll be there, When the roll is called up

yon - der, When the roll is called up yon - der, I'll be there.

557 Christ Returneth

Ye shall see the Son of man...coming in the clouds of heaven. Mark 14:6

H.L. TURNER   JAMES McGRANAHAN

1. It may be at morn, when the day is a-wak-ing, When
2. It may be at mid-day, it may be at twi-light, It
3. While hosts cry Ho-san-na, from heav-en de-scend-ing, With
4. O joy! O de-light! should we go with-out dy-ing, No

sun-light through dark-ness and shad-ow is break-ing, That Je-sus will
may be, per-chance, that the black-ness of mid-night Will burst in-to
glo-ri-fied saints and the an-gels at-tend-ing, With grace on His
sick-ness, no sad-ness, no dread and no cry-ing, Caught up through the

come in the full-ness of glo-ry, To re-ceive from the world His own.
light in the blaze of His glo-ry, When Je-sus re-ceives His own.
brow, like a ha-lo of glo-ry, Will Je-sus re-ceive His own.
clouds with our Lord in-to glo-ry, When Je-sus re-ceives His own.

Refrain

O Lord Je-sus, how long, how long Ere we shout the glad song, Christ re-

turn-eth! Hal-le-lu-jah! hal-le-lu-jah! A-men, Hal-le-lu-jah! A-men.

Is It the Crowning Day? 558

Unto them that look for Him shall He appear the second time...Heb 9:28

HENRY OSTROM

CHARLES H. MARSH

1. Je - sus may come to - day, Glad day! Glad day! And I would
2. I may go home to - day, Glad day! Glad day! Seem - eth I
3. Why should I anx - ious be? Glad day! Glad day! Lights ap - pear
4. Faith - ful I'll be to - day, Glad day! Glad day! And I will

see my Friend; Dan - gers and trou - bles would end If
hear their song; Hail to the ra - di - ant throng! If
on the shore, Storms will af - fright nev - er - more, For
free - ly tell Why I should love Him so well, For

Refrain

Je - sus should come to - day.
I should go home to - day.
He is "at hand" to - day.   Glad day! Glad day! Is it the crown-ing
He is my all to - day.

day? I'll live for to - day, nor anx - ious be, Je - sus my Lord I

soon shall see; Glad day! Glad day! Is it the crown - ing day?

559 Soon and Very Soon

"Yes, I am coming soon." Amen. Come, Lord Jesus. Rev. 22:20

ANDRAÉ CROUCH

ANDRAÉ CROUCH

Unison or Three-Part

1. 3. Soon and ver - y soon,   We are going to see the King;
2. No more dy - ing there,   We are going to see the King;

Soon and ver - y soon,   We are going to see the King;
No more dy - ing there,   We are going to see the King;

Soon and ver - y soon,   We are going to see the King;   Hal-le-
No more dy - ing there,   We are going to see the King;   Hal-le-

1,2

lu - jah!   Hal-le-lu - jah!   We're going to see the King.

going to see the King! Hal - le - lu - jah! Hal - le - lu - jah!

Every Eye Shall See 560

Behold, He comes with clouds and every eye shall see Him. Rev. 1:7

WILLIAM J. AND GLORIA GAITHER

WILLIAM J. GAITHER

Ev - ery eye shall see, Ev - ery knee shall

bow; Ev - ery tongue shall con -fess to the glo - ry of

God that Je - sus is Lord— He is Lord,

He is Lord, He is Lord.

561 The Trees of the Field

You shall go out with joy. Isa. 55:12

STEFFI GEISER RUBIN

STUART DAUERMANN

Unison

You shall go out with joy and be led forth with peace;

The moun-tains and the hills will break forth be-

fore you. There'll be shouts of joy, and all the trees of the

field Will clap, will clap their hands. And all the

claps

trees of the field will clap their hands, The trees of the

field will clap their hands, The trees of the field will

clap their hands While you go out with joy.

Seek the Lord

562

Isaiah 55:6-13 (NIV)

Seek the Lord while he may be found; call on him while he is near.
Let the wicked forsake his way and the evil man his thoughts.
Let him turn to the Lord, and he will have mercy on him,
and to our God, for he will freely pardon.

"For my thoughts are not your thoughts,
neither are your ways my ways," declares the Lord.
"As the heavens are higher than the earth, so are my ways higher than your ways
and my thoughts than your thoughts.

As the rain and the snow come down from heaven,
and do not return to it without watering the earth and making it bud and flourish,
so that it yields seed for the sower and bread for the eater,
so is my word that goes out from my mouth: It will not return to me empty,
but will accomplish what I desire and achieve the purpose for which I sent it.

You will go out in joy and be led forth in peace;
the mountains and the hills will burst into song before you,
and all the trees of the field will clap their hands.
Instead of the thornbush will grow the pine tree,
and instead of briers the myrtle will grow.
This will be for the Lord's renown, for an everlasting sign, which will not be destroyed."

563 When We See Christ

The sufferings (of this present time) are not worthy to be compared with the glory...Rom.8:18

ESTHER K. RUSTHOI   ESTHER K. RUSTHOI

1. Oft-times the day seems long, our tri-als hard to bear, We're tempt-ed
2. Some-times the sky looks dark with not a ray of light, We're tossed and
3. Life's day will soon be o'er, all storms for-ev-er past, We'll cross the

to com-plain, to mur-mur and de-spair; But Christ will soon ap-pear
driv-en on, no hu-man help in sight; But there is one in heav'n
great di-vide to glo-ry, safe at last; We'll share the joys of heav'n—

to catch His Bride a-way, All tears for-ev-er o-ver in
who knows our deep-est care, Let Je-sus solve your prob-lem—just
a harp, a home, a crown, The tempt-er will be ban-ished, we'll

Chorus

God's e-ter-nal day.
go to Him in pray'r. It will be worth it all when we see Je-sus,
lay our bur-den down.

Life's trials will seem so small when we see Christ; One glimpse of His dear face

all sor-row will e - rase, So brave-ly run the race till we see Christ.

Face to Face 564

Now we see through a glass, darkly; but then face to face...I Cor. 13:12

CARRIE E. BRECK   GRANT C. TULLAR

1. Face to face with Christ my Sav - ior, Face to face—what will it be—
2. On - ly faint-ly now I see Him, With the dark-ling veil be-tween;
3. What re - joic - ing in His pres - ence When are ban-ished grief and pain;
4. Face to face! O bliss-ful mo - ment! Face to face— to see and know;

When with rap - ture I be-hold Him, Je - sus Christ who died for me?
But a bless - ed day is com - ing When His glo - ry shall be seen.
When the crook-ed ways are straight-ened And the dark things shall be plain.
Face to face with my Re-deem - er, Je - sus Christ who loves me so.

Refrain

Face to face I shall be-hold Him, Far be-yond the star - ry sky;

Face to face in all His glo - ry, I shall see Him by and by!

565 Saved by Grace

Or ever the silver cord be loosed...Then shall the dust return to the earth. Eccl. 12:6,7

FANNY J. CROSBY   GEORGE C. STEBBINS

1. Some day the sil-ver cord will break, And I no more as now shall sing;
2. Some day my earth-ly house will fall, I can-not tell how soon 'twill be;
3. Some day, when fades the gold-en sun Be-neath the ro-sy-tint-ed west,
4. Some day: till then I'll watch and wait, My lamp all trimmed and burn-ing bright,

But oh, the joy when I shall wake With-in the pal-ace of the King!
But this I know—my All in All Has now a place in heav'n for me.
My bless-ed Lord will say, "Well done!" And I shall en-ter in-to rest.
That when my Sav-ior opes the gate, My soul to Him may take its flight.

Chorus

And I shall see Him face to face, And tell the sto-ry—Saved by grace;
shall see to face,

And I shall see Him face to face, And tell the sto-ry—Saved by grace.
shall see to face,

We Shall See His Lovely Face 566

They will see His face. Rev. 22:4

NORMAN J. CLAYTON

NORMAN J. CLAYTON

1. We shall see His love - ly face Some bright, gold - en morn - ing,
2. God shall wipe a - way all tears Some bright, gold - en morn - ing,
3. We shall meet to part no more, Some bright, gold - en morn - ing,

When the clouds have rift - ed, And the shades have flown;
When the jour - ney's end - ed, And the course is run;
At the gates of glo - ry Where our loved ones stand;

Sor - row will be turned to joy, Heart-aches gone for - ev - er;
No more cry - ing, pain or death In that hour of glad - ness,
Songs of vic - t'ry fill the skies In that hour of greet - ing,

No more night, on - ly light, When we see His face.
Tri - als cease, all is peace, When we see His face.
End - less days, end - less praise, When we see His face.

567 Jesus Is Coming Again

*Watch therefore, for ye know neither the day nor the hour...*Matt 25:13

JOHN W. PETERSON

JOHN W. PETERSON

1. Mar - vel - ous mes - sage we bring, Glo - ri - ous car - ol we sing,
2. For - est and flow - er ex - claim, Moun - tain and mead - ow the same,
3. Stand - ing be - fore Him at last, Tri - al and trou - ble all past,

Won - der - ful word of the King— Je - sus is com - ing a - gain! (a-gain!)
All earth and heav - en pro - claim— Je - sus is com - ing a - gain! (a-gain!)
Crowns at His feet we will cast— Je - sus is com - ing a - gain! (a-gain!)

Refrain — Unison

Com - ing a - gain, Com - ing a-

gain; May - be morn - ing, may - be noon,

May - be eve - ning and may - be soon! Com - ing a-

gain, Com - ing a - gain;

Parts

O what a won-der-ful day it will be— Je-sus is com-ing a - gain!

Beyond the Sunset 568

For there shall be no night there...Rev. 21:25

VIRGIL P. BROCK

BLANCHE KERR BROCK

1. Be - yond the sun - set, O bliss - ful morn - ing, When with our
2. Be - yond the sun - set no clouds will gath - er, No storms will
3. Be - yond the sun - set a hand will guide me To God, the
4. Be - yond the sun - set, O glad re - un - ion, With our dear

Sav - ior heav'n is be - gun. Earth's toil - ing end - ed, O glo - rious
threat - en, no fears an - noy; O day of glad - ness, O day un -
Fa - ther, whom I a - dore; His glo - rious pres - ence, His words of
loved ones who've gone be - fore; In that fair home - land we'll know no

dawn - ing; Be - yond the sun - set, when day is done.
end - ing, Be - yond the sun - set, e - ter - nal joy!
wel - come, Will be my por - tion on that fair shore.
part - ing, Be - yond the sun - set for ev - er - more!

569 O That Will Be Glory

We shall be like Him; for we shall see Him as He is. I John 3:2

CHARLES H. GABRIEL   CHARLES H. GABRIEL

1. When all my la-bors and tri-als are o'er, And I am safe on that
2. When by the gift of His in-fi-nite grace, I am ac-cord-ed in
3. Friends will be there I have loved long a-go; Joy like a riv-er a-

beau-ti-ful shore, Just to be near the dear Lord I a-dore
heav-en a place, Just to be there and to look on His face
round me will flow; Yet, just a smile from my Sav-ior, I know,

Refrain

Will through the a-ges be glo-ry for me. O that will be
                                          O   that will

glo-ry for me, Glo-ry for me, glo-ry for me; When by His grace
be glo-ry for me, Glo-ry for me, glo-ry for me;

rit.

I shall look on His face, That will be glo-ry, be glo-ry for me.

Sweet By and By 570

On either side of the river was there the tree of life...Rev. 22:2

SANFORD F. BENNETT

JOSEPH P. WEBSTER

1. There's a land that is fair - er than day, And by faith we can
2. We shall sing on that beau - ti - ful shore The me - lo - di - ous
3. To our boun - ti - ful Fa - ther a - bove We will of - fer our

see it a - far, For the Fa - ther waits o - ver the way To pre -
songs of the blest; And our spir - its shall sor - row no more— Not a
trib - ute of praise, For the glo - ri - ous gift of His love And the

Chorus

pare us a dwell - ing place there.
sigh for the bless - ing of rest.   In the sweet   by and
bless - ings that hal - low our days.   In the sweet

by,   We shall meet on that beau - ti - ful shore;   In the
by and by,   by and by,

sweet   by and by,   We shall meet on that beau - ti - ful shore.
In the sweet   by and by,

571 When He Comes

For the Lord Himself shall descend from heaven with a shout. I Thess. 4:16

TIMOTHY DUDLEY-SMITH   JAMES D. THORNTON

Unison

1. When He comes,   when He comes,   We shall see   the Lord in glo - ry   when He
2. When He comes,   when He comes,   We shall hear the trum-pet sound-ed   when He
3. When He comes,   when He comes,   We shall all   rise up   to meet Him when He

comes!   As   I   read the gos - pel sto - ry   we shall see the Lord in   glo - ry,
comes!   We shall hear the trum-pet sound-ed, see the Lord by saints sur-round-ed,
comes!   When He calls His own   to   greet Him we shall all   rise up   to   meet Him,

We shall see   the Lord in   glo - ry when He comes! With the Al - le-lu-ias ring-ing to the
We shall hear the trum-pet sound-ed when He comes! With the Al - le-lu-ias ring-ing to the
We shall all   rise up   to meet Him when He comes! With the Al - le-lu-ias ring-ing to the

sky,   With the Al - le-lu-ias ring-ing to the sky!   As   I   read the gos - pel sto - ry
sky,   With the Al - le-lu-ias ring-ing to the sky!   We shall hear the trum-pet sound-ed,
sky,   With the Al - le-lu-ias ring-ing to the sky!   When He calls His own   to   greet Him

we shall see the Lord in glo - ry With the Al - le - lu - ias ring-ing to the sky!
see the Lord by saints sur-round-ed, With the Al - le - lu - ias ring-ing to the sky!
we shall all rise up to meet Him With the Al - le - lu - ias ring-ing to the sky!

Lo, He Comes with Clouds Descending 572

Behold, He cometh with clouds; and every eye shall see Him. Rev. 1:7

CHARLES WESLEY

HENRY T. SMART

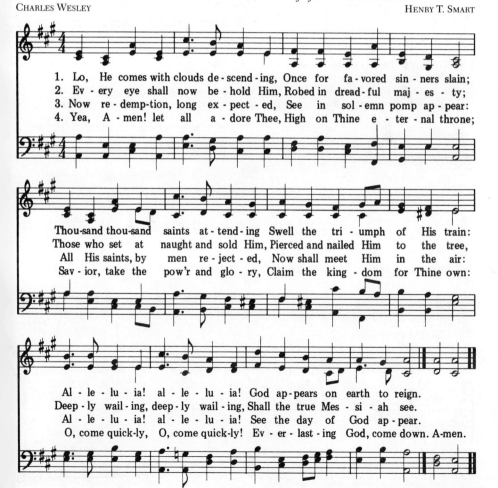

1. Lo, He comes with clouds de - scend - ing, Once for fa - vored sin - ners slain;
2. Ev - ery eye shall now be - hold Him, Robed in dread - ful maj - es - ty;
3. Now re - demp - tion, long ex - pect - ed, See in sol - emn pomp ap - pear:
4. Yea, A - men! let all a - dore Thee, High on Thine e - ter - nal throne;

Thou-sand thou-sand saints at - tend - ing Swell the tri - umph of His train:
Those who set at naught and sold Him, Pierced and nailed Him to the tree,
All His saints, by men re - ject - ed, Now shall meet Him in the air:
Sav - ior, take the pow'r and glo - ry, Claim the king - dom for Thine own:

Al - le - lu - ia! al - le - lu - ia! God ap-pears on earth to reign.
Deep - ly wail - ing, deep - ly wail - ing, Shall the true Mes - si - ah see.
Al - le - lu - ia! al - le - lu - ia! See the day of God ap - pear.
O, come quick - ly, O, come quick - ly! Ev - er - last - ing God, come down. A-men.

573 He the Pearly Gates Will Open

They that do His commandments...may enter in through the gates into the city. Rev. 22:14

FREDERICK A. BLOM
TR. NATHANIEL CARLSON

ATTR. ALFRED DULIN
ARR. ELSIE AHLWEN

1. Love di-vine, so great and won-drous, Deep and might-y, pure, sub-lime;
2. Like a dove when hunt-ed, fright-ened, As a wound-ed fawn was I,
3. Love di-vine, so great and won-drous— All my sins He then for-gave,
4. In life's e-ven-tide, at twi-light, At His door I'll knock and wait;

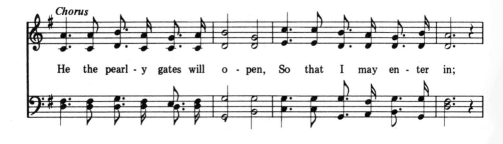

Com-ing from the heart of Je-sus— Just the same thro' tests of time.
Bro-ken heart-ed, yet He healed me— He will heed the sin-ner's cry.
I will sing His praise for-ev-er, For His blood, His pow'r to save.
By the pre-cious love of Je-sus, I shall en-ter heav-en's gate.

Chorus

He the pearl-y gates will o-pen, So that I may en-ter in;

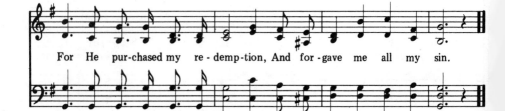

For He pur-chased my re-demp-tion, And for-gave me all my sin.

I Am Bound for the Promised Land 574

For He hath prepared for them a city. Heb. 11:16

SAMUEL STENNETT

TRADITIONAL AMERICAN MELODY
ARR. RIGDON M. MCINTOSH

1. On Jor-dan's storm-y banks I stand, And cast a wish-ful eye
2. All o'er those wide ex-tend-ed plains Shines one e-ter-nal day;
3. No chill-ing winds nor pois'nous breath Can reach that health-ful shore;
4. When shall I reach that hap-py place, And be for-ev-er blest?

To Ca-naan's fair and hap-py land, Where my pos-ses-sions lie.
There God the Son for-ev-er reigns And scat-ters night a-way.
Sick-ness and sor-row, pain and death Are felt and feared no more.
When shall I see my Fa-ther's face, And in His bos-om rest?

Refrain

I am bound for the prom-ised land, I am bound for the prom-ised land;

O who will come and go with me? I am bound for the prom-ised land.

575 Shall We Gather at the River?

A pure river of water of life...proceeding out of the throne of God. Rev. 22:1

ROBERT LOWRY   ROBERT LOWRY

1. Shall we gath - er at the riv - er, Where bright an-gel feet have trod;
2. On the bos-om of the riv - er, Where the Sav-ior-King we own,
3. Ere we reach the shin-ing riv - er, Lay we ev-ery bur-den down;
4. Soon we'll reach the shin-ing riv - er, Soon our pil-grim-age will cease;

With its crys - tal tide for - ev - er Flow-ing by the throne of God?
We shall meet, and sor - row nev - er, 'Neath the glo - ry of the throne.
Grace our spir - its will de - liv - er, And pro-vide a robe and crown.
Soon our hap - py hearts will quiv - er With the mel - o - dy of peace.

Chorus

Yes, we'll gath-er at the riv - er, The beau-ti - ful, the beau-ti - ful riv - er,

Gath-er with the saints at the riv - er That flows by the throne of God.

The River of Life 576

Then the angel showed me the river of the water of life, as clear as crystal, flowing from the throne of God and of the Lamb down the middle of the great street of the city.

On each side of the river stood the tree of life, bearing twelve crops of fruit, yielding its fruit every month. And the leaves of the tree are for the healing of the nations.

No longer will there be any curse. The throne of God and of the Lamb will be in the city, and his servants will serve him. They will see his face, and his name will be on their foreheads.

There will be no more night. They will not need the light of a lamp or the light of the sun, for the Lord God will give them light.

And they will reign for ever and ever.

Revelation 22:1-5 (NIV)

Evening
Hymns

From the rising of the sun
unto the going down of the same
the Lord's name is to be praised.
Psalm 113:3

Abide with Me 577

They constrained Him, saying, Abide with us. Luke 24:29

HENRY F. LYTE

WILLIAM H. MONK

1. A - bide with me: fast falls the e - ven - tide;
2. Swift to its close ebbs out life's lit - tle day;
3. I need Thy pres - ence ev - ery pass - ing hour;
4. I fear no foe, with Thee at hand to bless;
5. Hold Thou Thy cross be - fore my clos - ing eyes;

The dark - ness deep - ens; Lord, with me a - bide!
Earth's joys grow dim, its glo - ries pass a - way;
What but Thy grace can foil the tempt - er's power?
Ills have no weight, and tears no bit - ter - ness.
Shine through the gloom and point me to the skies:

When oth - er help - ers fail, and com - forts flee,
Change and de - cay in all a - round I see.
Who, like Thy - self, my guide and stay can be?
Where is death's sting? Where, grave, thy vic - to - ry?
Heav'n's morn - ing breaks, and earth's vain shad - ows flee;

Help of the help - less, O a - bide with me.
O Thou who chang - est not, a - bide with me.
Through cloud and sun - shine, Lord, a - bide with me.
I tri - umph still, if Thou a - bide with me.
In life, in death, O Lord, a - bide with me. A - men.

578 Wonderful Peace

Now the Lord of peace himself give you peace...II Thess. 3:16

W.D. CORNELL

W.G. COOPER

1. Far a - way in the depths of my spir - it to - night Rolls a
2. What a treas - ure I have in this won - der - ful peace, Bur - ied
3. I am rest - ing to - night in this won - der - ful peace, Rest - ing
4. And me - thinks when I rise to that Cit - y of peace, Where the
5. Ah! soul, are you here with - out com - fort or rest, March - ing

mel - o - dy sweet - er than psalm; In ce - les - tial - like strains it un -
deep in the heart of my soul; So se - cure that no pow - er can
sweet - ly in Je - sus' con - trol; For I'm kept from all dan - ger by
Au - thor of peace I shall see, That one strain of the song which the
down the rough path - way of time? Make Je - sus your friend ere the

ceas - ing - ly falls O'er my soul like an in - fi - nite calm.
mine it a - way, While the years of e - ter - ni - ty roll.
night and by day, And His glo - ry is flood - ing my soul.
ran - somed will sing, In that heav - en - ly king - dom shall be:
shad - ows grow dark; Oh, ac - cept this sweet peace so sub - lime.

Chorus

Peace! peace! won - der - ful peace, Com - ing down from the Fa - ther a - bove; Sweep

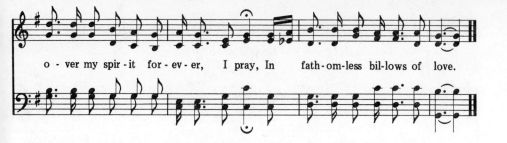

o - ver my spir - it for - ev - er, I pray, In fath - om - less bil - lows of love.

Benediction   579

The peace of God, which passeth all understanding, keep
your hearts and minds in the knowledge and love of God,
and of his Son Jesus Christ our Lord; and the blessing
of God Almighty, the Father, the Son, and the Holy
Ghost, be amongst you, and remain with you always.

Amen.

Peace, Perfect Peace   580

Thou wilt keep him in perfect peace, whose mind is stayed on Thee. Isa. 26:3

GEORGE T. CALDBECK
EDWARD H. BICKERSTETH
ARR. CHARLES J. VINCENT

1. Peace, per - fect peace, in this dark world of sin?
2. Peace, per - fect peace, by throng - ing du - ties pressed?
3. Peace, per - fect peace, with sor - rows surg - ing round?
4. Peace, per - fect peace, our fu - ture all un - known?
5. Peace, per - fect peace, death shad - owing us and ours?
6. It is e - nough: earth's strug - gles soon shall cease,

The blood of Je - sus whis - pers peace with - in.
To do the will of Je - sus, this is rest.
On Je - sus' bos - om naught but calm is found.
Je - sus we know, and He is on the throne.
Je - sus has van - quished death and all its po - wers.
And Je - sus, call us to heav'n's per - fect peace. A - men.

581 Lord, Dismiss Us with Your Blessing

May Your blessing be upon Your people. Psa. 3:8

JOHN FAWCETT

TATTERSALL'S PSALMODY

1. Lord, dis - miss us with your bless - ing, Fill our hearts with
2. Thanks we give and ad - o - ra - tion For the gos - pel's

joy and peace; Let us each, your love pos - sess - ing,
joy - ful sound; May the fruits of your sal - va - tion

Tri - umph in re - deem - ing grace. O re - fresh us,
In our hearts and lives a - bound. Ev - er faith - ful,

O re - fresh us, Trav - eling through this wil - der - ness.
ev - er faith - ful To the truth may we be found. A - men.

Savior, Again to Thy Dear Name 582

The Lord blesses His people with peace. Psa. 29:11

JOHN ELLERTON   EDWARD J. HOPKINS

1. Sav - ior a - gain to Thy dear name we raise
2. Grant us Thy peace up - on our home - ward way;
3. Grant us Thy peace, Lord, through the com - ing night,
4. Grant us Thy peace through - out our earth - ly life,

With one ac - cord our part - ing hymn of praise;
With Thee be - gan, with Thee shall end the day;
Turn Thou for us its dark - ness in - to light;
Our balm in sor - row, and our stay in strife;

We stand to bless Thee ere our wor - ship cease;
Guard Thou the lips from sin, the hearts from shame,
From harm and dan - ger keep Thy chil - dren free,
Then, when Thy voice shall bid our con - flict cease,

Then, low - ly kneel - ing, wait Thy word of peace.
That in this house have called up - on Thy name.
For dark and light are both a - like to Thee.
Call us, O Lord, to Thine e - ter - nal peace. A - men.

583 God Be with You

And now, brethren, I commend you to God...Acts 20:32

JEREMIAH E. RANKIN

WILLIAM G. TOMER

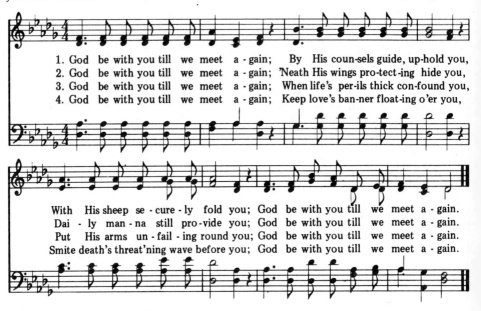

1. God be with you till we meet a - gain; By His coun-sels guide, up-hold you,
2. God be with you till we meet a - gain; 'Neath His wings pro-tect-ing hide you,
3. God be with you till we meet a - gain; When life's per-ils thick con-found you,
4. God be with you till we meet a - gain; Keep love's ban-ner float-ing o'er you,

With His sheep se - cure - ly fold you; God be with you till we meet a - gain.
Dai - ly man - na still pro-vide you; God be with you till we meet a - gain.
Put His arms un - fail - ing round you; God be with you till we meet a - gain.
Smite death's threat'ning wave before you; God be with you till we meet a - gain.

584 Now the Day Is Over

Thou shalt lie down, and thy sleep shall be sweet. Prov. 3:24

SABINE BARING-GOULD

JOSEPH BARNBY

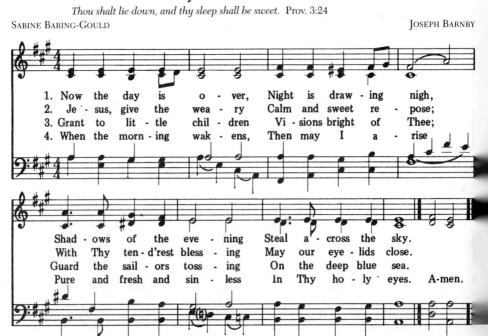

1. Now the day is o - ver, Night is draw - ing nigh,
2. Je - sus, give the wea - ry Calm and sweet re - pose;
3. Grant to lit - tle chil - dren Vi - sions bright of Thee;
4. When the morn - ing wak - ens, Then may I a - rise

Shad - ows of the eve - ning Steal a - cross the sky.
With Thy ten - d'rest bless - ing May our eye - lids close.
Guard the sail - ors toss - ing On the deep blue sea.
Pure and fresh and sin - less In Thy ho - ly eyes. A - men.

Day Is Dying in the West 585

Holy, holy, holy is the Lord...the whole earth is full of His glory. Isa. 6:3

MARY A. LATHBURY

WILLIAM F. SHERWIN

1. Day is dy - ing in the west, Heav'n is touch - ing
2. Lord of life, be - neath the dome Of the u - ni-
3. While the deep - 'ning sha - dows fall, Heart of Love, en-
4. When for - ev - er from our sight Pass the stars, the

earth with rest; Wait and wor - ship while the night Sets her
verse, Thy home, Gath - er us who seek Thy face To the
fold - ing all, Through the glo - ry and the grace Of the
day, the night, Lord of an - gels, on our eyes Let e-

Refrain

even - ing lamps a - light Through all the sky.
fold of Thy em-brace, For Thou art nigh.
stars that veil Thy face, Our hearts as - cend.
ter - nal morn - ing rise, And shad - ows end.

Ho - ly, ho - ly,

ho - ly, Lord God of Hosts! Heav'n and earth are full of Thee!

Heav'n and earth are prais - ing Thee, O Lord most high! A - men.

Thanksgiving

586

National
Thanksgiving Proclamation
OCTOBER 3, 1863

"I do, therefore, invite my fellow citizens,
in every part of the United States, and those who
are sojourning in foreign lands, to set apart and observe
the last Thursday in November next as a day of
thanksgiving praise to our beneficent
Father who dwelleth in the heavens."

Abraham Lincoln

Thanks to God for My Redeemer 587

In everything give thanks; for this is the will of God...I Thess. 5:18

AUGUST L. STORM
TR. CARL E. BACKSTROM

JOHN A. HULTMAN

1. Thanks to God for my Re-deem-er, Thanks for all Thou dost pro-vide!
2. Thanks for prayers that Thou hast an-swered, Thanks for what Thou dost de-ny!
3. Thanks for ros-es by the way-side, Thanks for thorns their stems con-tain!

Thanks for times now but a mem-'ry, Thanks for Je-sus by my side!
Thanks for storms that I have weath-ered, Thanks for all Thou dost sup-ply!
Thanks for homes and thanks for fire-side, Thanks for hope, that sweet re-frain!

Thanks for pleas-ant, balm-y spring-time, Thanks for dark and drear-y fall!
Thanks for pain and thanks for plea-sure, Thanks for com-fort in de-spair!
Thanks for joy and thanks for sor-row, Thanks for heav'n-ly peace with Thee!

Thanks for tears by now for-got-ten, Thanks for peace with-in my soul!
Thanks for grace that none can meas-ure, Thanks for love be-yond com-pare!
Thanks for hope in the to-mor-row, Thanks thro' all e-ter-ni-ty!

588 Come, Ye Thankful People, Come

The harvest is the end of the world; and the reapers are the angels. Matt. 13:39

HENRY ALFORD   GEORGE J. ELVEY

1. Come, ye thank-ful peo-ple, come, Raise the song of har-vest-home:
2. All the world is God's own field, Fruit un-to His praise to yield;
3. For the Lord our God shall come, And shall take His har-vest home;
4. E-ven so, Lord, quick-ly come To Thy fi-nal har-vest-home;

All is safe-ly gath-ered in, Ere the win-ter storms be-gin,
Wheat and tares to-geth-er sown, Un-to joy or sor-row grown;
From His field shall in that day All of-fens-es purge a-way;
Gath-er Thou Thy peo-ple in, Free from sor-row, free from sin;

God, our Ma-ker, doth pro-vide For our wants to be sup-plied:
First the blade, and then the ear, Then the full corn shall ap-pear:
Give His an-gels charge at last In the fire the tares to cast;
There, for-ev-er pu-ri-fied, In Thy pres-ence to a-bide:

Come to God's own tem-ple, come, Raise the song of har-vest-home.
Lord of har-vest, grant that we Whole-some grain and pure may be.
But the fruit-ful ears to store In His gar-ner ev-er-more.
Come, with all Thine an-gels come, Raise the glo-rious har-vest-home. A-men.

Summons to Thanksgiving   589

adapted from Psalm 145

Leader: Give thanks to the Lord for he is good!

People: **All your works shall give thanks to you, O Lord,**
and all your saints shall bless thee!

Leader: The Lord is gracious and compassionate,
slow to anger and rich in love.
The Lord is good to all,
he has compassion on all he has made.

People: **We give thanks to the Lord for he is good!**

Leader: The Lord is faithful to all his promises
and loving toward all he has made.

People: **The lord upholds all those who fall**
and lifts up all who are bowed down.

Leader: The eyes of all look to you,
and you give them their food at the proper time.

People: **You open your hand and satisfy the desires of every living thing.**

All: *We give thanks to the Lord for he is good!*

Leader: The Lord is righteous in all his ways
and loving toward all he has made.

People: **The Lord is near to all who call on him,**
to all who call on him in truth.

Leader: He fulfills the desires of those who fear him;
he hears their cry and saves them.

All: *We give thanks to the Lord for he is good!*

Leader: The Lord watches over all who love him,
but all the wicked he will destroy.

People: **Our mouths will speak in praise of the Lord.**
Let every creature praise his holy name for ever and ever.

All: *We give thanks to the Lord for he is good!*

590 In Thanksgiving Let Us Praise Him

With praise and thanksgiving they sang to the Lord. Ezra 3:11

CLAIRE CLONINGER

FRANZ JOSEPH HAYDN

1. From the first bright light of morn - ing, To the last warm
2. In the sea - son of our plen - ty, In the sea - son
3. Safe with - in His hand that guides us, Hid - den in His

glow of dusk; Ev - 'ry breath we take is sa - cred.
of our need; We will find His grace suf - fi - cient,
heal - ing wings; Day by day His love pro - vides us

For it is God's gift to us.
We will find His love com-plete. In thanks-giv -ing, let us praise Him;
Ev - 'ry good and per -fect thing.

In thanks - giv - ing, let us sing Songs of praise and

ad - o - ra - tion To our gra - cious Lord, and King. A - men.

For the Fruit of All Creation 591

Let them praise the name of the Lord; for He commanded, and they were created. Psa. 148:5

FRED PRATT GREEN

WELSH MELODY
HARM. L.O. EMERSON

1. For the fruit of all cre - a - tion, Thanks be to God.
2. In the just re - ward of la - bor, God's will is done.
3. For the har - vests of the Spir - it, Thanks be to God.

For His gifts to ev - ery na - tion, Thanks be to God.
In the help we give our neigh - bor, God's will is done.
For the good we all in - her - it, Thanks be to God.

For the plow - ing, sow - ing, reap - ing, Si - lent growth while we are
In our world-wide task of car - ing For the hun - gry and de -
For the won - ders that as - tound us, For the truths that still con -

sleep - ing, Fu - ture needs in earth's safe - keep - ing, Thanks be to God.
spair - ing, In the har - vests we are shar - ing, God's will is done.
found us, Most of all, that love has found us, Thanks be to God.

592 Now Thank We All Our God

Now therefore, our God, we thank Thee, and praise Thy glorious name. I Chron. 29:13

MARTIN RINKART
TR. CATHERINE WINKWORTH

JOHANN CRÜGER

1. Now thank we all our God With heart and hands and voic - es,
2. O may this boun-teous God Through all our life be near us,
3. All praise and thanks to God The Fa - ther now be giv - en,

Who won-drous things hath done, In whom His world re - joic - es;
With ev - er joy - ful hearts And bless - ed peace to cheer us;
The Son, and Him who reigns With them in high - est heav - en,

Who, from our moth - er's arms, Hath blessed us on our way
And keep us in His grace And guide us when per - plexed,
The one e - ter - nal God Whom earth and heav'n a - dore;

With count - less gifts of love, And still is ours to - day.
And free us from all ills In this world and the next.
For thus it was, is now, And shall be ev - er - more. A - men.

Sing to the Lord of Harvest 593

Blessed be the Lord who daily loadeth us with benefits. Psa. 68:19

JOHANN STEURLEIN
HARM. DONALD P. HUSTAD

JOHN S. B. MONSELL

1. Sing to the Lord of har - vest, Sing songs of love and praise;
2. God makes the clouds rain good - ness, The des - erts bloom and spring,
3. Bring to this sa - cred al - tar The gifts His good - ness gave,

With joy - ful hearts and voic - es Your al - le - lu - ias raise.
The hills leap up in glad - ness, The val - leys laugh and sing.
The gold - en sheaves of har - vest, The souls Christ died to save.

By Him the roll - ing sea - sons In fruit - ful or - der move;
God fills them with His full - ness, All things with large in - crease;
Your hearts lay down be - fore Him When at His feet you fall,

Sing to the Lord of har - vest A joy - ous song of love.
He crowns the year with bless - ing, With plen - ty and with peace.
And with your lives a - dore Him Who gave His life for all.

594 We Are So Blessed

God has blessed us with every spiritual blessing in Christ. Eph. 1:3

WILLIAM J. AND GLORIA GAITHER

WILLIAM J. GAITHER AND
GREG NELSON

We are so blessed by the gifts from Your hand, we just
so blessed, we just can't find a way or the

can't un-der-stand Why You've loved us so much. We are
words that can say, "Thank You,

Lord, for Your touch." When we're emp-ty You fill us till

we o-ver-flow, When we're hun-gry. You

feed us, and cause us to know; We are

So blessed, Take what we have to bring; Take it
all, ev-ery-thing, Lord, we love You so much.

Jesus, We Just Want to Thank You 595

Thanks be to God for His indescribable gift. II Cor. 9:15

WILLIAM J. AND GLORIA GAITHER

WILLIAM J. GAITHER

1. Je - sus, we just want to thank You, Je - sus, we just want to thank You, Je - sus, we just want to thank You, Thank You for be - ing so good.
2. Je - sus, we just want to praise You, Je - sus, we just want to praise You, Je - sus, we just want to praise You, Praise You for be - ing so good.
3. Je - sus, we just want to tell You, Je - sus, we just want to tell You, Je - sus, we just want to tell You, We love You for be - ing so good.

596 Count Your Blessings

Many, O Lord my God, are Thy wonderful works...Psa. 40:5

JOHNSON OATMAN, JR.

EDWIN O. EXCELL

1. When up-on life's bil-lows you are tem-pest-tossed, When you are dis-
2. Are you ev-er bur-dened with a load of care? Does the cross seem
3. When you look at oth-ers with their lands and gold, Think that Christ has
4. So a-mid the con-flict, wheth-er great or small, Do not be dis-

cour-aged, think-ing all is lost, Count your man-y bless-ings—name them
heav-y you are called to bear? Count your man-y bless-ings— ev-ery
prom-ised you His wealth un-told; Count your man-y bless-ings—mon-ey
cour-aged—God is o-ver all; Count your man-y bless-ings— an-gels

one by one, And it will sur-prise you what the Lord has done.
doubt will fly, And you will be sing-ing as the days go by.
can-not buy Your re-ward in heav-en nor your home on high.
will at-tend, Help and com-fort give you to your jour-ney's end.

Refrain

Count your bless-ings—name them one by one; Count your
Count your man-y bless-ings— name them one by one; Count your man-y

bless-ings—see what God has done; Count your bless-ings—
bless-ings— see what God has done; Count your man-y bless-ings—

name them one by one; Count your man - y bless - ings—see what God has done.

We Gather Together 597

If God be for us, who can be against us? Rom. 8:31

NETHERLANDS FOLK HYMN
TR. THEODORE BAKER

NETHERLANDS MELODY
ARR. EDWARD KREMSER

1. We gath - er to - geth - er to ask the Lord's bless - ing;
2. Be - side us to guide us, our God with us join - ing,
3. We all do ex - tol Thee, Thou Lead - er tri - um - phant,

He chas - tens and has - tens His will to make known;
Or - dain - ing, main - tain - ing His king - dom di - vine;
And pray that Thou still our De - fend - er wilt be.

The wick - ed op - press - ing now cease from dis - tress - ing,
So from the be - gin - ning the fight we were win - ning:
Let Thy con - gre - ga - tion es - cape trib - u - la - tion:

Sing prais - es to His name: He for - gets not His own.
Thou, Lord, wast at our side, all glo - ry be Thine!
Thy name be ev - er praised! O Lord, make us free! A - men.

National Hymns

Righteousness exalteth a nation:
but sin is a reproach to any people.
Prov. 14:34

God the Omnipotent 598

He maketh wars to cease unto the end of the earth...Psa. 46:9

HENRY F. CHORLEY AND
JOHN ELLERTON

ALEXIS F. LVOV

1. God the Om - nip - o - tent! King, who or - dain - est
2. God the All - mer - ci - ful! Earth hath for - sak - en
3. God the All - right - eous One! Man hath de - fied Thee;
4. So shall Thy peo - ple, with thank - ful de - vo - tion,

Thun - der Thy clar - ion, the light - ning Thy sword;
Meek - ness and mer - cy, and slight - ed Thy Word;
Yet to e - ter - ni - ty stand - eth Thy Word;
Praise Him who saved them from per - il and sword,

Show forth Thy pit - y on high where Thou reign - est;
Let not Thy wrath in its ter - rors a - wak - en;
False - hood and wrong shall not tar - ry be - side Thee;
Sing - ing in cho - rus from o - cean to o - cean,

Give to us peace in our time, O Lord.
Give to us peace in our time, O Lord.
Give to us peace in our time, O Lord.
Peace to the na - tions, and praise to the Lord. A - men.

599 God of Our Fathers

The Lord of hosts is with us; the God of Jacob is our refuge. Psa. 46:7

DANIEL C. ROBERTS

GEORGE W. WARREN

1. God of our fa - thers, whose al - might - y
2. Thy love di - vine hath led us in the
3. From war's a - larms, from dead - ly pes - ti -
4. Re - fresh Thy peo - ple on their toil - some

hand
past;
lence,
way;

Leads forth in beau - ty all the star - ry
In this free land by Thee our lot is
Be Thy strong arm our ev - er sure de -
Lead us from night to nev - er - end - ing

band
cast;
fense;
day;

Of shin - ing worlds in splen - dor through the
Be Thou our Rul - er, Guard - ian, Guide and
Thy true re - lig - ion in our hearts in -
Fill all our lives with love and grace di -

skies,
Stay,
crease,
vine;

Our grate - ful songs be - fore Thy throne a - rise.
Thy Word our law, Thy paths our cho - sen way.
Thy boun-teous good-ness nour-ish us in peace.
And glo - ry, laud, and praise be ev - er Thine. A - men.

America the Beautiful 600

Blessed is the nation whose God is the Lord. Psa. 33:12

KATHARINE L. BATES

SAMUEL A. WARD

1. O beau - ti - ful for spa - cious skies, For am - ber waves of grain,
2. O beau - ti - ful for pil - grim feet, Whose stern im-pas-sioned stress
3. O beau - ti - ful for he - roes proved In lib - er - at - ing strife,
4. O beau - ti - ful for pa - triot dream That sees be - yond the years

For pur - ple moun-tain maj - es - ties A - bove the fruit - ed plain!
A thor-ough-fare for free - dom beat A - cross the wil - der - ness!
Who more than self their coun - try loved, And mer - cy more than life!
Thine al - a - bas - ter cit - ies gleam, Un-dimmed by hu - man tears!

A - mer - i - ca! A - mer - i - ca! God shed His grace on thee,
A - mer - i - ca! A - mer - i - ca! God mend thine ev - ery flaw,
A - mer - i - ca! A - mer - i - ca! May God thy gold re - fine,
A - mer - i - ca! A - mer - i - ca! God shed His grace on thee,

And crown thy good with broth - er - hood From sea to shin-ing sea!
Con - firm thy soul in self - con - trol, Thy lib - er - ty in law!
Till all suc - cess be no - ble - ness, And ev - ery gain di - vine!
And crown thy good with broth - er - hood From sea to shin-ing sea! A - men.

601 The Star-Spangled Banner

It is better to trust in the Lord than to put confidence in princes. Psa. 118:9

FRANCIS SCOTT KEY

JOHN STAFFORD SMITH

1. O say, can you see, by the dawn's ear - ly light, What so
2. O thus be it ev - er, when free men shall stand Be -

proud - ly we hailed at the twi - light's last gleam - ing, Whose broad
tween their loved homes and the war's des - o - la - tion! Blest with

stripes and bright stars, thro' the per - il - ous fight, O'er the
vic - t'ry and peace, may the heav'n - res - cued land Praise the

ram - parts we watched, were so gal - lant - ly stream - ing? And the
Pow'r that hath made and pre - served us a na - tion! Then

602 America

Righteousness exalteth a nation; but sin is a reproach to any people. Prov. 14:34

SAMUEL F. SMITH

THESAURUS MUSICUS

1. My coun - try, 'tis of thee, Sweet land of lib - er - ty,
2. My na - tive coun - try, thee, Land of the no - ble free,
3. Let mu - sic swell the breeze, And ring from all the trees
4. Our fa - thers' God, to Thee, Au - thor of lib - er - ty,

Of thee I sing: Land where my fa - thers died, Land of the
Thy name I love: I love thy rocks and rills, Thy woods and
Sweet free - dom's song: Let mor - tal tongues a - wake, Let all that
To Thee we sing: Long may our land be bright With free - dom's

pil - grims' pride, From ev - ery moun - tain side Let free - dom ring!
tem - pled hills; My heart with rap - ture thrills Like that a - bove.
breathe par - take; Let rocks their si - lence break, The sound pro - long.
ho - ly light; Pro - tect us by Thy might, Great God, our King! A - men.

603 The Blessing of Almighty God

Before all else we seek, upon our common
  labor as a nation, the blessing of Almighty
  God. And the hopes in our hearts fashion
  the deepest prayers of our whole people.
May we pursue the right — without self-righteousness.
May we know unity — without conformity.
May we grow in strength — without pride in self.
May we, in our dealings with all peoples of the earth,
  may speak the truth and serve justice.
May the light of freedom, coming to all darkened
  lands, flame brightly — until at last the darkness is no more.
May the turbulence of our age yield to a true
  time of peace, when men and nations share a life that
  honors the dignity of each, the brotherhood of all.

Dwight D. Eisenhower

Battle Hymn of the Republic 604

He is terrible to the kings of the earth. Psa. 76:12

JULIA WARD HOWE

TRADITIONAL AMERICAN MELODY

1. Mine eyes have seen the glo-ry of the com-ing of the Lord; He is
2. I have seen Him in the watch-fires of a hun-dred cir-cling camps; They have
3. He has sound-ed forth the trum-pet that shall nev-er sound re-treat; He is
4. In the beau-ty of the lil-ies, Christ was born a-cross the sea, With a

trampling out the vin-tage where the grapes of wrath are stored; He hath loosed the
build-ed Him an al-tar in the eve-ning dews and damps; I can read His
sift-ing out the hearts of men be-fore His judg-ment seat; O be swift, my
glo-ry in His bos-om that trans-fig-ures you and me; As He died to

fate-ful light-ning of His ter-ri-ble swift sword; His truth is march-ing on.
right-eous sen-tence by the dim and flar-ing lamps; His day is march-ing on.
soul, to an-swer Him! be ju-bi-lant, my feet! Our God is march-ing on.
make men ho-ly, let us live to make men free, While God is march-ing on.

Refrain

Glo-ry! glo-ry, hal-le-lu-jah! Glo-ry! glo-ry, hal-le-lu-jah!

Glo-ry! glo-ry, hal-le-lu-jah! Our God is march-ing on.

605 O Canada!

In Thee shall all nations be blessed. Gal. 3:8

ROBERT STANLEY WEIR AND
ALBERT C. WATSON

MELODY BY CALIXA LAVALLEE
ARR. FREDERICK C. SILVESTER

1. O Can - a - da! our home and na - tive land! True pa - triot
2. Al - might - y Love, by Thy mys - ter - ious pow'r, In wis - dom

love in all thy sons com - mand. With glow - ing hearts we
guide, with faith and free - dom dow'r; Be ours a na - tion

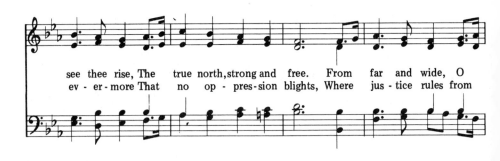

see thee rise, The true north, strong and free. From far and wide, O
ev - er - more That no op - pres - sion blights, Where jus - tice rules from

Can - a - da, We stand on guard for thee. God keep our land
shore to shore, From lakes to north - ern lights. May love a - lone

glo - rious and free, O Can - a - da, we stand on guard for
for wrong a - tone; Lord of the lands, make Can - a - da Thine

thee. O Can - a - da, we stand on guard for thee.
own! Lord of the lands, make Can - a - da Thine own.

Children of the Heavenly Father 606

As a father pitieth his children, so the Lord pitieth...Psa. 103:13

CAROLINA SANDELL BERG   TRAD. SWEDISH MELODY

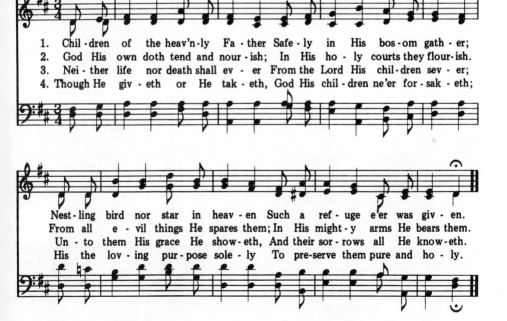

1. Chil - dren of the heav'n - ly Fa - ther Safe - ly in His bos - om gath - er;
2. God His own doth tend and nour - ish; In His ho - ly courts they flour - ish.
3. Nei - ther life nor death shall ev - er From the Lord His chil - dren sev - er;
4. Though He giv - eth or He tak - eth, God His chil - dren ne'er for - sak - eth;

Nest - ling bird nor star in heav - en Such a ref - uge e'er was giv - en.
From all e - vil things He spares them; In His might - y arms He bears them.
Un - to them His grace He show - eth, And their sor - rows all He know - eth.
His the lov - ing pur - pose sole - ly To pre - serve them pure and ho - ly.

607 Once to Every Man and Nation

Choose you this day whom ye will serve. Josh. 24:15

JAMES R. LOWELL

THOMAS J. WILLIAMS

1. Once to ev - ery man and na - tion Comes the mo - ment to de-cide,
2. Then to side with truth is no - ble, When we share her wretch-ed crust,
3. Though the cause of e - vil pros - per, Yet the truth a - lone is strong;

In the strife of truth with false-hood, For the good or e - vil side;
Ere her cause bring fame and prof - it, And 'tis pros-p'rous to be just;
Though her por - tion be the scaf - fold, And up - on the throne be wrong,

Some great cause, some great de - ci - sion, Of-f'ring each the bloom or blight,
Then it is the brave man choos-es While the cow - ard stands a - side,
Yet that scaf - fold sways the fu - ture, And, be - hind the dim un - known,

And the choice goes by for - ev - er 'Twixt that dark-ness and that light.
Till the mul - ti - tude make vir - tue Of the faith they had de - nied.
Stand-eth God with-in the shad - ow Keep-ing watch a - bove His own. A-men.

Music used by permission of Eluned Crump and Dilys Evans, representatives of the late Gwenlyn Evans.

Prayer for His Glory   608

Adapted from II Chronicles 7:14-15

Leader: If my people, who are called by my name,
People: **If my people, who are called by my name,**
Leader: Will humble themselves and pray,
People: **Will humble themselves and pray,**
Leader: And turn from their wicked ways,
People: **And turn from their wicked ways,**
Leader: Then will I hear from heaven and will forgive their sin,
People: **Then will I hear from heaven and will forgive their sin,**
Leader: And I will heal their land.
People: **And I will heal their land.**
All: *Humble us, O Lord, we pray.*
Convict us of sin.
Give us strength and desire to turn from wrongdoing.
So that your face may be turned toward us,
Your eyes opened unto us,
Your ears attentive to us,
So that your glory may again visit our land.
Amen.

Special
Days

Trust in the Lord with all thine heart;
and lean not unto thine own understanding.
In all thy ways acknowledge him,
and he shall direct thy paths.
Prov. 3:5,6

O Perfect Love 609

...And shall be joined unto his wife, and they two shall be one flesh. Eph. 5:31

DOROTHY F. GURNEY AND
JOHN ELLERTON

JOSEPH BARNBY

1. O per - fect Love, all hu - man thought tran - scend - ing,
2. O per - fect Life, be Thou their full as - sur - ance
3. Grant them the joy which bright - ens earth - ly sor - row;
4. Hear us, O Fa - ther, gra - cious and for - giv - ing,

Low - ly we kneel in prayer be - fore Thy throne,
Of ten - der char - i - ty and stead - fast faith,
Grant them the peace which calms all earth - ly strife,
Through Je - sus Christ, Thy co - e - ter - nal Word,

That theirs may be the love which knows no end - ing,
Of pa - tient hope, and qui - et, brave en - dur - ance,
And to life's day the glo - rious, un - known mor - row
Who, with the Ho - ly Ghost, by all things liv - ing

Whom Thou for - ev - er - more dost join in one.
With child - like trust that fears not pain nor death.
That dawns up - on e - ter - nal love and life.
Now and to end - less a - ges art a - dored. A - men.

610 Eternal Life

Yield yourselves unto God...and your members as instruments of righteousness...Rom. 6:13

OLIVE DUNGAN
ARR. DONALD P. HUSTAD

ST. FRANCIS OF ASSISI

Unison

Lord, make me an in-stru-ment of Thy peace;

Where there is ha - tred, let me sow love; Where there is in - ju - ry,

par - don; Where there is doubt, faith; Where there is des-pair,

hope; Where there is dark-ness, light; Where there is sad - ness,

joy. O Di-vine Mas-ter, grant that I may not so much

611 Happy the Home When God Is There

As for me and my house, we will serve the Lord. Josh. 24:15

HENRY WARE, JR.

JOHN B. DYKES

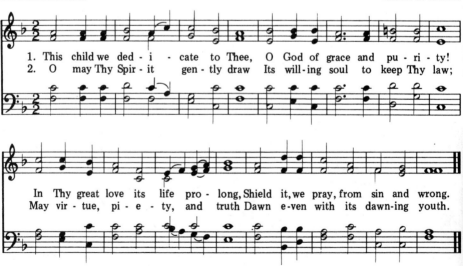

1. Hap - py the home when God is there, And love fills ev - ery breast;
2. Hap - py the home where Je - sus' name Is sweet to ev - ery ear;
3. Hap - py the home where prayer is heard, And praise is wont to rise;
4. Lord, let us in our homes a - gree This bless - ed peace to gain;

When one their wish and one their prayer, And one their heav'n-ly rest.
Where chil-dren ear - ly lisp His fame, And par - ents hold Him dear.
Where par-ents love the sa - cred Word, And all its wis - dom prize.
U - nite our hearts in love to Thee, And love to all will reign. A - men.

612 This Child We Dedicate to Thee

And the child...was in favor both with the Lord, and also with men. I Sam. 2:26

GERMAN HYMN
TR. SAMUEL GILMAN

HENRY K. OLIVER

1. This child we ded - i - cate to Thee, O God of grace and pu - ri - ty!
2. O may Thy Spir - it gen - tly draw Its will - ing soul to keep Thy law;

In Thy great love its life pro - long, Shield it, we pray, from sin and wrong.
May vir - tue, pi - e - ty, and truth Dawn e -ven with its dawn-ing youth.

Another Year Is Dawning 613

So teach us to number our days, that we may apply our hearts unto wisdom. Psa. 90:12

FRANCES R. HAVERGAL

SAMUEL S. WESLEY

1. An - oth - er year is dawn - ing! Dear Fa - ther, let it be,
2. An - oth - er year of mer - cies, Of faith - ful - ness and grace,
3. An - oth - er year of serv - ice, Of wit - ness for Thy love,

In work - ing or in wait - ing, An - oth - er year with Thee;
An - oth - er year of glad - ness, In the shin - ing of Thy face;
An - oth - er year of train - ing For ho - lier work a - bove;

An - oth - er year of prog - ress, An - oth - er year of praise,
An - oth - er year of lean - ing Up - on Thy lov - ing breast,
An - oth - er year is dawn - ing! Dear Fa - ther, let it be,

An - oth - er year of prov - ing Thy pres - ence all the days.
An - oth - er year of trust - ing, Of qui - et, hap - py rest.
On earth, or else in heav - en, An - oth - er year for Thee. A - men.

614 God of Our Life

Thou art the same, and Thy years shall have no end. Psa. 102:27

HUGH T. KERR   CHARLES H. PURDAY

1. God of our life, through all the cir - cling years, We trust in Thee;
2. God of the past, our times are in Thy hand; With us a - bide.
3. God of the com - ing years, through paths un-known We fol - low Thee;

In all the past, through all our hopes and fears, Thy hand we see.
Lead us by faith to hope's true prom-ised land; Be Thou our guide.
When we are strong, Lord, leave us not a - lone; Our ref - uge be.

With each new day, when morn - ing lifts the veil,
With Thee to bless, the dark - ness shines as light,
Be Thou for us in life our dai - ly bread,

We own Thy mer - cies, Lord, which nev - er fail.
And faith's fair vi - sion chang - es in - to sight.
Our heart's true home when all our years have sped. A-men.

Seek Ye First 615

Seek ye first the kingdom of God and His Righteousness...Matt. 6:33

MATT. 6:33

KAREN LAFFERTY

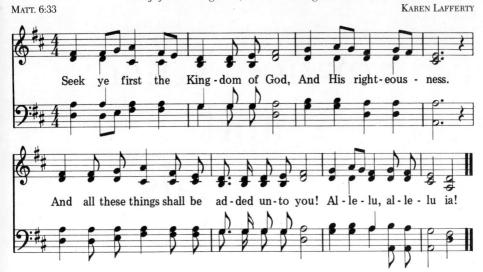

Seek ye first the King-dom of God, And His right-eous - ness.

And all these things shall be ad-ded un-to you! Al - le - lu, al - le - lu - ia!

God Is So Good 616

Truly God is good...to such as are of a clean heart. Psa. 73:1

TRADITIONAL

TRADITIONAL

1. God is so good, God is so good,
2. He cares for me, He cares for me,
3. I'll do His will, I'll do His will,
4. He loves me so, He loves me so,

God is so good, He's so good to me.
He cares for me, He's so good to me.
I'll do His will, He's so good to me.
He loves me so, He's so good to me.

Service Music and Materials

And let us consider how we may spur one another on
toward love and good deeds.
Let us not give up meeting together,
as some are in the habit of doing,
but let us encourage one another —
and all the more as you see the Day approaching.
Heb. 10:24,25

O Worship the Lord 617

O worship the Lord in the beauty of holiness. Psa. 96:9

PSALM 96:9

ROBERT G. McCUTCHAN

O wor-ship the Lord in the beau-ty of ho-li-ness;

Serve Him with glad - ness, all the earth. A - men.

Calls to Worship 618

— The earth is the Lord's, and the fullness thereof; the world, and they that dwell therein. Lift up your heads, O ye gates; even lift them up, ye everlasting doors; and the King of glory shall come in. Who is this King of glory? The Lord of hosts, he is the King of glory. (Psalm 24:1, 9, 10)

— Rejoice in the Lord, O ye righteous: for praise is comely for the upright. The counsel of the Lord standeth forever, the thoughts of his heart to all generations. Blessed is the nation whose God is the Lord; and the people whom he hath chosen for his own inheritance.
(Psalm 33:1, 11, 12)

— How amiable are thy tabernacles, O Lord of hosts! My soul longeth, yea, even fainteth for the courts of the Lord: my heart and my flesh crieth out for the living God. For the Lord God is a sun and shield: the Lord will give grace and glory: no good thing will he withhold from them that walk uprightly. (Psalm 84:1, 2, 11)

— O sing unto the Lord a new song: sing unto the Lord, all the earth. Declare his glory among the heathen, his wonders among all people. Give unto the Lord the glory due unto his name; bring an offering and come into his courts. O worship the Lord in the beauty of holiness: fear before him all the earth. (Psalm 96:1, 3, 8, 9)

— Make a joyful noise unto the Lord, all ye lands. Serve the Lord with gladness: come before his presence with singing. Enter into his gates with thanksgiving, and into his courts with praise; be thankful unto him, and bless his name. For the Lord is good; his mercy is everlasting; and his truth endureth to all generations.
(Psalm 100:1, 2, 4, 5)

6 — O give thanks unto the Lord; call upon his name: make known his deeds among the people. Sing unto him, sing psalms unto him: talk ye of all his wondrous works. Glory ye in his holy name: let the heart of them rejoice that seek the Lord. (Psalm 105:1-3)

7 — O give thanks unto the Lord for he is good: for his mercy endureth forever. Let the redeemed of the Lord say so, whom he hath redeemed out of the hand of the enemy. For he satisfieth the longing soul, and filleth the hungry soul with goodness. (Psalm 107:1, 2, 9)

8 — O praise the Lord, all ye nations: praise him, all ye people. For his merciful kindness is great toward us: and the truth of the Lord endureth forever. Praise ye the Lord.
(Psalm 117)

9 — Great is the Lord and greatly to be praised; and his greatness is unsearchable. The Lord is righteous in all his ways, and holy in all his works. The Lord is nigh unto all them that call upon him, to all that call upon him in truth. (Psalm 145:3, 17, 18)

10 — Praise ye the Lord: for it is good to sing praises unto our God; for it is pleasant; and praise is comely. Great is our Lord, and of great power: his understanding is infinite. The Lord taketh pleasure in them that fear him, in those that hope in his mercy. Praise the Lord, O Jerusalem; praise thy God, O Zion. (Psalm 147:1, 5, 11, 12)

11 — Praise ye the Lord. sing unto the Lord a new song, and his praise in the congregation of saints. Let Israel rejoice in him that made him: let the children of Zion be joyful in their King. for the Lord taketh pleasure in his people: He will beautify the meek with salvation.
(Psalm 149: 1, 2, 4)

619 Christ, We Do All Adore Thee

Thou are worthy, O Lord, to receive glory and honor, and power...Rev. 4:11

ADOREMUS TE
TR. THEODORE BAKER

THEODORE DUBOIS

Christ, we do all a - dore Thee, and we do praise Thee for - ev - er;

Christ, we do all a - dore Thee, and we do praise Thee for - ev - er,

For on the ho - ly cross hast Thou the world from sin re - deem - ed.

Christ, we do all a - dore Thee, and we do praise Thee for - ev - er.

(Organ ad lib.)

Christ, we do all a - dore Thee!

Gloria Patri 620

Give unto the Lord the glory due unto His name. I Chron. 16:29

TRADITIONAL

HENRY W. GREATOREX

Glo - ry be to the Fa - ther, and to the Son, and to the Ho - ly Ghost; As it was in the be - gin - ning, is now, and ev - er shall be, world with - out end. A - men, A - men.

Benedictions 621

1 — The Lord bless thee, and keep thee: the Lord make his face to shine upon thee, and be gracious unto thee: the Lord lift up his countenance upon thee, and give thee peace. Amen. (Numbers 6:24-26)

2 — Let the words of my mouth, and the meditation of my heart, be acceptable in thy sight, O Lord, my strength and my redeemer. Amen. (Psalm 19:14)

3 — God be merciful unto us, and bless us, and cause his face to shine upon us; that thy way may be known upon earth thy saving health among all nations. Amen. (Psalm 67: 1, 2)

4 — Now unto the King eternal, immortal, invisible, the only wise God, be honour and glory for ever and ever. Amen. (I Timothy 1:17)

5 — And the very God of peace sanctify you wholly; and I pray God your whole spirit and soul and body be preserved blameless unto the coming of our Lord Jesus Christ. The grace of our Lord Jesus Christ be with you. Amen. (I Thessalonians 5:23, 28)

6 — Now our Lord Jesus Christ himself, and God, even our Father, which hath loved us, and hath given us everlasting consolation and good hope through grace, comfort your hearts, and stablish you in every good word and work. Amen. (II Thessalonians 2:16, 17)

7 — Now unto him that is able to do exceeding abundantly above all that we ask or think, according to the power that worketh in us, unto him be glory in the church by Christ Jesus throughout all ages, world without end. Amen. (Ephesians 3:20, 21)

8 — And the peace of God, which passeth all understanding, shall keep your hearts and minds through Jesus Christ. Amen. (Philippians 4:7)

9 — Be perfect, be of good comfort, be of one mind, live in peace; and the God of love and peace shall be with you. The grace of the Lord Jesus Christ, and the love of God, and the communion of the Holy Ghost, be with you all. Amen. (II Corinthians 13:11, 14)

10 — Now the God of peace, that brought again from the dead our Lord Jesus, that great shepherd of the sheep, through the blood of the everlasting covenant, make you perfect in every good work to do his will, working in you that which is well pleasing in his sight, through Jesus Christ; to whom be glory for ever and ever. Amen. (Hebrews 13:20, 21)

11 — Now unto him that is able to keep you from falling, and to present you faultless before the presence of his glory with exceeding joy, to the only wise God our Saviour, be glory and majesty, dominion and power, both now and ever. Amen. (Jude 24, 25)

12 — The grace of our Lord Jesus Christ be with your spirit. Amen. (Philemon 25)

622 We Give Thee but Thine Own

Of Thine own have we given Thee. I Chron. 29:14

WILLIAM W. HOW

MASON AND WEBB'S *CANTICA LAUDIS*

1. We give Thee but Thine own, What-e'er the gift may be:
2. May we Thy boun - ties thus As stew - ards true re - ceive,
3. To com - fort and to bless, To find a balm for woe,
4. The cap - tive to re - lieve, To God the lost to bring,
5. And we be - lieve Thy word, Though dim our faith may be:

All that we have is Thine a - lone, A trust, O Lord, from Thee.
And glad - ly, as Thou bless - est us, To Thee our first-fruits give.
To tend the lone and fa - ther - less, Is an - gels' work be - low.
To teach the way of life and peace— It is a Christ-like thing.
What-e'er for Thine we do, O Lord, We do it un - to Thee. A-men.

623 Doxology

Let everything that hath breath praise the Lord. Psa. 150:6

THOMAS KEN

GENEVAN PSALTER

Praise God from whom all bless - ings flow; Praise Him, all crea - tures here be - low;

Praise Him a - bove, ye heav'n-ly host; Praise Fa-ther, Son, and Ho - ly Ghost. A-men.

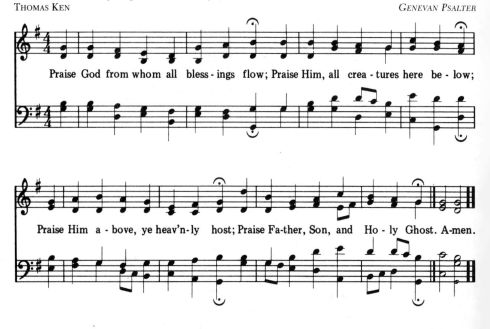

Amens 624

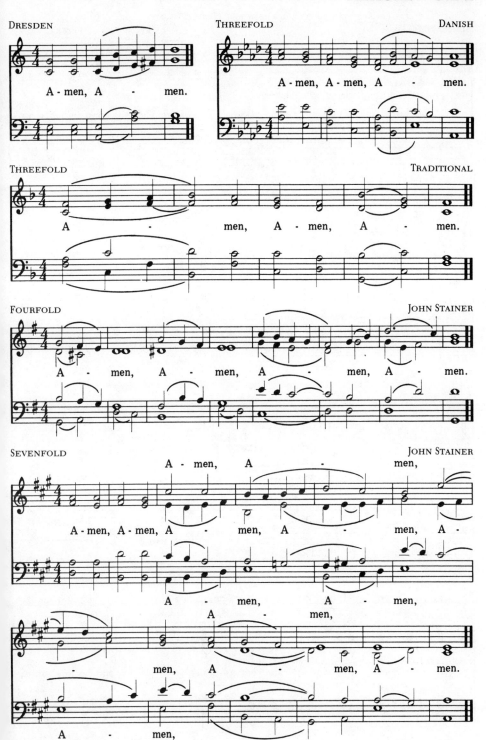

625 The Lord Bless You and Keep You

The Lord make His face to shine upon you. Num 6:25

NUMBERS 6:24-26

PETER C. LUTKIN

626   Nicene Creed

We believe in one God,
   the Father, the Almighty,
   maker of heaven and earth,
   of all that is, seen and unseen.

We believe in one Lord, Jesus Christ,
   the only Son of God,
   eternally begotten of the Father,
   God from God, Light from Light,
   true God from true God,
   begotten, not made,
   of one Being with the Father.
   Through him all things were made.
   For us and for our salvation
      he came down from heaven;
      by the power of the Holy Spirit
         he became incarnate from the virgin Mary, and was made man.
   For our sake he was crucified under Pontius Pilate;
      he suffered death and was buried.
   On the third day he rose again
      in accordance with the Scriptures;
      he ascended into heaven
         and is seated at the right hand of the Father.
   He will come again in glory to judge the living and the dead,
      and his kingdom will have no end.

We believe in the Holy Spirit, the Lord, the giver of life
   who proceeds from the Father and the Son.
   With the Father and the Son he is worshiped and glorified.
   He has spoken through the prophets.
   We believe in one holy catholic and apostolic Church.
   We acknowledge one Baptism for the forgiveness of sins.
   We look for the resurrection of the dead,
      and the life of the world to come. Amen

Apostles' Creed

I believe in God, the Father almighty,
　　creator of heaven and earth.

I believe in Jesus Christ, his only Son, our Lord.
　　He was conceived by the power of the Holy Spirit
　　　and born of the virgin Mary.
　　He suffered under Pontius Pilate,
　　　was crucified, died, and was buried.
　　He descended into hell.*
　　On the third day he rose again.
　　He ascended into heaven,
　　　and is seated at the right hand of the Father.
　　He will come again to judge the living and the dead.

I believe in the Holy Spirit,
　　the holy catholic Church,
　　the communion of saints,
　　the forgiveness of sins,
　　the resurrection of the body,
　　and the life everlasting. Amen
*Or, He descended to the dead

Psalm 150

Leader: A Call to Worship!
Praise the Lord.
Praise God in his sanctuary.
People: **Praise him in his mighty heavens.**
Leader: Praise him for his acts of power.
People: **Praise him for his surpassing greatness!**
All: Praise him with the sounding of the trumpet,
　　praise him with the harp and lyre.
Leader: Praise him with the tambourine and dancing,
People: **Praise him with the strings and flute.**
Leader: Praise him with the clash of cymbals,
People: **Praise him with resounding cymbals.**
All: Let everything that has breath praise the Lord.
　　Praise the Lord!

629 Responsive Prayer for the People of God

Leader: Hear our prayer, O Lord!

People: **Spare us good Lord**
from all sin, from all error, from all evil;
from the cunning assaults of the devil;
from unprepared and untimely death;
from war, bloodshed, and violence;
from corrupt and unjust government;
from sedition and treason;

Leader: Good Lord, deliver us.

Response: **Deliver us, O Lord.**

Leader: Hear our prayer, O Lord!

People: **Spare us, good Lord,**
from epidemic, drought, and famine;
from fire and flood, earthquake, lightning and storm.
In all time of our tribulation;
in all time of our prosperity;
in the hours of living and the hours of dying;
preserve our souls against the day of judgment.

Leader: Hear our prayer, O Lord!

People: **Though unworthy, we implore you**
to rule and govern your universal Church;
to guide all servants of your Church in the love
of your Word and in the holiness of life;
to put an end to all schisms,
to cease the causes of offense to those who would believe;
and to bring into truth all who have gone astray.

Leader: We implore you to hear us, good Lord.

People: **To beat down Satan under our feet;**
to send faithful workers into your harvest;
to accompany your Word with your Spirit and power;
to raise up those who fall and to strengthen those who stand;
to comfort and help the fainthearted and the distressed.

Leader: We implore you to hear us, good Lord.
People: **To give to all nations justice and peace;**
to preserve our country from discord and strife;
to direct and guard those who have civil authority;
and to bless and guide all our people.
Leader: We implore you to hear us, good Lord.
People: **To behold and help all who are in danger, need, or tribulation;**
to protect and guide all who travel;
to preserve and provide for all women in childbirth;
to watch over children and to guide the young;
to heal the sick and to strengthen their families and friends;
to bring reconciliation to families in discord;
to provide for the unemployed and for all in need;
to free prisoners from the bondages of their lives and prisons;
to support, comfort, and guide all orphans, widowers, and widows;
and to have mercy on all your people.
Leader: Dear Lord, Jesus Christ, take away the sins of the world.
People: **Give us the strength to forgive our enemies, persecutors, and slanderers and to be reconciled to them.**
Help us not to be alien to our own selves, but to accept with joy our place as works of redemption and creatures of your love.
Help us not to rebel against your created order;
but to wisely use the fruits and treasures of the earth, sea and air.
Leader: Grant us, O Lord, your peace.
People: **Make known to us, in greater depths, the mystery of your incarnation, Christ among us, our Hope;**
Give us grace to understand and experience your death, burial and resurrection.
Leader: Help us, dear Lord, we implore you.
People: **O Christ, hear us:**
In all things, may we be
the people of God. *Amen.*

Adapted

Responsive
Readings

Open thou mine eyes,
that I may behold wondrous things
out of thy law.
Psalm 119:18

630 GOD THE CREATOR

In the beginning God created the heavens and the earth.

Now the earth was formless and empty, darkness was over the surface of the deep, and the Spirit of God was hovering over the waters.

And God said, "Let there be light," and there was light.

God saw that the light was good, and he separated the light from the darkness.

God called the light "day," and the darkness he called "night."

And there was evening, and there was morning—the first day. Genesis 1:1-5

By the word of the Lord were the heavens made, their starry host by the breath of his mouth.

He gathers the waters of the sea into jars; he puts the deep into storehouses.

Let all the earth fear the Lord; let all the people of the world revere him.

For he spoke, and it came to be; he commanded, and it stood firm.

Psalm 33:6-9

Let us come before him with thanksgiving and extol him with music and song.

For the Lord is the great God, the great King above all gods.

In his hand are the depths of the earth, and the mountain peaks belong to him.

The sea is his, for he made it, and his hands formed the dry land.

Come, let us bow down in worship, let us kneel before the Lord our Maker;

For he is our God and we are the people of his pasture, the flock under his care. Psalm 95:2-7

(NIV)

631 GOD'S OMNISCIENCE

0 Lord, you have searched me and you know me.

You know when I sit and when I rise; you perceive my thoughts from afar.

You discern my going out and my lying down; you are familiar with all my ways.

Before a word is on my tongue you know it completely, 0 Lord.

You hem me in—behind and before; you have laid your hand upon me.

Such knowledge is too wonderful for me, too lofty for me to attain.

Where can I go from your Spirit? Where can I flee from your presence?

If I go up to the heavens, you are there; if I make my bed in the depths, you are there.

If I rise on the wings of the dawn, if I settle on the far side of the sea,

Even there your hand will guide me, your right hand will hold me fast.

If I say, "Surely the darkness will hide me and the light become night around me,

Even the darkness will not be dark to you; the night will shine like the day, for darkness is as light to you."

I praise you because I am fearfully and wonderfully made; your works are wonderful, I know that full well.

Search me, O God, and know my heart; test me and know my anxious thoughts. See if there is any offensive way in me, and lead me in the way everlasting. Psalm 139:1-12, 14, 23, 24

(NIV)

632 GOD'S CARE

I lift up my eyes to the hills—where does my help come from?

My help comes from the Lord, the Maker of heaven and earth.

He will not let your foot slip - he who watches over you will not slumber;

Indeed, he who watches over Israel will neither slumber nor sleep.

The Lord watches over you - the Lord is your shade at your right hand;

The sun will not harm you by day, nor the moon by night.

The Lord will keep you from all harm —he will watch over your life;

The Lord will watch over your coming and going both now and forevermore. Psalm 121

(NIV)

633 DIVINE PROVIDENCE

I will extol the Lord at all times; his praise will always be on my lips.

My soul will boast in the Lord; let the afflicted hear and rejoice.

Glorify the Lord with me; let us exalt his name together.

I sought the Lord, and he answered me; he delivered me from all my fears.

Those who look to him are radiant; their faces are never covered with shame.

This poor man called, and the Lord heard him; he saved him out of all his troubles.

The angel of the Lord encamps around those who fear him, and he delivers them.

Taste and see that the Lord is good; blessed is the man who takes refuge in him.

Fear the Lord, you his saints, for those who fear him lack nothing.

The lions may grow weak and hungry, but those who seek the Lord lack no good thing.

The righteous cry out, and the Lord hears them; he delivers them from all their troubles.

The Lord is close to the brokenhearted and saves those who are crushed in spirit.

A righteous man may have many troubles, but the Lord delivers him from them all;

The Lord redeems his servants; no one will be condemned who takes refuge in him. Psalm 34:1-10, 17-19,22

(NIV)

634 GOD'S COMMANDMENTS

I am the Lord thy God, which have brought thee out of the land of Egypt, out of the house of bondage. Thou shalt have no other gods before me.

Thou shalt not make unto thee any graven image, or any likeness of any thing that is in heaven above, or that is in the earth beneath, or that is in the water under the earth: thou shalt not bow down thyself to them, nor serve them.

Thou shalt not take the name of the Lord thy God in vain;

For the Lord will not hold him guiltless that taketh his name in vain.

Remember the sabbath day, to keep it holy. For in six days the Lord made heaven and earth, the sea, and all that in them is, and rested on the seventh day:

Wherefore, the Lord blessed the sabbath day, and hallowed it.

Honour thy father and thy mother: that thy days may be long upon the land which the Lord thy God giveth thee.

Thou shalt not kill.

Thou shalt not commit adultery.

Thou shalt not steal.

Thou shalt not bear false witness against thy neighbour.

Thou shalt not covet thy neighbor's house, thou shalt not covet thy neighbour's wife, nor his manservant, nor his maidservant, nor his ox, nor his ass, nor any thing that is thy neighbour's. Exodus 20:2-5, 7, 8, 11-17.

Thou shalt love the Lord thy God with all thy heart, and with all thy soul, and with all thy mind. This is the first and great commandment.

And the second is like unto it. Thou shalt love thy neighbour as thyself. On these two commandments hang all the law and the prophets. Matthew 22:37-40

635 WORSHIP OF GOD

Sing to the Lord a new song; sing to the Lord, all the earth.

Sing to the Lord, praise his name; proclaim his salvation day after day.

Declare his glory among the nations, his marvelous deeds among all peoples.

For great is the Lord and most worthy of praise; he is to be feared above all gods.

For all the gods of the nations are idols, but the Lord made the heavens.

Splendor and majesty are before him; strength and glory are in his sanctuary.

Ascribe to the Lord, O families of nations, ascribe to the Lord glory and strength.

Ascribe to the Lord the glory due his name; bring an offering and come into his courts.

Worship the Lord in the splendor of his holiness; tremble before him, all the earth.

Say among the nations, "The Lord reigns." The world is firmly established, it cannot be moved; he will judge the peoples with equity.

Let the heavens rejoice, let the earth be glad; let the sea resound, and all that is in it;

Let the fields be jubilant, and everything in them. Then all the trees of the forest will sing for joy;

They will sing before the Lord, for he comes, he comes to
judge the earth.

He will judge the world in righteousness and the peoples in his truth. Psalm 96

(NIV)

Who satisfies your desires with good things so that your youth is renewed like the eagle's.

The Lord works righteousness and justice for all the oppressed.

He made known his ways to Moses, his deeds to the people of Israel:

The Lord is compassionate and gracious, slow to anger, abounding in love.

He will not always accuse, nor will he harbor his anger forever;

He does not treat us as our sins deserve or repay us according to our iniquities.

For as high as the heavens are above the earth, so great is his love for those who fear him;

As far as the east is from the west, so far has he removed our transgressions from us.

As a father has compassion on his children, so the Lord has compassion on those who fear him;

Praise the Lord, all his works everywhere in his dominion. Praise the Lord, O my soul. Psalm 103:1-13, 22

(NIV)

636 THANKSGIVING TO GOD

Praise the Lord, O my soul; all my inmost being, praise his holy name.

Praise the Lord, O my soul, and forget not all his benefits - Who redeems your life from the pit and crowns you with love and compassion,

637 OBEDIENCE TO GOD

You have laid down precepts that are to be fully obeyed. Oh, that my ways were steadfast in obeying your decrees!

Then I would not be put to shame when I consider all your commands.

I will praise you with an upright heart as I learn your righteous laws.

I will obey your decrees; do not utterly forsake me.

How can a young man keep his way pure? By living according to your word.

I seek you with all my heart; do not let me stray from your commands.

I have hidden your word in my heart that I might not sin against you.

Praise be to you, 0 Lord; teach me your decrees.

With my lips I recount all the laws that come from your mouth.

I rejoice in following your statutes as one rejoices in great riches.

I meditate on your precepts and consider your ways.

I delight in your decrees; I will not neglect your word.

Do good to your servant, and I will live; I will obey your word.

Open my eyes that I may see wonderful things in your law.

Psalm 119:4-18

(NIV)

638 THE INCARNATE CHRIST

In the beginning was the Word, and the Word was with God, and the Word was God.

He was with God in the beginning.

Through him all things were made; without him nothing was made that has been made.

In him was life, and that life was the light of men.

The light shines in the darkness, but the darkness has not understood it.

There came a man who was sent from God; his name was John.

He came as a witness to testify concerning that light, so that through him all men might believe.

He himself was not the light; he came only as a witness to the light.

The true light that gives light to every man was coming into the world.

He was in the world, and though the world was made through him, the world did not recognize him.

He came to that which was his own, but his own did not receive him.

Yet to all who received him, to those who believed in his name, he gave the right to become children of God—

Children born not of natural descent, nor of human decision or a husband's will, but born of God.

The Word became flesh and made his dwelling among us. We have seen his glory, the glory of the One and Only, who came from the Father, full of grace and truth. John 1:1-14

For God so loved the world that he gave his one and only Son, that whoever believes in him shall not perish but have eternal life.

For God did not send his Son into the world to condemn the world, but to save the world through him.

John 3:16, 17

(NIV)

639 THE SAVIOR'S ADVENT

And there were shepherds living out in the fields nearby, keeping watch over their flocks at night.

An angel of the Lord appeared to them, and the glory of the Lord shone around them, and they were terrified.

But the angel said to them, "Do not be afraid. I bring you good news of great joy that will be for all the people.

Today in the town of David a Savior has been born to you; he is Christ the Lord.

This will be a sign to you: You will find a baby wrapped in cloths and lying in a manger."

Suddenly a great company of the heavenly host appeared with the angel, praising God and saying,

"Glory to God in the highest, and on earth peace to men on whom his favor rests."

When the angels had left them and gone into heaven, the shepherds said to one another,

"Let's go to Bethlehem and see this thing that has happened, which the Lord has told us about."

So they hurried off and found Mary and Joseph, and the baby, who was lying in the manger.

When they had seen him, they spread the word concerning what had been told them about this child,

And all who heard it were amazed at what the shepherds said to them.

But Mary treasured up all these things and pondered them in her heart.

The shepherds returned, glorifying and praising God for all the things they had heard and seen, which were just as they had been told.

Luke 2:8-20

(NIV)

640 ADORATION OF THE MAGI

After Jesus was born in Bethlehem in Judea, during the time of King Herod, Magi from the east came to Jerusalem and asked,

"Where is the one who has been born king of the Jews? We saw his star in the east and have come to worship him."

When King Herod heard this he was disturbed, and all Jerusalem with him.

When he had called together all the people's chief priests and teachers of the law, he asked them where the Christ was to be born.

"In Bethlehem in Judea," they replied, "for this is what the prophet has written:

"'But you, Bethlehem, in the land of Judah, are by no means least among the rulers of Judah; for out of you will come a ruler who will be the shepherd of my people Israel.'"

Then Herod called the Magi secretly and found out from them the exact time the star had appeared.

He sent them to Bethlehem and said, "Go and make a careful search for the child. As soon as you find him, report to me, so that I too may go and worship him."

After they had heard the king, they went on their way, and the star they had seen in the east went ahead of them until it stopped over the place where the child was.

On coming to the house, they saw the child with his mother Mary, and they bowed down and worshiped him.

Then they opened their treasures and presented him with gifts of gold and of incense and of myrrh.

And having been warned in a dream not to go back to Herod, they returned to their country by another route. Matthew 2:1-12

(NIV)

641 BAPTISM OF JESUS

In those days John the Baptist came, preaching in the Desert of Judea and saying,

"Repent, for the kingdom of heaven is near."

This is he who was spoken of through the prophet Isaiah: "A voice of one calling in the desert, 'Prepare the way for the Lord, make straight paths for him.' "

John's clothes were made of camel's hair, and he had a leather belt around his waist. His food was locusts and wild honey.

People went out to him from Jerusalem and all Judea and the whole region of the Jordan.

Confessing their sins, they were baptized by him in the Jordan River.

But when he saw many of the Pharisees and Sadducees coming to where he was baptizing, he said ot them: "You brook of vipers! Who warned you to flee from the coming wrath?

Produce fruit in keeping with repentance."

"I baptize you with water for repentance. But after me will come one who is more powerful than I, whose sandals I am not fit to carry. He will baptize you with the Holy Spirit and with fire."

Then Jesus came from Galilee to the Jordan to be baptized by John.

But John tried to deter him, saying, "I need to be baptized by you, and do you come to me?"

Jesus replied, "Let it be so now; it is proper for us to do this to fulfill all righteousness." Then John consented.

As soon as Jesus was baptized, he went up out of the water. At that moment heaven was opened, and he saw the Spirit of God descending like a dove and lighting on him.

And a voice from heaven said, "This is my Son, whom I love; with him I am well pleased." Matthew 3:1-8, 11, 13-17

(NIV)

642 LAMB OF GOD

Who has believed our message and to whom has the arm of the Lord been revealed?

He grew up before him like a tender shoot, and like a root out of dry ground. He had no beauty or majesty to attract us to him, nothing in his appearance that we should desire him.

He was despised and rejected by men, a man of sorrows, and familiar with suffering. Like one from whom men hide their faces he was despised, and we esteemed him not.

Surely he took up our infirmities and carried our sorrows, yet we considered him stricken by God, smitten by him, and afflicted.

But he was pierced for our transgressions, he was crushed for our iniquities; the punishment that brought us peace was upon him, and by his wounds we are healed.

We all, like sheep, have gone astray, each of us has turned to his own way; and the Lord has laid on him the iniquity of us all.

He was oppressed and afflicted, yet he did not open his mouth; he was led like a lamb to the slaughter, and as a sheep before her shearers is silent, so he did not open his mouth.

By oppression and judgment he was taken away. And who can speak of his descendants? For he was cut off from the land of the living; for the transgression of my people he was stricken.

He was assigned a grave with the wicked, and with the rich in his death, though he had done no violence, nor was any deceit in his mouth.

Yet it was the Lord's will to crush him and cause him to suffer, and though the Lord makes his life a guilt offering, he will see his offspring and prolong his days, and the will of the Lord will prosper in his hand.

After the suffering of his soul, he will see the light of life and be satisfied; by his knowledge my righteous servant will justify many, and he will bear their iniquities.

Therefore, I will give him a portion among the great, and he will divide the spoils with the strong, because he poured out his life unto death, and was numbered with the transgressors. For he bore the sin of many, and made intercession for the transgressors. Isaiah 53

(NIV)

643 THE LAST SUPPER

So the disciples did as Jesus had directed them and prepared the Passover.

When evening came, Jesus was reclining at the table with the Twelve.

And while they were eating, he said, "I tell you the truth, one of you will betray me."

They were very sad and began to say to him one after the other, "Surely not I, Lord?"

Jesus replied, "The one who has dipped his hand into the bowl with me will betray me.

The Son of Man will go just as it is written about him. But woe to that man who betrays the Son of Man! It would be better for him if he had not been born."

Then Judas, the one who would betray him, said, "Surely not I, Rabbi?" Jesus answered, "Yes, it is you."

While they were eating, Jesus took bread, gave thanks and broke it, and gave it to his disciples, saying, "Take and eat; this is my body."

Then he took the cup, gave thanks and offered it to them, saying, "Drink from it, all of you. This is my blood of the covenant, which is poured out for many for the forgiveness of sins.

I tell you, I will not drink of this fruit of the vine from now on until that day when I drink it anew with you in my Father's kingdom."

Matthew 26:19-29

(NIV)

644 THE TRIUMPHAL ENTRY

As they approached Jerusalem and came to Bethphage and Bethany at the Mount of Olives, Jesus sent two of his disciples, saying to them,

"Go to the village ahead of you, and just as you enter it, you will find a colt tied there, which no one has ever ridden. Untie it and bring it here.

If anyone asks you, 'Why are you doing this?' tell him, 'The Lord needs it and will send it back here shortly.'"

They went and found a colt outside in the street, tied at a doorway. As they untied it, some people standing there asked, "What are you doing, untying that colt?"

They answered as Jesus had told them to, brought the colt to Jesus and threw their cloaks over it, he sat on it.

Many people spread their cloaks on the road, while others spread branches they had cut in the fields.

Those who went ahead and those who followed shouted, "Hosanna!" "Blessed is he who comes in the name of the Lord!" "Blessed is the coming kingdom of our father David!" "Hosanna in the highest!"

Jesus entered Jerusalem and went to the temple. He looked around at everything, but since it was already late, he went out to Bethany with the Twelve. Mark 11:1-11

When Jesus entered Jerusalem, the whole city was stirred and asked, "Who is this?"

The crowds answered, "This is Jesus, the prophet from Nazareth in Galilee." Matthew 21:10, 11

(NIV)

645 CRUCIFIXION OF CHRIST

Finally Pilate handed him over to them to be crucified. So the soldiers took charge of Jesus.

Carrying his own cross, he went out to the place of the Skull (which in Aramaic is called Golgotha).

Here they crucified him, and with him two others - one on each side and Jesus in the middle.

Pilate had a notice prepared and fastened to the cross. It read: JESUS OF NAZARETH, THE KING OF THE JEWS.

When the soldiers crucified Jesus, they took his clothes, dividing them into four shares, one for each of them, with the undergarment remaining. This garment was seamless, woven in one piece from top to bottom.

"Let's not tear it," they said to one another. "Let's decide by lots who will get it."

This happened that the scripture might be fulfilled which said, "They divided my garments among them and cast lots for my clothing." So this is what the soldiers did.

Near the cross of Jesus stood his mother, his mother's sister, Mary the wife of Clopas, and Mary Magdalene.

When Jesus saw his mother there, and the disciple whom he loved standing nearby, he said to his mother, "Dear woman, here is your son," and to the disciple, "Here is your mother." From that time on, this disciple took her into his home.

Later, knowing that all was now completed, and so that the Scripture would be fulfilled, Jesus said, "I am thirsty."

A jar of wine vinegar was there, so they soaked a sponge in it, put the sponge on a stalk of the hyssop plant, and lifted it to Jesus' lips.

When he had received the drink, Jesus said, "It is finished." With that, he bowed his head and gave up his spirit. John 19:16-19, 23-30

(NIV)

646 THE RISEN LORD

After the Sabbath, at dawn on the first day of the week, Mary Magdalene and the other Mary went to look at the tomb.

There was a violent earthquake, for an angel of the Lord came down from heaven and, going to the tomb, rolled back the stone and sat on it.

The angel said to the women, "Do not be afraid, for I know that you are looking for Jesus, who was crucified.

He is not here; he has risen, just as he said. Come and see the play where he lay.

Then go quickly and tell his disciples: 'He has risen from the dead and is going ahead of you into Galilee. There you will see him.' Now I have told you."

So the women hurried away from the tomb, afraid yet filled with joy, and ran to tell his disciples.

Suddenly Jesus met them. "Greetings," he said. They came to him, clasped his feet and worshiped him.

Then Jesus said to them, "Do not be afraid. Go and tell my brothers to go to Galilee; there they will see me." Matthew 28:1, 2, 5-10

On the evening of that first day of the week, when the disciples were together, with the doors locked for fear of the Jews, Jesus came and stood among them and said, "Peace be with you!"

After he said this, he showed them his hands and side. The disciples were overjoyed when they saw the Lord. John 20:19, 20

(NIV)

647 GREAT COMMISSION

Then the eleven disciples went to Galilee, to the mountain where Jesus had told them to go.

When they saw him, they worshiped him; but some doubted.

Then Jesus came to them and said, "All authority in heaven and on earth has been given to me.

Therefore, go and make disciples of all nations, baptizing them in the name of the Father and of the Son and of the Holy Spirit, and teaching them to obey everything I have commanded you. And surely I am with you always, to the very end of the age." Matthew 28:16-20

So when they met together, they asked him, "Lord, are you at this time going to restore the kingdom to Israel?"

He said to them: "It is not for you to know the times or dates the Father has set by his own authority.

But you will receive power when the Holy Spirit comes on you; and you will be my witnesses in Jerusalem, and in all Judea and Samaria, and to the ends of the earth."

After he said this, he was taken up before their very eyes, and a cloud hid him from their sight. Acts 1:6-9

(NIV)

648 THE BEATITUDES

And seeing the multitudes, he went up into the mountain: and when he was set, his disciples came unto him:

And he opened his mouth, and taught them, saying,

Blessed are the poor in spirit: for theirs is the kingdom of heaven.

Blessed are they that mourn: for they shall be comforted.

Blessed are the meek: for they shall inherit the earth.

Blessed are they which do hunger and thirst after righteousness: for they shall be filled.

Blessed are the merciful: for they shall obtain mercy.

Blessed are the pure in heart: for they shall see God.

Blessed are the peacemakers: for they shall be called the children of God.

Blessed are they which are persecuted for righteousness' sake: for theirs is the kingdom of heaven.

Blessed are ye, when men shall revile you, and persecute you, and shall say all manner of evil against you falsely, for my sake.

Rejoice, and be exceedingly glad: for great is your reward in heaven: for so persecuted they the prophets which were before you.

Ye are the light of the world.

Let your light so shine before men, that they may see your good works, and glorify your Father which is in heaven Matthew 5:1-12, 14, 16

649 THE VINE AND BRANCHES

I am the true vine, and my Father is the husbandman.

Every branch in me that beareth not fruit he taketh away: and every branch that beareth fruit, he purgeth it, that it may bring forth more fruit.

Now ye are clean through the word which I have spoken unto you.

Abide in me, and I in you. As the branch cannot bear fruit of itself, except it abide in the vine; no more can ye, except ye abide in me.

I am the vine, ye are the branches: He that abideth in me, and I in him, the same bringeth forth much fruit: for without me ye can do nothing.

If a man abide not in me, he is cast forth as a branch, and is withered; and men gather them, and cast them into fire, and they are burned.

If ye abide in me, and my words abide in you, ye shall ask what ye will, and it shall be done unto you.

Herein is my Father glorified, that ye bear much fruit; so shall ye be my disciples.

These things have I spoken unto you, that my joy might remain in you, and that your joy might be full.

Ye are my friends, if ye do whatsoever I command you.

Henceforth I call you not servants; for the servant knoweth not what his lord doeth: but I have called you friends: for all things that I have heard of my Father I have made known unto you.

Ye have not chosen me, but I have chosen you, and ordained you, that ye should go and bring forth fruit, and that your fruit should remain: that whatsoever ye shall ask of the Father in my name, he may give it you. John 15:1-8, 11, 14-16

650 COMFORT FROM CHRIST

"Do not let your hearts be troubled. Trust in God; trust also in me.

In my Father's house are many rooms; if it were not so, I would have told you. I am going there to prepare a place for you.

And if I go and prepare a place for you, I will come back and take you to be with me that you also may be where I am.

You know the way to the place where I am going."

Thomas said to him, "Lord, we don't know where you are going, so how can we know the way?"

Jesus answered, "I am the way and the truth and the life. No one comes to the Father except through me."

Philip said, "Lord, show us the Father and that will be enough for us."

Jesus answered: "Don't you know me, Philip, even after I have been among you such a long time? Anyone who has seen me has seen the Father. How can you say, 'Show us the Father'?

Don't you believe that I am in the Father, and that the Father is in me? The words I say to you are not just my own. Rather, it is the Father, living in me, who is doing his work.

Believe me when I say that I am in the Father and the Father is in me; or at least believe on the evidence of the miracles themselves.

I tell you the truth, anyone who has faith in me will do what I have been doing. He will do even greater things than these, because I am going to the Father."

"Peace I leave with you; my peace I give you. I do not give to you as the world gives. Do not let your hearts be troubled and do not be afraid." John 14:1-6, 8-12, 27

(NIV)

651 THE HOLY SPIRIT

"And I will ask the Father, and he will give you another Counselor
to be with you forever—

The Spirit of truth. The world cannot accept him, because it neither sees him nor knows him.

But you know him, for he lives with you and will be in you. I will not leave you as orphans; I will come to you.

Before long, the world will not see me anymore, but you will see me. Because I live, you also will live." John 14:16-19

"Because I have said these things, you are filled with grief.

But I tell you the truth: It is for your good that I am going away.

Unless I go away, the Counselor will not come to you; but if I go, I will send him to you.

When he comes, he will convict the world of guilt in regard to sin and righteousness and judgment: in regard to sin, because men do not believe in me;

In regard to righteousness, because I am going to the Father, where you can see me no longer;

And in regard to judgment, because the prince of this world now stands condemned.

I have much more to say to you, more than you can now bear.

But when he, the Spirit of truth, comes, he will guide you into all truth. He will not speak on his own; he will speak only what he hears, and he will tell you what is yet to come.

He will bring glory to me by taking from what is mine and making it known to you.

"I have told you these things, so that in me you may have peace. In this world you will have trouble. But take heart! I have overcome the world." John 16:6-14, 33

(NIV)

652 HOLY SCRIPTURES

Above all, you must understand that no prophecy of Scripture came about by the prophet's own interpretation.

For prophecy never had its origin in the will of man, but men spoke from God as they were carried along by the Holy Spirit. 2 Peter 1:20, 21

All Scripture is God-breathed and is useful for teaching, rebuking, correcting and training in righteousness,

So that the man of God may be thoroughly equipped for every good work 2 Timothy 3:16, 17

Do your best to present yourself to God as one approved, a workman who does not need to be ashamed and who correctly handles the word of truth.
2 Timothy 2:15

For everything that was written in the past was written to teach us, so that through endurance and the encouragement of the Scriptures we might have hope. Romans 15:4

Your word, 0 Lord, is eternal; it stands firm in the heavens.

Your word is a lamp to my feet and a light for my path.

The unfolding of your words gives light; it gives understanding to the simple.

Great peace have they who love your law, and nothing can make them stumble. Psalm 119:89, 105, 130, 165

(NIV)

653 TRUE WISDOM

Blessed is the man who finds wisdom, the man who gains understanding,

For she is more profitable than silver and yields better returns than gold.

She is more precious than rubies; nothing you desire can compare with her.

Long life is in her right hand; in her left hand are riches and honor.

Her ways are pleasant ways, and all her paths are peace.

She is a tree of life to those who embrace her; those who lay hold of her will be blessed.

By wisdom the Lord laid the earth's foundations, by understanding he set the heavens in place;

By his knowledge the deeps were divided, and the clouds let drop the dew.

My son, preserve sound judgment and discernment, do not let them out of your sight;

They will be life for you, an ornament to grace your neck.

Then you will go on your way in safety, and your foot will not stumble;

When you lie down, you will not be afraid; when you lie down, your sleep will be sweet.

Have no fear of sudden disaster or of the ruin that overtakes the wicked,

For the Lord will be your confidence and will keep your foot from being snared.

Trust in the Lord with all your heart and lean not on your own understanding;

In all you ways acknowledge him, and he will make your paths straight. Proverbs 3:13-26, 5, 6

(NIV)

654 THE CHURCH

When Jesus came to the region of Caesarea Philippi, he asked his disciples, "Who do people say the Son of Man is?"

They replied, "Some say John the Baptist; others say Elijah; and still others, Jeremiah or one of the prophets."

"But what about you?" he asked. "Who do you say I am?"

Simon Peter answered, "You are the Christ, the Son of the living God."

Jesus replied, "Blessed are you, Simon son of Jonah, for this was not revealed to you by man, but by my Father in heaven.

And I tell you that you are Peter, on this rock I will build my church, and the gates of Hades will not overcome it. Matthew 16:13-18

Consequently, you are no longer foreigners and aliens, but fellow citizens with God's people and members of God's household,

Built on the foundation of the apostles and prophets, with Christ Jesus himself as the chief cornerstone.

In him the whole building is joined together and rises to become a holy temple in the Lord.

And in him you too are being built together to become a dwelling in which God lives by his Spirit. Ephesians 2:19-22

There is one body and one Spirit — just as you were called to one hope when you were called —

One Lord, one faith, one baptism; one God and Father of all, who is over all and through all and in all. Ephesians 4:4-6

(NIV)

655 CHRISTIAN MINISTRY

"Everyone who calls on the name of the Lord will be saved."

How, then, can they call on the one they have not heard? And how can they hear without someone preaching to them?

And how can they preach unless they are sent? As it is written, "How beautiful are the feet of those who bring good news!" Romans 10:13-15

Just as each of us has one body with many members, and these members do not all have the same function, so in Christ we who are many form one body, and each member belongs to all the others.

We have different gifts, according to the grace given us. If a man's gift is prophesying, let him use it in proportion to his faith.

If it is serving, let him serve; if it is teaching, let him teach; if it is encouraging, let him encourage.

If it is contributing to the needs of others, let him give generously; if it is leadership, let him govern diligently; if it is showing mercy, let him do it cheerfully. Romans 12:4-6

Each one should use whatever gift he has received to serve others, faithfully administering God's grace in its various forms.

If anyone speaks, he should do it as one speaking the very words of God.

If anyone serves, he should do it with the strength God provides, so that in all things God may be praised through Jesus Christ. To him be the glory and the power for ever and ever. Amen. 1 Peter 4:10, 11

(NIV)

656 CHRISTIAN UNITY

After Jesus said this, he looked toward heaven and prayed: "Father, the time has come. Glorify your Son, that your Son may glorify you.

"I have revealed you to those whom you gave me out of the world. They were yours; you gave them to me and they have obeyed your word."

"I pray for them. I am not praying for the world, but for those you have given me, for they are yours.

All I have is yours, and all you have is mine. And glory has come to me through them."

"My prayer is not for them alone. I pray also for those who will believe in me through their message,

That all of them may be one, Father, just as you are in me and I am in you. May they also be in us so that the world may believe that you have sent me." John 17:1, 6, 9, 10, 20, 21

I appeal to you, brothers, in the name of our Lord Jesus Christ, that all of you agree with one another so that there may be no divisions among you and that you may be perfectly united in mind and thought. 1 Corinthians 1:10

Be completely humble and gentle; be patient, bearing with one another in love. Make every effort to keep the unity of the Spirit through the bond of peace.

There is one body and one Spirit— just as you were called to one hope when you were called—one Lord, one faith, one baptism;

One God and Father of all, who is over all, and through all, and in all. Ephesians 4:2-6

(NIV)

657 SIN AND FORGIVENESS

Blessed is the man who perseveres under trial, because when he has stood the test, he will receive the crown of life that God has promised to those who love him.

When tempted, no one should say, "God is tempting me." For God cannot be tempted by evil, nor does he tempt anyone;

But each one is tempted when, by his own evil desire, he is dragged away and enticed.

Then, after desire has conceived, it gives birth to sin; and sin, when it is full-grown, gives birth to death. James 1:12-15

But if we walk in the light, as he is in the light, we have fellowship with one another, and the blood of Jesus, his Son, purifies us from all sin.

If we claim to be without sin, we deceive ourselves and the truth is not in us.

If we confess our sins, he is faithful and just and will forgive us our sins and purify us from all unrighteousness.

1 John 1:7-9

Blessed is he whose transgressions are forgiven, whose sins are covered.

Blessed is the man whose sin the Lord does not count against him and in whose spirit is no deceit.

Then I acknowledged my sin to you and did not cover up my iniquity. I said, "I will confess my transgressions to the Lord"—and you forgave the guilt of my sin.

Many are the woes of the wicked, but the Lord's unfailing love surrounds the man who trusts in him.

Rejoice in the Lord and be glad, you righteous; sing, all you who are upright in heart!

Psalm 32:1, 2, 5, 10, 11
(NIV)

658 LAW AND GOSPEL

Now we know that whatever the law says, it says to those who are under the law, so that every mouth may be silenced and the whole world held accountable to God.

Therefore, no one will be declared righteous in his sight by observing the law, rather, through the law we become conscious of sin.

But now a righteousness from God, apart from law, has been made known, to which the Law and the Prophets testify.

This righteousness from God comes through faith in Jesus Christ to all who believe. There is no difference,

For all have sinned and fall short of the glory of God, and are justified freely by his grace through redemption that came by Christ Jesus.

Romans 3:19-24

Before this faith came, we were held prisoners by the law, locked up until faith should be revealed.

So the law was put in charge to lead us to Christ that we might be justified by faith.

Now that faith has come, we are no longer under the supervision of the law.

You are all sons of God through faith in Christ Jesus,

For all of you who were baptized into Christ have clothed yourselves with Christ.

Galatians 3:23-27

Therefore, since we have been justified through faith, we have peace with God through our Lord Jesus Christ,

Through whom we have gained access by faith into this grace in which we now stand. And we rejoice in the hope of the glory of God.

Romans 5:1, 2
(NIV)

659 GOD'S INVITATION

"Come, all you who are thirsty, come to the waters; and you who have no money, come, buy and eat! Come, buy wine and milk without money and without cost.

Why spend money on what is not bread, and your labor on what does not satisfy? Listen, listen to me, and eat what is good, and your soul will delight in the richest of fare.

Give ear and come to me; hear me, that your soul may live. I will make an everlasting covenant with you, my faithful love promised to David."

Seek the Lord while he may be found; call on him while he is near.

Let the wicked forsake his way and the evil man his thoughts. Let him turn to the Lord, and he will have mercy on him, and to our God, for he will freely pardon.

"For my thoughts are not your thoughts, neither are your ways my ways," declares the Lord.

So is my word that goes out from my mouth: It will not return to me empty, but will accomplish what I desire and achieve the purpose for which I sent it.

"You will go out in joy and be led forth in peace; the mountains and hills will burst into song before you, and all the trees of the field will clap their hands.

Instead of the thornbush will grow the pine tree, and instead of briers, the myrtle will grow.

This will be for the Lord's renown, for an everlasting sign, which will not be destroyed." Isaiah 55:1-3, 6-8, 11-13

660 THE WAY OF LIFE

Blessed is the man who does not walk in the counsel of the wicked or stand in the way of sinners or sit in the seat of mockers.

But his delight is in the law of the Lord, and on his law he meditates day and night.

He is like a tree planted by streams of water, which yields it fruit in season and whose leaf does not wither. Whatever he does prospers.

Not so the wicked! They are like chaff that the wind blows away.

Therefore, the wicked will not stand in the judgment, nor sinners in the assembly of the righteous.

For the Lord watches over the way of the righteous, but the way of the wicked will perish. Psalm 1

There is a way that seems right to a man, but in the end it leads to death.
Proverbs 14:12

Trust in the Lord with all your heart and lean not on your own understanding;

In all your ways acknowledge him, and he will make your paths straight.
Proverbs 3:5, 6

"Enter through the narrow gate. For wide is the gate and broad is the road that leads to destruction, and many enter through it.

But small is the gate and narrow the road that leads to life, and only a few find it."
Matthew 7:13, 14

Jesus answered, "I am the way and the truth and the life. No one comes to the Father except through me." John 14:6

661 FAITH IN CHRIST

Now faith is being sure of what we hope for and certain of what we do not see.

And without faith it is impossible to please God, because anyone who comes to him must believe that he exists and that he rewards those who earnestly seek him. Hebrews 11:1, 6

"For my Father's will is that everyone who looks to the Son and believes in him shall have eternal life, and I will raise him up at the last day." John 6:40

For everyone born of God overcomes the world. This is the victory that has overcome the world, even our faith.

Who is it that overcomes the world? Only he who believes that Jesus is the Son of God.

And this is the testimony: God has given us eternal life, and this life is in his Son.

We know also that the Son of God has come and has given us understanding, so that we may know him who is true.

And we are in him who is true— even in his Son, Jesus Christ. He is the true God and eternal life.

1 John 5:4, 5, 11, 13, 20

662 PRAYER OF PENITENCE

Have mercy on me, O God, according to your unfailing love; according to your great compassion, blot out my transgressions.

Wash away all my iniquity and cleanse me from my sin.

For I know my transgressions, and my sin is always before me.

Against you, you only, have I sinned and done what is evil in your sight, so that you are proved right when you speak and justified when you judge.

Surely I was sinful at birth, sinful from the time my mother conceived me.

Surely you desire truth in the inner parts; you teach me wisdom in the inmost place.

Cleanse me with hyssop, and I will be clean; wash me, and I will be whiter than snow.

Let me hear joy and gladness; let the bones you have crushed rejoice.

Hide your face from my sins and blot out all my iniquity.

Create in me a pure heart, 0 God, and renew a steadfast spirit within me.

Do not cast me from your presence or take your Holy Spirit from me.

Restore to me the joy of your salvation and grant me a willing spirit, to sustain me.

Then I will teach transgressors your ways, and sinners will turn back to you.

0 Lord, open my lips, and my mouth will declare your praise.

You do not delight in sacrifice, or I would bring it; you do not take pleasure in burnt offerings.

The sacrifices of God are a broken spirit; a broken and contrite heart, 0 God, you will not despise.

Psalm 51:1-13, 15-17

(NIV)

663 CONFESSION OF CHRIST

If anyone acknowledges that Jesus is the Son of God, God lives in him and he in God. 1 John 4:15

But what does it say? "The word is near you; it is in your mouth and in your heart," that is, the word of faith we are proclaiming:

That if you confess with your mouth, "Jesus is Lord," and believe in your heart that God raised him from the dead, you will be saved.

For it is with your heart that you believe and are justified, and it is with your mouth that you confess and are saved. Romans 10:8-10

Therefore, God exalted him to the highest place and gave him the name that is above every name, that at the name of Jesus every knee should bow, in heaven and on earth and under the earth,

And every tongue confess that Jesus Christ is Lord, to the glory of God the Father. Philippians 2:9-11

"I tell you, whoever acknowledges me before men, the Son of Man will also acknowledge him before the angels of God.

But he who disowns me before men will be disowned before the angels of God. Luke 12:8, 9

(NIV)

664 CHRISTIAN BAPTISM

Then Jesus came to them and said, "All authority in heaven and on earth has been given to me.

Therefore, go and make disciples of all nations, baptizing them in the name of the father and of the Son and of the Holy Spirit,

And teaching them to obey everything I have commanded you. And surely I am with you always, to the very end of the age." Matthew 28:18-20

We were, therefore, buried with him through baptism into death in order that, just as Christ was raised from the dead through the glory of the Father, we too may live a new life.

If we have been united with him like this in his death, we will certainly also be united with him in his resurrection.

For we know that our old self was crucified with him so that the body of sin might be done away with, that we should no longer be slaves to sin—

Because anyone who has died has been freed from sin. Now if we died with Christ, we believe that we will also live with him.

For we know that since Christ was raised from the dead, he cannot die again; death no longer has mastery over him.

The death he died, he died to sin once for all; but the life he lives, he lives to God.

In the same way, count yourselves dead to sin, but alive to God in Christ Jesus. Romans 6:4-11

(NIV)

665 THE MIND OF CHRIST

If there be, therefore, any consolation in Christ, if any comfort of love, if any fellowship of the Spirit, if any bowels and mercies,

Fulfill ye my joy, that ye be like-minded, having the same love, being of one accord, of one mind.

Let nothing be done through strife or vainglory; but in lowliness of mind let each esteem other better than themselves.

Look not every man on his own things, but every man also on the things of others.

Let this mind be in you, which was also in Christ Jesus:

Who, being in the form of God, thought it not robbery to be equal with God:

But made himself of no reputation, and took upon him the form of a servant, and was made in the likeness of men:

And being found in fashion as a man, he humbled himself, and became obedient unto death, even the death of the cross.

Wherefore, God also hath highly exalted him, and given him a name which is above every name:

That at the name of Jesus every knee should bow, of things in heaven, and things in earth, and things under the earth;

And that every tongue should confess that Jesus Christ is Lord, to the glory of God the Father.

For it is God which worketh in you both to will and to do of his good pleasure.

Do all things without murmurings and disputings: that ye may be blameless and harmless, the sons of God, without rebuke, in the midst of a crooked and perverse nation,

Among whom ye shine as lights in the world; holding forth the word of life. Philippians 2:1-11, 13-16.

666 GROWTH IN GRACE

Grace and peace be yours in abundance through the knowledge of God and of Jesus our Lord.

His divine power has given us everything we need for life and godliness through our knowledge of him who called us by his own glory and goodness.

Through these he has given us his very great and precious promises, so that through them you may participate in the divine nature and escape the corruption in the world caused by evil desires.

For this very reason, make every effort to add to your faith goodness; and to goodness, knowledge;

And to knowledge, self-control; and to self-control, perseverance;

And to perseverance, godliness; and to godliness, brotherly kindness; and to brotherly kindness, love.

For if you possess these qualities in increasing measure, they will keep you from being ineffective and unproductive in your knowledge of our Lord Jesus Christ.

But if anyone does not have them, he is nearsighted and blind, and has forgotten that he has been cleansed from his past sins.

Therefore, my brothers, be all the more eager to make your calling and election sure. For if you do these things, you will never fall,

And you will receive a rich welcome into the eternal kingdom of our Lord and Savior Jesus Christ.

2 Peter 1:2-11

(NIV)

667 PRACTICAL CHRISTIANITY

Therefore, I urge you, brothers, in view of God's mercy, to offer your bodies as living sacrifices, holy and pleasing to God - this is your spiritual act of worship.

Do not conform any longer to the pattern of this world, but be transformed by the renewing of your mind. Then you will be able to test and approve what God's will is - his good, pleasing and perfect will.

For by the grace given me I say to every one of you: Do not think of yourself more highly than you ought, but rather think of yourself with sober judgment, in accordance with the measure of faith God has given you.

Love must be sincere. Hate what is evil; cling to what is good.

Be devoted to one another in brotherly love. Honor one another above yourselves.

Never be lacking in zeal, but keep your spiritual fervor, serving the Lord.

Be joyful in hope, patient in affliction, faithful in prayer.

Share with God's people who are in need. Practice hospitality.

Bless those who persecute you; bless and do not curse.

Rejoice with those who rejoice; mourn with those who mourn.

Live in harmony with one another. Do not be proud, but be willing to associate with people of low position. Do not be conceited.

Do not repay anyone evil for evil. Be careful to do what is right in the eyes of everybody.

If it is possible, as far as it depends on you, live at peace with everyone.

Do not take revenge, my friends, but leave room for God's wrath, for it is written: "It is mine to avenge; I will repay," says the Lord.

On the contrary: "If your enemy is hungry, feed him; if he is thirsty, give him something to drink. In doing this, you will heap burning coals on his head."

Do not be overcome by evil, but overcome evil with good.

Romans 12:1-3, 9-21

(NIV)

668 TEMPERANCE

Wine is a mocker and beer a brawler; whoever is led astray by them is not wise. Proverbs 20:1

Who has woe? Who has sorrow? Who has strife? Who has complaints? Who has needless bruises? Who has bloodshot eyes?

Those who linger over wine, who go to sample bowls of mixed wine.

Proverbs 23:29, 30

For the sinful nature desires what is contrary to the Spirit, and the Spirit what is contrary to the sinful nature. They are in conflict with each other, so that you do not do what you want.

But if you are led by the Spirit, you are not under law.

The acts of the sinful nature are obvious; sexual immorality, impurity and debauchery;

Idolatry and witchcraft; hatred, discord, jealousy, fits of rage, selfish ambition, dissensions, factions and envy; drunkenness, orgies, and the like.

I warn you, as I did before, that those who live like this will not inherit the kingdom of God.

But the fruit of the Spirit is love, joy, peace, patience, kindness, goodness, faithfulness, gentleness and self-control. Against such things there is no law.

Galatians 5:17-23

And whatever you do, whether in word or deed, do it all in the name of the Lord Jesus, giving thanks to God the Father through him.

Colossians 3:17
(NIV)

669 CHRISTIAN GIVING

"Do not store up for yourselves treasures on earth, where moth and rust destroy, and where thieves break in and steal.

But store up for yourselves treasures in heaven, where moth and rust do not destroy, and where thieves do not break in and steal. For where your treasure is, there your heart will be also." Matthew 6:19-21

On the first day of every week, each one of you should set aside a sum of money in keeping with his income, saving it up, so that when I come no collections will have to be made.

1 Corinthians 16:2

But just as you excel in everything —in faith, in speech, in knowledge, in complete earnestness and in your love for us - see that you also excel in this grace of giving.

I am not commanding you, but I want to test the sincerity of your love by comparing it with the earnestness of others.

For you know the grace of our Lord Jesus Christ, that though he was rich, yet for your sakes he became poor, so that you through his poverty might become rich.

2 Corinthians 8:7-9

Remember this: Whoever sows sparingly will also reap sparingly, and whoever sows generously will also reap generously.

Each man should give what he has decided in his heart to give, not reluctantly or under compulsion, for God loves a cheerful giver.

2 Corinthians 9:6-7
(NIV)

670 CHRISTIAN ASSURANCE

Because those who are led by the Spirit of God are sons of God.

For you did not receive a spirit that makes you a slave again to fear, but you received the Spirit of sonship. And by him we cry, "Abba, Father."

The Spirit himself testifies with our spirit that we are God's children.

Now if we are children, then we are heirs - heirs of God and co-heirs with Christ, if indeed we share in his sufferings in order that we may also share in his glory.

I consider that our present sufferings are not worth comparing with the glory that will be revealed in us.

And we know that in all things God works for the good of those who love him, who have been called according to his purpose.

What, then, shall we say in response to this? If God is for us, who can be against us?

He who did not spare his own Son, but gave him up for us all - how will he not also, along with him, graciously give us all things?

Who shall separate us from the love of Christ? Shall trouble or hardship or persecution or famine or nakedness or danger or sword?

No, in all these things we are more than conquerors through him who loved us.

For I am convinced that neither death nor life, neither angels nor demons, neither the present nor the future, nor any powers,

Neither height nor depth, nor anything else in all creation, will be able to separate us from the love of God that is in Christ Jesus our Lord.

Romans 8:14-18, 28, 31, 32, 35, 37-39

(NIV)

671 LOVE

Though I speak with the tongues of men and of angels, and have not love, I am become as sounding brass, or a tinkling cymbal.

And though I have the gift of prophecy, and understand all mysteries, and all knowledge:

And though I have all faith, so that I could remove mountains, and have not love, I am nothing.

And though I bestow all my goods to feed the poor, and though I give my body to be burned, and have not love, it profiteth me nothing.

Love suffereth long, and is kind; love envieth not; love vaunteth not itself, is not puffed up,

Doth not behave itself unseemly, seeketh not her own, is not easily provoked, thinketh no evil;

Rejoiceth not in iniquity, but rejoiceth in the truth;

Beareth all things, believeth all things, hopeth all things, endureth all things.

Love never faileth: but whether there be prophecies, they shall fail; whether there be tongues, they shall cease; whether there be knowledge, it shall vanish away.

For we know in part, and we prophesy in part.

But when that which is perfect is come, then that which is in part shall be done away.

When I was a child, I spake as a child, I understood as a child, I thought as a child: but when I became a man, I put away childish things.

For now we see through a glass, darkly; but then face to face: now I know in part; but then shall I know even as also I am known.

And now abideth faith, hope, love, these three; but the greatest of these is love.   1 Corinthians 13

For thine is the kingdom, and the power, and the glory, for ever. Amen.   Matthew 6:7-13

Continue in prayer, and watch in the same with thanksgiving.   Colossians 4:2

Confess your faults one to another, and pray one for another, that ye may be healed. The effectual fervent prayer of a righteous man availeth much.   James 5:16

Be careful for nothing; but in every thing by prayer and supplication with thanksgiving let your requests be made known unto God.

And the peace of God, which passeth all understanding, shall keep your hearts and minds through Christ Jesus.   Philippians 4:6, 7.

672 PRAYER

When ye pray, use not vain repetitions, as the heathen do: for they think that they shall be heard for their much speaking.

But not ye therefore, like unto them: for your Father knoweth what things ye have need of, before ye ask him.

After this manner, therefore, pray ye:

Our Father which art in heaven, hallowed be thy name.

Thy kingdom come. Thy will be done in earth, as it is in heaven.

Give us this day our daily bread. And forgive us our debts, as we forgive our debtors.

And lead us not into temptation, but deliver us from evil:

673 CIVIL POWER

Everyone must submit himself to the governing authorities, for there is no authority except that which God has established. The authorities that exist have been established by God.

Consequently, he who rebels against the authority is rebelling against what God has instituted, and those who do so will bring judgment on themselves.

For rulers hold no terror for those who do right, but for those who do wrong. Do you want to be free from fear of the one in authority? Then do what is right and he will commend you.

For he is God's servant to do you good. But if you do wrong, be afraid for he does not bear the sword for nothing. He is God's servant, an agent of wrath to bring punishment on the wrongdoer.

Therefore, it is necessary to submit to the authorities, not only because of possible punishment but also because of conscience.

This is also why you pay taxes, for the authorities are God's servants, who give their full time to governing.

Give everyone what you owe him: If you owe taxes, pay taxes; if revenue, then revenue; if respect, then respect; if honor, then honor.

Let no debt remain outstanding, except the continuing debt to love one another, for he who loves his fellow man has fulfilled the law.

Romans 13:1-8

(NIV)

674 SPIRITUAL WARFARE

Finally, be strong in the Lord and in his mighty power.

Put on the full armor of God so that you can take your stand against the devil's schemes.

For our struggle is not against flesh and blood, but against the rulers, against the authorities, against the powers of this dark world and against the spiritual forces of evil in the heavenly realms.

Therefore, put on the full armor of God, so that when the day of evil comes, you may be able to stand your ground, and after you have done everything, to stand.

Stand firm then, with the belt of truth buckled around your waist, with the breastplate of righteousness in place,

And with your feet fitted with the readiness that comes from the gospel of peace.

In addition to all this, take up the shield of faith, with which you can extinguish all the flaming arrows of the evil one.

Take the helmet of salvation and the sword of the Spirit, which is the word of God.

And pray in the Spirit on all occasions with all kinds of prayers and requests. With this in mind, be alert and always keep on praying for all the saints. Ephesians 6:10-18

The night is nearly over; the day is almost here. So let us put aside the deeds of darkness and put on the armor of light.

Let us behave decently, as in the daytime, not in orgies and drunkenness, not in sexual immorality and debauchery, not in dissension and jealousy.

Rather, clothe yourselves with the Lord Jesus Christ, and do not think about how to gratify the desires of the sinful nature. Romans 13:12-14

(NIV)

675 THE RETURN OF CHRIST

Brothers, we do not want you to be ignorant about those who fall asleep, or to grieve like the rest of men, who have no hope.

We believe that Jesus died and rose again and so we believe that God will bring with Jesus those who have fallen asleep in him.

According to the Lord's own word, we tell you that we who are still alive, who are left till the coming of the Lord, will certainly not precede those who have fallen asleep.

For the Lord himself will come down from heaven, with a loud command, with the voice of the archangel and with the trumpet call of God, and the dead in Christ will rise first.

After that, we who are still alive and are left will be caught up together with them in the clouds to meet the Lord in the air. And so we will be with the Lord forever.

Therefore, encourage each other with these words. Now, brothers, about times and dates we do not need to write to you,

For you know very well that the day of the Lord will come like a thief in the night.

So then, let us not be like others, who are asleep, but let us be alert and self-controlled.

For those who sleep, sleep at night, and those who get drunk, get drunk at night.

But since we belong to the day, let us be self-controlled, putting on faith and love as a breastplate, and the hope of salvation as a helmet.

For God did not appoint us to suffer wrath but to receive salvation through our Lord Jesus Christ.

He died for us so that, whether we are awake or asleep, we may live together with him. 1 Thessalonians 4:13--5:2, 6-10
(NIV)

676 CHRIST AND IMMORTALITY

But Christ has indeed been raised from the dead, the first fruits of those who have fallen asleep.

For since death came through a man, the resurrection of the dead comes also through a man.

For as in Adam all die, so in Christ all will be made alive.

So it is written: "The first man Adam became a living being", the last Adam, a life-giving spirit.

The first man was of the dust of the earth, the second man from heaven.

As was the earthly man, so are those who are of the earth; and as is the man from heaven, so also are those who are of heaven.

And just as we have borne the likeness of the earthly man, so shall we bear the likeness of the man from heaven.

For the perishable must clothe itself with the imperishable, and the mortal with immortality.

When the perishable has been clothed with the imperishable, and the mortal with immortality, then the saying that is written will come true: "Death has been swallowed up in victory."

"Where, 0 death, is your victory? Where, 0 death, is your sting?"

The sting of death is sin, and the power of sin is in the law.

But thanks be to God! He gives us the victory through our Lord Jesus Christ. 1 Corinthians 15:20-22, 45, 47-49, 53-57
(NIV)

677 THE JUDGMENT

Then I saw a great white throne and him who was seated on it. Earth and sky fled from his presence, and there was no place for them.

And I saw the dead, great and small, standing before the throne, and books were opened.

Another book was opened, which is the book of life. The dead were judged according to what they had done, as recorded in those books.

The sea gave up the dead that were in it, and death and Hades gave up the dead that were in them, and each person was judged according to what he had done.

Then death and Hades were thrown into the lake of fire. The lake of fire is the second death.

If anyone's name was not found written in the book of life, he was thrown into the lake of fire.

Revelation 20:11-15

"As the weeds are pulled up and burned in the fire, so it will be at the end of the age.

The Son of Man will send out his angels, and they will weed out of his kingdom everything that causes sin and all who do evil.

They will throw them into the fiery furnace, where there will be weeping and gnashing of teeth.

Then the righteous will shine like the sun in the kingdom of their Father. He who has ears, let him hear."

Matthew 13:40-43

(NIV)

678 THE NEW CREATION

Then I saw a new heaven and a new earth, for the first heaven and the first earth had passed away, and there was no longer any sea.

I saw the Holy City, the new Jerusalem, coming down out of heaven from God, prepared as a bride beautifully dressed for her husband.

And I heard a loud voice from the throne saying, "Now the dwelling of God is with men, and he will live with them. They will be his people, and God himself will be with them and be their God.

He will wipe every tear from their eyes. There will be no more death or mourning or crying or pain, for the old order of things has passed away."

He who was seated on the throne said, "I am making everything new!" Then he said, "Write this down, for these words are trustworthy and true."

He said to me: "It is done. I am the Alpha and the Omega, the Beginning and the End. To him who is thirsty I will give to drink without cost from the spring of the water of life.

He who overcomes will inherit all this, and I will be his God and he will be my son."

And he carried me away in the Spirit to a mountain great and high, and showed me the Holy City, Jerusalem, coming down out of heaven from God.

It shone with the glory of God, and its brilliance was like that of a very precious jewel, like a jasper, clear as crystal.

I did not see a temple in the city, because the Lord God Almighty and the Lamb are its temple.

The city does not need the sun or the moon to shine on it, for the glory of God gives it light, and the Lamb is its lamp.

The nations will walk by its light, and the kings of the earth will bring their splendor into it.

On no day will its gates ever be shut, for there will be no night there. The glory and honor of the nations will be brought into it.

Nothing impure will ever enter it, nor will anyone who does what is shameful or deceitful, but only those whose names are written in the Lamb's book of life.

Revelation 21:1-7, 10, 11, 22-27

(NIV)

679 THE IDEAL MOTHER

A wife of noble character who can find? She is worth far more than rubies.

Her husband has full confidence in her and lacks nothing of value.

She brings him good, not harm, all the days of her life.

She selects wool and flax and works with eager hands.

She is like the merchant ships, bringing her food from afar.

She gets up while it is still dark; she provides food for her family and portions for her servant girls.

She considers a field and buys it; out of her earnings she plants a vineyard.

She sets about her work vigorously; her arms are strong for her tasks.

She sees that her trading is profitable, and her lamp does not go out at night.

In her hand she holds the distaff and grasps the spindle with her fingers.

She opens her arms to the poor and extends her hands to the needy.

When it snows, she has no fear for her household; for all of them are clothed in scarlet.

She makes coverings for her bed; she is clothed in fine linen and purple.

Her husband is respected at the city gate, where he takes his seat among the elders of the land.

She makes linen garments and sells them, and supplies the merchants with sashes.

She is clothed with strength and dignity; she can laugh at the days to come.

She speaks with wisdom, and faithful instruction is on her tongue.

She watches over the affairs of her household and does not eat the bread of idleness.

Her children arise and call her blessed; her husband also, and he praises her: "Many women do noble things, but you surpass them all."

Charm is deceptive, and beauty is fleeting; but a woman who fears the Lord is to be praised. Proverbs 31:10-30

(NIV)

680 CHRIST AND CHILDREN

At that time the disciples came to Jesus and asked, "Who is the greatest in the kingdom of heaven?"

He called a little child and had him stand among them. And he said: "I tell you the truth, unless you change and become like little children, you will never enter the kingdom of heaven.

Therefore, whoever humbles himself like this child is the greatest in the kingdom of heaven. And whoever welcomes a little child like this in my name welcomes me.

But if anyone causes one of these little ones who believe in me to sin, it would be better for him to have a large millstone hung around his neck and to be drowned in the depths of the sea."

"See that you do not look down on one of these little ones. For I tell you that their angels in heaven always see the face of my Father in heaven."

Matthew 18:1-6, 10

"Whoever welcomes one of these little children in my name welcomes me; and whoever welcomes me does not welcome me but the one who sent me." Mark 9:37

People were bringing little children to Jesus to have him touch them, but the disciples rebuked them.

When Jesus saw this, he was indignant. He said to them, "Let the little children come to me, and do not hinder them, for the kingdom of God belongs to such as these.

I tell you the truth, anyone who will not receive the kingdom of God like a little child will never enter it."

And he took the children in his arms, put his hands on them and blessed them. Mark 10:13-16

(NIV)

Indexes

ALPHABETICAL INDEX OF READINGS

SUBJECT INDEX OF READINGS

INDEX OF AUTHORS AND COMPOSERS

Crouch, Andraé(b. 1954) w/m 15, 102, 298, 304, 559
Crüger, Johann (1598-1662) m 288, 592
Cull, Robert (b. 1949) w/m 132
Cummings, William H., Arr. (1831-1915) m 191
Cushing, William O. (1823-1902) w 484, 491, 509
Cutler, Henry S. (1824-1902) m 236, 515, 530

D

Darwall, John (1731-1789 m 55, 282, 289
Dauermann, Stuart (b. 1944) m 561
Davis, Geron (b. 1960) w/m 83
De Giardini, Felice (1716-1796) m 88, 545
Dix, William C. (1837-1898) w 202, 219
Dixon, Helen C. (1877-1969) w 468
Doane, William H. (1832-1915) m 79, 257, 370, 378, 412, 428, 470, 504
Doddridge, Philip (1702-1751) w 350
Dorsey, Thomas A., Adapt. (1899-1965) w/m 494
Doudney, Sarah (1841-1926) w 502
Dubois, Theodore (1837-1924) m 619
Dudley-Smith, Timothy (b. 1926) w 20, 258, 571
Duffield, George (1818-1888) w 510
Dunbar, C.R. (19th century) m 440
Dungan, Olive (b. 1903) m 610
Dunlop, Merrill (b. 1905) m 251, 529
Dwight, John S. (1813-1893) w 195
Dwight, Timothy (1752-1817) w 135
Dykes, John B. (1823-1876) m 2, 89, 155, 170, 332, 459, 554, 611

E

Edmunds, Lidie H. (19th century) w 308
Ellerton, John (1826-1893) w 582, 598, 609
Elliott, Charlotte (1789-1871) w 387
Elliott, Emily E.S. (1836-1897) w 218
Ellor, James (1819-1899) m 56
Elvey, George J. (1816-1893) m 3, 458, 516
Emerson, L.O. (1820-1915) m 591
English Carol, Traditional w 205
English Melody, Traditional m 65, 202
Evans, David, Arr. (1874-1948) m 70,
Everett, Asa B. (1828-1875) m 467
Excell, Edwin O. (1851-1921) w/m 335 m 240, 299, 596

F

Faber, Frederick W. (1814-1863) w 118, 379
Farjeon, Eleanor (1881-1965) w 274
Fawcett, John (1740-1817) w 138, 581
Featherstone, William R. (1846-1873) w 262
Ferguson, Manie P. (19th century) w 147
Fettke, Tom (b. 1941) m 222
Fillmore, James H. (1849-1936) m 271
Fischer, William G. (1835-1912) m 322, 368
Flemming, Friedrich F. (1778-1813) m 47
Flint, Annie Johnson (1866-1932) w 311
Folk Melody From India m 427 .
Fosdick, Harry E. (1878-1969) w 514
Foundery Collection (1742) m 26
Fox, Baynard L. (b. 1932) w/m 326
Francis of Assisi, St. (1182-1226) w 33, 610
Francis, Samuel Trevor (1834-1925) w 72
French Carol, Traditional w/m 206

G

Gabriel, Charles H. (1856-1932) w/m 318, 338, 351, 540, 569 w 538 m 158, 374, 448, 465, 476
Gaelic Melody, Traditional m 72

Gaither, Gloria (b. 1942) w 19, 105, 128, 129, 133, 227, 246, 275, 312, 429, 450, 512, 560, 594, 595
Gaither, William J. (b. 1936) m 75, 105, 128, 129, 246, 275, 312, 314, 429, 450, 499, 500, 551, 560, 594, 595
Garrett, Les (b. 1944) w/m 84
Gauntlett, Henry J. (1805-1876) m 217
Geistliche Kirchengesang (1623) m 33, 196
Gellert, Christian F. (1715-1769) w 288
Genevan Psalter (1551) m 42, 623
George, Bill (b. 1953) m 227
Gerhardt, Paul (1607-1676) w 458
German Carol w 196 m 221
German Carol, Traditional w 192
German Hymn w 612
German Melody, Traditional m 99, 192, 214
Gibbs, Ada R. (1865-1905) m 405
Gillman, Bob (20th century) w/m 130
Gilman, Samuel, Tr. (1791-1858) w 612
Gilmore, Joseph H. (1834-1918) w 447
Gilmour, Henry L. (1837-1920) w 489
Girard, Chuck (b. 1943) w/m 80
Gladden, Washington (1836-1918) w 542
Gläser, Carl G. (1784-1829) m 93, 396
Gordon, Adoniram J. (1836-1895) m 262, 331
Goss, John, Arr. (1800-1880) m 518
Gottschalk, Louis M. (1829-1869) m 159
Graham, David (20th century) w/m 97
Grant, Amy (b. 1960) w/m 178
Grant, Robert (1779-1838) w 90
Grape, John T. (1835-1915) m 255
Gray, James M. (1851-1935) w 333
Greatorex, Henry W. (1813-1858) m 109, 620
Greatorex, Walter (1877-1949) m 20
Green, Fred Pratt (b. 1903) w 25, 591
Green, Harold (1871-1930) m 157
Greenwell , Dora (1821-1882) w 287
Grétry, André (1741-1831) m 308
Grieg, Edvard, Harm. (1843-1907) m 553
Grimes, E. May (1864-1927) w 157
Grimes, Katherine A. (b. 1877) w 420
Grindal, Gracia, Tr. (b. 1943) w 553
Grose, Howard B. (1851-1939) w 422
Groves, Kandela (20th century) w/m 454
Grüber, Franz (1787-1863) m 189
Grundtvig, Nicolai F.S. (1783-1872) w 114
Gurney, Dorothy F. (1858-1932) w 609

H

Hall, Elvina M. (1820-1889) w 255
Hammond, Mary J. (1878-1964) m 152
Hammontree, Homer (1878-1965) m 423
Hanby, Benjamin R. (1833-1867) w/m 226
Handel, George Frederick (1685-1759) m 194, 197, 281
Hankey, A. Catherine (1834-1911) w 322, 378
Hanks, Jr., Billie (b. 1944) w/m 525
Harkness, Robert, Arr. (1880-1961) m 63
Harris, Carol (b. 1945) w/m 125
Harris, Margarett J. (19th century) w/m 62
Harris, Ron (b. 1941) w/m 125
Harris, Thoro (1874-1955) w/m 430
Hassler, Hans Leo (1564-1612) m 238, 258
Hastings, Thomas (1784-1872) m 490
Hatch, Edwin (1835-1889) w 139
Hatton, John (1710-1793) m 536
Havergal, Frances R. (1836-1879) w 419, 436, 451, 518, 535, 613
Hawks, Annie S. (1835-1918) w 169

Haydn , Franz Joseph (1732-1809) m 116, 590
Hayford, Jack W. (b. 1934) w/m 4
Head, Bessie P. (1850-1936) w 152
Hearn, Naida (b. 1944) w/m 57
Heber, Reginald (1783-1826) w 2, 515
Hebrew Folk Song, Ancient m 291
Hebrew Melody m 21
Helmore, Thomas (1811-1890) m 186
Hemy, Henri F. (1818-1888) m 118
Herrell, N.B. (20th century) w/m 280
Herring, Anne (b. 1945) w/m 272
Herrington, Lee, Arr. (b. 1941) m 120
Hewitt, Eliza E. (1851-1920) w 182, 487, 555
Hickman, Roger M. (1888-1968) m 349
Hicks , Roy (20th century) w/m 37
Hine, Stuart K. (b. 1899) w/m 16
Hoffman, Elisha A. (1839-1929) w/m 96, 164, 376 w
382, 492
Holden, Oliver (1765-1844) m 68
Homer, Charlotte G. (1856-1932) w 158
Hopkins, Edward J. (1818-1901) m 398, 582
Hopkins, John H. (1861-1945) w/m 220
Hopson, Hal (b. 1933) w/m 126
Houghton, Will H. (1887-1947) w 506
How, William W. (1823-1897) w 180, 548, 622
Howe, Julia Ward (1819-1910) w 604
Hoyle, Richard B. (1875-1939) w 281
Hudson, Ralph E. (1843-1901) w 440 m 59, 301, 323
Hugg, George C. (1848-1907) m 477
Hughes, John (1873-1932) m 442, 514
Hull, Eleanor, Ed . (1860-1935) w 400
Hultman, John A. (1861-1942) m 587
Husband, John J. (1843-1908) m 95
Hussey, Jennie E. (1874-1958) w 426
Hustad, Donald P. (b. 1918) m 210, 409, 439, 593,
610
Hutson, Wihla (b. 1901) w 201, 215

I

Irish Hymn w 400
Irish Melody, Traditional m 400
Irvine, Jessie S. (1836-1887) m 444
Iverson, Daniel (b. 1890) w/m 150

J

Jackson, Robert (1842-1914) m 139
James, Mary D. (1810-1883) w 421
Johnston, Julia H. (1849-1919) w 383
Jones, Lewis E. (1865-1936) w/m 334
Joy, Edward Henry (1871-1949) w/m 471
Jude, William H. (1851-1922) m 533
Judson, Adoniram (1788-1850) w 151

K

Kaan, Fred (b. 1926) w 127
Kaiser, Kurt (b. 1934) w/m 254, 406, 503
Katholisches Gesangbuch (c. 1774) m 28, 107
Keble, John (1792-1866) w 107
Kelly, Thomas (1769-1855) w 99, 284
Ken, Thomas (1637-1710) w 623
Kerr, Hugh T. (1872-1950) w 614
Ketchum, Albert A. (b. 1894) w/m 321
Kethe, William (d. c.1600) w 42
Key, Francis Scott (1779-1843) w 601
Kilpatrick, Bob (b. 1952) w/m 528
Kirk, James M., Arr. (1854-1945) m 147
Kirkpatrick, William J. , Arr. (1838-1921) m 59, 308
Kitchin, George W. (1827-1912) w 523
Klein, Laurie (b. 1950) w/m 228

Knapp, Phoebe P. (1839-1908) m 295
Kocher, Conrad (1786-1872) m 64, 219
Kremser, Edward, Arr. (1838-1914) m 27, 597

L

Lafferty, Karen (b. 1948) m 615
Lathbury, Mary A. (1841-1913) w 175, 585
Latin Carol w 214
Latin Hymn w 186, 188, 270
Lavalee, Calixa (1842-1891) m 605
Ledner, Michael (20th century) w/m 53
Lee, George E. (19th century) m 550
Leech, Bryan Jeffery (b. 1931) w 117, 221, w/m 260
LeFevre, Mylon R. (b. 1944) w/m 393
Lehman, Frederick M. (1869-1953) w/m 305
Lemmel, Helen H. (1864-1961) w/m 363
Lillenas, Haldor (1885-1959) w/m 319, m 327
Lindeman, Ludvig M. (1812-1887) m 114
Loes, Harry D. (1892-1965) m 248
Long, Lela B. (20th century) w/m 296
Longfellow, Henry W. (1807-1882) w 208
Longstaff, William D. (1822-1894) w 171
Loveless, Wendell P. (1892-1987) m 384, 506
Lowden, C. Harold (1883-1963) m 413
Lowell, James R. (1819-1891) w 607
Lowry , Robert (1826-1899) w/m 264, 269, 575 m
136, 169, 441, 481
Luther, Arthur A. (1891-1960) w/m 473
Luther, Martin (1483-1546) w/m 1
Lutkin, Peter C. (1858-1931) m 625
Lvov, Alexis F. (1799-1870) m 598
Lynch, Thomas T. (1818-1871) w 149
Lyon, Meyer, Arr. (1751-1797) m 21
Lyra Davidica, (1708) m 268
Lyte, Henry F. (1793-1847) w 22, 577

M

Mackay, William P. (1839-1885) w 95
Maker, Frederick C. (1844-1927) m 239, 418
Malan, Henri·A. César (1787-1864) m 436
Malotte, Albert Hay (1895-1964) w 168
Mann, Arthur H. (1850-1929) m 466
Maori Melody, Traditional m 410
March, Daniel (1816-1909) w 544
Marlatt, Earl (1892-1976) w 507
Marsh, Charles H. (1886-1956) m 225, 558
Marsh, Donald (b. 1923) w/m 229
Marshall, W.S. (19th century) m 147
Martin, Civilla D. (1869-1948) w 485
Martin, W. Stillman (1862-1935) m 485
Mason and Webb's Cantica Laudis (1850) m 622
Mason, Harry S. (1881-1964) w 507
Mason, Lowell (1792-1872) m 46, 93, 138, 194, 253
300, 396, 437, 462
Matheson, George (1842-1906) w 409, 439
Matthews, Timothy R. (1826-1910) m 218
Maxwell, Mary E. (20th century) w 405
Mays, Claudia Lehman, Arr. (20th century) m 305
McAfee, Cleland B. (1866-1944) w/m 433
McCutchan, Robert G. (1877-1958) m 617
McDaniel, Rufus H. (1850-1940) w 351
McGee, Bob (b. 1949) w/m 185
McGranahan, James (1840-1907) w/m 537 m 160,
310, 324, 355, 557
McGuire, Dony (b. 1951) w/m 293
McHugh, Phill (b. 1951) w 19 w/m 241, 527
McIntosh, Rigdon M., Arr. (1836-1899) m 574
McKinney, B.B. (1886-1952) w/m 87, 543 m 493
McSpadden, Gary (b. 1943) w/m 330

page 658

Williams, Ralph Vaughan, Arr. (1872-1958) m 6, 187,
548
Williams, Robert (c.1781-1821) m 270
Williams, Thomas J. (1781-1821) m 607
Williams, William (1717-1791) w 442
Willis, Richard S. (1819-1900) m 104, 199
Wilson, Emily D. (1865-1942) m 555
Wilson, Hugh (1766-1824) m 263
Wilson, Ira B. (1880-1950) w 525
Winkworth, Catherine, Tr. (1827-1878) w 10, 497,
592
Wohlgemuth, Paul, Arr. (1927-1988) m 193
Wolcott, Samuel (1813-1886) w 545
Wolfe, Lanny (20th century) w/m 146, 173
Work, John W. (1872-1925) w 216
Wurtemburg Gesangbuch m 233
Wyrtzen, Don (b. 1942) w/m 244, m 249, 344
Wyrtzen, Jack (b. 1913) w 344

Y
Yales, John H. (1837-l900) w 519
Young, G. A. (19th century) w/m 479

Z
Zelley, Henry J. (1859-1942) w 488
Zinzendorf, Nikolaus Von (1700-1760) w 325
Zundel, John (1815-1882) m 71

INDEX OF SCRIPTURES APPEARING WITH HYMN TITLES

LeFEVRE-SONG PUBLISHING COMPANY, P.O. Box 460, Smyrna, GA 30081; Hymn: 393.

LILLENAS PUBLISHING COMPANY, Box 419527, Kansas City, MO 64141–(816) 931-1900; Hymns: 94, 123, 280, 305, 311, 399, 430, 561.

MANNA MUSIC, INC., 25510 Avenue Stanford, Valencia, CA 91355–(805) 257-1191: Hymns: 16, 60, 153, 298, 304, 460.

MARANATHA! MUSIC, P.O. Box 31050, Laguna Hills, CA 92654-1050–(714) 586-5778; Hymns: 48, 53, 54, 57, 61, 84, 91, 120, 130, 132, 228, 291, 415, 454, 472, 615.

MEADOWGREEN MUSIC, 8 Music Square West, Nashville, TN 37203–(615) 255-2718; Hymns: 7, 9, 19, 83, 178, 241, 330, 527, 594.

NAZARENE PUBLISHING HOUSE–See Lillenas Publishing Company.

NEW JERUSALEM MUSIC, P.O. Box 225, Pine Mill Road, Clarksboro, NJ 08020–(609) 423-0066; Hymn: 290.

NEW SONGS MINISTRIES, P.O. Box 11662, Costa Mesa, CA 92627–(714) 675-8756; Hymn: 69.

ORTLUND, ANNE, Renewal Ministries, 4500 Campus Drive, Suite 662, Newport Beach, CA 92660–(714) 756-1313; Hymn: 530.

OXFORD UNIVERSITY PRESS, Ely House, 37 Dover Street, London, W1X 4AH, England–01-493 2661; Hymns: 6, 20, 33, 70, 187, 548.

PATHWAY PRESS, P.O. Box 2250, Cleveland, TN 37320–(615) 476-4512; Hymns: 146, 173.

PEARCE, MRS. ALMEDA J., 503 Shortridge Drive, Wynnewood, PA 19096; Hymn: 552.

RIVER OAKS MUSIC CO.–See Meadowgreen Music.

ROCKSMITH MUSIC, c/o Trust Music Management, Inc., P.O. Box 9256, Calabasas, CA 91302–(818) 347-2473; Hymn: 4.

RON HARRIS PUBLICATIONS, 22643 Paul Revere Drive, Woodland Hills, CA 91364–(818) 888-0753; Hymn: 125.

SALVATIONIST PUBLISHING AND SUPPLIES LTD., 117-221 Judd Street, King's Cross, London, WC1H 9NW, England; Hymn: 471.

SANDI'S SONGS MUSIC, P.O. Box 2940, Anderson, IN 46018; Hymn: 19.

SHEPHERD'S FOLD MUSIC–See Meadowgreen Music.

SINGSPIRATION MUSIC–See The Benson Company.

SOUND III, INC., c/o Tempo Music Publications, Inc., 3773 W. 95th Street, Leawood, KS 66206; Hymns 36, 101.

SPARROW CORPORATION, THE, P.O. Box 2120, 9225 Deering Avenue, Chatsworth, CA 91311–(818) 709-6900; Hymns: 37, 106, 272.

SPECTRA COPYRIGHT MANAGEMENT, INC., 23 Music Square East, Suite 101, Nashville, TN 37203–(615) 259-4000; Hymns: 15, 50, 86, 102, 165, 293, 357, 364, 371, 443, 482, 503, 559.

THORNTON, JAMES D., 10A North Road, Hertford, Hertfordshire, SG14 1LS, England; Hymn: 571.

TREE PUBLICATIONS–See Meadowgreen Music.

TRUSTEES OF VINCENT (HAZEON) TRUST, c/o Withers, Crossman & Block, 20 Essex Street, London, WC2R 3AL, England–01-836-8400; Hymn: 580.

WESTMINSTER/JOHN KNOX PRESS, 925 Chestnut Street, Philadelphia, PA 19107–(215) 928-2700; Hymn: 614.

WHOLE ARMOR PUBLISHING COMPANY, 3609 Donna Kay Drive, Nashville, TN 37211–(615) 331-6056; Hymn: 18.

WORD, INC., 5221 N. O'Connor Blvd., Suite 1000, Irving, TX 75039–(214) 556-1900; Hymns: 121, 143, 186, 222, 245, 254, 279, 285, 294, 302, 320, 346, 351, 367, 392, 406, 413, 505, 508, 525, 566, 568, 590.

WORLD STUDENT CHRISTIAN FEDERATION, Ecumenical Centre, 5 route des Morrillons, 1218 Grand-Saconnex, Geneva, Switzerland; Hymn: 281.

YELLOW HOUSE MUSIC–See The Benson Company.

TOPICAL INDEX OF HYMNS

page 665

page 666

page 672

ALPHABETICAL INDEX OF HYMNS

81 Savior, I Pray for Blessing This Hour

D. H. N.

Dolores Henderson Nash

1. Sav - ior, I pray for bless - ing this hour — Fill me with wis - dom, en -
2. Take all my plans and show me Thy way, Give me the cour - age Thy
3. Give me a glimpse of souls I must seek, Souls dai - ly dy - ing for

due me with pow'r; Take all of self — my pride and my shame,
will to o - bey; Send me the light Thy path - way to see,
words I should speak; Use me each day, wher - e'er I may be,

Chorus

That I may hon - or Thy won - der - ful name.
Know - ing my foot - steps are or - dered by Thee. Take all I have — it's the
Know - ing my weak - ness is strengthened by Thee.

least I can do! Speak thru my lips and a - noint me a - new; Shine thru my

life, that oth - ers may see Thy ho - ly pres - ence a - bid - ing in me.